# THE FINEST OF THE WHEAT

# II

# THE FINEST OF THE WHEAT

*Selected Excerpts from*
*the Published Works of Watchman Nee*

# II

WATCHMAN NEE

Christian Fellowship Publishers, Inc.
New York

*THE FINEST OF THE WHEAT*

(Vol. 2 of 2 vols.)



ISBN 0-935008-77-2 Cloth Edition
ISBN 0-935008-78-0 Paper Edition

Available from the Publishers at:

11515 Allecingie Parkway
Richmond, Virginia 23235

Printed in the United States of America

# PREFACE

As the psalmist Asaph sang one day about the goodness of the Lord towards His people, he was wont to conclude his song by declaring that Jehovah "would feed them also with the finest of the wheat" (Ps. 81.16a). The apostle James reenforced this statement by noting that "every good gift and every perfect gift is from above, coming from the Father of lights, with whom can be no variation, neither shadow that is cast by turning" (James 1.17). Whatever God gives is always the best. Ultimately, He gave us His only begotten Son, and with Him all things (see Rom. 8.32).

We are thankful to the Lord that because of His great love for the Church He has sent throughout the centuries many of His choice servants to help build up our holy faith. Their lives and teachings become the heritage of the Church which ought to be preserved. In our own time, Watchman Nee was one such choice servant given by God to His Church. He was called to serve the Lord in his youth; and from the time he was saved in 1920 to the time he was imprisoned in 1952, he faithfully and diligently served the Master he loved. Moreover, Watchman Nee was a man with deep spiritual insight, and was given great understanding of the word of God. He traveled far and wide and delivered many messages from the Lord to the Church. Because of his faith he was jailed. But though his voice was silenced during twenty long years of imprisonment, he nonetheless still speaks today. The messages and writings which he presented in the days of freedom have over the years been published in Chinese and also translated into many other languages. In the English version alone, there are some seventy volumes of varying size that have been published. Many are the testimonies of lives transformed and God glorified.

In order to preserve the best of Mr. Nee's thoughts and teachings, we have taken excerpts from nearly all his published works and now offer this final volume of a two-volume collection of *The Finest of the Wheat* to our readers. These extracts are grouped together under about fifty topics and are appropriately introduced by a sketch of the life of their author that has been provided by the Publishers' translator (see volume one for the text of the sketch).

We want to express our thanks to Dr. Angus I. Kinnear of London for giving us permission to print extracts taken from his copyrighted materials of some of Mr. Nee's books, and to extend our thanks also to Sure Foundation in Indiana (USA) for allowing us to do the same with Mr. Nee's *The Release of the Spirit* which is copyrighted by that Foundation. The bulk of the excerpts appearing in this collection, however, have been culled from our own publications of Watchman Nee's works. A few remaining ones have been derived from fresh translations into English made by the Publishers' translator from particular portions of the Chinese originals. (See the Translator's Note for additional details about this and for a complete Code List of Nee Published Materials to which the reader can refer to learn the source of any given excerpt in the entire collection.)

May the blessed Lord take, as it were, this "five loaves and two fishes," bless it, break it and give to His own—that it may multiply even further the glory to His name.

**CHRISTIAN FELLOWSHIP PUBLISHERS**

## Translator's Note

As was intimated in the Preface, there are a few excerpts from Watchman Nee's works appearing in *The Finest of the Wheat* which—though previously translated and published in English—have for this present publication been derived from new translations made from the pertinent sections of the original or subsequent Chinese-language editions of his works. These several works, whose Chinese titles have been transliterated into English, are indicated by an asterisk (*) in the following Code List of Nee Published Materials that has been provided for the readers' use by Christian Fellowship Publishers. It will be noticed, too, that full bibliographical data have been given for each item listed in the Code (with the abbreviation, NY: CFP, standing for New York: Christian Fellowship Publishers).

It should be added here that the codes for these published items excerpted from which have been compiled and/or edited by Dr. Kinnear are marked with a dagger (†) for easy identification, while all other codes listed (except ROS) are for those titles of Mr. Nee's published material whose copyrights belong to Christian Fellowship Publishers

### Code List of All Nee Published Materials Cited in the Collection of Excerpts

| | |
|---|---|
| **ALS** | A Living Sacrifice (v. 1 of Basic Lesson Series). (NY: CFP, 1972) |
| **AT** | Assembling Together (v. 3 of BLS). (NY: CFP, 1973) |
| **ATR** | Aids to "Revelation" (NY: CFP, 1983) |
| **BC** | The Better Covenant (NY: CFP, 1982) |
| **BCL** | A Balanced Christian Life (NY: CFP, 1981) |
| **BOC** | The Body of Christ: A Reality (NY: CFP, 1978) |
| **BTC** | Back to the Cross (NY: CFP, 1988) |
| **CGW** | The Character of God's Workman (NY: CFP, 1988) |
| **†CHL** | Changed into His Likeness (Fort Washington, PA: Christian Literature Crusade, 1980). Originally published 1967. |
| **CLJ** | "Come, Lord Jesus" (NY: CFP, 1976) |
| **CS** | Christ the Sum of All Spiritual Things (NY: CFP, 1973) |
| **CW** | The Church and the Work. 3 vols. [I: Assembly Life; II. Rethinking the Work (known also as The Normal Christian Church Life); III: Church Affairs]. (NY: CFP, 1982) |
| **DA** | Do All to the Glory of God (v. 5 of BLS). (NY: CFP, 1974) |

**FF** FROM FAITH TO FAITH (NY: CFP, 1984)
**FGG** FROM GLORY TO GLORY (NY: CFP, 1985)
**GC** THE GOOD CONFESSION (v. 2 of BLS). (NY: CFP, 1973)
**GD** GOSPEL DIALOGUE (NY: CFP, 1975)
**GFB** GLEANINGS IN THE FIELDS OF BOAZ (NY: CFP, 1987)
**GG** GRACE FOR GRACE (NY: CFP, 1983)
**GL** THE GLORY OF HIS LIFE (NY: CFP, 1976)
***GOC** "The Ground of the Church," *The Open Door* (a Chinese-language magazine published at Shanghai), Issue No. 20 dated 30 June 1950. This article is the Chinese text of a talk given by the author to the brethren in Shanghai on 1 April 1950. A new translation of excerpted selections.
**GP** GOD'S PLAN AND THE OVERCOMERS (NY: CFP, 1977)
**GW** GOD'S WORK (NY: CFP, 1974)
***HWB** HOLY AND WITHOUT BLEMISH (Shanghai: Gospel Book Room, 1953). A series of messages given in Chinese by the author at Shanghai between the autumn of 1937 and the autumn of 1942. A new translation of excerpted selections.
**IM** INTERPRETING MATTHEW (NY: CFP, 1989)
**KKH** THE KING AND THE KINGDOM OF HEAVEN (NY: CFP, 1978)
**†LNW** LOVE NOT THE WORLD (Fort Washington, PA: Christian Literature Crusade, 1984). Originally published 1968.
**LOA** LOVE ONE ANOTHER (v. 6 of BLS). (NY: CFP, 1975)
**LPS** THE LATENT POWER OF THE SOUL (NY: CFP, 1972)
**LUP** LET US PRAY (NY: CFP, 1977)
**LW** THE LIFE THAT WINS (NY: CFP, 1986)
**MC** THE MESSENGER OF THE CROSS (NY: CFP, 1980)
**MGW** THE MINISTRY OF GOD'S WORD (NY: CFP, 1971)
***MHMG** MINISTRY UNTO THE HOUSE OR MINISTRY UNTO GOD (Taipei: Gospel Book Room, 1953). A booklet-length publication in Chinese. A new translation of excerpted selections.
**†NCL** THE NORMAL CHRISTIAN LIFE (Fort Washington, PA: Christian Literature Crusade, 1985). Originally published 1957.
**NI** NOT I BUT CHRIST (v. 4 of BLS). (NY: CFP, 1974)
***OC** THE ORTHODOXY OF THE CHURCH (Shanghai: Gospel Book Room, 1951). A series of messages given by the author in 1945 among the gathered saints at Chungking and published there in Chinese the same year. Reprinted in subsequent years in Chinese. A new translation of excerpted selections.
**PI** PRACTICAL ISSUES OF THIS LIFE (NY: CFP, 1975)
**PM** THE PRAYER MINISTRY OF THE CHURCH (NY: CFP, 1973)

| | |
|---|---|
| **ROS** | THE RELEASE OF THE SPIRIT (Indianapolis: Sure Foundation, 1965) |
| **SA** | SPIRITUAL AUTHORITY (NY: CFP, 1972) |
| **SG** | THE SPIRIT OF THE GOSPEL (NY: CFP, 1986) |
| **SJ** | THE SPIRIT OF JUDGMENT (NY: CFP, 1984) |
| **SK** | SPIRITUAL KNOWLEDGE (NY: CFP, 1973) |
| ***SOS** | SONG OF SONGS (First published at Chungking in Chinese in 1945; reprint ed., Tsingtao: Church Book Department, 1948). Notes from a Bible reading on Solomon's Song of Songs conducted by the author with about ten fellow-workers at Hangchow in 1935. A new translation of excerpted selections. |
| **SRO** | SPIRITUAL REALITY OR OBSESSION (NY: CFP, 1970) |
| **SS** | THE SALVATION OF THE SOUL (NY: CFP, 1978) |
| **SWR** | THE SPIRIT OF WISDOM AND REVELATION (NY: CFP, 1980) |
| **†SWS** | SIT, WALK, STAND (Fort Washington, PA: Christian Literature Crusade, 1987). Originally published 1957. |
| ***TEV** | "The Treasure and the Earthen Vessel," *The Present Testimony* (a Chinese-language magazine published at Shanghai), Issue No. 38 dated 1 March 1951. Excerpts selected have been derived from the Combined Edition of Issue Nos. 37, 38 and 39 of the magazine and published at Taichong (Taiwan) by Readers Information Supplies in 1977. A new translation of excerpted selections. |
| **TG** | THE TESTIMONY OF GOD (NY: CFP, 1979) |
| ***TPL** | TWO PRINCIPLES OF LIVING (Taipei: Gospel Book Room, 1952). A booklet-length publication in Chinese. A new translation of excerpted selections. |
| **TSM** | THE SPIRITUAL MAN. 3 vols. (NY: CFP, 1968) |
| **WG** | WORSHIP GOD (NY: CFP, 1990) |
| **†WSM** | WHAT SHALL THIS MAN DO? (Fort Washington, PA: Christian Literature Crusade, 1975). Originally published 1961. |
| **WSS** | WHOM SHALL I SEND? (NY: CFP, 1979) |
| **YS** | YE SEARCH THE SCRIPTURES (NY: CFP, 1974)* |

*Those works of Watchman Nee's listed above *which have been published by Christian Fellowship Publishers* are still available and can be ordered from the Publishers at the address indicated on the Copyright Page of the present volume. Four other works of Mr. Nee's published by CFP but not cited above are also still available from the Publishers: *Full of Grace and Truth* (2 vols.), *The Mystery of Creation*, *Take Heed*, and *The Lord My Portion* (a Daily Devotional).

## Sources for the Scripture Quotations

For those works excerpted from in the present volume whose Codes are CW v.II, LNW, NCL, SWS and WSM, the English Revised Version of the Bible (1881-5) was used.

For MGW, the American Standard Version of the Bible of 1901 (ASV) was used for all quotations taken from the Old Testament, while the New American Standard Bible: The New Testament (1960) was the version used for all quotations taken from the New Testament—unless, in both instances, it was otherwise indicated.

For ROS, the Bible version (or versions?) used was unidentifiable.

For TSM, the Revised Standard Version of the Bible (1952) was used, unless otherwise indicated.

For all other works excerpted from in the present volume, the ASV was used, unless otherwise indicated.

# CONTENTS—Volume II

# 25 | Man

## *God's Purpose in Creating Man*

Why did God create man? What purpose did He have in doing so? This He has already told us in Genesis 1.26–27. These two verses are exceedingly important. The creation of man was truly a special creation, hence it required a council of the Godhead. When God created light, He gave the word and it was done. In creating the air, He again merely pronounced the word and it was done. He created all the living creatures by mere acts of creating. But in the creation of man, it was totally different. Before that creation there was a council among the Godhead: "God said, Let us make man in our image, after our likeness; and let them have dominion over the fish of the sea, and over the birds of the heavens, and over the cattle, and over all the earth, and over every creeping thing that creepeth upon the earth" (v.26). This was a plan decided in that Divine council: "Let us . . . " This brief phrase reveals the fact of consultation in the Godhead. In other words, here was the blueprint for the creation of man. Then, verse 27 gives us God's construction work: "And God created man in his own image, in the image of God created he him; male and female created he them." This is followed by verse 28: "And God blessed them: and God said unto them, Be fruitful, and multiply, and replenish the earth, and subdue it; and have dominion over the fish of the sea, and over the birds of the heavens, and over every living thing that creepeth upon the earth" (mg.).

Here we see that God wants to have a man, a man who has dominion over this earth. This will satisfy His heart.

The man whom God created had not only the Divine likeness but also the Divine image. Likeness bespeaks what is external; image, what is internal. God wants man to be like Him in nature as well as in appearance. God wants man to have the same senses, the same actions, the same manner of life and the same holiness. He wants man to be like Him so that when people touch one another they may touch the character of God. Such, then, was the substance and implication of this decision made in the Divine council.

Here is another amazing thing. Verse 26 reads: "Let us make man in our image, after our likeness." But verse 27 tells us that "God created man in his image, in the image of God created he him; male and female created he them." In verse 26 the word "us" signifies plurality whereas in verse 27 the word "his" indicates singular number. Grammatically speaking, if the phrase "let *us* make man in *our* image" in verse 26 reveals a consultation among the Father, Son, and Holy Spirit of the Godhead, then verse 27 should have similarly read the following: "And God created man in *their* image . . . ; male and female created *they* them." What is the explanation for this apparent discrepancy? It is because of the fact that in the Godhead there is but One who has image, and that One is the Son. For this reason, at the consultation of the Godhead the Divine utterance came forth: "Let us make man in our image" (for They are one), but in describing the actual construction of man the Scriptures declared: "in his image." This shows us that Adam was created in the image of the Lord Jesus. It is not a case of first Adam and then the Lord Jesus. Rather is it a case of first the Lord Jesus and then Adam. When God created Adam He created him in the image of the Lord Jesus. And hence we read: "in his image" and not "in their image."

The purpose of God is to obtain a people who are like the Son. "For whom he foreknew, he also foreordained to be conformed to the image of his Son, that he might be the firstborn among many brethren" (Rom. 8.29). This is God's purpose. He wants many sons, and these many sons are to be like His only Son. That only Son of His has an image, He also has a likeness. And these many sons are therefore to be conformed to the image of His only begotten Son. With the result that His Son is no longer the only begotten but has become the Firstborn among many brethren. God's purpose is to obtain such a people. From all this we should recognize the preciousness of man. Each time when we mention man, we should rejoice. How highly God regards man! He himself even came to be a man! And when He obtains men like this One Man, His plan is realized.

The plan of God is to be carried out by man. He wishes to use man as the solution to His own demand. What, then, did God want man to do after creating him? It was that man should have dominion. In creating man, God had not foreordained man to fall. The fall of man came after the creation of man—it happening in the time of Genesis 3. And it was due to man's own doing, since God had not foreordained man to sin. Even redemption was not God's foreordination. This does not mean that redemption is not important; it simply means that redemption was not foreordained. For had it been foreordained, then man could not help but have sinned. In the Divine council, what God *did* foreordain was for man to have dominion. This is what Genesis 1.26 reveals to us. There in His Scriptures God disclosed His own mind to us. He told us the secret of that Divine council: "Let us make man in our image, after our likeness: and let them have dominion over the fish of the sea, and over the birds of the heavens, and over the cattle, and over all the earth, and over every creeping thing that creepeth upon the earth." This, then, is the purpose of God for man: that he has dominion.

Perhaps some will ask: Why did God conceive this purpose in His mind? It was because before God proposed to create man, an angel of light had rebelled and had turned himself into the devil. Satan had committed sin and had fallen. From having been a brilliant created star he became God's adversary (see Is. 14.12). God therefore decided to take away from Satan the authority to rule and give it to man. Consequently, He created man so that man and not Satan might rule. Therein do we see the greatness of God's grace in creating man.

God not only desired man to have dominion but also wanted him to rule over a special territory. This too is shown in Genesis 1.26: "let them [the created man, both male and female] have dominion over the fish of the sea, and over the birds of the heavens, and over the cattle, and over all the earth." All the earth was to be the sphere of man's rule: not just over the fish of the sea, over the birds of the heavens, and over the cattle, but over all the earth. The boundary, therefore, within which God gives man to rule is the entire earth. Hence, there is a special relationship between man and earth, and God made special note of it. Yet God took note of this relationship between man and the earth at the time of the creation of man as well as during the consultation within the council of the Godhead: "God created man in his own image, in the image of God created he him; male and female created he them. And God blessed them: and God said unto them, Be fruitful, and multiply, and replenish the earth, and subdue it" (vv.27–28b). As to God's intention for man to "have dominion over the fish of the sea, and over the birds of the heavens . . . ," these are secondary matters: for to have dominion over these creatures is but work that is supplementary to the central design of God for man. No, what God lays emphasis upon is for man to "replenish the earth, and subdue it." But in God so stating it this way, He has revealed to us that there is a primary problem on the earth.

In that connection, let us review some other relevant Scriptures. "In the beginning God created the heavens and the earth. And the earth was waste and void; and darkness was upon the face of the deep" (Gen 1.1–2b). When at the beginning God created the heavens and the earth, there was no problem whatsoever. Later, however, a plight arose: "the earth was waste and void." The word "was" here is the same word in Hebrew as the word "became" found in Genesis 19.26, where we read that Lot's wife "looked back from behind him, and she became a pillar of salt." Lot's wife was not born as a pillar of salt; she became one later on. Likewise, the earth when created was not waste and void, but *became* so later on. God had created the heavens and the earth, "and the earth [became] waste and void." And thus a problem arose that was not in the heavens but on the earth.

Consequently, the earth is the site of the problem. What God contends for is the earth. In the prayer which our Lord Jesus taught us to pray, it reads in part: "Hallowed be thy name. Thy kingdom come. Thy will be done, as in heaven, so on earth" (Matt. 6.9b–10). According to the grammatical construction in the original Greek, this phrase "as in heaven, so on earth" is actually a part of all three petitions and not merely applicable to the last petition. In other words, the most accurate rendering of the original should be: "Hallowed be thy name, as in heaven, so on earth. Thy kingdom come, as in heaven, so on earth. Thy will be done, as in heaven, so on earth." So that from this prayer we can readily discern that there is no problem in heaven but that a great problem exists on earth. Let us recall that after the fall of man, God had said to the serpent: "upon thy belly shalt thou go, and dust shalt thou eat all the days of thy life" (Gen. 3.14b). This was to signify that thereafter the earth was to be the serpent's boundary and that he was to crawl upon it. Hence the sphere of Satan's work was no longer to be in heaven but on the earth. Accordingly, if ever the kingdom of God was to come, Satan must be driven out from the earth; if ever the will of God was to be done, it must be done on the earth; and if ever the name of God was to be hallowed, it must be hallowed on the earth. Hence, all the problem is centered on the earth.

Among many important words to be found in Genesis, there are especially two that are full of meaning. One is "subdue" (1.28); the other is "keep" or "guard" (2.15). From a consideration of these two words we may see that God appointed man both to subdue and to guard the earth. For God's original idea concerning the earth was that He had "created it not a waste, [but] formed it to be inhabited" (Is. 45.18b). God gave the earth to man to dwell upon and to guard it against the intrusion of Satan. Since after Satan's fall God had limited him to the earth, and since further

Satan is intent upon doing the work of destruction here, God has chosen man to recover the earth from Satan's hand.

Another thing to be noticed here is that, more accurately speaking, such recovery extends not only to the earth but also to the heaven that is related to the earth. In the Scriptures there is a distinction made between "heavens" and "heaven." The "heavens" is where the throne of God is, the sphere in which His authority is respected. "Heaven," on the other hand, refers at times in the Bible to the heaven which is akin to the earth. This heaven, too, like the earth, needs to be recovered (see Rev. 12.7–10).

Some may ask why God does not himself cast Satan immediately into the bottomless pit and the lake of fire. Our answer is that God is most surely able to do it, but He prefers not to do it himself. We do not know why He himself will not do it, but we do know *how* He will do it: He wants to use man to deal with His enemy, and hence this is one of the reasons why He created man: He will use the created to deal with the created: and the instrument He shall use is man.

Let us read Genesis 1.26 again. "God said, Let us make man in our image, after our likeness: and let them have dominion over the fish of the sea, and over the birds of the heavens, and over the cattle, and over all the earth . . ." It would seem that the word was about to be ended at this point; but no, another phrase is added: "and over every creeping thing that creepeth upon the earth." Here we can learn about the significant place that is occupied by the creeping things. God specifically listed the creeping things upon the earth, thus indicating that in order to rule or to subdue the earth, special attention must be paid to them. Genesis 3 mentions the serpent. Luke 10 mentions both the serpent and the scorpion. These both are creeping things: the serpent, which represents Satan; and scorpions, which represent the sinful, unclean spirits. The sphere of the scorpions as well as of the serpent is the earth. Hence the entire problem is to be found on the earth.

We need, therefore, to distinguish between the work of saving souls and the work of God. Many a time the former may not be the latter. For saving souls is for solving man's problem; whereas God's work is for man to rule, that is to say, to have dominion over all God's created things. In other words, there is a need to have a ruler over God's created things; and God chooses man to be that ruler. Had the decision about work been left up to us humans, then what we would pursue after would be confined to the expectations of our loving the Lord more, of our being more holy, and of our being more zealous in winning souls. Although all these are good, they are nonetheless too much centered on man. They are mindful of the welfare of men, but are not mindful of God's need and work. We must be brought to see that God has His need. Our lives on earth are not to be centered merely on human requirements but even more so on God's requirement.

We thank the Lord for giving us the ministry of reconciliation in persuading men to be reconciled to God. Nevertheless, were we to be successful in winning the whole world back to God, there would still be a work of God for us to do because the requirement of God would have remained unsatisfied. Here is a matter called the work of God, the need of God. When God created man, He had already disclosed what His need was. He had shown us that His need is for man to have dominion over all the created things of His hand. Let us understand that to rule is not a small matter; it is a very large issue. God is in need of a people who can be trusted and who will not themselves create problems. This, then, is God's work, God's requirement, that which He is after.

Let me make it clear here that we do not despise the preaching of the gospel at all. But if all our works are confined to preaching the gospel and winning souls, then Satan has not been dealt a fatal blow. For if men do not regain the earth from the hand of Satan, we shall fail to arrive at God's purpose in creating man. To win souls back to the Lord is for the benefit of men; to be used of the Lord to deal with Satan is for the advantage of God. To win souls is to solve man's need, but to deal with Satan is to satisfy God's need. But brethren should realize that this demands a price be paid! We know demons can speak. For on one occasion the evil spirit had said, "Jesus I know, and Paul I know, but who are ye?" (Acts 19.15) The issue centers on whether or not demons flee when they meet us. True, preaching the gospel is indeed costly, but dealing with Satan is much more costly.

This that is being said here is not sermonizing; what is being said needs to be put into practice. And when done so, we shall find that the cost is exceedingly high indeed. If God greatly desires men to overthrow all the works and authority of Satan, then we men must absolutely and completely surrender ourselves to the Lord. In performing other spiritual works, the consequence of our making provision for ourselves may not be that grave. But in God's work of dealing with Satan, we cannot retain any place at all for ourselves. We may hold back something of ourselves in reading the Bible, in preaching the gospel, helping the church, or in helping the brethren; but in this matter of dealing with Satan, we cannot keep anything of ourselves back at all. For if we do, we will not be able to dislodge him from his wrongful rule. May the Lord open our eyes that we may see that God's purpose is for us to be wholly His. All who are double-minded cannot be used to deal with Satan. May God speak to our hearts.

### *God's Purpose Never Changes*

God wishes to obtain a man who can rule over the earth, yet man has not attained to God's purpose. We find in Genesis 3 that man failed, sin came into the world, and that the earth came under the power of Satan. In fact, it appeared that all was now lost. Satan seemed to have overcome all, and God appeared as though defeated. But we still have that portion of Genesis 1, earlier discussed, to encourage our hearts; and also, there are two other portions of Scripture—Psalm 8 and Hebrews 2—which have a direct bearing on this matter, and they, too, can encourage us.

#### Psalm 8

Psalm 8 shows us that God's foreordained plan never changes.

After the fall of man, God's will and demand on man remain the same. His purpose has not changed. What will and purpose which God had concerning man in the Divine council reported in Genesis 1 remained the same after man's sin and fall. Psalm 8 was composed after the fall of man. Man had fallen, but the psalmist could still sing praises because his eyes were fixed on Genesis 1. The Holy Spirit had not forgotten Genesis 1; the Holy Son had not forgotten Genesis 1; God the Father had not forgotten Genesis 1.

Let us look into the contents of Psalm 8. "O Jehovah, our Lord, how excellent is thy name in all the earth . . . !" (v.1) All who are moved by the Holy Spirit will declare: "How excellent is Thy name in all the earth!" In spite of that name being blasphemed and rejected by men, the psalmist can still shout aloud, "O Jehovah, our Lord, how excellent is Thy name in all the earth!" He did not just say, "Excellent is Thy name in all the earth." For there is quite a difference between saying "excellent" and "*How* excellent." Simply to say "excellent" would suggest that the psalmist could still describe Jehovah's name, but to say "*How* excellent" signifies that the writer of the psalm did not know what to say or how to describe its excellency. He could therefore only cry out, "O Jehovah, our Lord, how excellent is Thy name in all the earth!" Not only is His name excellent beyond description, but His name is par excellence in *all the earth*. The significance of this latter phrase is the same as the "all the earth" phrase found in Genesis 1.26. If we know the plan of God, our heart will be moved each time we read concerning "man" and "earth."

"Out of the mouth of babes and sucklings hast thou established strength, because of thine adversaries, that thou mightest still the enemy and the avenger" (v.2). Babes and sucklings refer to man. The emphasis here is how God uses man to deal with the enemy. Later the Lord Jesus himself quoted this very word, saying, "Out of the mouth of babes and sucklings thou hast perfected praise" (Matt. 21.16b). This means that no matter what the enemy may do, God has no need to deal with him since God's plan calls for the use of babes and sucklings to deal with him. What might these babes and sucklings do? "Out of the mouth of babes and sucklings hast thou established strength." God desires to obtain a people who are able to praise. By the renewed strength which comes from praising God, such people can deal with the enemy.

"When I consider thy heavens, the work of thy fingers, the moon and the stars, which thou hast ordained; what is man, that thou art mindful of him? and the son of man, that thou visitest him? For thou hast made him but little lower than God [or, *the angels*], and crownest him with glory and honor. Thou makest him to have dominion over the works of thy hands; thou hast put all things under his feet: all sheep and oxen, yea, and the beasts of the field, the birds of the heavens, and the fish of the sea, whatsoever passeth through the paths of the seas" (vv.3–8). Had we composed this psalm we would most probably have added a parenthesis, saying, "Alas, man has fallen, has sinned and been driven out of the garden of Eden, thus man can never attain to this place of dominion and rule." Yet thank God, here in the mind of the poet there was no such thought. In the eyes of God, the earth can still be regained: the position He gave to man is still there: and the task He had entrusted into man's hands to destroy the work of the devil is still in force. And hence, from verse 3 onward the psalmist is seen retelling the old story, but ignoring completely the failure and fall of man found in Genesis 3. This in itself constitutes the most characteristic feature of Psalm 8. God's purpose is for man to rule. Is man worthy? No, he is truly unworthy. But if God's purpose is for man to rule, and if God's purpose has not changed, then man shall most certainly rule.

"O Jehovah, our Lord, how excellent is thy name in all the earth!" (v.9) The psalmist praises as though he has never been made aware of the fall of man. Notwithstanding their having sinned, Adam and Eve could not withstand God's plan. Man might fall into sin, but he cannot overturn God's will of wanting man to have dominion and to overthrow the authority of Satan. After the fall of man, God's determined will for man remained the same. Oh, God is eternally the same! God's path is a straight one which never deviates no matter what may happen. We must know that God is unbeatable. In this world some people may receive many blows, yet none takes constant, daily blows as does God, but still His will has never been overturned. What God had decided before man's fall remained the same even after sin came into the world. What yesterday He had ordained stays the same today. He does not change.

### Hebrews 2

Genesis 1 discloses God's foreordained will at the time of creation; Psalm 8 reiterates God's will after the fall of man; and Hebrews 2 reveals God's will in redemption. Let us now look at Hebrews 2. In redemption and victory, God still wants man to have authority to deal with Satan, as Hebrews 2.5–8a—quoting at the outset from Psalm 8—makes clear: "For not unto angels did he subject the world to come, whereof we speak. But one hath somewhere testified, saying, What is man, that thou art mindful of him? or the son of man, that thou visitest him? Thou madest him a little lower than the angels; thou crownedst him with glory and honor, and didst set him over the works of thy hands: thou didst put all things in subjection under his feet. [All up to this point is a quotation from Psalm 8.] For in that he subjected all things unto him, he left nothing that is not subject to him." All things must be in subjection to man, for this is what God had originally ordained.

However, the matter is not as straightforward as one would wish. For in the second part of verse 8 and the first part of verse 9 we read: "But now we see not yet all things subjected to him. But we behold him who hath been made a little lower than the angels, even Jesus, because of the suffering of death crowned with glory and honor." Here the reference is only applied to Jesus. In Psalm 8 we learn that God has made man a little lower than the angels, but here in Hebrews 2 the apostle changes "man" to "Jesus." He interprets "man" as Jesus: It was Jesus who was made a little lower than the angels. Redemption comes from this source. Originally God had ordained man to be made a little lower than the angels that he might drive out for God the enemy from the earth and its immediate heaven. Man was to destroy all the powers of Satan and be crowned with glory and honor that he might rule over God's creation. But man had fallen and was thus not able to rule. It was for this cause, then, that the Lord Jesus came. He took upon himself man's body of flesh and blood and became the "last Adam" (1 Cor. 15.45b).

Continuing with Hebrews 2, we next read this: "that by the grace of God he [Jesus] should taste of death for every man" (v.9b). The phrase "every man" in Greek can be translated "every thing." The Lord Jesus was born as a man and accomplished the work of redemption—yet not just for men but for all created beings, except the angels. Hence He occupies two positions. In the first, towards God, Jesus is the original man, the man whom God has foreordained; in the second, towards men, He is the Savior. On the one hand, the Lord Jesus is the man whom God had foreordained to have dominion and to overturn Satan. And this man is now seated on the throne! For hallelujah! this man has already overthrown the powers of Satan. This is the man of God's expectation and possession. On the other hand, this man is also related to us. We have sinned and fallen, but God set forth Jesus to be a propitiation. He not only became our propitiation, He also was judged for all created things. This fact is demonstrated by what happened at Jesus' crucifixion with the renting of the veil in the Temple sanctuary (see Mark 15.38). For according to Hebrews 10.20 that veil points to the flesh of the Lord Jesus. On the sanctuary veil had been embroidered cherubim who were representative of created things. So that inherent in the flesh of our Lord Jesus were all created things. And on the day the Lord died, the veil, we are told, was rent into two from top to bottom. Naturally, the cherubim embroidered on the veil were also rent. Hence, in the death of the Lord Jesus, all created things were judged. He has thus tasted death not only for every *man* but also for every *thing*.

Reading further in Hebrews 2, we learn this: "For it became him [God] for whom are all things, and through whom are all things, in bringing many sons unto glory" (v.10a). All things belong to God; all things are through God; and all things are unto God. In other words, what is *of* Him will be what is *unto* Him. Thank God, His purpose of creation has not changed. What He had foreordained at the time of creation remains the same after the fall of man. In redemption God's foreordination is secured. He has not changed His plan because of the fall of man. Thank God, He will lead many sons into glory. He wants His many sons to have glory. He will obtain a new mankind after the image and likeness of His Son. The Lord Jesus becomes a representative man. As He is, so are the rest of men who are redeemed. Together with Him, they will enter into glory.

How is this matter implemented? The next verse supplies the answer. "For both he that sanctifieth, and they that are sanctified are all of one" (v.11a). Who is He who sanctifies? He is the Lord Jesus. Who are the sanctified? We are the sanctified. So we may read the verse in this manner: "For both Jesus that sanctifieth and we that are sanctified are all of one." Both the Lord Jesus and we come from the one Father—the one source with the same life and the one indwelling Holy Spirit. God is the Father of us as well as of our Lord Jesus. "For which cause he is not ashamed to call them brethren" (v.11b). The "he" here points to the Lord Jesus, and the "them" here refers to us who have been redeemed. "For which cause he is not ashamed to call them brethren." It is because He comes from the Father, and so do we.

We are the many sons of God. Our destiny will be brought by God into glory. Redemption does not alter God's purpose; it instead fulfills that purpose which creation had earlier failed to fulfill. God had originally designed for man to have dominion and to rule over the earth; but, alas, man fell. Nevertheless, not everything was finished and done for because the first man had fallen. What God could not obtain in the first man (Adam), He achieved in the second man (Christ). Due to God's determined will and purpose for man to rule, regain the earth, and destroy Satan as one created (man) against another created (Satan), there occurs the birth in Bethlehem. For God *will* have a man to defeat His enemy. So the Lord Jesus now comes forth.

The first man failed to achieve God's purpose and fell into sin. He not only failed to regain the earth but was even taken captive by Satan He not only could not rule, he fell under the rule and power of Satan. Moreover, man even became Satan's food, for Genesis 2 tells us that man was made of dust and Genesis 3 tells us that dust was to be Satan's food. The consequence of all this, then, is that man has no way to deal with Satan. In short, it would appear that man is finished. Or is he? Can anything be done about this? Or does this truly mean that God's eternal purpose will never be fulfilled? that God cannot obtain what He has desired? that He cannot recover the earth? No, He sent His own Son to become a man. He specifically comes as a man and is truly a man. The Lord Jesus is truly God, but at the same time He is truly a man.

In this whole world, there is one man who truly desires after God. There is One who can truly say: "the prince of the world . . . hath nothing in me" (John 14.30). In other words, in the Lord Jesus you cannot find anything that belongs to the prince of the world—the devil. Let us take note of the fact that the Lord Jesus came to the world not to be God but to be man. For what God needs is a man. If God in himself had wanted to deal with Satan, He could have done it quickly and Satan could never have stood against it. But God did not wish to do it himself. Instead He desired to have man deal with Satan. He arranges to have a created being to deal with another created being. But with the failure of the first man, the Lord Jesus came forth to be the second man. He was tempted just like the rest of mankind; and what He experienced was not any different from what other men have experienced. Yet today *this* man has ascended to heaven, *this* man has already seated himself at the right hand of God; *this* man has already received glory.

Yet the glory which Hebrews 2 speaks about is not the glory of Jesus as God but His glory as a man. (This does not mean to imply that Jesus does not have the glory that belongs to Him as God; it simply means that here in Hebrews 2 this is not the focus.) He who was made a little lower than the angels is now crowned with glory and honor because of the suffering of death. The Lord ascended to heaven in the likeness of man. Today there is one Man already in heaven; in the future many other men—His brethren—will also be there in heaven. Today, one Man has already been seated on the throne; one day, many other men will likewise sit on thrones. This is most certainly to come.

At the time of resurrection the Lord Jesus gave His life to us. We who now believe in Him have His life. We all become the sons of God. We all belong to God. Due to the fact that we have His life in us, we are able to accept the charge of God to achieve His purpose also, as did His Son. Hence, the Scripture reads: "bringing many sons to glory." To rule is glory; glory is to rule. Many other sons are brought into glory because they, like *the* Son, have authority, because they—like *the* Son—have regained the earth from the hands of the enemy.

In the light of all this, we must not assume that what God has purposed is only to save us out of hell into the blessing of heaven. We should ever be mindful that God wants men to reign together with His Son over the earth. Above all else, God desires to accomplish this one thing, but He will not do it himself, He wants us men to do it. If we do this work, God will gain what He desires. God wants to have a people who will do His work that He might rule over the earth through them.

### *The Relation between Redemption and Creation*

Let us notice the relation between redemption and creation. Do not ever imagine that there is nothing in the entire Bible besides the matter of redemption. We thank God that there is also creation. God's heart desire is truly expressed in His creation: for His purpose, plan and foreordained will are all intimated there. Creation discloses God's eternal purpose. It tells us what God is really after.

First of all, we must understand and acknowledge that the position of redemption is not higher than that of creation. What is the purpose of redemption? Redemption is to recover that which God had not obtained in creation. Redemption does not give us any new thing; on the contrary, it only gives us in restored form what was already there. Through redemption God finally achieves the purpose of creation which man had failed to achieve. Hence we may say that redemption is to restore and recover, whereas creation is to will and determine. Redemption is but a step after creation in order to arrive at God's purpose of creation. May God's children not despise creation. May they not consider redemption as everything. Redemption is related to us for it causes us to be saved, to receive eternal life and to be benefited. Creation is related to God for it is connected to the will and work of God. Our relationship with redemption is a matter of man's benefit, but our relationship to creation is for God's benefit. May God do a new thing on earth, which is, to cause men to take note of not only the gospel but also the work of God, the affairs of God, the eternal plan of God.

To be a Christian is on the one hand receiving the benefit of redemption but on the other hand arriving at God's purpose of creation. Without redemption there can be no relationship with God. But once having been redeemed, we need to consecrate ourselves to God so that His original purpose in creating man might be achieved. If we only notice the gospel, then that is only taking in half of the matter. There is another half which God desires; and that is, He wants man to drive out Satan from this earth and to rule here for Him. This other half the Church must likewise possess. Hebrews 2 shows us that the end of redemption is not simply for man's sins to be forgiven and for him to be saved; it is also to recover him back to the original purpose of creation.

We may say, then, that redemption is like the valley between two peaks. Coming down from one mountain peak you are enabled to go up the other peak. Redemption is at the lowest place of the valley. It stops man from falling farther down and enables him to be lifted up to the highest peak. On the one side is God's purpose which is eternal, traveling in a straight line, and without the slightest deviation or point of depression. His purpose for creation must be arrived at. On the other side something terrible has happened: man has fallen, having departed from God and falling farther and farther away from God's eternal purpose for him. The purpose of God is a straight line from eternity to eternity. But man has fallen and failed to follow the line. Thank God, here is a way of salvation which is called redemption. Redemption emerges as a means to keep man from going farther downward. Once having been redeemed, man is transformed and he commences going upward. He keeps ascending till one day he touches the straight line of God's purpose again. This is the time of the arrival of the Kingdom.

Thank God that we do indeed have redemption. If there were no redemption, we would fall lower and lower and be oppressed more and more by Satan. We would have no way of rising up. Thank the Lord that His redemption causes us to return to the eternal purpose of God. That which God had not obtained in creation and which had been lost in man's fall is now being recovered through redemption.

Let us ask God to open our eyes to see what He has done so that it will change our life and work. If all our works are circumscribed by only the winning of souls, then we have failed because we have not satisfied God's heart. Both redemption and creation are for His purpose of obtaining glory and overthrowing all the powers of the enemy. May we on the one hand proclaim the love and authority of God and on the other hand exercise spiritual authority to overturn the authority of the devil. The mission of the Church is to testify to the salvation of Christ on the one hand and to the victory of Christ on the other. And thus shall men be benefited and Satan suffer loss.

### *God's Sabbath*

Among the six days of creation, that of man was special, for all the other works of God in these six days were but preparations for the creation of man. God's ultimate purpose in all these other preparatory labors lay in His creating man: in order to create man, God must first restore the ruinous earth and heaven. "These are the generations of the heavens and of the earth when they were created, in the day that Jehovah God made earth and heaven" (Gen. 2.4). (Please note that the statement "the generations of the heavens and of the earth when they were created" refers to the original creation, for in the beginning God created the heavens and then the earth; but the succeeding statement—"in the day that Jehovah God made earth and heaven"—points to repair and restoration, because at the time of restoring, God first repaired the earth and then heaven.) But once He had restored the ruinous earth and heaven, God could create the man He had originally had in mind. And following these six days of creation came the seventh day—a day on which God "rested . . . from all his work which he had made" (2.2b).

Rest follows work. Only after the work is satisfactorily done can there be rest. If the work is not completed or satisfactory, there can be no rest. Consequently, we must not regard God's rest after six days of creation as a small matter. For God to have rested signified a momentous event. He can only rest after He has obtained that which He desired. Who can measure the power that causes the God of creation—the God who has a plan and who is so full of life—to rest? That power had to have been tremendous to have moved Him to rest. Genesis 2 shows us that God rested on the seventh day. Why could He rest? This is revealed to us in the last verse of Genesis 1: "And God saw everything that he had made, and, behold, it was very good" (v.31).

So God rested on the seventh day. Before that day He had worked; and before He had worked, He had had a purpose in mind. Romans 11 mentions the mind, the judgments and the ways of the Lord (see vv.33–34). Ephesians 1 speaks of the mystery of God's will, His good pleasure and His foreordination. Ephesians 3 talks of God's predetermined will. God is therefore not just the One who works but the One who wills as well. He works out from His good pleasure. He works out from what He desires in His heart. And after He is satisfied with His work, He rests.

By noticing the occasion that prompted God to rest, we can understand God's mind, will, plan, good pleasure and foreordained purpose. By observing the particular thing which gives God rest, we shall know that that is the very thing for which He had originally planned. No one can rest in matters which remain unsatisfactory to him. He must obtain what he desires before he can ever rest. Hence, we cannot despise or belittle this rest of God, as though it were something inconsequential. On the contrary, rest here is most meaningful. During the first six days God had no rest. On the seventh day He rested. This rest therefore tells us that God had accomplished a work which satisfied and gladdened His heart. And hence, He rested.

Notice the words "saw" and "behold" here. What do they signify? After we have purchased something, for example, we are so pleased with it that we look at it over and over again. This is something of the meaning of "saw . . . behold." God saw and beheld everything He had made, and to Him it was not just good, it was *very* good. "And he rested" (2.2). By this very statement is declared God's satisfaction and pleasure in having achieved His purpose: God's good pleasure has been fully met, and His work has been totally accomplished.

For this reason, God told the children of Israel to keep the sabbath from generation to generation. This implies that the one thing which God had hoped for and sought after had now been obtained, and therefore there could be rest. The meaning of sabbath lies not in the buying of fewer things or the walking of fewer miles; rather, it declares that God is now at rest because He has possessed that which He had originally conceived and looked for. Sabbath is not a matter of a particular day and one's conduct thereon. It speaks instead of God's heart satisfaction in having accomplished His plan and having achieved His purpose. God needs to be satisfied, and now He *is* satisfied. And when that happens—when He obtains what He desires—He enters into rest.

Precisely what, here, had gladdened His heart? What, specifically, had given Him satisfaction? On the first day, there came forth light; on the second day, there was firmament; on the third day, the earth came out of the waters; on the fourth day, sun, moon and stars appeared; on the fifth day, there appeared living creatures in the waters and living birds in the air; and finally, on the sixth day, God created man. All works before the creation of man were but God's preparatory labors, for all His hope lay ultimately in man. Now it was this man that gave God satisfaction and allowed Him to enter into rest.

Let us read again Genesis 1.27–28: "God created man in his own image, in the image of God created he him; male and female created he them. And God blessed them: and God said unto them, Be fruitful, and multiply, and replenish the earth, and subdue it; and have dominion over the fish of the sea, and over the birds of the heavens, and over every living thing that creepeth upon the earth." This is followed by 1.31–2.3 which reads: "And God saw everything that he had made, and, behold, it was very good. . . . And God blessed the seventh day, and hallowed it; because that in it he rested from all his work which God had created and made." God has a purpose which is to obtain the man who can exercise dominion over the earth. This alone can satisfy His heart. And when He possesses this man, to Him everything will be very good. When finally on the sixth day the purpose of God was arrived at, "God saw everything that he had made, and, behold, it was very good." Thus did He rest on the seventh day from all His work! His foreordained will and expectation had been fulfilled; therefore, He could rest. In short, God's rest rests upon the fact of man's dominion.

—HWB 2-23

### *The Creation of Man*

"And Jehovah God formed man of dust from the ground, and breathed into his nostrils the breath of life; and man became a living soul" (Gen. 2.7 ASV). When God first created man He formed him of dust from the ground, and then breathed "the breath of life" into his nostrils. As soon as the breath of life, which became man's spirit, came into contact with man's body, the soul was produced. Hence the soul is the combination of man's body and spirit. The Scriptures therefore call man "a living soul." The breath of life became man's spirit; that is, the principle of life within him. The Lord Jesus tells us "it is the spirit that gives life" (John 6.63). This breath of life comes from the Lord of Creation. However, we must not confuse *man's* spirit with God's Holy Spirit. The latter differs from our human spirit. Romans 8.16 demonstrates their difference by declaring that "it is the Spirit himself bearing witness *with* our spirit that we are children of God." The original of the word "life" in "breath of life" is *chay* and is in the *plural.* This may refer to the fact that the inbreathing of God produced a twofold life, soulical and spiritual. When the inbreathing of God entered man's body it became the spirit of man; but when the spirit reacted with the body the soul was produced. This explains the source of our spiritual and soulical lives. We must recognize, though, that this spirit is not God's *own* life, for "the breath of the Almighty gives me life" (Job 33.4). It is not the entrance of the uncreated life of God into man, neither is it that life of God which we receive at regeneration. What we receive at new birth is God's own life as typified by the tree of life. But our human spirit, though permanently existing, is void of "eternal life."

"Formed man of dust from the ground" refers to man's body; "breathed into his nostrils the breath of life" refers to man's spirit as it came from God; and "man became a living soul" refers to man's soul when the body was quickened by the spirit and brought into being a living and self-conscious man. A complete man is a trinity—the composite of spirit, soul and body. According to Genesis 2.7, man was made up of only two independent elements, the corporeal and the spiritual; but when God placed the spirit within the casing of the earth, the soul was produced. The spirit of man touching the dead body produced the soul. The body apart from the spirit was dead, but with the spirit man was made alive. The organ thus animated was called the soul.

### *Respective Functions of Spirit, Soul and Body*

It is through the corporal body that man comes into contact

with the material world. Hence we may label the body as that part which gives us *world-consciousness.* The soul comprises the intellect which aids us in the present state of existence and the emotions which proceed from the senses. Since the soul belongs to man's own self and reveals his personality, it is termed the part of *self-consciousness.* The spirit is that part by which we commune with God and by which alone we are able to apprehend and worship Him. Because it tells us of our relationship with God, the spirit is called the element of *God-consciousness.* God dwells in the spirit, self dwells in the soul, while senses dwell in the body. . . .

The spirit is the noblest part of man and occupies the innermost area of his being. The body is the lowest and takes the outermost place. Between these two dwells the soul, serving as their medium. The body is the outer shelter of the soul, while the soul is the outer sheath of the spirit. The spirit transmits its thought to the soul and the soul exercises the body to obey the spirit's order. This is the meaning of the soul as the medium. Before the fall of man the spirit controlled the whole being through the soul. . . .

According to the teaching of the Bible and the experience of believers, the human spirit can be said to comprise three parts; or, to put it another way, one can say it has three main functions. These are conscience, intuition and communion The *conscience* is the discerning organ which distinguishes right and wrong; not, however, through the influence of knowledge stored in the mind but rather by a spontaneous direct judgment. Often reasoning will justify things which our conscience judges. The work of the conscience is independent and direct; it does not bend to outside opinions. If man should do wrong it will raise its voice of accusation. *Intuition* is the sensing organ of the human spirit. It is so diametrically different from physical sense and soulical sense that it is called intuition. Intuition involves a direct sensing independent of any outside influence. That knowledge which comes to us without any help from the mind, emotion or volition comes intuitively. We really "know" through our intuition; our mind merely helps us to "understand." The revelations of God and all the movements of the Holy Spirit are known to the believer through his intuition. A believer must therefore heed these two elements: the voice of conscience and the teaching of intuition. *Communion* is worshiping God. The organs of the soul are incompetent to worship God. God is not apprehended by our thoughts, feelings or intentions, for He can only be known *directly* in our spirits. Our worship of God and God's communications with us are directly in the spirit. They take place in "the inner man," not in the soul or outward man.

We can conclude then that these three elements of conscience, intuition and communion are deeply interrelated and function coordinately. The relationship between conscience and intuition is that conscience judges according to intuition; it condemns all conduct which does not follow the directions given by intuition. Intuition is related to communion or worship in that God is known by man intuitively and reveals His will to man in the intuition. No measure of expectation or deduction gives us the knowledge of God. . . .

That which constitutes man's personality are the three main faculties of volition, mind and emotion. Volition is the instrument for our decisions, revealing our power to choose. It expresses our willingness or unwillingness: "we will" or "we won't." Without it, man is reduced to an automaton. Mind, the instrument for our thoughts, manifests our intellectual power. Out of this arise wisdom, knowledge and reasoning. Lack of it makes a man foolish and dull. The instrument for our likes and dislikes is the faculty of emotion. Through it we are able to express love or hate and to feel joyful, angry, sad or happy. Any shortage of it will render man as insensitive as wood or stone. . . .

"The fruit of the knowledge of good and evil" uplifts the human soul and suppresses the spirit. God does not forbid man to eat of this fruit merely to test man. He forbids it because He knows that by eating this fruit man's soul life will be so stimulated that his spirit life will be stifled. This means man will lose the true knowledge of God and thus be dead to Him. God's forbiddance shows God's love. The knowledge of good and evil in this world is itself evil. Such knowledge springs from the intellect of man's soul. It puffs up the soul life and consequently deflates the spirit life to the point of losing any knowledge of God, to the point of becoming as much as dead. . . .

Satan moved Adam to sin by seizing the latter's will through his emotion, while he tempted Eve to sin by grasping her will through the channel of a darkened mind. When man's will and mind and emotion were poisoned by the serpent and man followed after Satan instead of God, his spirit, which was capable of communing with God, suffered a fatal blow. Here we can see the law which governs the work of Satan. He uses the things of the flesh (eating fruit) to entice man's soul into sin; as soon as the soul sins, the spirit descends into utter darkness. The order of his working is always such: from the outside to the inside. If he does not start with the body, then he begins by working on the mind or the emotion in order to get to the will of man. The moment man's will yields to Satan he possesses man's whole being and puts the spirit to death. But not so the work of God; His is always from the inside to the outside. God begins working in man's spirit and continues by illuminating his mind, stirring his emotion, and causing him to exercise his will over his body for carrying into execution the will of God. All satanic works are performed from the outside inward; all divine works, from the inside outward. We may in this way distinguish what comes from God and what from Satan. All this additionally teaches us that once Satan seizes man's will, then is he in control over that man

We should carefully note that the soul is where man expresses his free will and exerts his own mastery. The Bible therefore often records that it is the soul which sins. For example, Micah 6.7 says, "the sin of my soul." Ezekiel 18.4,20 reads, "the soul that sins." And in the books of Leviticus and Numbers mention frequently is made that the soul sins. Why? Because it is the soul which chooses to sin. Our description of sin is: "The will acquiesces in the temptation." Sinning is a matter of the soul's will; atonement accordingly must be for the soul. "Ye give the heave-offering of Jehovah to make atonement for your souls" (Ex. 30.15 Darby). "For the soul of the flesh is in the blood; and I have given it to you upon the altar to make atonement for your souls, for it is the blood that maketh atonement for the soul" (Lev. 17.11 Darby). "To make atonement for our souls before Jehovah" (Num. 31.50 Darby). Since it is the *soul* which sins, it follows that the *soul* needs to be atoned. And it can only be atoned, moreover, by a soul:

> it pleased Jehovah to bruise him; he hath subjected him to suffering . . . thou shalt make his soul an offering for sin . . . He shall see of the fruit of the travail of his soul, and shall be satisfied . . . he hath poured out his soul unto death . . .; and he bore the sin of many, and made intercession for the transgressors. (Is. 53.10–12 Darby) . . .

Henceforth Adam's spirit (as well as the spirit of all his descendants) fell under the oppression of the soul until it gradually merged with the soul and the two parts became closely united. The writer of Hebrews declares in 4.12 that the word of God shall pierce and divide soul and spirit. The dividing is necessary because spirit and soul have become one. While they are intimately knit they plunge man into a psychic world. Everything is done according to the dictates of intellect or feeling. The spirit has lost its power and sensation, as though dead asleep. What instinct it has in knowing and serving God is entirely paralyzed. It remains in a coma as if non-existent. This is what is meant in Jude 19 by "natural, not having spirit" (literal).* This certainly does not mean the human spirit ceases to exist, for Numbers 16.22

*The spirit here does not point to the Holy Spirit but to the human spirit, for it is preceded by the word "natural," which literally is, "soulish." As "soulish" pertains to man, so "spirit" also pertains to man. —*Author* distinctly states that God is "the God of the spirits of all flesh." Every human being still has in his possession a spirit, although it is darkened by sin and impotent to hold communion with God. . . .

*Regeneration*

The concept of regeneration as found in the Bible speaks of the process of passing out of death into life. A man's spirit before regeneration is far away from God and is considered dead, for death is dissociation from life and from God who is the fountain of life. Death is hence separation from God. Man's spirit is dead and therefore unable to commune with Him. Either his soul controls him and plunges him into a life of ideas and imaginations, or the lusts and habits of his body stimulate him and reduce his soul to servitude.

Man's spirit needs to be quickened because it is born dead. The new birth which the Lord Jesus spoke about to Nicodemus is the new birth of the spirit. It certainly is not a physical birth as Nicodemus suspected, nor is it a soulical one. We must note carefully that new birth imparts God's life to the *spirit* of man. Inasmuch as Christ has atoned for our soul and destroyed the principle of the flesh, so we who are joined to Him participate in His resurrection life. We have been united with Him in His death; consequently it is in our spirit that we first reap the realization of His resurrection life. New birth is something which happens entirely within the spirit; it has no relation to soul or body. . . .

The writer of Proverbs tells us that "the spirit of man is the lamp of the Lord" (20.27). During the time of regeneration the Holy Spirit comes into man's spirit and quickens it as though kindling a lamp. This is the "new spirit" mentioned in Ezekiel 36.26; the dead old spirit is quickened into life when the Holy Spirit infuses it with God's uncreated life.

Before regeneration the soul of man is in control of his spirit while his own "self" rules his soul and his passion governs his body. Soul has become the life of the body. At regeneration man receives God's own life into his spirit and is born of God. As a consequence, the Holy Spirit now rules man's spirit which in turn is equipped to regain control over the soul and, through the soul, to govern his body. Because the Holy Spirit becomes the life of man's spirit, the latter becomes the life of man's whole being. The spirit, soul and body are restored to God's original intention in every born-again person. . . .

A life relationship is established with God in new birth. It resembles the old birth of the flesh in that it is once and for all. Once a man is born of God he can never be treated by God as not having been so born of Him. However endless eternity may be, this relationship and this position cannot be annulled. This is because what a believer receives at new birth is not contingent upon a progressive, spiritual and holy pursuit after he believes but is the pure gift of God. What God bestows is eternal life. No possibility exists for this life and position to be abrogated. . . .

For those who are born anew, there is great potentiality for spiritual growth. Regeneration is the obvious first step in spiritual development. Though the life received is perfect, it waits to be matured. At the moment of new birth life cannot be full-grown. It is like a fruit newly formed: the life is perfect but it is still unripe. There is therefore boundless possibility for growth. The Holy Spirit is able to bring the person into complete victory over body and soul.

—TSM, I: 23–4, 26, 27, 31–2, 36, 44–5, 48–9, 51, 61, 63, 67

The dividing of soul and spirit is exceedingly essential since it concerns the Christian's spiritual growth. How can a Christian seek for that which is spiritual if he does not even know the distinction between spirit and soul? He will often mistake the soulish for the spiritual, and thus stay long in the realm of soulish living instead of seeking for the spiritual. The word of God cites many times the features of the spirit as well as those of the soul. For instance, the Bible records being sorrowful in the spirit as well as being sorrowful in the soul, it mentions being joyful in the spirit as much as being joyful in the soul. Hence people draw the conclusion that since the expressions of the spirit and the soul are the same, the spirit must be the soul. This is like saying, "Because you eat food and I too eat food, therefore you must be me." Yet Hebrews 4.12 says that "the word of God is living, and active, and sharper than any two-edged sword, and piercing even to the *dividing* of soul and spirit." Since soul and spirit may be separated, soul must be soul and spirit must be spirit.

We are shown in Genesis 2 that when God first created man He "formed man of the dust of the ground, and breathed into his nostrils the breath of life; and man became a living soul" (v.7). This breath of life is man's spirit since it came directly from God. As it touched man's body, the soul was produced—and man became a living soul. Man's spirit has God-consciousness, knows God's voice, and is able to communicate with Him. But after the fall of Adam, his spirit became dead to God. Thereafter the spirit of Adam (and of all his descendants) was so oppressed by the soul that his spirit was knit intimately with the soul. When a person is saved, though, his spirit becomes alive to God; but due to the close uniting of the spirit with the soul for such a long period, it requires the word of God to divide or separate them. . . .

What therefore is soulish? Soulish is that which is done by oneself. And what therefore is spiritual? It is that which is done by God. And these two are radically different. A person can do something without any need for waiting upon God and trusting in Him. Such action is fleshly and it is soulish. But if a person cannot speak before God speaks, cannot move except God moves first; if he must look to God, wait and depend on Him—then that person and that action is spiritual. Let us thus ask ourselves if all we do is in the Holy Spirit? This is such an important question. Frequently there is nothing wrong in what we do, nevertheless there is condemnation registered within us when we do it. The reason for this inward sense is not that what we do outwardly is necessarily wrong but because the thing we do is not initiated from God—that is to say, it is not the outcome of the working of the Holy Spirit in us. . . .

The lady who powders herself needs to look at the mirror frequently, but Moses' face shone often without his even being conscious of it. Whoever manifests the effects of God's working in him, that can be called spiritual. But the one who attempts to manufacture something must employ much strength; therefore he feels weary at being a Christian, although a Christian should never exercise his own strength in any case. We often judge that so long as a thing looks good it is probably all right, but God looks at the source as to whether it is of Him or an imitating in the power of the flesh. . . .

In spiritual things, self-analysis will not only fail to show us the reality, it will even create spiritual paralysis. Real seeing and understanding comes only from God's illumination. As light shines, we just naturally see. We therefore do not need to ask ourselves questions; all we need to do is to ask God to cause His word to shine in us, for the word of God is living and most effective; it is sharper than any two-edged sword and pierces even to dividing between soul and spirit, between both joints and marrow. As soon as the word of God enters, you can immediately perceive what is soulish from what is spiritual. There is a judgment within you which is sharper than any human judgment. If you make a move, your inward sense tells you that this move is not right or not deep enough, or that it is you who are doing things and you who are trying to influence people. When you see inwardly, you really see. May God have mercy upon us by granting the inner light by which we may distinguish inwardly.

The dividing of soul and spirit is the foundation for a Christian to have discerning power. Yet whether we have this discerning power or not depends on inward illumination and not on outward instruction. What we should expect before God is that the entry of His word will give light so that He may show us what in our personal life and work is soulish or what is spiritual.

—MC 91-2, 94, 97, 99-100

### *The True Nature of the Fall*

If we have even a little revelation of the plan of God we shall always think much of the word "man." We shall say with the Psalmist, "What is man, that thou art mindful of him?" The Bible makes it clear that what God desires above all things is a man—a man who will be after His own heart.

So God created a man. In Genesis 2.7 we learn that Adam was created *a living soul*, with a *spirit* inside to commune with God and with a *body* outside to have contact with the material world. (Such New Testament verses as 1 Thessalonians 5.23 and Hebrews 4.12 confirm this threefold character of man's being.) With his spirit Adam was in touch with the spiritual world of God; with his body he was in touch with the physical world of material things. He gathered up these two sides of God's creative act into himself to become a personality, an entity living in the world, moving by itself and *having powers of free choice.* Viewed thus as a whole, he was found to be a self-conscious and self-expressing being, "a living soul."

We saw earlier that Adam was created perfect—by which we mean that he was without imperfections because created by God—but that he was not yet perfected. He needed a finishing touch somewhere. God had not yet done all that He intended to do in Adam. There was more in view, but it was as yet in abeyance. God was moving towards the fulfillment of His purpose in creating man, a purpose which went beyond man himself, for it had in view the securing to God of all His rights in the universe through man's instrumentality. But how could man be instrumental in this? Only by a cooperation that sprang from living union with God. God was seeking to have not merely a race of men of one blood upon the earth, but a race which had, in addition, His life resident within its members. Such a race will eventually compass Satan's downfall and bring to fulfillment all that God has set His heart upon. It is this that was in view with the creation of man.

Then again, we saw that Adam was created neutral. He had a spirit which enabled him to hold communion with God, but as man he was not yet, so to speak, finally orientated; he had powers of choice and he could, if he liked, turn the opposite way. God's goal in man was "sonship," or, in other words, the expression of His life in human sons. That divine life was represented in the garden, as we saw, by the tree of life, bearing a fruit that could be accepted, received, taken in. If Adam, created neutral, were voluntarily to turn that way and, choosing dependence upon God, were to receive of the tree of life (representing God's own life), God would then have that life in union with men; He would have secured His spiritual sons. But if instead Adam should turn to the tree of the knowledge of good and evil, he would as a result be "free," in the sense of being able to develop himself on his own lines apart from God. Because, however, this latter choice involved complicity with Satan, Adam would thereby put beyond his reach the attaining of his God-appointed goal.

### *The Human Soul*

Now we know the course that Adam chose. Standing between the two trees, he yielded to Satan and took of the fruit of the tree of knowledge. This determined the lines of his development. From then on he could command a knowledge; he "knew." But—and here we come to the point—the fruit of the tree of knowledge made the first man *over-developed in his soul.* The emotion was touched, because the fruit was pleasant to the eyes, making him "desire"; the mind with its reasoning power was developed, for he was "made wise"; and the will was strengthened, so that in future he could always decide which way he would go. The whole fruit ministered to the expansion and full development of the soul, so that not only was the man a living soul, but from henceforth man will *live by the soul.* It is not merely that man has a soul, but that from that day on, the soul, with its independent powers of free choice, usurps the place of the spirit as the animating power of man.

We have to distinguish here between two things, for the difference is most important. God does not mind—in fact He of course intends—that we should have a soul such as He gave to Adam. But what God has set himself to do is to reverse something. There is something in man today which is not just the fact of having and exercising a soul, but which constitutes a living by the soul. It was this that Satan brought about in the Fall. He trapped man into taking a course by which he could develop his soul so as to derive from it his very spring of life.

We must, however, be careful. To remedy this does not mean that we are going to cross out the soul altogether. You cannot do that. When today the Cross is really working in us, we do not become inert, insensate, characterless. No, we still possess a soul, and whenever we receive something from God the soul will still be used in relation to it, as an instrument, a faculty, in a true subjection to Him. But the point is: Are we keeping within God's appointed limit, that is to say, within the bounds set by Him in the Garden at the beginning, with regard to the soul, or are we getting outside those bounds?

What God is now doing is the pruning work of the vinedresser. In our souls there is an uncontrolled development, an untimely growth, that has to be checked and dealt with. God must cut that off. So now there are two things before us to which our eyes must be opened. On the one hand God is seeking to bring us to the place where we live by the life of His Son. On the other hand He is doing a direct work in our hearts to undo that other natural resource that is the result of the fruit of knowledge. Every day we are learning these two lessons: a rising up of the life of this One, and a checking and a handing over to death of that other soul-life. These two processes go on all the time, for God is seeking the fully developed life of His Son in us in order to manifest himself, and to that end He is bringing us back, as to our soul, to Adam's starting-point. So Paul says: "We which live are alway delivered unto death for Jesus' sake, that the life also of Jesus may be manifested in our mortal flesh" (2 Cor. 4.11).

What does this mean? It simply means that I will not take any action without relying on God. I will find no sufficiency in myself. I will not take any step just because I have the power to do so. Even though I have that inherited power within me, I will not go ahead solely upon it as basis; I will put no reliance on myself. By taking the fruit, Adam became possessed of an inherent power to act, but a power which, by its independence of God, played right into Satan's hands. You lose that power to act when you come to know the Lord. The Lord cuts it off and you find you can no longer act on your own initiative. You have to live by the life of another; you have to draw everything from Him

—NCL 224-8

### *The Human Heart*

The heart, according to the Biblical concept, is the conscience of man's spirit plus the mind in man's soul. The spirit communes with God and is the organ for knowing His will, whereas the heart is the steward of the spirit, working towards the expression of all which is in the spirit. Whatever is in the spirit is expressed through the heart. The heart is therefore the link or the place of exchange for the workings of the spirit and of the soul. It is like the operating center of a telephone system where all the lines will converge and be connected. All that enters the spirit enters from the heart. Hence the heart is the connecting point of all communications. The spirit reaches the soul via the heart; and through the heart the soul conveys to the spirit what it has gathered from outside. The heart is where our personality is located. It is our real self. Since it is the link between the spirit and the soul, the heart may be considered as the real "I." Knowing the scriptural concept of the heart, we may then judge its significance to us. Let us read a few passages from the Scriptures which deal with the heart.

"Commune with your own heart upon your bed, and be still" (Ps. 4.4). In other words, the heart is myself. So that communing with one's heart suggests what is commonly known as the consultation of heart and mouth.

"Keep thy heart with all diligence; for out of it are the issues of life" (Prov. 4.24). We need to do nothing else but to keep our heart, for out of it come forth the issues of life. Whatever fruit we see in man is produced by the heart. Hence the heart is man's real self.

"Ye offspring of vipers, how can ye, being evil, speak good things? for out of the abundance of the heart the mouth speaketh. The good man out of his good treasure bringeth forth good things: and the evil man out of his evil treasure bringeth forth evil things" (Matt. 12.34–35). The Lord declares that out of the fullness of the heart does the mouth speak; for the heart is the man's own self. Whatever a sinner does comes from his heart; all sins issue from the heart.

"But the things which proceed out of the mouth come forth out of the heart; and they defile the man. For out of the heart come forth evil thoughts, murders, adulteries, fornications, thefts, false witness, railings" (Matt. 15.18–19). What springs from the heart defiles the man, for the heart is unclean.

Is it not rather surprising that though man is a composite of spirit, soul, and body, yet in regeneration God only gives us a new spirit and a new heart but not a new soul? God gives us a new spirit so that we may commune with Him by having our dead spirit quickened into functioning before Him. He also gives us a new heart so as to enable us to live a new life and to have a new desire.

Although the heart and the spirit have a number of things in common, even so, the Bible does not mix up these two but keeps them in their respective place. It is said in Ezekiel, "A new heart also will I give you, and a new spirit will I put within you; and I will take away the stony heart out of your flesh, and I will give you a heart of flesh" (36.26). God does not say, I will give you a new spirit and a new soul, for He deems the soul to be an organ not needing to be remade. Only man's heart must be recreated, because out of it flow the issues of life.

What is to be done to a believer's spirit and heart after he has sinned? "Create in me a clean heart, O God; and renew a right spirit within me" (Ps. 51.10). This verse reveals how God looks upon the heart and the spirit of a believer. If defiled, he ought to ask God to create in him a clean heart. Our heart must be clean; our spirit must be made right.

Since the Bible lays so much stress on the heart, we can see what a significant place it occupies in the Word. The heart is of exceeding importance, for it is our real self. What our heart is is what we really are. It is the source of life. It includes the conscience of the spirit and the mind of the soul. We commune with God by the spirit, but what God looks at is our heart. It is the most essential factor in our lives. We say we are saved: but how *are* we saved after all? It is when we believe in our heart. How are we now serving God? It is serving God with the heart. Whom does God bless? Those who are upright in heart. What shall be judged in the future? God will judge the hidden things in the heart of man. For this reason, we must have a good heart when we come near to God. But a good mind is prerequisite to a good heart. And this brings us to a consideration especially of this matter of the mind or "nous." . . .

### *What Is Nous?*

What is this nous which the New Testament speaks of? We may view this subject from three different angles: physically viewed, we may say that we human beings possess brain; psychologically considered, we have nous; and speaking spiritually, we have intuition. That which pertains to matter is termed the brain; and that which pertains to intellect or reasoning is called nous. Though we dare not say that nous represents the whole of the mind, it certainly occupies a major part of the mind nonetheless. Through the intuition of our spirit we receive an impression from God. By the nous of the soul that impression in the intuition is being interpreted and made known to us. We know the will of God through intuition, but intuition, being unrational and unsystematic, needs to be explained by the nous.

Now let us further say that man has three different organs for knowledge. In the body is the brain, in the spirit is the intuition, and in the soul is the nous. When we dissect the brain, we see nothing but the gray and white substance. And intuition is something which we sometimes sense and sometimes do not sense. At times it seems to constrain, at other times it seems to restrain. It is that entity which is deep down in us. But the nous stands between the intuition and the brain. It interprets the meaning in the intuition and directs the brain to express it in words. Should a believer's nous be defective, and even though he has strong intuition and a good brain, his life will be lived devoid of any standard. He will spend his days foolishly. And he will not be able to express what is within him, even at the time of preaching. All this is due to his nous not being renewed.

—SK 85–8, 90–1

There is a rather awesome problem among God's children: we may encounter many good-hearted and well-behaved people, but they carry with them heads which still belong to the old creation. To put it another way, their life is the life of Christ but their head is the head of Adam. This curtails their ability to know the will of God. Therefore, in measuring the spiritual life of a person, we need only measure his head. To the degree that his head is delivered, to that degree is he delivered from Adam and hence delivered from the old creation. The basic difference between living in the old and living in the new creation is seen in the relationship between one's head and God. . . .

Hence we must ask God to deliver us from our head: that our head may be saved by our taking the helmet of salvation.

Whenever we encounter anything, we must first confess to God: "God, my head or my cleverness is not the principle of my Chris tian living. All that matters to me is to seek Your will." This does not mean that you need to pretend to be a fool. Let us say again that God has no more use for the fool than He does for the wise. We only insist that as Christians live in this world they are not to live by the deliberation of their heads but by proving what is the good and acceptable and perfect will of God. . . .

"They that are after the flesh mind the things of the flesh; but they that are after the Spirit the things of the Spirit. For the mind of the flesh is death; but the mind of the Spirit is life and peace" (Rom. 8.5–6). What is the mind of the flesh? It has one chief characteristic: believing in oneself as all-knowing and all capable. The mind of the Spirit in a believer has its chief characteristic too: not believing in himself nor daring to say or do anything but always being in fear and trembling. The mind of the flesh is constantly busy and swift, self-wise, and restless. And the result is death. The mind of the Spirit is not controlled by fleshly wisdom but is governed by the command of God, it having no confidence in the flesh nor daring to follow its own idea, with the result being life and peace. Our head needs to be delivered so that we will no longer be directed by fleshly thought but be guided by spiritual will instead.

—MC 147, 149–50, 152–3

# 26 Soul and Spirit

Chapter 6 [of Romans] begins with a call to reminisce, not to anticipate. It directs our attention to the past, to what is already ours: "Knowing this, that our old man has been crucified with him, that the body of sin might be annulled, that we should no longer serve sin" (v.6 Darby). In this single verse we find three major elements—

(1) "sin" (singular in number);
(2) "old man"; and
(3) "body" (the body of sin).

These three are vastly different in nature and play unique roles in the act of sinning. Sin here is that which commonly is called the *root* of sin. The Bible informs us that we were formerly slaves of sin. Sin had been the master. First of all, therefore, we need to recognize that sin possesses power, for it enslaves us. It emits this power incessantly to draw us into obedience to its old man so that we might sin. The old man represents the sum total of everything we inherit from Adam. We can recognize the old man by knowing what the new man is, because whatever is not of the new man must belong to the old. Our new man embraces everything which flows newly from the Lord at our regeneration. Hence the old man betokens everything in our personality which is outside the new—our old personality and all which belongs to the old nature. We sin because this old man loves sin and is under its power. Now the body of sin refers to this body of ours. This corporeal part of man has become the inevitable puppet in all our sinning. It is labeled the body of sin because it likewise is subject to the power of sin, fully laden with the lusts and desires of sin. And it is through this body that sin manages to express itself, else it will be merely an invisible power.

To recapitulate then, sin is the power which pulls us to do sin. Old man is the non-corporeal part of what we inherit from Adam. The body of sin is the corporeal element we inherit from him.

The process of sinning follows this order: first, sin; next, the old man; lastly, the body. Sin exudes its power to attract man and force him to sin. Since the old man delights in sin, he condones sin and bends to it, instigating the body to sin. Wherefore the body serves as the puppet and actually practices sin. It is through the joint enterprise of these three elements that sin is committed. Present always are the compulsion of sin's power, the inclination of the old man, and the practice of the body. . . .

### *God's Fact*

The Lord Jesus in going to the cross took with Him not only our sins but also our beings. Paul enunciates this fact by proclaiming "that our old man has been crucified with him." The verb "crucified" in the original is in the aorist tense, connoting that our old man was once and forever crucified with Him. As the cross of Christ is a fact accomplished, so our being crucified with Him is additionally an accomplished fact. Who ever questions the reality of the crucifixion of Christ? Why, then, should we doubt the reality of the crucifixion of our old man? . . .

Mere mental assimilation of these truths cannot withstand temptation, however. The revelation of God is positively essential. The Spirit of God must reveal how we are in Christ and how we are united with Him in one. He must also show us distinctly how our old man was crucified with Christ for the simple reason that we are in Christ. This cannot be simply a mental comprehension; it must be a disclosure of the Holy Spirit. When a truth is unfolded by God it most naturally becomes a power in man, who then finds himself able to believe. Faith comes through revelation. Without the latter the former is impossible. This explains why many do not have faith, for though they mentally understand they do not have God's revelation. Therefore, brethren, pray until God gives us revelation so that "knowing this" in our spirit we may truly confess "that our old man has been crucified with him."

What is the consequence of the crucifixion of our old man? Again the answer comes to us unequivocally—"that the body of sin might be annulled." "Annulled" should be rendered "withered" or "unemployed." Beforehand when sin stirred, our old man responded and consequently the body practiced sin. With the crucifixion of the old man and its replacement by the new man, sin may still stir within and attempt to exert its pressure, but it fails to find the consent of the old man in driving the body to sin. Sin can no longer tempt the believer for he is a new man; the old has died. The body's occupation was formerly that of sinning, but this body of sin is now disemployed because the old man was set aside. It is not able to sin and hence has been denied its job. Praise the Lord, this is what He has furnished us.

Why does God crucify our old man with Christ and render our body jobless? His purpose is that "we should no longer serve sin." What God has done in this regard makes it possible for us not to yield thereafter to the pressure of sin nor to be bound by its power. Sin will exercise no dominion over us. Hallelujah! We must praise God for this deliverance.

### *The Two Essentials*

How shall we enter into such blessing? Two elements are indispensable. First, "reckon yourselves dead to sin and alive to God in Christ Jesus" (Rom. 6.11 Darby). This is the essential of faith. When God avows that our old man was crucified with Christ we believe His word and "reckon ourselves as dead." How then do we die? "We reckon ourselves as dead to sin." When God affirms that we are resurrected with Christ we again trust His word and "reckon ourselves alive." How then do we live? "We reckon ourselves as alive to God." This reckoning is none other than believing God according to His word. When God says our old man was crucified, we account ourselves dead; when He insists we are made alive, we reckon ourselves as alive. The failure of many lies in the desire to feel, to see and to experience this crucifixion and resurrection before trusting in the word of God. These do not realize God has done it already in Christ and that if only they would believe His word by reckoning that what He has done is true, His Holy Spirit would give them the experience. His Spirit would communicate to them what is in Christ.

Second, "neither yield your members instruments of unrighteousness to sin, but yield yourselves to God as alive from among the dead and your members instruments of righteousness to God" (Rom. 6.13 Darby). This is the essential of consecration. If we persist in holding on to something which God wants us to relinquish, sin shall have dominion over us, and our reckoning shall be futile. If we fail to yield our members as godly instruments of righteousness to speak and do what He desires and go where He directs, should we be surprised we are not yet delivered from sin? Whenever we refuse to relinquish or we offer resistance to God, sin shall return to its dominion. Under such circumstances we naturally lose the power to reckon, that is, to believe God's word. In our ceasing to exercise faith and to reckon, can we still be said to be positionally in Christ? Yes, but we are living no longer in Him according to the sense of the "abide in me" of John 15. Accordingly we are unqualified to experience what is factual in Christ, even our crucifixion. . . .

Christians who thrive on the soul life are very proud. This is because they make self the center. However much they may try to give the glory to God and acknowledge any merit as of God's grace, carnal believers have their mind set upon self. Whether accounting their lives good or bad their thoughts revolve around themselves. They have not yet lost themselves in God. These feel greatly hurt if they are laid aside either in work or in the judgment of others. They cannot bear to be misunderstood or criticized because they—unlike their more spiritual brethren—still have not learned to accept gladly God's orderings, whether resulting in uplift or in rejection. Unwilling are they to appear inferior, as being despised. Even after they have received grace to know the actual state of their natural life as most corrupt and even after they may have humbled themselves before God—counting their lives to be the worst in the world—these nevertheless ironically end up regarding themselves more humble than the rest. They boast in their humility! Pride is deeply bred in the bone. . . .

A vaunting ambition marks out those who live in the realm of the soul. The first place is often their desire. They are vainglorious in the Lord's work. They aspire to be powerful workers, greatly used by the Lord. Why? That they may gain a place, obtain some glory. They like to compare themselves with others: probably not so much with those whom they do not know as with those with whom they work. Such contending and striving in the dark can be very intense. Those who are spiritually behind they despise, regarding them as too laggard; those who are spiritually great they downgrade, visualizing themselves as almost equal. Their unceasing pursuit is to be great, to be the head. They hope their work will prosper so that they may be well spoken of. These desires of course are deeply concealed in their hearts, barely detectable by others. Although these longings may indeed be well-nigh hidden and mingled with other and purer motives, the presence of such base desires is nonetheless an irrefutable fact. . .

God's children are awakened to the folly of holding fast their soul life only after they have been enlightened by the Holy Spirit as to the abhorrent character of that life. Such enlightenment does not arrive all at once; it proceeds gradually; not once for all but on many occasions. When believers are illumined by the Spirit for the first time they repent beneath the Light and voluntarily deliver their self life to death. But human hearts are exceedingly deceitful. After a while, perhaps but a few days later, self-confidence, self-love and self-pleasure are reinstated. Hence, periodic illumination must continue so that believers may be willing to deny their natural life. What is truly distressing is to find few believers so possessed of the Lord's mind that they are amenable to yielding voluntarily to Him in these matters. Multiplied defeats and no less shame are always required to render believers willing and ready to forsake their natural propensities. How imperfect is our willingness and how fickle is our condition! . . .

Renunciation of our natural life is not something which is done once and forever. As for sin, we only need take the ground of the cross (Rom. 6.6) and immediately we are freed from its power and our servitude to it. In a moment this can be experienced with a full and perfect victory. But the self life must be overcome step by step. The deeper the word of God penetrates (Heb. 4.12), the deeper works the cross and the further the Holy Spirit completes the union of the life of our spirit with the Lord Jesus. How can believers deny the self when it is yet unknown to them? They can deny only that part of the soul life which they already recognize. God's word must lay bare more and more of our natural life so that the work of the cross can probe deeper and deeper. That is why the cross must be borne daily. To know more of God's will and to know more of the self furnishes the cross increased ground to operate. . . .

The cleaving of soul and spirit means not only their separation but also a cracking open of the soul itself. Since the spirit is enveloped in the soul, it cannot be reached by the Word of life save through a cracked shell. The Word of the cross plunges in and splits open a way into and through the soul so that God's life can reach the spirit within and liberate it from the bondage of its soulish shell. Having received the mark of the cross, the soul now can assume its proper position of subjection to the spirit.

But if the soul fails to become a "thoroughfare" to the spirit, then the former surely will become the latter's chain. These two never agree on any matter. Before the spirit achieves its rightful place of pre-eminence it is challenged persistently by the soul. While the spirit is striving to gain freedom and mastery the strong soul power exerts its utmost strength to suppress the spirit. Only after the cross has done its work on the soulish life is the spirit liberated. If we remain ignorant of the damage this discord between the spirit and soul can bring or remain unwilling to forsake the pleasure of a sensuous walk, we shall make hardly any spiritual progress. As long as the seige thrown up by the soul is not lifted the spirit cannot be freed.

Upon carefully studying the teaching of this fragment of Scripture, we may conclude that the dividing of spirit and soul hinges upon two factors: the cross and God's word. Before the priest could use his knife the sacrifice had to be placed on the altar. The altar in the Old Testament speaks of the cross in the New Testament. Believers cannot expect their High Priest to wield God's sharp Sword, His word which pierces to the separation of soul and spirit, unless first they are willing to come to the cross and accept its death. Lying on the altar always precedes the plunging of the sword. Hence all who desire to experience the parting of soul and spirit must answer the Lord's call to Calvary and lay themselves unreservedly on the altar, trusting their High Priest to operate with His keen Sword to the dividing asunder of their spirit and soul. For us to lie on the altar is our free-will offering well-pleasing to God; to use the sword to divide is the work of the priest. We should fulfill our part with all faithfulness, and commit the rest to our merciful and faithful High Priest. And at the appropriate time He shall lead us into a complete spiritual experience.

We need to follow the footsteps of our Lord. As He was dying, Jesus poured out His soul to death (Is. 53.12) but committed His spirit to God (Luke 23.46 ). We must do now what He did before. If we truly pour out the soul life and commit our spirit to God we too shall know the power of resurrection and shall enjoy a perfect spiritual way in the glory of resurrection. . . .

This brings us to the other, and equally significant, aspect of the dividing of spirit and soul. Insofar as the soul's influence and control of the spirit is concerned, the work of the cross is to effect the division of the two; but insofar as the spirit's filling and reigning is concerned, the cross works towards the surrender of the soul's independence so that it may be reconciled completely to the spirit. Believers should seek to experience oneness of spirit and soul. Were we to allow the cross and the Holy Spirit to operate thoroughly in us we would discover that what the soul has relinquished is scarcely a fraction of what it ultimately gains: the dead has now come into fruition, the lost is now kept for eternal life. When our soul is brought under the reins of the spirit it undergoes an immense change. Beforehand it seems to be useless and lost to God because it is employed for self and often moves independently; afterwards God gains our soul, though to man it may appear to be crushed. We become as "those who have faith and keep their souls" (Heb. 10.39). This is much more profound than what we commonly term "saved," because it points especially to life. Since we have learned not to walk by sensation and sight, we are now able to save our life by faith into serving and glorifying God. "Receive with meekness the implanted word, which is able to save your souls" (James 1.21). As God's word is implanted we receive its new nature into us and are thus enabled to bear fruit. We obtain the life of the word from the Word of life. Although the organs of the soul still remain, these organs no longer function through its power; rather, they operate by the power of God's word. This is "the salvation of your souls" (1 Peter 1.9).

—TSM, I: 134–8, 158, 163–4, 171–2, 186–7, 197–8, 203–4

The Spirit alone can render believers spiritual. It is His work to bring men into spirituality. In the arrangement of God's redemptive design the cross performs the negative work of destroying all which comes from Adam while the Holy Spirit executes the positive work of building all which comes from Christ. The cross makes spirituality possible to believers; but it is the Holy Spirit who renders them spiritual. The meaning of being spiritual is to belong to the Holy Spirit. He strengthens with might the human spirit so as to govern the entire man. In our pursuit of spirituality, therefore, we must never forget the Holy Spirit. Yet we must not set aside the cross either, because the cross and the Spirit work hand in hand. The cross always guides men to the Holy Spirit, while the Latter without fail conducts men to the cross. These two never operate independently of each other. A spiritual Christian must experimentally know the Holy Spirit in his spirit. . . .

The various experiences of having his outer and inner man divided will make a believer spiritual. A spiritual believer differs from others for the simple reason that his entire being is governed by his spirit. Such spirit-control connotes more than the Holy Spirit's authority over the soul and body of man; it also signifies that man's *own* spirit, upon being elevated as head over the whole man through the working of the Holy Spirit and the cross, is no longer ruled by the soul and body but is powerful enough to subject them to its rule.

The division of these two organs is necessary for entering spiritual life. It is that preparation without which believers shall continue to be affected by the soul and hence shall always pursue a mixed course: sometimes walking according to the spirit life but at other times walking according to the natural life. Their pathway fails to be marked by purity, for both spirit *and* soul are their life principles. This mixture holds believers fast within a soulish framework which damages their walk as well as hinders the important work of the Spirit.

Were a believer's outer and inner life definitely separated so that he walks not according to the former but according to the latter, he would sense instantaneously any movement in his soul and immediately shake off its power and influence as though being defiled. Indeed, everything belonging to the soulish is defiled and can defile the spirit. But upon experiencing the partition of soul and spirit, the latter's intuitive power becomes most keen. As soon as the soul stirs, the spirit suffers and will resist right away. The spirit may even be grieved at the inordinate stirring of the soul in others. It will in fact repulse a person's soulish love or natural affection as something unbearable. Only after experiencing such separation do Christians come into possession of a genuine sense of cleanliness. They then know that not sin alone, but all which belongs to the soulish, is defiled and defiling and ought to be resisted. Nay, it is far more than simply knowing, for any contact with what is soulish—whether in themselves or in others—causes their intuitive spirit to feel defiled and to demand instant cleansing. . . .

How marvelous is the cross! It is the foundation for everything spiritual. The purpose and end of its working is to unite the believer's spirit with the resurrected Lord into one spirit. The cross must go deeply to rid him of the sinful and the natural within him that he may be joined to the positive resurrection life of the Lord and thus become one spirit with Him. A believer's spirit, together with all which is natural and transient in him, needs to pass through death so that it may be purified and then united to become one spirit with the Lord in the freshness and purity of resurrection. Spirit is joined with Spirit to become one spirit. And the outcome will be: to serve the Lord in "newness of spirit" (Rom. 7.6 Darby). What is of the natural, of self, and of animal activities has no more place in the believer's walk and labor. Both the soul and the body may then but exhibit the purpose, work, and life of the Lord. The Spirit life leaves its imprint on everything, and everything speaks of the outflowing of the Spirit of the Lord. . . .

### *Knowing the Indwelling of the Holy Spirit*

God's children already have the Holy Spirit abiding in them, but they may not recognize Him or obey Him. They need to do so completely. They must realize that this indwelling presence is a Person, One who teaches, guides, and communicates the reality of Christ to them. Until they are willing to acknowledge the foolishness and dullness of their soul and are ready to be taught, they block the way of this Person. It is necessary for them to let Him regulate everything so as to reveal the truth. Except they know in the depth of their being that God's Holy Spirit is indwelling them and unless with their spirit they wait for His teaching, they will not welcome His operation upon their soul life. Only as they cease to seek anything by themselves and only as they take the position of the teachable shall they be taught by the Spirit truth which they are able to digest. We know He verily abides in us when we understand that our spirit, which is deeper than thought and emotion, is God's Holy of Holies by which we commune with the Holy Spirit and in which we wait for His communication. As we acknowledge Him and respect Him, He manifests His power out from the hidden part of our being by extending His life to our soulical and conscious life.

The Christians at Corinth were of the flesh. In exhorting them to depart from their carnal state, Paul repeatedly reminded them of the fact that they were God's temple and that the Holy Spirit lived in them. Knowing He indwells them helps Christians to overcome their carnal condition. . . .

### *The Strengthening of the Holy Spirit*

In order for man's innermost organ to gain dominion over the soul and the body and thus serve as channel for the life of the Spirit to be transmitted to others, there must be His strengthening. Paul prays for believers "that according to the riches of his glory he may grant you to be strengthened with might through his Spirit in the inner man" (Eph. 3.16). He so prays because he considers it infinitely important. He asks God to strengthen by His Spirit their "inner man," which is the new man in them after they have trusted in the Lord. Therefore the prayer is that the believer's spirit may be strengthened by God's Spirit. . . .

In order for the inner man to be strengthened with power through the Holy Spirit, the children of God must discharge their responsibility. They need to yield specifically to the Lord, forsake every doubtful aspect in their life, be willing to obey fully God's will, and believe through prayer that He will flood their spirit with His power. Without delay God will answer the expectation of their heart, once all obstacles on their part are removed. Believers do not need to wait for the Holy Spirit's filling, because He has descended already. What they need only wait for is for themselves to fulfill the condition for His filling, which is, they must let the cross perform a deeper incision upon them. Should they be faithful in believing and obeying, then within a very short time the power of the Holy Spirit will saturate their spirit and strengthen their inner man for living and for laboring. Some may receive His filling immediately upon once surrendering themselves to the Lord, for they already have met the conditions for such filling. . . .

The Apostle Paul has described the authentic condition of a spiritual man in I Thessalonians: "May the God of peace himself sanctify you wholly; and may your spirit and soul and body be kept sound and blameless at the coming of our Lord Jesus Christ" (5.23). Hence the portrait of the spiritual man which can be drawn from everything which has been said is as follows:

(1) He has God dwelling in his spirit, sanctifying him totally. Its life inundates his entire person so that his every component lives by the spirit life and functions in the spirit's strength.

(2) He does not live by soul life. His every thought, imagination, feeling, idea, affection, desire and opinion is renewed and purified by the Spirit and has been brought into subjection to his spirit. These no longer operate independently.

(3) He still possesses a body, for he is not a disembodied spirit; yet physical weariness, pain, and demand do not impel the spirit

to topple from its ascended position. Every member of the body has become an instrument of righteousness.

★ To conclude, then, a spiritual man is one who belongs to the spirit: the whole man is governed by the inner man: all the organs of his being are subject completely to it. His spirit is what stamps his life as unique—everything proceeds from his spirit, while he himself renders absolute allegiance to it. No word does he speak nor act does he perform according to himself; rather does he deny his natural power each time in order to draw power from the spirit. In a word, a spiritual man lives by the spirit. . . .

It is often observed that Calvary precedes Pentecost. The Holy Spirit is not willing to dispense power to men and women who have not been dealt with by the cross. The path which leads to the upper room in Jerusalem winds by way of Calvary. Only those who are conformed to the death of the Lord can receive the power of the Lord. The word of God affirms that "upon man's flesh shall it (holy anointing oil) not be poured" (Ex. 30.32 Darby). God's Holy Oil will not be poured upon the flesh, whether it be exceedingly defiled or highly refined. Where the mark of the cross is lacking, there the oil of the Spirit is absent. Through the death of the Lord Jesus God pronounces His verdict upon all who are in Adam: "all must die." Just as the Heavenly Power did not descend until the Lord Jesus died, even so should the believer not expect that Power if he has yet to know the death of the Lord Jesus in experience. Historically, Pentecost followed Calvary; experientially, being filled with the power of the Holy Spirit follows the bearing of the cross. . . .

Not only should we pray with the spirit; we should "pray with the mind also" (1 Cor. 14.15). In praying, these two must work together. A believer receives in his spirit what he needs to pray and understands in his mind what he has received. The spirit accepts the burden of prayer while the mind formulates that burden in prayerful words. Only in this way is the prayer of a believer perfected. How often the Christian prays according to the thought in his mind without possessing any revelation in his spirit. He becomes the origin of the prayer himself. But true prayer must originate from the throne of God. It initially is sensed in the person's spirit, next is understood by his mind, and finally is uttered through the power of the Spirit. Man's spirit and prayer are inseparable.

To be able to pray with the spirit a Christian must learn first to walk according to the spirit. No one can pray with his spirit if during the whole day he walks after the flesh. The state of one's prayer life cannot be too greatly disconnected from the condition of his daily walk. The spiritual condition of many too often disqualifies them from praying in the spirit. The quality of a man's prayer is determined by the state of his living. How could a fleshly person offer spiritual prayer? A spiritual person, on the other hand, does not necessarily pray spiritually either, for unless he is watchful he also shall fall into the flesh. Nonetheless, should the spiritual man pray often with his spirit, his very praying shall keep his spirit and mind continually in tune with God. Praying exercises the spirit which in turn is strengthened through such exercising. Negligence in prayer withers the inner man. Nothing can be a substitute for it, not even Christian work. Many are so preoccupied with work that they allow little time for prayer. Hence they cannot cast out demons. Prayer enables us first inwardly to overcome the enemy and then outwardly to deal with him. All who have fought against the enemy on their knees shall see him routed upon their rising up.

Now the spiritual man grows stronger through such exercises. For if a believer prays often with his spirit, his spiritual efficiency shall be increased greatly. He will develop sharp sensitivity in spiritual affairs and will be delivered from all spiritual dullness. . .

### *The Functions of the Spirit*

Mention was made previously that the functions of the spirit could be classified as intuition, communion, and conscience.

While these three *can* be distinguished, still, they are closely entwined. It is therefore difficult to treat of one without touching upon the others. When we talk for example about intuition, we naturally must include communion and conscience in our discussion. Thus in dissecting the spirit we necessarily must look into its triple functions. Since we have seen already how the spirit comprises these three abilities, we shall proceed next to uncover what these exactly are in order that we may be helped to walk according to the spirit. We may say that such a walk is a walk by intuition, communion and conscience.

These three are merely the *functions* of the spirit. (Furthermore, they are not the *only* ones; according to the Bible, they are but the *main* functions of the spirit). None of them *is* the spirit, for the spirit itself is substantial, personal, invisible. It is beyond our present comprehension to apprehend the substance of the spirit. What we today know of its substance comes via its various manifestations in us. We will not attempt here to solve future mysteries but only attempt to discover spiritual life; sufficient for us is the knowledge of these abilities or functions and of the way to follow the spirit. Our spirit is not material and yet it exists independently in our body. It must therefore possess its own spiritual substance, out of which arise various abilities for the performance of God's demands on man. Hence what we desire to learn is not the substance but the functions of the spirit. . . .

It is while a Christian lives spiritually that his spiritual sense develops fully. Before he experiences the dividing of soul and spirit and union with the Lord in one spirit, his spiritual sense is rather dull. But once he has had the power of the Holy Spirit poured into his spirit, his inner man is strengthened and it possesses the sense of the matured. Only then can he fathom the various senses of his spirit.

This spiritual sensing is called "intuition," for it impinges *directly* without reason or cause. Without passing through any procedure, it comes forth in a *straight* manner. Man's ordinary sensing is caused or brought out by people or things or events.

We rejoice when there is reason to rejoice, grieve if there is justification to grieve and so forth. Each of these senses has its respective antecedent; hence we cannot conclude them to be expressions of intuition or direct sense. Spiritual sense, on the other hand, does not require any outside cause but emerges directly from within man.

Great similarities do exist between the soul and the spirit. But believers should not walk according to the soul, that is, they should not follow its thoughts, feelings and desires. The way God ordains for His children is a walk after the spirit; all other paths belong to the old creation and hence possess no spiritual value. But how to walk after the spirit? It is living by its intuition because the latter expresses the thought of the spirit which in turn expresses the mind of God.

Oftentimes we think of a certain thing we have good reason to do and our heart delights in it and finally our will decides to execute it; yet somehow, in the inner sanctuary of our being there seems to arise *an unuttered and soundless voice* strongly opposing what our mind, emotion or volition has entertained, felt, or decided. This strange complex seems to infer that this thing ought not to be done. Now such an experience as this may change according to altered conditions. For at other times we may sense in the inner depths that same wordless and noiseless monitor greatly urging, moving and constraining us to perform a certain thing which we view as highly unreasonable, as contrary to what we usually do or desire, and as something which we do not like to do.

What is this complex which is so unlike our mind, emotion and will? It is the intuition of the spirit: the spirit is expressing itself through our intuition. How distinctive the intuition is from our emotional feeling. Frequently we feel inclined to execute a certain act, but this inward, unarticulated intuition sharply warns against it. It is totally counter to our mind. The latter is located in the brain and is of a reasoning nature, while intuition is lodged elsewhere and is often opposed to reasoning. The Holy Spirit expresses His thought through this intuition. What we commonly refer to as being moved by the Spirit is but the Holy Spirit making us know His will intuitively by working upon our spirit. Just here can we differentiate between what comes from God's Spirit and what from ourselves and Satan. Because the Holy Spirit dwells in our spirit which is at the center of our being, His thought, expressed through our intuition, must arise from that innermost region. How contrary this is to thought which originates at the periphery of our being. If a notion should come from our outward man—that is, from the mind or emotion—then we realize it is but our own and not that of the Holy Spirit; for whatever is His must flow from the depths. The same distinction applies to what comes forth from Satan (those of demon possession excepted). He dwells not in our spirit but in the world: "he who is in you [the Holy Spirit] is greater than he who is in the world [Satan]" (1 John 4.4). Satan can only attack us from the outside in. He may work through the lust and sensations of the body or through the mind and emotion of the soul, for those two belong to the outward man. It therefore behooves us to learn to distinguish our feelings as to whether they originate with the inner, or come from the outer, man.

### *The Anointing of God*

The intuition of which we have been speaking is exactly the locus where occurs the anointing that teaches: "you have been anointed by the Holy One, and you all *know*. . . . But the anointing which you received from him *abides in you,* and you have *no need that any one should teach you*; as his anointing teaches you about everything, and is true, and is no lie, just as it has taught you, abide in him" (1 John 2.20,27). This portion of Scripture informs us quite lucidly where and how the anointing of the Holy Spirit teaches us. . . .

The Apostle John speaks of the operation of intuition when he asserts that the anointing of the Lord, who dwells in the believer, shall instruct him in all things and enable him to know all so that he has no need for anyone to teach him. The Lord gives the Holy Spirit to every saint in order that He may dwell in him and lead him into all truth. How does He lead? Through the intuition. He unfolds His mind in the believer's spirit. Intuition possesses the inherent ability to discern His movement and its meaning. Just as the mind instructs us in mundane affairs, so intuition teaches us in spiritual affairs. Anointing in the original signifies "applying ointment." This suggests how the Holy Spirit teaches and speaks in man's spirit. He does not speak thunderously from heaven nor does He cast the believer to the ground by an irresistible force. Rather does He work very quietly in one's spirit to impress something upon our intuition. In the same way that a man's body feels soothed when ointment is applied, so our spirit gently senses the anointing of the Holy Spirit. When intuition is aware of something, the spirit is apprehending what He is saying. . . .

We communicate with the material world through the body. We communicate with the spiritual world through the spirit. This communication with the spiritual is not carried on by means of the mind or emotion but through the spirit or its intuitive faculty. It is easy for us to understand the nature of the communion between God and man if we have seen the operation of our intuition. In order to worship and fellowship with God man must possess a nature similar to His. "God is *spirit,* and those who worship him must worship in *spirit* and truth" (John 4.24). There can be no communication between different natures; hence both the unregenerate whose spirit obviously has not been quickened and the regenerate who does not use his spirit to worship are equally unqualified to have genuine fellowship with God. Lofty sentiments and noble feelings do not bring people into spiritual reality nor do they forge personal communion with God. Our fellowship with Him is experienced in the deepest place of our entire being, deeper than our thought, feeling and will, even in the intuition of our spirit. . . .

In our communion with God He frequently gives revelation.

We ought to pray for such. The spirit of revelation implies that God reveals in the spirit. The spirit of wisdom and revelation signifies where God reveals himself and how He imparts to us His wisdom. An impulsive thought is not to be interpreted as belonging to the spirit of revelation. Only what we intuitively know of the mind of God through the operation of the Holy Spirit in our spirit ever constitutes the spirit of revelation. God communes with us there and nowhere else. . . .

Besides the functions of intuition and communion, our spirit performs still another important task—that of correcting and reprimanding so as to render us uneasy when we fall short of the glory of God. This ability we call conscience. As the holiness of God condemns evil and justifies good, so a believer's conscience reproves sin and approves righteousness. Conscience is where God expresses His holiness. If we desire to follow the spirit (and since we never reach a stage of infallibility), we must heed what our inward monitor tells us regarding both inclination and overt action. For its works would be decidedly incomplete if it were only *after* we have committed error that conscience should rise up to reprove us. But we realize that even before we take any step—while we are still considering our way—our conscience together with our intuition will protest immediately and make us uneasy at any thought or inclination which is displeasing to the Holy Spirit. If we were more disposed today to mind the voice of conscience we would not be as defeated as we are. . . .

### *Conscience and Communion*

"How much more shall the blood of Christ, who through the eternal Spirit offered himself without blemish to God, purify your conscience from dead works to serve the living God" (Heb. 9.14). In order to commune with God and to serve Him one first must have his conscience cleansed by the precious blood. As a believer's conscience is cleansed he is regenerated. According to the Scriptures the cleansing by the blood and the regeneration of the spirit occur simultaneously. Here we are informed that before one can serve God he must receive a new life and have his intuition quickened through the cleansing of the conscience by the blood. A conscience so cleansed makes it possible for the intuition of the spirit to serve God. Conscience and intuition are inseparable.

"Let us *draw near* with a true heart in full assurance of faith, with our hearts sprinkled clean from an evil conscience and our bodies washed with pure water" (Heb. 10.22). We do not draw near to God physically as did the people in the Old Testament period, for our sanctuary is in heaven; nor do we draw near soulically with our thoughts and feelings since these organs can never commune with God. The regenerated spirit alone can approach Him. Believers worship God in their quickened intuition. The verse above affirms that a sprinkled conscience is the basis for communion with God intuitively. A conscience tinged with offense is under constant accusation. That naturally will affect the intuition, so closely knit to the conscience, and discourage its approach to God, even paralyzing its normal function. How infinitely necessary to have "a true heart in full assurance of faith" in a believer's communion with God. When conscience is unclear one's approach to Him becomes forced and is not true because he cannot fully believe that God is for him and has nothing against him. Such fear and doubt undermine the normal function of intuition, depriving it of the liberty to fellowship freely with God. The Christian must not have the slightest accusation in his conscience; he must be assured that his every sin is entirely atoned by the blood of the Lord and that now there is no charge against Him (Rom. 8.33–34). A single offense on the conscience may suppress and suspend the normal function of intuition in communing with God, for as soon as a believer is conscious of sin his spirit gathers all its powers to eliminate that particular sin and leaves no more strength to ascend heavenward. . . .

Only an unconditional and unrestricted acceptance of the reproach of conscience with a corresponding willingness to do what is revealed can show how perfect is our consecration, how truly we hate sin, how sincerely we desire to do God's will. Often we express a wish to please God, to obey the Lord, to follow the Spirit; here is the test as to whether our wish is real or fancied, perfect or incomplete. If we are yet entangled in sin and not completely severed from it, most likely our spirituality is largely a pretense. A believer who is unable to follow his conscience wholly is unqualified to walk after the spirit. Before conscience has its demand realized, what else but an imaginary spirit will lead the person, since the true spirit within him continues to petition him to listen to the monitor within? A believer can make no genuine spiritual progress if he is reluctant to have his evil conscience judged in God's light and clearly dealt with. The truth or falsity of his consecration and service depends on his willing obedience to the Lord—both to His command and to His reproach.

After one has permitted conscience to begin operating, he should allow it to perfect its work. Sins must be treated progressively one by one until all have been eliminated. If a child of God is faithful in his dealing with sin and faithfully follows his conscience, he shall receive light increasingly from heaven and have his unnoticed sins exposed; the Holy Spirit shall enable him to read and to understand more of the law written upon his heart. Thus is he made to know what is holiness, righteousness, purity and honesty, concerning which he had had only vague ideas before. Moreover, his intuition is strengthened greatly in its ability to know the mind of the Holy Spirit. Whenever a believer is therefore reproved by his conscience his immediate response should be: "Lord, I am willing to obey." He should let Christ once again be the Lord of his life; he should be teachable and should be taught by the Holy Spirit. The Spirit shall surely come and help if a person is honestly minding his conscience.

Conscience is like a window to the believer's spirit. Through it the rays of heaven shine into the spirit, flooding the whole being with light. Heavenly light shines in through the conscience to expose fault and to condemn failure whenever we wrongfully think or speak or act in a way not becoming saints. If by submitting to its voice and eliminating the sin it condemns we allow it to do its work, then the light from heaven will shine brighter next time; but should we not confess nor extirpate the sin, our conscience will be corrupted by it (Titus 1.15), because we have not walked according to the teaching of God's light. With sin accumulating, conscience as a window becomes increasingly clouded. Light can barely penetrate the spirit. And there finally comes a day when that believer can sin without compunction and with no grief at all, since the conscience has long been paralyzed and the intuition dulled by sin. The more spiritual a believer is the more keenly alert is his inner monitor. No Christian can be so spiritual as to have no further necessity to confess his sin. He must be fallen spiritually if his conscience is dull and insensitive. Excellent knowledge, hard labor, excited feeling and strong will cannot substitute for a sensitive conscience. He who does not heed it but seeks mental and sensational progress is retrogressing spiritually.

The sensitivity of the conscience can be increased as well as decreased. Should anyone give ground to his conscience to operate, his spirit's window will let in more light next time; but should he disregard it or answer it with reason or works other than what it demands, then his conscience will speak more and more softly each time it is rejected until ultimately it ceases to speak. Every time a believer does not listen to conscience he damages his spiritual walk. If this self-inflicted wounding of his spiritual life continues unabated, he shall sink into the state of being fleshly. He will lose all his former distaste for sin and former admiration of victory. Until we learn to face squarely the reproach which arises from conscience, we do not actually appreciate how meaningful to our walk in the spirit this heeding of the voice of conscience is. . . .

### *Conscience and Knowledge*

In abiding by the spirit and listening to the voice of conscience we should remember one thing, and that is, conscience is limited by knowledge. It is the organ for distinguishing good and evil, which means it gives us the knowledge of good and evil. This knowledge varies with different Christians. Some have more while others have less. The degree of knowledge may be determined by individual environment or perhaps by the instruction each has received. Thus we can neither live by the standard of others nor ask other people to live by the light we have. In a Christian's fellowship with God an unknown sin does *not* hinder communion. Whoever observes all the will of God known to him and forsakes everything known to be condemned by God is qualified to enjoy perfect fellowship with Him. A young Christian frequently concludes that due to his lack of knowledge he is powerless to please God. *Spiritual* knowledge is indeed quite important, but we also know that the lack of such knowledge does not hinder one's fellowship with God. In the matter of fellowship God looks not at how much we apprehend of His will but rather at what our *attitude* towards His will is. If we honestly seek and wholeheartedly obey His desires, our fellowship remains unbroken, even though there should be many unknown sins in us. Should fellowship be determined by the holiness of God, who among all the most holy saints in the past and the present would be qualified to hold a moment's perfect communion with Him? Everyone would be banished daily from the Lord's face and from the glory of His might. That sin which is unknown to us is under the covering of the precious blood.

On the other hand, were we to permit to remain even the tiniest little sin which we know our conscience has condemned, we instantly would lose that perfect fellowship with God. Just as a speck of dust disables us from seeing, so our known sin, no matter how infinitesimal, hides God's smiling face from us. The moment the conscience is offended immediately fellowship is affected. A sin unknown to the saint may persist long in his life without affecting his fellowship with God; but as soon as light (knowledge) breaks in, he forfeits a day's fellowship with Him for every day he allows that sin to remain. God fellowships with us according to the level of the knowledge of our conscience. We shall be very foolish if we assume that, since a certain matter has not hindered our fellowship with God for so many years, it cannot later be of any consequence.

This is because conscience can condemn only to the extent of its newest light; it cannot judge as sinful that of which it is not conscious. As the knowledge of a believer grows, his conscience too increases in its consciousness. The more his knowledge advances the more his conscience judges. One need not worry about what he does not know if he but completely follows what he already does know. "If we walk in the light" — that is, if we are walking in the light which *we have already*—"as he is in the light, we have fellowship with *one another*, and the blood of Jesus his Son cleanses us from all sin [though many are still unknown to us]" (1 John 1.7). God has unlimited light. Although our light is limited, we shall have fellowship with God and the blood of His Son shall cleanse us if we walk according to the light we have. Perhaps there are still sins today unremoved from our life, but we are not conscious of them; hence we can continue to have fellowship with God today. Let us keep in mind that, important as conscience is, it nevertheless is not our standard of holiness, because it is closely related to knowledge. *Christ himself* is alone our single standard of holiness. But in the matter of fellowship with God, His one condition is whether or not we have maintained a conscience void of offense. Yet, having fully obeyed the dictates of conscience, we must not visualize ourselves as now "perfect." A good conscience merely assures us that so far as our knowledge goes we are perfect, that is, we have arrived at the *immediate* goal, but not the ultimate one. . .

### *Burdens of the Spirit*

The burdens of the spirit differ from the weights on the spirit. The latter proceed from Satan with the intent of crushing the believer and making him suffer, but the former issue from God in His desire to manifest His will to the believer so that he may cooperate with Him. Any weight on the spirit has no other objective than to oppress; it therefore usually serves no purpose and produces no fruit. A burden of the spirit, on the other hand, is given by God to His child for the purpose of calling him to work, to pray, or to preach. It is a burden with purpose, with reason, and for spiritual profit. We must learn how to distinguish the burden of the spirit from the weight on the spirit.

Satan never burdens Christians with anything; he only encircles their spirit and presses in with a heavy weight. Such a load binds one's spirit and throttles his mind from functioning. A person with a burden or concern from God merely carries it; but the one who is oppressed by Satan finds his total being bound. With the arrival of the power of darkness, a believer instantaneously forfeits his freedom. A God-given burden is quite the reverse. However weighty it may be, God's concern is never so heavy as to throttle him from praying. The *freedom* of prayer will never be lost under any burden from God: yet the enemy's weight which forces itself upon one's spirit invariably denies one his freedom to pray. The burden imparted by God is lifted once we have prayed, but the heaviness from the enemy cannot be raised unless we fight and resist in prayer. The weight on the spirit steals in unawares, whereas the concern of the spirit results from God's Spirit working in our spirit. The load upon the spirit is most miserable and oppressive, while the burden of the spirit is very joyous (naturally the flesh does not deem it so), for it summons us to walk together with God (see Matt. 11.30). It turns bitter only when opposed and its demand is not met.

All real works begin with burdens or concerns in the spirit. (Of course, when the spirit lacks any concern we need to exercise our minds.) When God desires us to labor or speak or pray, He first implants a burden in our spirit. Now if we are acquainted with the laws of the spirit we will not continue on carelessly with the work in hand and allow the burden to accrue. Nor will we neglectfully disregard the burden until it is no longer sensed. We should lay everything aside immediately to ferret out *the meaning of this burden.* Once we have discerned its import, we can act accordingly. And when the work called for is done, the burden then leaves us.

In order to receive burdens from God our spirit has to be kept continuously free and untrampled. Only an untrammeled spirit can detect the movement of the Holy Spirit. Any spirit which is already full of concerns has lost the sharpness of its intuitive sense and hence cannot be a good vessel. Due to his failure to act according to the burden which he already has received from God, the believer often finds himself painfully burdened for many days. During this period God is unable to give him any new one. Consequently, it is highly necessary to search out the meaning of a burden through prayer, with the help of the Holy Spirit and the exercise of one's mind.

Frequently the burden or concern in the spirit is for prayer (Col. 4.12). As a matter of fact we are not able to pray beyond our burden. To continue to pray without it can produce no fruit because the prayer must be emanating from our mind. But the *prayer* burden in the spirit can only be lightened *through prayer.* Whenever God concerns us with something, such as prayer, preaching the Word, and so forth, the only way to lessen that concern or burden is to do what it calls for. The prayer burden in the spirit alone enables us to pray in the Holy Spirit with sighs too deep for words. When our spirit is concerned with prayer burdens nothing can discharge that burden except prayer. It is lifted soon after the work is performed. . . .

The Bible is not silent about the normalcy of a believer's spirit. Many matured ones have experienced what the Bible exhorts; they recognize that to retain their triumphant position and to cooperate with God they must preserve their spirit in the proper conditions laid down in the Word. We shall shortly see how it is to be controlled by the renewed will of the believer. This is a principle of great consequence, for by the will one is able to set his spirit in its proper place.

### *A Contrite Spirit*

> Jehovah is nigh unto them that are of a broken heart, and saveth such as are of a contrite spirit. (Ps. 34.18 ASV)
>
> For thus says the high and lofty One who inhabits eternity, whose name is Holy: I dwell in the high and holy place, and also with him who is of a contrite and humble spirit. (Is. 57.15)

God's people often erroneously think that they need a contrite spirit only at the time they repent and believe in the Lord or whenever they subsequently fall into sin. We should know, however, that God wishes us to keep our spirit in a state of contrition at all times. Although we do not daily sin we are nonetheless required by Him to be of humble spirit constantly, because our flesh still exists and may be stirred up at any moment. Such contrition precludes our losing watchfulness. We ought never sin; yet we always should have sorrow for sin. The presence of God is felt in such a spirit. . . .

### *A Broken Spirit*

> The sacrifice acceptable to God is a broken spirit. (Ps. 51.17)

A broken spirit is one which trembles before God. Some Christians do not sense any uneasiness in their inner man after they have sinned. A healthy spirit will be broken before God—as was David's—upon once having sinned. It is not difficult to restore to God those who have a broken spirit.

### *An Afflicted Spirit*

> But to this man will I look: to the afflicted and contrite in spirit, and who trembleth at my word. (Is. 66.2 Darby)

The spirit with which God is delighted is an afflicted one because it reverences Him and trembles at His word. Our spirit must be kept in continual reverential fear of the Lord. All self-reliance and self-conceit must be shattered; the word of God must be accepted as the sole guide. The believer must possess within him a holy fear: he must have absolutely no confidence in himself: he must be as one whose spirit is so stricken that he dare not raise his head but humbly follows the command of God. A hard and haughty spirit always impedes the way of obedience. But when the cross is working deeply a believer comes to know himself. He realizes how undependable are his ideas, feelings and desires. Hence he dare not trust himself but trembles in all matters, acknowledging that except he be sustained by the power of God he shall unquestionably fail. We must never be independent of God. The moment our spirit ceases to tremble before Him at that precise moment it declares its independence from Him. Except we sense our helplessness we shall never trust in God. A spirit which trembles before Him shields one from defeat and helps him to truly apprehend God.

### *A Lowly Spirit*

> It is better to be of a lowly spirit with the poor than to divide the spoil with the proud. (Prov. 16.19)
>
> He who is lowly in spirit will obtain honor. (Prov. 29.23)
>
> And also with him who is of a contrite and humble spirit, to revive the spirit of the humble. (Is. 57.15)

Lowliness is not a looking down on one's self; rather is it a not looking at one's self at all. As soon as a believer's spirit becomes haughty he is liable to fall. Humility is not only Godward but is manward as well. A lowly spirit is demonstrated when one associates with the poor. It is this spirit alone which does not despise any who are created by God. God's presence and glory is manifested in the life of the spiritually humble.

A lowly person is a teachable person, easily entreated and open to explanation. Many of our spirits are too arrogant: they can teach others but can never themselves be taught. Many possess a stubborn spirit: they stick to their opinions even if they realize they are wrong. Many are too hard in spirit to listen to an explanation for a misunderstanding. Only the humble have the capacity to bear and forbear. God needs a lowly man to express His virtue. How can a proud man hear the voice of the Holy Spirit and then cooperate with God? No trace of pride should be found in our spirit: tenderness, delicacy, flexibility—these shall be the norm. A tiny bit of harshness in the inner man may hinder fellowship with the Lord, for this certainly is most unlike Him. To walk with the Lord the spirit must be lowly, forever waiting on Him and offering no resistance to Him.

### *Poor in Spirit*

Blessed are the poor in spirit. (Matt. 5.3)

The poor in spirit views himself as possessing nothing. A believer's peril lies in his having too many things in his spirit. Only the poor in spirit can be humble. How often the experience, growth and progress of a Christian become such precious matters to him that he loses his lowliness. The most treacherous of all dangers for a saint is to meditate on what he appropriates and to pay attention to what he has experienced. Sometimes he engages in this unconsciously. What, then, is the meaning of being poor? Poor bespeaks having nothing. If one endlessly reflects upon the deep experience which he has passed through, it soon shall be debased to a commodity of his spirit and hence become a snare. An emptied spirit enables a person to lose himself in God whereas a wealthy spirit renders him self-centered. Full salvation delivers a believer *out* of himself and into God. Should a Christian retain something for himself his spirit immediately shall turn inward, unable to break out and be merged in God.

### *A Gentle Spirit*

In a spirit of gentleness. (Gal. 6.1)

Gentleness is a most necessary feature of the inner man. It is the opposite of harshness. God requires us to cultivate a gentle spirit. Amid the most prosperous work anyone with a gentle spirit can instantly stop on short notice from God, just as Philip did when sent from Samaria to the desert. A gentle spirit turns easily in God's hand however He wills. It knows not how to resist God nor how to follow its own will. God needs such a yielding spirit to accomplish His purpose.

A gentle spirit is no less important in human relationships. It is the spirit of a lamb which characterizes the spirit of the cross. "When he was reviled, he did not revile in return; when he suffered, he did not threaten" (1 Peter 2.23). This is a description of a gentle spirit. Such gentleness is willing to suffer loss; though it has the power of revenge and the protection of the law, it nevertheless has no wish to avenge itself with the arm of flesh. It is a spirit which in suffering harms no one. The one who can boast such a spirit as this lives righteously himself but never demands righteousness from others. He is full of love and mercy; wherefore he can melt the heart of those around him.

### *A Fervent Spirit*

> In diligence not slothful; fervent in spirit; serving the Lord. (Rom. 12.11 ASV)

For a time the flesh may be fervent when it is emotionally excited, but this fervency does not endure. Even when the flesh seems most diligent it actually may be quite lazy, since it is diligent solely in those things with which it agrees; hence the flesh is impelled by emotion. It cannot serve God in matters which do not appeal to it nor when emotion is cold and low. It is impossible for the flesh to labor with the Lord in cloud as well as in sunshine, step by step, slowly but steadily. "Fervent in spirit" is a permanent feature; he therefore who possesses this spirit is qualified to serve the Lord endlessly. We should avoid all fervency of the flesh but allow the Holy Spirit to so fill our inner man that He may keep it perpetually fervent. Then our spirit will not turn cold when our emotion becomes chilled, nor will the work of the Lord collapse into a seemingly immovable state.

What the Apostle stresses here amounts to an order. This

order must be taken up by our renewed will. We should exercise it to choose to be fervent. We should say to ourselves, "I want my spirit to be fervent and not to be cold." We should not be overwhelmed by our icy and indifferent feeling; instead we should permit our fervent spirit to control everything, even where our emotion is extremely unconcerned. The sign of a fervent spirit is serving the Lord *always*.

### *A Cool Spirit*

> He who has a cool spirit is a man of understanding. (Prov. 17.27)

Our spirit needs to be fervent yet also to be cool. Fervency is related to "diligence in serving the Lord" whereas coolness is related to knowledge.

If our spirit lacks coolness we often take inordinate action. The enemy purposes to drive us off track in order that our spirit may be deprived of its contact with the Holy Spirit. Frequently we observe saints who, in the hour of a feverish spirit, change their principled life into a sensational one. The spirit is closely knit with the mind. The moment the spirit loses its composure the mind is excited; when the mind becomes heated the conduct of the believer grows abnormal and goes out of control. Consequently it is always profitable to keep the inner man calm and collected. By disregarding the ardor of the emotion, the increase of desire, or the confusion of thought and by measuring every problem with a cool spirit instead, we shall maintain our feet on the pathway of the Lord. Any action taken when our spirit is excited is likely to be against the will of God. . . .

The key, therefore, is the rule of the will. Our spirit must accept this rule. Fervency is what our will desires, but so is coolness. We should never permit our spirit to be in such a condition as to extend beyond the control of the will. We must will both to have a fervent spirit towards the Lord's work and to maintain a cool spirit in executing that work.

### *A Joyful Spirit*

My spirit rejoices in God my Savior. (Luke 1.47)

Towards himself a Christian should have a broken spirit (Ps. 51.17), but towards God it should be one of rejoicing always in Him. He rejoices not for its own sake nor because of any joyful experience, work, blessing or circumstance, but exclusively because God is his center. Indeed, no saint can genuinely rejoice out of any cause other than God himself.

If our spirit is oppressed by worry, weight and sorrow it will commence to be irresponsible, next sink down, then lose its proper place, and finally become powerless to follow the leading of the Holy Spirit. When pressed down by a heavy load the spirit loses its lightness, freedom and brightness. It quickly topples from its ascendant position. And should the time of sorrow be prolonged, damage to spiritual life is incalculable. Nothing can save the situation except to rejoice in the Lord—rejoice in what God is and how He is our Savior. The note of hallelujah must never be in short supply in the spirit of the believer.

### *A Spirit of Power*

For God did not give us a spirit of timidity but a spirit of power and love and self-control. (2 Tim. 1.7)

Timidity is not humility. While humility is self-forgetfulness completely—a forgetting both its weakness and strength—timidity recalls all the weakness and hence is self-remembering. God does not delight in our cowardice and withdrawal. He wants us, on the one hand, to tremble before Him because of our emptiness, yet on the other hand, to proceed courageously in His might. He requires us to bear Him witness fearlessly, to suffer pain and shame for Him valiantly, to accept loss of all things with courage, and to rely on the Lord's love, wisdom, power and faithfulness with confidence. Whenever we discover ourselves shrinking from witnessing for the Lord or withdrawing in other ways where boldness is demanded, we should realize that our spirit has abandoned its normal state. We ought to preserve it in a condition of "dauntlessness."

We need to have a spirit of power, of love, and of self-control. It should be strong, but not to the point of becoming unloving. It is also mandatory that it be quiet ancl controlled so that it may not be excited easily. We must have a spirit of power towards the enemy, a spirit of love towards men, and a spirit of self-control towards ourselves.

### *A Quiet Spirit*

> Let it be the hidden person of the heart with the imperishable jewel of a gentle and quiet spirit, which in God's sight is very precious. (1 Peter 3.4)

Granted that this is a word directed towards the sisters, it nonetheless is spiritually applicable to the brothers as well.

"To aspire to live quietly" (1 Thess. 4.11). This is the duty of every Christian. Modern Christians talk far too much. Sometimes their unuttered words surpass in number those that are spoken. Confused thought and endless speech set our spirits to wandering away from the control of our wills. A "wild spirit" often leads people to walk according to the flesh. How hard for believers to restrain themselves from sinning when their spirits become unruly. An errant spirit invariably ends up with an error in conduct.

Before one can display a quiet mouth he first must possess a quiet spirit, for out of the abundance of the spirit does the mouth speak. We ought to carefully keep our spirit in stillness; even in time of intense confusion our inner being should nevertheless be able to sustain an independent quietude. A placid spirit is essential to anyone walking after the spirit: without it he shall quickly fall into sin. If our spirit is hushed we can hear the voice of the Holy Spirit there, obey the will of God, and understand what we cannot understand when confused. Such a quiet inner life constitutes the Christian's adornment which betokens something manifested outwardly.

### *A Newness of Spirit*

> We should serve in newness of spirit. (Rom. 7.6 Darby)

This too is a serious facet of spiritual life and work. An old spirit cannot inspire people: the best it can do is pass on some thought to others: even so, it is weak and therefore powerless to stimulate earnest consideration. An aged spirit can only produce aged thought. Never can dynamic life flow out from an old spirit. Whatever issues from a decrepit spirit (words, teaching, manner, thought, life) are but old, stale and traditional. Perhaps many doctrines do in fact reach another believer's mind, but they gain no footing in his spirit; as a consequence, it is impossible to touch the spirits of others because there is no spirit behind one's teaching. It is conceivable that the one who harbors an old spirit has once experienced some of the truths, but they have now become mere remembrances of the past, purely pleasant memories. These truths have been transferred from the spirit to the mind. Or perhaps they have just been new ideas freshly conceived in his mind, and due to lack of confirmation in life they simply do not impart the touch of a fresh spirit to the audience.

Time and again we meet various Christians who habitually convey something new from the Lord. While we are with them we feel they have *just* left the Lord's presence, as though they would bring us right back to the Lord. This is what newness means; anything else is oldness. Such ones appear to enjoy renewed strength all the time, soaring like eagles and running like youths. Instead of imparting dried, corrupted, and worm-eaten manna of the mind to people, these give fish and bread freshly cooking on the fire of the spirit. Deep and wonderful thoughts never move people as a fresh spirit can.

## A Holy Spirit

To be holy in body and spirit. (1 Cor. 7.34)
Let us cleanse ourselves from every defilement of body and spirit. (2 Cor. 7.1)

For anyone to walk in a spiritual manner it will be necessary for him to keep his spirit holy at all times. An unholy spirit leads people into error. Inordinate thought towards men or things, assessing the evil of others, a lack of love, loquacity, sharp criticism, self-rightousness, refusing entreaty, jealousy, self-pride, and so forth—all these can defile the spirit. An unholy spirit cannot be fresh and new.

In our pursuit of spiritual life we must not overlook any sin, because sin inflicts more harm upon us than does anything else. Even though we already have learned how to be delivered from sin and how to walk by the spirit, we nevertheless must guard against unknowingly returning to the old sinful ways. For such a return renders a walk after the spirit utterly impossible. The child of God therefore needs to maintain an attitude of death towards sin lest it overcome him and poison his spirit. Without holiness no one can see the Lord (Heb. 12.14).

## A Strong Spirit

Become strong in spirit. (Luke 1.80)

Our spirit is capable of growth and should increase gradu ally in strength. This is indispensable to spiritual life. How often we sense our spirit is not strong enough to control our soul and body, especially the moment the soul is stimulated or the body is weak. Sometimes in helping others we notice how heavily weighed down they are in their spirit, yet ours lacks the power to release them. Or when battling with the enemy we discover our spiritual strength is inadequate to wrestle long enough with the enemy until we win. Numberless are those occasions when we feel the spirit losing its grip; we have to force ourselves to proceed in life and in work. How we long for a more robust inner man!

As the spirit waxes stronger the power of intuition and discernment increases. We are fit to resist everything not of the spirit. Some who wish to walk after the spirit cannot because their inner man lacks the strength to control the soul and the body. We cannot expect the Holy Spirit to do anything for us; our regenerated spirit must instead cooperate with Him. We should learn how to *exercise* our spirit and use it to the limit of our understanding. Through exercise it will become progressively sturdier till it possesses the strength to eliminate all obstructions to the Holy Spirit; such hindrances as a stubborn will, a confused mind, or an undisciplined emotion. . . .

### *One Spirit*

Ye stand fast in one spirit. (Phil 1.27 ASV)

We have observed previously how the life of a spiritual man flows with that of other Christians. Oneness of the spirit is a matter of great moment. If by His Spirit God dwells in the believer's spirit and He fully unites with him, how can his spirit not be one with other believers? A spiritual man is not only one with Christ in God but also one with God indwelling each of His children. Should a Christian permit thought or feeling to control his spirit, it will not be one with that of other saints. Only when mind and emotion are subject to the spirit's rule can he disregard or restrain differences in thought and feeling and so be one in the spirit with all children of God. It is necessary for him to guard unceasingly the oneness of spirit with *all* believers. We are not united with a small group—those who share the same interpretation and outlook as we—but with the body of Christ. Our spirit should harbor neither harshness nor bitterness nor bondage but be completely open and entirely free, thus creating no wall in our contact with all other brethren.

### *A Spirit Full of Grace*

> The grace of our Lord Jesus Christ be with your spirit. (Gal. 6.18)
>
> The grace of the Lord Jesus Christ be with your spirit. (Philemon 25)

The grace of the Lord Jesus Christ is exceedingly precious to our spirit. There we find the Lord's grace to help us in time of need. This is a word of benediction: but this also represents the peak a believer's spirit can ever reach. We should always season our spirit with the grace of our lovely Lord.

### *A Spirit of Rapture*

One other facet of the normal spirit needs to be discussed besides those features mentioned already. This one we would term the spirit of rapture. Christians ought to have a spirit which is perpetually in an out-of-this-world and ascending-into-heaven state. Such a spirit as this is deeper than one of ascension, for those who possess the former not only live on earth as though in heaven but also are truly led of the Lord to wait for His return and their own rapture. When a believer's spirit is united to the Lord's and they become one spirit, he commences to live in the world as a sojourner, experiencing the life of a heavenly citizen. Following that, the Holy Spirit will call him to take one further step and will give him the spirit of rapture. Formerly his impetus was "Go forward!"—now it becomes "Ascend up!" Everything about him rises heavenward. The spirit of rapture is that spirit which has tasted the powers of the age to come (Heb. 6.5). . . .

### *The Proper Use of Emotion*

If God's children permit the cross to operate deeply upon their emotion they shall find afterwards that it no longer obstructs, but rather cooperates with, their spirit. The cross has dealt with the natural life in the emotion, has renewed it, and has made it a channel for the spirit. A spiritual man we have said before is not a spirit, but neither is he a person devoid of emotion; on the contrary, the spiritual man will use his feeling to express the divine life in him. Before it is touched by God emotion follows its own whim. And hence it habitually fails to be an instrument of the spirit. But once it is purified it can serve as the means of the spirit's expression. The inner man needs emotion to express its life: it needs emotion to declare its love and its sympathy towards man's suffering: and it also needs emotion to make man sense the movement of its intuition. Spiritual sensing is usually made known through the feeling of a quiet and pliable emotion. If emotion is pliably subject to the spirit the latter, through the emotion, will love or hate exactly as God wishes.

Some Christians, upon discerning the truth of not living by feeling, mistake spiritual life as one without it. They accordingly try to destroy it and to render themselves as insensate as wood and stone. Because of their ignorance of the meaning of the death of the cross, they do not understand what is meant by handing over one's emotion to death and living by the spirit. We do not say that, in order to be spiritual, a Christian must become exceedingly hard and void of affection like inanimate objects—as though the term spiritual man means for him to be emptied of feeling. Quite the contrary. The most tender, merciful, loving, and sympathetic of persons is a spiritual man. To be entirely spiritual by delivering his emotion to the cross does not denote that henceforth he is stripped of his feeling. We have observed numerous spiritual saints and have noticed that their love is greater than that of others, which demonstrates that a spiritual man is not without emotion and additionally that it differs from that of the ordinary man.

In committing our soul to the cross we must remember that what is lost is the soul *life*, not its *function*. Were its function nailed to the cross we then could no longer think, choose, or feel. We must therefore remember this basic fact: to lose soul life means to doggedly, resolutely, and continuously deny the natural power and to walk exclusively by the power of God; it means to live no longer after self and its desires but to submit unexceptionally to the will of God. Moreover the cross and resurrection are two inseparable facts: "for if we have become united with him in the likeness of his death, we shall be also in the likeness of his resurrection" (Rom. 6.5 ASV). The death of the cross does not connote annihilation; hence the emotion, mind and will of the soul are not extinguished upon passing through the cross. They only relinquish their natural life in the death of the Lord and are raised again in His resurrection life. Such death and resurrection cause the various operating organs of the soul to lose their life, to be renewed, and to be used by the Lord. Consequently a spiritual man is not emotionally deprived; rather, his emotion is the most perfect and the most noble, as though newly created out of God's hand. In short, if anyone has trouble here, the trouble lies with his theory and not with his experience, for the latter will bear out the truth.

Emotion must go through the cross (Matt. 10.38–39) in order to destroy its fiery nature, with its confusion, and to subject it totally to the spirit. The cross aims to accord the spirit authority to rule over every activity of emotion.

### *God's Demand*

Yielding one's affection to the Lord may be viewed by the Christian to be a most difficult task, yet the Lord is concerned with one's affection more than with any other matter. He demands him to present his affection wholly to Him and let Him lord over it. The Lord asks for first place in our affection. We often hear people talk about consecration, but this act is simply the first step in one's spiritual walk. Consecration is not the destination of spirituality, it is but its beginning. It leads a Christian to a sanctified position. In a word, without consecration there can be no spiritual life. Even so, nothing is more paramount in one's consecration than is his affection. Whether or not this has been yielded determines the truth or falsity of consecration. Its acid test is affection. Relatively easy is it for us to hand over our time, money, power, and countless other items; but to offer our affection is exceedingly difficult. This is not to imply we do not love Christ; perhaps we love our Lord very much. Nevertheless, if we grant first place in our affection to another and relegate Christ to second place, or if we love someone else while loving the Lord, or if we ourselves direct our affection, then what we have offered is not considered consecration for we have not yielded our affection. Every spiritual believer appreciates the necessity for affection to be offered first. For without that, nothing really is offered.

God the Father demands absolute love from His children. He is unwilling to share our heart with anyone or anything else: even if He should receive the bigger share, He is still not pleased. God demands all our love. Naturally this strikes a fatal blow to one's soul life. The Lord bids us part with what we ourselves cling to, for it divides our heart. He asks us to love Him totally and to utterly follow Him in love: "You shall love the Lord your God with all your heart, and with all your soul, and with all your mind" (Matt. 22.37). "All" denotes every ounce of it for the Lord. He enjoins us to reserve not one tiny particle of affection which we ourselves can direct. He calls for all. He is a jealous God (Ex. 20.5), therefore He does not allow anybody to steal the love of His children. . . .

Actually, only God can satisfy a Christian's heart; man cannot. The failure of many is to seek from man what can be found only in God. All human affection is empty; the love of God alone is able to fully satisfy one's desire. The moment a Christian seeks a love outside God his spiritual life immediately falls. We can only live by the love of God.

What then? Does this indicate we need not love man? The Bible repeatedly charges us to love the brethren and even to love our enemies. Accordingly we know it is not God's will we should not love man, but He does desire to *manage* our affection towards all men. God does not want us to love others for our sake but to love for His sake and in Him. Our natural likes and dislikes do not have any part here; natural affection must lose its power. God wants us, for love's sake, to accept His control. When He wishes us to love someone, we instantly are able to; should He also desire us to terminate our relationship with someone, we can do that too.

This is the pathway of the cross. Only as we allow it to cut deeply so that we have our soul life delivered to death can we be rid of self in our affections. If we genuinely have undergone death we will not be *attached* to anyone but will be guided solely by the command of God. Our soul life, as it experiences death, loses its power and becomes as much as dead in the matter of affection. God will then direct us how in Him to renew our love for men. God wants us to create in Him a new relationship with those we formerly loved. Every natural relationship has been terminated. New relationships are established through death and resurrection. . . .

To sum up, a Christian's affection must be entirely offered to God. Whenever we feel it too difficult to hand someone over to God, we know our soul life has ruled in that area. Where our affection is unable to yield fully to God's will, much unspiritual mixture must be there. All soulish affections lead us to sin and draw us to the world. An affection which is not inspired by the Lord will soon be transformed into lust. Samson is not alone in the history of man in failing in this regard. Delilah is still cutting the hair of man today!

We stated earlier that affection is the hardest element for a believer to offer: *ergo,* its consecration becomes the sign of true spirituality: *ergo,* this is the greatest test. He who has not died to worldly affection has not died to anything. Death to natural affection proves one's death to the world. To covet and to lust after man's affection demonstrates that the Christian has not yet died to self life. His death to soul life is substantiated by his forsaking every affection other than that for God. How transcendent is a spiritual man! He walks far above human natural affection.

Desire occupies the largest part of our emotional life: it joins forces with our will to rebel against God's will. Our innumerable desires create such confused feelings in us that we cannot quietly follow the spirit. They arouse our feelings and make for many turbulent experiences. Before one is set free from the power of sin his desire unites with sin in making him love sin and in depriving the new man of his freedom. After he is liberated from sin's outward manifestations the same desire drives him to seek for *himself* many things outside God. And while a person is still in the emotional state he is controlled mainly by his desire. Not until the cross has performed its deeper work and one's desire has been judged in the light of the cross can he wholly live in the spirit and for God.

When a Christian remains carnal he is ruled vigorously by his desire. All natural or soulish desires and ambitions are linked with *self* life. They are for self, by self, or after self. While carnal, one's will is not yielded fully to the Lord, and so he holds many ideas of his own. His desire then works together with his ideas to make him delight in what he wills to have and to expect to have his own ideas realized. All self-delight, self-glory, self-exaltation, self-love, self-pity and self-importance issue from man's desire and render self the center of everything. Can we conjure up anything man himself desires which is not linked to something of self? If we examine ourselves in the light of the Lord we shall see that all our aspirations, no matter how noble, cannot escape the bounds of self. All are for it! If they are not self-pleasing, then they are self-glorifying. How can a Christian live in the spirit if he is engulfed in such a condition? . . .

If anyone wishes to maintain a true spiritual course he must cooperate with God in putting to death his own desire. All interests, inclinations and preferences must be denied. We should gladly accept man's contradicting, despising, discounting, misunderstanding, and harsh criticizing and permit these matters which are so antagonistic to natural desire to deal with our soul life. We should learn how to receive suffering, pain, or a lowly place as apportioned us by God. However much our self life feels pained or our natural feeling is hurt, we must bear them patiently. If we bear the cross in practical matters we shall shortly see our self life crucified on the cross we bear. For to carry the cross is to be crucified thereon. Every time we silently accept what goes against our natural disposition we receive another nail which pins our soul life more firmly to the cross. All vainglory has to die. Our longing to be seen, respected, worshiped, exalted and proclaimed needs to be crucified. Any heart for self-display must equally be crucified. Every pretension to spirituality in order to be praised must be cut down; so must all self-importance and self-exaltation. Our desire, whatever its expression, must be denied. Anything which is initiated by ourselves is defiled in the sight of God.

The practical cross which God dispenses runs counter to our desires. The cross aims at crucifying them. Nothing in our total make-up suffers more wounding under the lash of the cross than does our emotion. It cuts deeply into everything pertaining to ourselves. How then can our emotion be happy when our desire is dying? The redemption of God requires a thorough setting aside of the old creation. God's will and our soul's delight are incompatible. For anyone to pursue the Lord he must oppose his own desire. . . .

Once he loses his heart for "self" the believer can be wholly God's. He is ready to be molded into any form God wishes. His desire no longer strives against God; nay, he relishes nothing but God. His life has now become quite simple: he has no expectations, no requests, no ambitions other than to be willingly obedient to the Lord's will. A life of obedience to His intent is the simplest kind on earth, because he who so lives seeks nothing but to quietly follow God. . . .

A Christian should recognize that "feeling" is exclusively a part of the soul. When he lives by sensation, no matter what the kind, he is being soulish. During the period that he feels joyful, is loving the Lord and senses His presence, he is walking by feeling; likewise, during the period that he feels just the opposite he is *still* walking by feeling. Just as he is soulish whose life and labor are dictated by a refreshing, bright and joyous sensation, so is he equally soulish whose walk and work are determined by a dry, gloomy and painful one. A real spiritual life is never dominated by, nor lived in, feeling. Rather does it regulate feeling. Nowadays Christians mistake a life of feeling for spiritual experience. This is because many have never entered into genuine spirituality and hence interpret happy sensation to be spiritual experience. They do not know that such feeling is still soulical. Only what occurs in the intuition is spiritual experience—the rest merely soulical activity. . . .

The life of faith is not only totally different from, but also diametrically opposite to, a life of feeling. He who lives by sensation can follow God's will or seek the things above purely at the time of excitement; should his blissful feeling cease, every activity terminates. Not so with one who walks by faith. Faith is anchored in the One whom he believes rather than in the one who exercises the believing, that is, himself. Faith looks not at what happens to him but at Him whom he believes. Though he may completely change, yet the One in whom he trusts never does—and so he can proceed without letting up. Faith establishes its relationship with God. It regards not its feeling because it is concerned with God. Faith follows the One believed while feeling turns on how one feels. What faith thus beholds is God whereas what feeling beholds is one's self. God does not change: He is the same God in either the cloudy day or the sunny day. Hence he who lives by faith is as unchanging as is God; he expresses the same kind of life through darkness or through light. But one who dwells by feeling must pursue an up-and-down existence because his feeling is ever changing.

What God expects of His children is that they will not make enjoyment the purpose of their lives. God wants them to walk by believing Him. As they run the spiritual race they are to carry on whether they feel comfortable or whether they feel painful

They never alter their attitude towards God according to their sensations. However dry, tasteless or dark it may be, they continue to advance—trusting God and advancing as long as they know this is God's will. Frequently their feeling appears to rebel against this continuation: they grow exceedingly sorrowful, melancholic, despondent, as though their emotions were pleading with them to halt every spiritual activity. They nonetheless go on as usual, entirely ignoring their adverse feeling; for they realize work must be done. This is the pathway of faith, one which pays no heed to one's emotion but exclusively to the purpose of God. If something is believed to be God's mind, then no matter how uninterested one's feeling is he must proceed to execute it. One who walks by sensation undertakes merely what he feels interested in; the one however who walks by faith obeys the complete will of God and cares not at all about his own interest or indifference.

The life of feeling draws people away from abiding in God to finding satisfaction in joy, while the life of faith draws believers into being satisfied with God by faith. They having possessed God, their joyful feelings do not add to their joy nor do their painful sensations render them woeful. A life of emotion induces the saint to exist for himself but a life of faith enables him to exist for God and cedes no ground to his self life. When self is entertained and pleased it is not a life of faith but simply a life of feeling. Exquisite feeling does indeed please the self. If one walks according to sensation it indicates he has not yet committed his natural life to the cross. He still reserves some place for self—wishing to make it happy—while simultaneously continuing to tread the spiritual path. . . .

### *The Life of the Will*

The life of faith can be called the life of the will since faith is impervious to how one feels but chooses through volition to obey God's mind. Though the Christian may not *feel* like obeying God, even so he *wills* to obey Him. We find two opposite kinds of Christians: one depends on emotion, the other relies on the *renewed* will. A Christian who trusts in feeling can obey God solely while he is deriving stimulus from his feeling, that is, excitable feeling. The one however who depends on volition determines that he shall serve God amid whatever circumstance or feeling. His will reflects his real opinion whereas his feeling is only activated by outside stimulus. From God's viewpoint not much value accrues in doing His will out of a pleasurable sensation: to do so is merely to be persuaded by the joy of God and not by a wholehearted aspiration to do His will. Except he neither feels a bit of joy nor is stimulated by some wonderful feeling and yet decides to do God's will can the Christian's obedience be counted truly valuable, because it flows from his honest heart and expresses his respect for God and disregard of self. The distinction between the spiritual and the soulish Christian lies precisely there: the soulish primarily considers himself and therefore only obeys God when he feels his desire is satisfied; the spiritual has a will fully cooperating with God and hence accepts His arrangement without wavering even though he has no outside help or stimulus. . . .

### *In Battling the Enemy*

Those who live by feeling are even more worthless in spiritual warfare, because to battle the enemy in prayer is truly a self-denying work. What incalculable suffering is involved! Nothing for satisfying one's self can be found here; it is pouring out one's all for the body of Christ and the kingdom of God. How unbearable must be this resisting and wrestling in the spirit! What pleasure is there for the spirit to be laden with indescribable burden for the sake of God? Is it interesting to attack the evil spirit with every ounce of strength one can summon? This is a prayer warfare. But for whom is the believer praying? Not for himself surely, but for the work of God. Such prayer is for warfare which is thoroughly lacking in interest one usually encounters during ordinary prayer. Is there anything in this that can make him feel comfortable when he must travail in his soul and pray to destroy and to build? No element in spiritual warfare can gladden the flesh—unless of course one is contending merely in his imagination.

An emotional Christian is easily defeated in conflict with Satan. While he is praying to assault the enemy the latter by his evil spirit will attack his emotion. He will set the Christian to feeling that such contesting is painful and such prayer is lifeless. So as he becomes sorrowful, insipid, dark and dry, he immediately stops fighting. An emotional Christian is powerless to war against Satan, for as soon as his feeling comes under attack by Satan he quits the field of battle. If one's emotion has not experienced death, he may provide opportunity to Satan to strike at any hour. Each time he rises to oppose the enemy he is defeated by a satanic touch upon his feeling. Can anyone expect victory over Satan unless he has first overcome his life of sensation?

Spiritual warfare accordingly demands an attitude of total death to feeling and an absolute trust in God. Only a person with this attitude can bear up alone and not seek companions or man's approval in fighting the enemy. Only this caliber of Christian can proceed under all sorts of anguished feelings. He cares not at all for his life nor about death but only cares for the leading of God. He indulges no personal interest, desire or longing. He has offered himself to death already and then lives exclusively for God. He neither blames nor misunderstands Him because he considers all His ways to be loving. This is the class of person who is able to fill the breach. Though he may appear to be deserted by God and forgotten by men, yet he mans his battle station. He is a prayer warrior. He overcomes Satan.

—TSM, II: 18–19, 20–1, 23, 24, 25–6, 27, 33–4, 37, 53–4, 68, 71–3, 74, 86, 101–2, 106, 108–9, 113–4, 119–21, 153–5, 173, 174–8, 179–83, 184–5, 200–3, 205–6, 211–3, 219–20, 229–30, 240–1, 247–8, 253–4

According to the Bible the mind of man is unusual in that it constitutes a battlefield where Satan and his evil spirits contend against the truth and hence against the believer. We may illustrate as follows. Man's will and spirit are like a citadel which the evil spirits crave to capture. The open field where the battle is waged for the seizure of the citadel is man's mind. Note how Paul the Apostle describes it: "though we live in the world we are not carrying on a worldly war, for the weapons of our warfare are not worldly but have divine power to destroy strongholds. We destroy *arguments* and every proud obstacle to the knowledge of God, and take every *thought* captive to obey Christ" (2 Cor. 10.3–5). He initially tells us of a battle—then where the battle is fought—and finally for what objective. This struggle pertains exclusively to man's mind. The Apostle likens man's arguments or reasonings to an enemy's strongholds. He pictures the mind as held by the enemy; it must therefore be broken into by waging war. He concludes that many rebellious thoughts are housed in these strongholds and need to be taken captive to the obedience of Christ. All this plainly shows us that the mind of man is the scene of battle where the evil spirits clash with God. . . .

*Passivity*

The passivity of the mind is due to a misconception of the meaning of consecration and obedience to the Holy Spirit. Many take for granted that the thoughts in their head hinder their spiritual walk. They do not perceive that it is a brain which ceases to function or which functions chaotically that hinders spiritual life, whereas one which functions properly is not only profitable but also essential. Such a mind as this can alone cooperate with God. As has been emphasized previously, the normal path of guidance is in the spirit's intuition and not in the mind. An appreciation of this principle is exceedingly necessary and should never be forgotten. The believer must follow the revelation in his intuition, not the thought in his head. He who heeds the mind is walking after the flesh and is accordingly led astray. Nevertheless, we have not said that the mind is utterly useless, that it does not even exercise a secondary role. True, we make a grave mistake if we elevate the mind as *the* organ for direct fellowship with God and for receiving revelation from Him; yet it *does* have a role assigned to it. That role is to *assist* intuition. Yes, it is by intuition that we come to know God's will, but we additionally need the mind to inspect our inner sense to determine whether it is from our intuition or is a counterfeit of our emotions, whether or not it is of God and harmonizes with the Word. We know by intuition; we prove by the mind. How easy it is for us to err! Without the assistance of the mind we shall find it hard to decide what is authentically of God. . . .

### *The Mind Renewed*

God desires not only a change in the mind of His children at the time of conversion; He desires also a mind that is totally renewed, which is transparent as crystal. We find this commanded in the word of God. The reason Satan can work is that the Christian has not been liberated entirely from a carnal mind. He may start out with a narrow mentality which cannot tolerate others or a darkened mentality that cannot comprehend deeper truth or a foolish mentality which cannot bear any important responsibility; and afterwards he slips into deeper sins. This is because "the mind that is set on the flesh is hostile to God" (Rom. 8.7). Once knowing the teaching of Romans 6 many Christians see themselves as having already been freed from their carnal mind. What they do not appreciate is that the cross must operate minutely in every area of the man. "Consider yourselves dead to sin" must be followed by "let not sin therefore reign in your mortal bodies" (Rom. 6.11–12). Following the change of mentality there must be the bringing of "*every* thought captive to obey Christ" (2 Cor. 10.5). The mind must be renewed completely, since any residue of its carnality is hostile to God.

For us to have our intellects renewed we must draw near to the cross. This is plainly called for in Ephesians 4. The Apostle Paul describes the darkness of man's carnal mentality in verses 17 and 18; but in verses 22 and 23 he informs us how the mind can be renewed: "Put off your old nature which belongs to your former manner of life and is corrupt through deceitful lusts, and be renewed in the spirit of your mind." We know our old man has been crucified with the Lord already (Rom. 6.6). Here we are exhorted to "put off" so that our mind might be renewed. This brings the cross into view as the instrument for its renewal. A believer should understand that his old brain too is part of that old man which God wants us to put off entirely. The salvation which God imparts through the cross includes not only a new life but the renewal of every *function* of our soul as well. The salvation which is rooted deeply in our being must gradually be "worked out." A serious lack among Christians today is in not perceiving the need for their minds to be saved (Eph. 6.17); they conceive salvation in general and somewhat vague terms. They fail to recognize that God desires to save them to the uttermost in that all their abilities are to be renewed and fit for His use. The mind is one of man's natural endowments. God calls His own to believe that their old man was crucified on the cross; thereafter they need to accept single-mindedly God's judgment towards the old man and exercise their will to resist or to put off its deeds including their old thoughts. They must come to the foot of the cross, willing to forsake their traditional mentalities and trusting God to give them a new mind. Brethren, the old one needs to be thoroughly put off. Yes, its renewal is God's work, but the putting off—the denial, the forsaking—of your old organ of thought is what you must do. If you perform your part, God will fulfill His. And once you put off specifically, you should just as thoroughly believe that God will renew your mind, despite the fact you know not how. . . .

### *Mind, the Spirit, and a Spiritual Mind*

The more spiritual a child of God becomes the more he is conscious of the significance of walking according to the spirit and the dangers of walking according to the flesh. But how is he actually to walk by the spirit? The answer given in Romans 8 is to mind the spirit and to possess a spiritual mind: "they that are after the flesh mind the things of the flesh; but they that are after the Spirit the things of the Spirit. For the mind of the flesh is death; but the mind of the Spirit is life and peace" (vv.5–6 ASV). To walk after the spirit means to have the mind set on the things of the spirit; it also means to have the spirit rule the mind. Those who act according to the spirit are none other than those who are occupied with the things of the inner man and whose mind is therefore spiritual. Walking by the spirit simply denotes that a mind under the control of the spirit sets itself on the things of the spirit. This implies that our mentality has been renewed and has become spirit-controlled and thus qualified to detect every movement and silence of the spirit.

Here we see once more the relationship between these two component parts—"they that are after the flesh mind the things of the flesh; but they that are after the spirit the things of the spirit." Man's head is able to mind the flesh as well as the spirit. Our mental faculty (soul) stands between the spirit and the flesh (specifically here, the body). Whatever the mind sets itself on is what the man walks after. If it occupies itself with the flesh, we walk after that; conversely, if it sets itself upon the spirit, we follow after it. It is therefore unnecessary to ask whether or not we are walking after the spirit. We need only inquire if we are minding the spirit, that is, noticing the movement or silence therein. Never can it be that we set ourselves on the things of the flesh and yet walk after the spirit. On whatever the mind sets itself, that do we follow. This is an unchangeable law. What does our mind think and notice in our daily experience? What do we obey? Are we heeding the inner man or do we obey the flesh? Being occupied with the affairs of the spirit will make us spiritual men, whereas occupying ourselves with the affairs of the flesh will turn us into fleshly people. If our mind is not governed by the spirit, it must be governed by the flesh; if not guided by heaven, it must be guided by earth; if not regulated from above, it must be regulated from beneath. Following the spirit produces life and peace, while following the flesh results in death. From God's point of view, nothing arising from the flesh contains any spiritual value. A believer is capable of living in "death" though he still possesses life. . . .

A man's will is his organ for decision-making. To want or not to want, to choose or not to choose are the typical operations of the will. It is his "helm" by which he sails upon the sea of life.

The will of a man can be taken as his real self, for it truthfully represents him. Its action is the action of the man. When we declare "*I* will," it is actually our volition which wills. When we say "*I* want, *I* decide," again it is our volition which wants and decides. Our volition acts for the entire man. Our emotion merely expresses how we feel; our mind simply tells us what we think; but our will communicates what we *want*. Hence, it is the most influential component of our entire person. It is deeper than emotion and mind. So in seeking spiritual growth the believer must not neglect the volitional element in him. . . .

### *A Submissive Will*

What is salvation? It is none other than God saving man out of himself into Himself. Salvation has two facets: a cutting off and a uniting with. What is cut off is self; the uniting is with God. Whatever does not aim at deliverance from self and union with Him is not genuine salvation. Anything which cannot save man from self and join him to God is vanity. A true spiritual beginning involves release from animal life and entry into divine life. Everything belonging to the created one must be relinquished so that the created one will enjoy all things solely in the Creator. The created one must vanish in order that true salvation may be manifested. Real greatness rests not on how much we have but on how much we have lost. Authentic life can be seen only in the abandonment of self. If the nature, life and activities of the created one are not denied, the life of God has no way to express itself. Our "self" is often the enemy of God's life. Our spiritual growth shall be stunted severely if we have no intention nor experience of losing ourselves.

What is self? That is extremely difficult to answer, nor can our answer be fully correct. But were we to say "self" is "self-will," we would not be too far from the mark. Man's essence is in his volition because it expresses what man fundamentally is, desires, and is willing for. Before God's grace has done its work in man all which a man has, whether he be sinner or saint, is generally contrary to God. It is because man belongs to the natural, which is exceedingly antithetical to God's life.

Salvation, then, is to deliver man from his created, natural, animal, fleshly, and self-emanating will. Let us make a special note of this: that aside from God giving us a new life, the turning of our will to Him is the greatest work in salvation. We may even say that God imparts new life in order for us to abandon our will to Him. The gospel is to facilitate the union of our will with God. Anything short of this is failure of the mission. God aims his arrow of salvation not so much at our emotion or our mind but at our will, for once the latter is saved, the rest are included. Man may be united with God in mind to a certain degree; he may agree with Him in his feeling towards numerous things; but the most consequential and most perfect union is that of his will with the divine will. This accord embraces all other unions between God and man. Anything short of the union of wills is inadequate. Since our total being moves according to our will, it is obvious that it constitutes the most influential part of man. Even so noble an organ as the spirit must yield to the rule of the will. (We shall enlarge on this subsequently). The spirit does not symbolize the whole man, for it is but his organ for communication with God. The body cannot stand for man either, because it is only his apparatus by which to communicate with the world. But the will embodies man's authentic attitude, intention and condition. It is the mechanism in him that most nearly corresponds to the man himself. Now unless this will is united with God, all other unions are shallow and empty. Once this ruling will of man is joined completely to God, the man is spontaneously and fully submissive to Him.

Our union with the Lord has two steps: the union of life and the union of will. We are united with Him in life at the time we are regenerated and receive His life. As He lives by His Spirit so shall we thereafter live by the Holy Spirit. This is the bond of life. It indicates we share one life with God. This uniting is an internal one. But what *expresses* that life is the will; consequently there needs to be an external union, one of the will. To be joined with the Lord in will simply denotes that we have one will with Him. These two unions are related, neither is independent of the other. The one of new life is spontaneous, for this new life is the life of God; but the one of will is neither so simple nor spontaneous because our will is clearly our self.

—TSM, III: 7-8, 23-4, 51-2, 67-8, 75, 81-3

Adam is a soul. His spirit and body are joined in his soul. That astonishing power which we have just mentioned is present in Adam's soul. In other words, the living soul, which is the result of the coming together of the spirit and the body, possesses unthinkable supernatural power. At the fall, though, the power which distinguishes Adam from us is lost. Yet this does not mean there is no longer such power; it only denotes that though this ability is still in man, it is nonetheless "frozen" or immobilized. According to Genesis 6, after the fall man becomes flesh. The flesh envelops the whole being and subjugates him. Man was originally a living soul; now, having fallen, he becomes flesh. His soul had been meant to submit to the spirit's control; now it is subject to the dominion of the flesh. Hence the Lord said, "My Spirit shall not strive with man for ever, for that he also is flesh" (Gen. 6.3). When God here mentioned man, He called him flesh, for in His eyes that was now what he was. Consequently it is recorded in the Bible that "all flesh had corrupted their way upon the earth" (Gen. 6.12); and again, "upon the flesh of man shall it [the holy anointing oil, representing in type the

Holy Spirit] not be poured" (Ex. 30.32); and further, "by the works of the law shall no flesh be justified in his sight" (Rom. 3.20).

Why do I dwell at some length on this? In Revelation 18 things are mentioned which shall come to pass in the last days. I indicated at the very beginning how man's soul will become a commodity in Babylon—that which can be sold and bought. But why is man's soul treated as a commodity? Because Satan and his puppet the Antichrist wish to use the human soul as an instrument for their activities at the end of this age. When Adam fell in the garden of Eden his power was immobilized. He had not lost this power altogether, only it was now buried within him. He had become flesh, and his flesh now enclosed tightly this marvelous power within it. Generation has succeeded generation with the result that this primordial ability of Adam has become a "latent" force in his descendants. It has turned to become a kind of "hidden" power. It is not lost to man, it is simply bound up by the flesh.

Today in each and every person who lives on earth lies this Adamic power, though it is confined in him and is not able to freely express itself. Yet such power is in every man's soul just as it was in Adam's soul at the beginning. Since today's soul is under siege by the flesh, this power is likewise confined by the flesh. The work of the devil nowadays is to stir up man's soul and to release this latent power within it as a deception for spiritual power. . . .

These miraculous phenomena in religion and science are but the manifestation of man's latent power which in turn is used by the evil spirit. They all follow one common rule: to break through the bonds of the flesh and release the power of the soul. The difference between us (the Christians) and them lies in the fact that all our miracles are performed by God through the Holy Spirit. Satan makes use of man's soul force to manifest his strength. Man's soul power is Satan's working instrument, through which he works out his evil end.

God, though, never works with man's soul power, for it is unusable to Him. When we are born again, we are born of the

Holy Spirit. God works by the Holy Spirit and our renewed spirit. He has no desire to use soul power. Since the Fall God has forbidden man to again use his original power of the soul. It is for this reason that the Lord Jesus often declares how we need to lose our soul life, that is, our soul power. God wishes us today not to use this soul power at all. . . .

Satan is now engaging this soul power to serve as a substitute for God's gospel and its power. He tries to blind people's hearts, through the marvel of soul force, into accepting a bloodless religion. He also uses the discoveries of psychic sciences to cast doubt upon the value of supernatural occurrences in Christianity—causing people to consider the latter as likewise being nothing but the latent power of the soul. He aims at substituting Christ's salvation with psychic force. The modern attempt to change evil habits and bad temperaments by hypnosis is a forerunner to this objective. . . .

### *Four Facts*

(1) There is in Adam an almost unlimited power, a near miraculous ability. This we call soul power. Modern psychic researchers have proved the existence of such ability within man. Since the discovery of [Franz Anton] Mesmer in 1778 [of what is called mesmerism or hypnotism], all kinds of latent power have been exhibited—whether expressed psychically or religiously. These are but the release of man's soul force. We should not forget that these powers of the soul were in man before his fall but became latent in him afterwards.

(2) Satan desires to control man's latent soul power. He is well aware that there is this power in man's soul which is capable of doing many things. He therefore wishes to bring it under his control instead of God's. Satan wants to use it for his own purpose. The purpose of his tempting Adam and Eve in the garden was to gain control of their soul power.

I have frequently spoken on the spiritual meanings of the tree of the knowledge of good and evil and the tree of life. The meaning of the tree of the knowledge of good and evil is *in*dependence, the taking of independent action. The tree of life, though, signifies *de*pendence or reliance on God. The significance of this tree further tells us that Adam's original life is but a human life, and that therefore he needs to depend on God and receive God's life in order to live. But the tree of the knowledge of good and evil discloses that man does not need to depend on God but he can work and live and bear fruit all by himself. Why do I bring up these matters? Simply to show you the cause of Adam and Eve's fall. If we can release Adam's latent power we too may work wonders. But are we permitted to do so?

Satan knew there was such wonder-working strength in man, hence he tempted man to declare his independence from God. The fall in the Edenic garden was none other than man taking independent action, separating himself from God. Upon learning the story of the fall in the garden, we can perceive what the purpose of Satan was. He aimed at gaining the soul of man. And when man fell, his original ability and miraculous strength all fell into Satan's hand.

(3) Today Satan desires to release and display the latent power of the soul. As soon as man fell, God imprisoned man's psychic powers in his flesh. His many powers became confined and hidden in the flesh as a latent force—present but inactive. After the Fall, all which belongs to the soul comes under the control and bondage of that which belongs to the flesh. All psychological forces are thus governed by physiological forces. Satan's objective is to liberate man's soul power through the breakdown of the outer shell of his flesh so as to free his soul from its fleshly bonds, thereby manifesting his latent power. This is what Revelation 18.13 means by making merchandise of men's souls. Indeed, man's soul has become one of the many items of the enemy's commodities. The enemy desires especially to have man's psychological abilities as his merchandise.

At the end of the age, particularly during the present moment, Satan's intention is to carry through what he at the beginning aimed at in the garden of Eden. Although he initiated the work of controlling man's soul in the garden, he had not fully succeeded. For after his fall, man's whole being, including his soul power, came under the flesh. In other words, man's psychological forces came under the dominion of his physiological forces. The enemy failed to make use of man's soul power; accordingly his plan was foiled.

Throughout these thousands of years, Satan has been exerting himself to influence men into expressing their latent power. He has found, now and then, here and there, persons from whom he succeeds in drawing out their soul force. These have become wonder-working religious leaders of the ages. But in the last hundred years, since the discovery of Mesmer in parapsychology, many new discoveries of psychic phenomena have followed. All these are due to but one reason: the enemy is attempting to finish his previously unsuccessful work. He intends to release all the latent powers of men. This is his singular purpose which he has been cultivating for thousands of years. This is why he trades in the souls of men besides such merchandise as gold, silver, precious stones, pearls, and cattle and horses. As a matter of fact, he has exerted his utmost strength to obtain this special commodity [see again Rev. 18.13].

(4) How does Satan make use of these latent powers? What are the various advantages for him?

(a) He will be able to fulfill his original promise he made to man that "ye shall be as God." In their ability to work so many wonders, men will consider themselves as gods, and worship not God but themselves.

(b) He will confuse God's miracles. He wishes mankind to believe that all the miracles in the Bible are but psychological in their origin, thus lowering their value. He wants men to think that they are able to do whatever the Lord Jesus did.

(c) He will confound the work of the Holy Spirit. The Holy Spirit works in man through the human spirit, but now Satan forges in man's soul many phenomena similar to the workings of the Holy Spirit, causing man to experience false repentance, false salvation, false regeneration, false revival, false joy, and other counterfeits of Holy Spirit experiences.

(d) He will use man as his instrument for his final resistance against God's plan in this last age. The Holy Spirit is God's miracle-working power; but man's soul is Satan's wonder-working power. The last three years and a half (during the great tribulation) will be a period of great wonders performed by man's soul under Satan's direction.

In summary, then, we see that (1) all these miraculous powers are already in Adam, (2) Satan's objective is to control these powers, (3) in the end time Satan is, and will continue to be, especially engaged in manifesting these powers, and (4) this is his attempt to finish his earlier unsuccessful task.

### *The Point of Difference in the Workings of God and Satan*

How should we guard against deception? We need to discern what is God's operation and what is the enemy's operation, what work is done by the Holy Spirit and what work is done by the evil spirit. All the works of the Holy Spirit are done through man's spirit; but the works of the enemy are all done through man's soul. The Holy Spirit moves the human spirit while the enemy spirit moves the human soul. This is the basic point of difference between the operations of God and those of the enemy. God's work is initiated by the Holy Spirit, but the enemy's work is commenced in man's soul. . . .

There are two classes of people who hold to two extremes respectively. One class insists there is no wonder. When they hear about wonders such as divine healing, they refuse to listen. Another class lays stress on wonders so much that they do not care from what source come these wonders—from God or from the enemy. Today we should be careful not to bend to either extreme. Each time we see or hear of a wonder performed we must ask, Is this God's doing or the enemy's? Is it done by the Holy Spirit of God or by the law of human psychology?

Today we should use our abilities—such as that of the mind, the will and the emotion—to do things, but we ought not express the latent power that is in our soul. The mind, emotion and will are man's psychic organs which he cannot help but use. For if *man* does not use them the evil spirit will take over their usage. However, if man desires to use *the latent power behind* these abilities, the evil spirit will begin to give him all kinds of counterfeit miracles. All works done by the soul and its psychic law are counterfeits. Only what is done by the power of the Holy Spirit is real. The Holy Spirit has His own law of operation. For it is stated in Romans 8.2, "the law of the Spirit of life." Thank God, the Holy Spirit is real, and the law of the Holy Spirit is factual. Wonders performed according to the law of the Holy Spirit come from God. . . .

### *Differences in Effects*

What is the difference in effects between the operation of the spirit and that of the soul? This will afford us a major clue in differentiating between what is of the spirit and what is of the soul. "The first man Adam became a living soul. The last Adam became a life-giving spirit" (1 Cor. 15.45). Paul says here that the first Adam became a living soul. The soul is alive. It has its life, therefore it enables man to do all sorts of things. This refers to the position which Adam had. Then the Apostle continues with: "the last Adam became a life-giving spirit." This word is worthy of close attention; it is most precious and significant. The difference in effects between the operations of the spirit and the soul is clearly given right here. The soul is itself alive and has life in itself. The spirit, however, is able to give life to others and cause them to live. The soul is itself living, yet it cannot make others live. But the spirit is not only living in itself, it can also make others live. Only the spirit is capable of quickening people into life. The soul, no matter how strong it is, cannot impart life to others. "It is the spirit," says the Lord, "that giveth life; the flesh profiteth nothing" (John 6.63).

We must distinguish these two operations very clearly, for this is of the utmost importance. None can work satisfactorily if he is confused on this point. Let me repeat: the soul is itself truly alive, but it cannot make others to live. The spirit, on the other hand, is not only itself living but in addition gives life to others. This is why I state with such emphasis that we must lay down our soul power. All that is of the soul is of no avail. We are not quarreling over terminologies, for this is too great a principle. Although the soul is alive, it has no way to make others live. Hence in helping people, we should aim at the depth of their beings instead of merely aiding their minds. We must not work according to psychic force, since it can neither save nor profit anyone. How very careful we need to be. How we must deny whatever comes out of the soul. For it not only cannot help people, it also hinders God's work. It offends God as well as deprives Him of His glory.

—LPS 18–20, 32–3, 35, 38–42, 57–8, 76–8

According to 1 Thessalonians 5.23 the Scriptures clearly portray man as possessing three important elements: "your spirit and soul and body." Briefly speaking, the spirit is that faculty by which man is able to commune with God and which none of the lower animals possess. For this reason, the lower animals cannot worship God. The soul, on the other hand, is the organ in man for thought, will, and emotion—something of which the lower animals also share: for the soul speaks of one animal (or animated) life. And lastly, the body is that part of man which communicates with the material world. Since we human beings are composed of spirit, soul and body, our salvation must accordingly reach all these parts.

"That the spirit may be saved in the day of the Lord Jesus" (1 Cor. 5.5). This speaks of the salvation of the spirit. "To wit, the redemption of our body" (Rom. 8.23). This tells of the salvation of the body. But what we would presently like to examine pertains to the salvation of the soul. And to this end, let us carefully examine every place in the New Testament where the salvation of the soul is mentioned so as to enable us to understand what it really means.

> Then said Jesus unto his disciples, If any man would come after me, let him deny himself, and take up his cross, and follow me. For whosoever would save his life shall lose it: and whosoever shall lose his life for my sake shall find it. For what shall a man be profited, if he shall gain the whole world, and forfeit his life? or what shall a man give in exchange for his life? For the Son of man shall come in the glory of his Father with his angels; and then shall he render unto every man according to his deeds. Verily I say unto you, there are some of them that stand here, who shall in no wise taste of death, till they see the Son of man coming in his kingdom. (Matt. 16.24–28)

"Then said Jesus unto his disciples"—By this we know that the following words which the Lord Jesus utters are spoken to His disciples and not to outsiders. If disciples, then they are saved ones. Let us therefore keep in mind that the words which follow are directed at saved saints, not unsaved sinners.

"If any man would come after me"—That is, if any man among the saved would follow the Lord. The man is a saved disciple who wishes especially to follow the Lord. "Follow me" gives the clue to the conditions which are thereafter set forth.

"Let him deny himself"—Denying the self means disregarding one's self or renouncing one's privileges. To deny oneself denotes a setting aside of the self in seeking the mind of God, so that in all things he may not follow his own mind nor be self-centered. Only such kind of people can follow the Lord. This is of course self-evident, for how can anyone follow the Lord if he follows after himself?

"And take up his cross, and follow me"—This is even deeper than denying the self. For self-denying is only the disregarding of self whereas taking up the cross is obeying God. To take up the cross means to accept whatever God has decided for the person and to be willing to suffer according to the will of God. By denying self and taking up the cross we may truly follow the Lord.

"For whosoever would save his life shall lose it: and whosoever shall lose his life for my sake shall find it" —The word "life" here is *psuche* in the Greek original, which means "soul"; and hence this scripture verse tells us about the saving or the losing of our soul. It will give us light on the subject under examination.

"For" connects the following word with what has preceded it. Such connective will help us to see that the phrase "deny himself and take up his cross" in the earlier verse is one and the same thing as saving or losing the soul mentioned in the verse which follows.

"For whosoever would save his *soul*" —Such a rendering therefore means that although he has the desire to follow the Lord he nevertheless is not willing to deny himself and take up his cross. This helps us to understand somewhat the meaning of saving one's soul. It reveals how a person is reluctant to disregard himself, to renounce his privileges and to allow himself to suffer for the sake of obeying God. And thus we can recognize that the meaning of the saving of the soul is just the opposite to the denying of self and the taking up of the cross. If anyone knows what self-denying is and what cross-bearing is, he will also know what saving one's own soul signifies.

The Lord tells us that if any man would be so mindful of himself as to be unwilling to deny his self, take up his cross, and suffer for the sake of obeying God, that one will eventually lose his soul. In trying to save his soul in the above manner, he will as a result lose it in the future. To lose his soul means he will at the end suffer and lose whatever he delights in. He will not obtain what he looks for.

"Whosoever shall lose his life for my sake" —This is the self-denial and cross-bearing spoken of in the preceding verse. Losing the soul is the same as denying the self. The Lord concedes that if for His sake anyone is willing to forsake all the pleasures of the soul and to suffer according to the will of God, he will find the soul. It simply means that whoever is willing for the sake of the Lord to deny his own thoughts and desires so as not to be satisfied with the things of the world but instead to undergo much suffering, he will at another time be given by the Lord his heart desire with full blessing and joy.

By studying this verse we ought to be able to understand what is the meaning of the salvation of the soul. To save the soul denotes gaining for oneself happiness and joy to his heart's fullest satisfaction. To lose the soul, on the other hand, speaks of losing one's joy, desire and satisfaction.

Hence to lose the soul (which requires self-denial and cross-bearing) is definitely not what we commonly term "to perish"; instead, the Lord shows us that to save one's soul is in not denying self and taking up the cross. This concept has no relationship to the ordinary idea of "save" or "perish"—a fact which is quite evident, because if saving one's soul means having eternal life, why does the Lord Jesus declare that a person must lose his soul for the Lord's sake? If losing one's soul suggests a going to the lake of fire, then in requiring us to lose our souls for His sake would He want us to go down to the lake of fire for Him? Consequently, this passage has absolutely nothing to do with the issue of eternal life or the lake of fire. The phrase "shall lose it [the soul]" in the first half of the verse and "shall lose his life [soul]" in the second half of the verse must mean the same. If "whosoever would save his life shall lose it" means that whoever does not deny self will go to the lake of fire, then the words "whosoever shall lose his life for my sake shall find it" would mean that whoever goes to the lake of fire for the Lord's sake shall have eternal life. But this would be absurd. Therefore, what is meant here is simply this: that if a saved Christian will not permit his soul to suffer now his soul will suffer in the future, but that if he is willing to let his soul suffer for the Lord's sake now his soul shall not suffer in the future.

Moreover, if the salvation of the soul *did* mean having eternal life (which it does not), then the losing of the soul would have to denote a going into the lake of fire. But then what the Lord

Jesus says would not be consistent with what is said before. For the Lord is here speaking to the disciples, who have already been given eternal life; and we know that a non-Christian can neither deny himself nor take up his cross and follow the Lord. If the Lord desires a person to have eternal life He would no doubt ask that one to believe rather than demand him to deny himself in order to possess eternal life. Only one who has had eternal life is able to deny himself, take up the cross, and follow the Lord. For a sinner who has not yet possessed eternal life, what he needs to do is not to try to follow the Lord but to believe in the Lord.

"For what shall a man be profited, if he shall gain the whole world, and forfeit his life? or what shall a man give in exchange for his life?"—Again, the word "life" is "soul" in the original. Here our Lord continues to explain how unprofitable it is for a man to save his soul now and lose his soul later. What He means is that if one does not deny himself, take up the cross and closely follow the Lord but instead does things according to the desires of his soul in order to satisfy it, there will come a time when he shall lose his soul even though he may have gained the entire world. Though man may gain many pleasures by following his own desires, eventually, says the Lord, he will have to pay back through losing all pleasures to his soul. According to the Lord's viewpoint, it would be far better to gain one's soul at the last than to gain it at the first. Nothing can be exchanged for the final satisfaction of the soul. So that to lose the soul now is far better than to lose it at the end.

"Whosoever would save his life shall lose it"—If a man saves his soul now, when will he lose it? "And whosoever shall lose his life for my sake shall find it"—Again, when will a man find his soul? We see from this same passage that the Lord answers these questions with these words: "For the Son of man shall come in the glory of his Father with his angels; and *then* shall he render unto every man according to his deeds" (v.27).

"According to his deeds" means according to what each does in this present life. Such deeds are divided into two categories: (1) saving his own soul now, and (2) losing his soul now for the

Lord's sake. "He shall render unto every man according to his deeds" means that the Lord shall cause the one who saves his soul now to lose it and cause the other who loses his soul now for the Lord's sake to gain it. And when will this happen? At the time of His coming. Therefore, let us be perfectly clear that if a person should mind the things of the flesh, cater to his own pleasure, and refuse to suffer for Christ, he will receive the Lord's reproof instead of receiving the Lord's glory and may even weep and gnash his teeth at the coming of the Lord. But if he should be willing to forfeit his own rights, be wholly separated from the world, and be faithfully obedient to the will of God, he shall be praised by the Lord and shall enjoy the joy of the Lord to his heart's full satisfaction.

The coming of the Lord and His recompense relate especially to reigning with Him in the kingdom. For the Lord himself informs us immediately with respect to where He is coming. In this same passage He states that "the Son of man [is] coming in his kingdom" (v.28). What the Lord Jesus means to say is that when He shall come to earth to reign for a thousand years, some of the believers will reign with Him while some of them will not. . . .

The spirit is saved because Christ lays down His life for me; the soul is saved because I deny myself and follow the Lord.

The spirit is saved on the basis of faith: once having believed, the matter is forever settled, never again to be shaken. The soul is saved on the basis of following: it is a lifelong matter, a course to be finished.

By faith the spirit is saved, because "he that believeth on the Son hath eternal life" (John 3.36). Through works the soul is saved, because "then shall [the Lord] render unto every man according to his deeds" (Matt. 16.27). Once the spirit is saved, eternal life is assured. Though all the demons in hell may rise up to tempt me, they cannot cause me to perish. Though the angels in heaven come down to smite me, neither can they cause me to perish. Nay, even the triune God cannot cause me to perish.

Yet as to the salvation of the soul nothing can be assured today, for whether or not the soul will be gained shall be decided at the coming again of the Lord.

The salvation of the spirit is decided today, because by believing in the Lord one has eternal life. The salvation of the soul, however, is to be decided at the coming of the Son of man.

The salvation of the spirit is a current *gift*, for "God so loved the world, that he gave his only begotten Son" (John 3.16). The salvation of the soul, though, is a future *reward* given at the time of the Lord's return to those who have faithfully followed Him.

In order for the soul to be saved a person must have the spirit saved first. Without the salvation of the spirit, there is no possibility of having the soul saved. . . .

Let us recognize that the meaning of the gaining of the soul today applies equally to the gaining of the soul in the future; and the meaning of the losing of the soul now is the same as the losing of the soul then. Their meanings must remain the same. In other words, to lose the soul for the Lord's sake denotes the refusal to allow the soul to be gratified and pleased today, and to lose the soul in the future signifies the denial to the soul of satisfaction and enjoyment in the kingdom. When that day shall come, that is to say, when the kingdom shall arrive, some people will have their souls fulfilled while others will have their souls unfulfilled. All who in this age have catered to their soul's desires by excessive enjoyment beyond the natural needs shall not obtain anything in the future kingdom. Similarly, all who for the Lord's sake lose these things in this age shall be fully satisfied in the kingdom age to come. Everyone who overcomes the world shall be rewarded in the kingdom. This is absolutely certain. . . .

When will his soul suffer loss? At the time when the Lord shall set up the kingdom. Whoever loves his soul in this age will not be able to enjoy glory with the Lord in that future time. We believe that the possession of eternal life as well as our entering heaven are matters both certain and positive. But as to the matters of reigning in the millennial kingdom and experiencing future enjoyment in the soul—these require us that we not love our souls today.

I have stated before and I will now state it again that just as God places heaven and hell before the *sinner* for him to choose (and if a sinner can see clearly, he no doubt will choose heaven), so God also places the kingdom and the world before the *Christian* for him to choose. Do we choose the kingdom? Or do we choose the world? How sad that a sinner likes to choose heaven, whereas numerous Christians would rather have the world! Too many of us think being saved is enough; yet let us realize that after we are born again God places the future kingdom before us for us to choose.

He who is full now shall lose fullness in the glory and shall enjoy no more. "He that loveth his life loseth it," declared the Lord, "and he that hateth his life in this world shall keep it unto life eternal"—How closely knit is our soul to the world! To love the soul in this world is to gratify oneself in this world. Eating and dressing well, having many friends and fans, and enjoying fame and praises among men—all these are desirable, but how they do nourish one's soul! Yet whoever nourishes his soul now shall lose it in the kingdom.

*To lose the soul is not a going to hell but a causing the soul to suffer in that it cannot reign with the Lord.* During the kingdom age the Lord will assign ten cities or five cities to His disciples to rule. According to Old Testament prophecies, this will be the golden age. How very good and pleasant will the ruling over ten or five cities be at such a time! Yet he who has gained his soul in this world shall lose his soul in this regard during the kingdom age. And how serious must this be! All who are filled in this present age—that is to say, all who have their souls satisfied now—will have nothing in the kingdom. I have said many times and I will continue to say it: He who hates his own soul in this age—by which I mean not allowing his soul to be filled and gratified in this age but instead turning his back on the world and turning his face towards God and always arming himself with the will to suffer—shall gain his soul in the kingdom; but he who gains on this side shall lose on the other side. Whoever possesses today shall possess nothing in the future. In order to gain in the future, one must forfeit something today.

—SS 3–10, 11–2, 25, 38–40

# 27 The Flesh

The word "flesh" is *basar* in Hebrew and *sarx* in Greek. Seen often in the Bible, it is used in various ways. Its most significant usage, observed and made most clear in Paul's writings, has reference to the unregenerated person. Speaking of his old "I," he says in Romans 7: "I am fleshly" (v.14 Darby). Not merely his nature or a particular part of his being is fleshly; the "I"—Paul's whole being—is fleshly. He reiterates this thought in verse 18 by asserting "within me, that is, in my flesh." It follows clearly that "flesh" in the Bible points to all an unregenerated person is. In connection with this usage of "flesh" it must be remembered that in the very beginning man was constituted spirit, soul and body. As it is the site of man's personality and consciousness, the soul is connected to the spiritual world through man's spirit. The soul must decide whether it is to obey the spirit and hence be united with God and His will or is to yield to the body and all the temptations of the material world. On the occasion of man's fall the soul resisted the spirit's authority and became enslaved to the body and its passions. Thus man became a fleshly, not a spiritual, man. Man's spirit was denied its noble position and was reduced to that of a prisoner. Since the soul is now under the power of the flesh, the Bible deems man to be fleshly or carnal. Whatever is soulical has become fleshly. . . .

### *How Does Man Become Flesh?*

"That which is born of the flesh is flesh." So asserted the Lord

Jesus to Nicodemus long ago (John 3.6). Three questions are answered by this succinct statement: (1) what flesh is; (2) how man becomes flesh; and (3) what its quality or nature is.

(1) *What is flesh?* "That which is born of the flesh is flesh." What is born of the flesh? Man; therefore man is flesh; and everything a man naturally inherits from his parents belongs to the flesh. No distinction is made as to whether the man is good, moral, clever, able and kind or whether he is bad, unholy, foolish, useless and cruel. Man is flesh. Whatever a man is born with pertains to the flesh and is within that realm. All with which we are born or which later develops is included in the flesh.

(2) *How does man become flesh?* "That which is *born* of the flesh is flesh." Man does not become fleshly by learning to be bad through gradual sinning, nor by giving himself up to licentiousness, greedy to follow the desire of his body and mind until finally the whole man is overcome and controlled by the evil passions of his body. The Lord Jesus emphatically declared that as soon as a man is born he is fleshly. He is determined neither by his conduct nor by his character. But one thing decides the issue: through whom was he born? Every man of this world has been begotten of human parents and is consequently judged by God to be of the flesh (Gen. 6.3). How can anyone who is born of the flesh not be flesh? According to our Lord's word, a man is flesh because he is born of blood, of the will of the flesh, and of the will of man (John 1.13) and not because of how he lives or how his parents live.

(3) *What is the nature of flesh?* "That which is born of the flesh *is* flesh." Here is no exception, no distinction. No amount of education, improvement, cultivation, morality or religion can turn man from being fleshly. No human labor or power can alter him. Unless he is not generated of the flesh, he will remain as flesh. No human device can make him other than that of which he was born. The Lord Jesus said "is"; with that the matter was forever decided. The fleshliness of a man is determined not by himself but by his birth. If he is born of flesh, all plans for his transformation will be unavailing. No matter how he changes

outwardly, whether from one form to another or through a daily change, man remains flesh as firmly as ever. . . .

God knows no good resides in man; no flesh can please Him. It is corrupted beyond repair. Since it is so absolutely hopeless, how then can man please God after he has believed in His Son unless He gives him something new? Thank God, He has bestowed a new life, His uncreated life, upon those who believe in the salvation of the Lord Jesus and receive Him as their personal Savior. This is called "regeneration" or "new birth." Though He cannot alter our flesh God gives us His life. Man's flesh remains as corrupt in those who are born anew as in those who are not. The flesh in a saint is the same as that in a sinner. In regeneration the flesh is not transformed. New birth exerts no good influence on the flesh. It remains as is. God does not impart His life to us to educate and train the flesh. Rather, it is given to overcome the flesh. . . .

The Galatian letter of Paul delineates the relationship between the flesh and the believer. He tells us on the one hand that "those who belong to Christ Jesus have crucified the flesh with its passions and desires" (5.24). On the very day one becomes identified with the Lord Jesus then his flesh also is crucified. Now one might think, without the Holy Spirit's instruction, that his flesh is no longer present, for has it not been crucified? But no, on the other hand the letter says to us to "walk by the Spirit, and do not gratify the desires of the flesh. For the desires of the flesh are against the Spirit, and the desires of the Spirit are against the flesh" (5.16–17). Here we are told openly that one who belongs to Christ Jesus and has already the indwelling Holy Spirit still has the flesh in him. Not only does the flesh exist; it is described as being singularly powerful as well.

What can we say? Are these two Biblical references contradictory? No, verse 24 stresses the sin of the flesh, while verse 17 the self of the flesh. The cross of Christ deals with sin and the Holy Spirit through the cross treats of self. Christ delivers the believer completely from the power of sin through the cross that sin may not reign again; but by the Holy Spirit who dwells in the believer, Christ enables him to overcome self daily and obey Him perfectly. Liberation from sin is an accomplished fact; denial of self is to be a daily experience. . . .

The flesh demands full sovereignty; so does the spiritual life. The flesh desires to have man forever attached to itself; while the spiritual life wants to have man completely subject to the Holy Spirit. At all points the flesh and spiritual life differ. The nature of the former is that of the first Adam, the nature of the latter belongs to the last Adam. The motive of the first is earthly; that of the second, heavenly. The flesh focuses all things upon self; spiritual life centers all upon Christ. The flesh wishes to lead man to sin, but spiritual life longs to lead him to righteousness. Since these two are so essentially contrary, how can a person avoid clashing continually with the flesh? Not realizing the full salvation of Christ, a believer constantly experiences such a struggle. . . .

Here [in 1 Cor. 3.1–3] the Apostle divides all Christians into two classes: the spiritual and the fleshly or carnal. The spiritual Christians are not at all extraordinary; they are simply normal. It is the fleshly who are out of the ordinary, because they are abnormal. . . .

We have observed that we cannot yield to the flesh; nor can we repair, regulate, or educate it, because none of our methods can ever alter in the slightest the nature of the flesh. What then can be done? The flesh must die. This is God's way. Not through any other avenue but death is it to be. We would prefer to tame the flesh by striving, by changing it, by exercising the will, or by innumerable other means; but God's prescription is death. If the flesh is dead, are not all problems automatically solved? The flesh is not to be conquered; it is to die. This is most reasonable when considered in relation to how we became flesh in the first place: "that which is born of the flesh is flesh." We became flesh by being born of it. Now the exit simply follows the entrance. The way of possessing is the way of losing. Since we became flesh by being born of the flesh, it naturally follows that we shall be freed from it if the flesh dies. Crucifixion is the one and only way. "For he who has died is freed from sin" (Rom. 6.7). Anything less than death is insufficient. Death is the only salvation. . . .

### *The Deliverance of the Cross*

Upon reciting many deeds of the flesh in his Galatian letter, the Apostle Paul then points out that "those who belong to Christ Jesus have crucified the flesh with its passions and desires" (Gal. 5.24). Here is deliverance. Is it not strange that what concerns the believer vastly differs from what concerns God? The former is concerned with "the works of the flesh" (Gal. 5.19), that is, with the varying sins of the flesh. He is occupied with today's anger, tomorrow's jealousy, or the day after tomorrow's strife. The believer mourns over a particular sin and longs for victory over it. Yet all these sins are but fruits from the same tree. While plucking one fruit (actually one cannot pick off any), out crops another. One after another they grow, giving him no chance for victory. On the other hand God is concerned not with the *works* of the flesh but with "the flesh" itself (Gal. 5.24). Had the tree been put to death, would there be any need to fear lest it bear fruit? The believer busily makes plans to handle sins—which are the fruits, while forgetting to deal with the flesh itself—which is the root. No wonder that before he can clear up one sin, another has burst forth. We must therefore deal today with the source of sin. . . .

It may be helpful to be more explicit here. We have indicated that the crucifixion of the flesh is not dependent upon experiences, however different they may be; rather is it contingent upon the fact of God's finished work. "Those who belong to Christ Jesus"—the weak as well as the strong—"have crucified the flesh with its passions and desires." You say you still sin, but God says you have been crucified on the cross. You say your temper persists, but

God's answer is that you have been crucified. You say your lusts remain very potent, but again God replies that your flesh has been crucified on the cross. For the moment will you please not look at your experience, but just hearken to what God says to you. If you do not listen to His word and instead look daily upon your situation, you will never enter into the reality of your flesh having been crucified on the cross. Disregard your feelings and experience. God pronounces your flesh crucified; it therefore *has* been crucified. Simply respond to God's word and you shall have experience. When God tells you that "your flesh has been crucified" you should answer with "Amen, indeed my flesh has been crucified." In thus acting upon His word you shall see your flesh is dead indeed. . . .

Our union with Christ in His death signifies that it is an accomplished fact in our spirits. What a believer must do now is to bring this sure death out of his spirit and apply it to his members each time his wicked lusts may be aroused. Such spiritual death is not a once for all proposition. Whenever the believer is not watchful or loses his faith, the flesh will certainly go on a rampage. If he desires to be conformed completely to the Lord's death, he must unceasingly put to nought the deeds of his members so that what is real in the spirit may be executed in the body.

But whence comes the power to so apply the crucifixion of the Lord to our members? It is "by the Spirit," insists Paul, that "you put to death the deeds of the body" (Rom. 8.13). To put away these deeds the believer must rely upon the Holy Spirit to translate his co-crucifixion with Christ into personal experience. He must believe that the Holy Spirit will administer the death of the cross on whatever needs to die. In view of the fact that the believer's flesh was crucified with Christ on the cross, he does not need today to be crucified once again. All which is required is to apply, by the Holy Spirit, the accomplished death of the Lord Jesus for him on the cross to any particular wicked deed of the body which now tries to rise up. It will then be put aside by the power of the Lord's death. The wicked works of the flesh may spring up at any time and at any place; accordingly, unless the child of God by the Holy Spirit continually turns to account that power of the holy death of our Lord Jesus, he will not be able to triumph. But if in this way he lays the deeds of the body to rest, the Holy Spirit who indwells him will ultimately realize God's purpose of putting the body of sin out of a job (Rom. 6.6). By thus appropriating the cross the babe in Christ will be liberated from the power of the flesh and will be united with the Lord Jesus in resurrection life. . . .

The opposition manifested by the flesh against the spirit and against the Holy Spirit is two-fold: (1) by way of committing sin—rebelling against God and breaking the law of God; and (2 ) by way of performing good—obeying God and following the will of God. The body element of the flesh, full of sin and lust, naturally cannot but express itself in many sins, much to the grief of the Holy Spirit. The soul part of the flesh, however, is not as defiled as the body. Soul is the life principle of man; it is his very self, comprising the faculties of will, mind and emotion. From the human viewpoint the works of the soul may not be all defiled. They merely center upon one's thought, idea, feeling, and like or dislike. Though these all are focused upon self, they are not necessarily defiling sins. The basic characteristic of the works of the soul is independence or self-dependence. Even though the soul side is therefore not as defiled as the body side, it nonetheless is hostile to the Holy Spirit. The flesh makes self the center and elevates self-will above God's will. It may serve God, but always according to its idea, not according to God's. It will do what is good in its own eyes. Self is the principle behind every action. It may not commit what man considers sin: it may even try to keep God's commandments with all its power: yet "self" never fails to be at the heart of every activity. Who can fathom the deceitfulness and vitality of this self? The flesh opposes the spirit not just in sinning against God, but now even in the matter of serving Him and pleasing Him. It opposes and quenches the Holy

Spirit by leaning upon its own strength without wholly relying upon God's grace and simply being led by the Spirit.

We can find many believers around us who are by nature good and patient and loving. Now what the believer hates is sin; therefore if he can be delivered from it and from the works of the flesh as described in Galatians 5, verses 19 through 21, then is he content. But what the believer *admires* is righteousness; therefore he will try hard to act righteously, longing to possess the fruits of Galatians 5, verses 22 and 23. Yet, just here lies the danger. For the Christian has not come to learn how to hate the *totality* of his flesh. He merely desires to be liberated from the sins which spring from it. He knows how to resist somewhat the deeds of the flesh, but he does not realize that the entire flesh itself needs to be destroyed. What deceives him is that the flesh not only can produce sin but can also perform good. If it is still doing good it is evident it is yet alive. Had the flesh definitely died the believer's ability both to do good and to do evil would have perished with it. An ability to undertake good manifests that the flesh has not yet died. . . .

Self-confidence and self-reliance, as we have said, are the notable traits of the good works of the flesh. It is impossible for the flesh to lean upon God. It is too impatient to tolerate any delay. So long as it deems itself strong it will never depend upon God. Even in a time of desperation the flesh continues to scheme and to search for a loophole. It never has the sense of utter dependency. This alone can be a test whereby a believer may know whether or not a work is of the flesh. Whatever does not issue from waiting upon God, from depending upon the Holy Spirit, is unquestionably of the flesh. Whatever one decides according to his pleasure in lieu of seeking the will of God emanates from the flesh. Whenever a heart of utter trust is lacking, there is the labor of the flesh. Now the things done may not be evil or improper; they in fact may be good and godly (such as reading the Bible, praying, worshiping, preaching); but if they are not undertaken in a spirit of complete reliance upon the Holy Spirit, then the flesh is the source of all. The old creation is willing to do anything—even to submit to God—if only it is permitted to live and to be active! However good the deed of the flesh may appear to be, "I," whether veiled or seen, always looms large on the horizon. The flesh never acknowledges its weakness nor admits to its uselessness; even should it become a laughingstock, the flesh remains unshaken in the belief in its ability. . . .

### *God's View of the Flesh*

We Christians need to be reminded once again of God's judgment upon the flesh. "The flesh," says the Lord Jesus, "is of no avail" (John 6.63). Whether it be the sin of the flesh or the righteousness of the flesh, it is futile. That which is born of the flesh, whatever it may be, is flesh, and can never be "unfleshed." Whether it be the flesh in the pulpit, the flesh in the audience, the flesh in prayers, the flesh in consecration, the flesh in reading the Bible, the flesh in singing hymns, or the flesh in doing good—none of these, asserts God, can avail. However much believers may lust in the flesh, God declares it all to be unprofitable; for neither does the flesh profit the spiritual life nor can it fulfill the rigtheousness of God. . . .

### *The Cross and the Deeper Work of the Holy Spirit*

Because the flesh is grossly deceitful, the believer requires the cross and the Holy Spirit. Once having discerned how his flesh stands before God, he must experience each moment the deeper work of the cross through the Holy Spirit. Just as a Christian must be delivered from the sin of the flesh through the cross, so he must now be delivered from the righteousness of the flesh by the same cross. And just as by walking in the Holy Spirit the Christian will not follow the flesh unto sin, so too by walking in the Holy Spirit he will not follow the flesh unto self-righteousness.

As a fact outside the believer the cross has been accomplished perfectly and entirely: to deepen it is not possible. As a process within the believer the cross is experienced in an ever deepening way: the Holy Spirit will teach and apply the principle of the cross in point after point. If one is faithful and obedient he will be led into continually deeper experiences of what the cross has indeed accomplished for him. The cross objectively is a finished absolute fact to which nothing can be added; but subjectively it is an unending progressive experience that can be realized in an ever more penetrating way.

—TSM, I: 69–70, 71–2, 75–6, 78–9, 80–1, 83, 93, 95–6, 97–8, 100–1, 109–10, 114, 119, 124

# 28 Body and Sickness

We should recognize the place of the body in God's design of redemption. Christ sets apart our fleshly frames that we may be filled with the Holy Spirit and become His instruments. Because He has died, been resurrected and been glorified, He is now qualified to give His Holy Spirit to our body. As in the past our soul life permeated our body, so now His Spirit shall permeate it. His life will flow into every member, and He will give us life and power far abundantly beyond what we can think.

That our body constitutes a temple of the Holy Spirit is a sure fact; and it can be livingly experienced as well. Yet many are like the Corinthian believers who forgot this glorious possibility. Though God's Spirit does dwell in them, He seems nonexistent to them. We need to exercise faith to believe, to acknowledge and to accept this fact of God. If we *draw* on this fact by faith we shall discover that the Spirit will bring not only the holiness, joy, righteousness and love of Christ to our souls, but also life, power, health and strength to our weak, weary and sick bodies. He will give to our earthen vessels the life of Christ together with the vital elements of His glorious body. When our body has truly died with Christ, that is, when it is subject completely to Him, all self-will and independent action denied and nothing sought but to be a temple of the Lord, then the Holy Spirit shall assuredly manifest the life of the risen Christ in our mortal frame. How good it is for us to genuinely experience the Lord in healing and in strengthening, in His being our health and life! If we see our tent as a temple of the Holy Spirit we shall follow Him in wonderment and in love! . . .

*The Lord's Work and Sickness*

"Surely he has borne our griefs and carried our sorrows; yet we esteemed him stricken, smitten by God, and afflicted. But he was wounded for our transgressions, he was bruised for our iniquities" (Is. 53.4–5). Of all the Old Testament writings this 53rd chapter of Isaiah is quoted most often in the New Testament. It alludes to the Lord Jesus Christ, especially to Him as our Savior. Verse 4 affirms that "he has borne our griefs and carried our sorrows" whereas Matthew 8.17 declares that "this was to fulfil what was spoken by the prophet Isaiah, 'He took our infirmities and bore our diseases'." The Holy Spirit indicates here that the Lord Jesus came to the world to take our infirmities and bear our diseases. Prior to His crucifixion He had already taken our infirmities and borne our diseases; which is to say that during His earthly ministry the Lord Jesus made healing His burden and task. He not only preached, He also healed. He preached the glad tidings on the one hand, but on the other hand strengthened the weak, restored the withered hand, cleansed the leper and raised the palsied. While on earth the Lord Jesus devoted himself to the performance of miracles as well as to the ministry of the Word. He went about doing good, He healed the sick, and cast out demons. The purpose of His work was to overthrow sickness, the result of sin. He came to deal with death and sickness as well as with sin.

Psalm 103 is familiar to many of God's children; I myself love to read it. David proclaims, "Bless the Lord, O my soul; and all that is within me, bless his holy name!" Why bless the Lord? "Bless the Lord, O my soul, and forget not all his benefits." What are His benefits? "Who forgives all your iniquity, who heals all your diseases." (vv.1–3) I wish brothers and sisters to see that sickness is coupled with two elements: death on the one side, sin on the other. We have mentioned earlier how death is the result of sin, with sickness included therein. Both sickness and death flow from sin. Here in Psalm 103 we find that sickness is coupled with sin. Because of sin in the soul there is disease in the body. Along with the forgiveness of our iniquity comes the healing of our disease. The trouble in the body is sin within and disease without. But the Lord takes both away.

There is a basic dissimilarity, however, between God's treatment of our iniquity and His treatment of our disease. Why this difference? Our Lord Jesus bore our sins in His body on the cross. Does any sin remain unforgiven? Absolutely none, for the work of God is so complete that sin is entirely destroyed. But in taking our infirmities and bearing our diseases while He lived on earth, the Lord Jesus did not eradicate all diseases and all infirmities. For note that Paul never says "when I sin, then am I sanctified," but he does declare that "when I am weak, then I am strong" (2 Cor. 12.10). Hence sin is thoroughly and unlimitedly dealt with whereas sickness is only limitedly treated.

In God's redemption the handling of sickness is unlike that of sin. With the latter, its destruction is totally uncircumscribed; with the former, this is just not so. Timothy, for instance, continued to have a weak stomach. The Lord permitted this weakness to remain with His servant. So in God's salvation sickness has not been eradicated as totally as has sin. Some maintain that the Lord Jesus deals solely with sin and not with illness too: others conceive the scope of His treatment of disease to be as broad and inclusive as His treatment of sin. Yet the Scriptures manifestly indicate to us that the Lord Jesus deals with both sin and sickness; only His dealing with sin is limitless while that with sickness is limited. We must behold the Lamb of God taking away *all* the sin of the world—He has borne the sin of each and every person. Sin's problem is therefore already solved. But meanwhile sickness still pervades God's children.

Nonetheless, we contend that since the Lord Jesus has actually borne our diseases there should not be so much sickness as there is among the children of God. While Jesus was on earth he unmistakably devoted himself to the healing of the sick. He included healing in His work. Isaiah 53.4 is fulfilled in Matthew 8, not in Matthew 27. It is realized *before* Calvary. Had it been realized on the cross, healing would be unbounded. But no, the Lord Jesus bore our diseases prior to crucifixion, with the result that this aspect of His work is not as unlimited as was His bearing of our sins.

Even so, numberless saints remain ill because they have missed the opportunity of being healed; they do not see that the Lord has borne our diseases. Let me add a few more words on this point. Unless we have the assurance as did Paul upon praying thrice that his weakness would stay on because it was profitable to him, we should ask for healing. Paul accepted his weakness only after he had prayed the third time and had been shown distinctly by the Lord that His grace was sufficient for him and that His strength would be made perfect in his weakness. Until we are sure that God wants us to bear our weakness, we should boldly ask the Lord himself to bear it and take away our disease. The children of God live on earth not to be sick but to glorify God. If to be sick will bring God glory, well and good; but many diseases do not necessarily glorify Him. Consequently, we must learn to trust the Lord while sick and must realize that He bears our sickness too. He healed a great number while He was on earth. And He is the same yesterday, today and forever. Let us commit our infirmity to Him and ask for His healing.

### *The Believer's Attitude towards Sickness*

Every time the believer falls ill the first thing he should do is to inquire after its cause before the Lord. He should not be overanxious in seeking healing. Paul sets a good example in showing us how he was most clear about his weakness. We must examine whether we have disobeyed the Lord, have sinned anywhere, owe anybody a debt, have violated some natural law, or have neglected some special duty. We ought to know that frequently our violation of natural law can constitute a sin against God, for God sets up these natural laws by which to govern the universe. Many are afraid to die; upon becoming sick they hurriedly seek out physicians, for they are anxious to be cured. Such ought not to be the Christian's attitude. He should first attempt to isolate the cause for his malady. Alas, how many brothers and sisters do not possess any patience. The moment they fall sick they search for a remedy. Are you so afraid to lose your precious life that through prayer you lay hold of God for healing yet simultaneously lay hold of a physician for drugs and an injection? This reveals how full of self you are. But then how could you be less full of self in sickness if you are filled with self during ordinary days? Those who are ordinarily full of self will be those who anxiously seek for healing just as soon as they get sick.

May I tell you that anxiety avails nothing. Since you belong to God, your healing is not so simple. Even if you are cured this time, you will be ailing again. One must solve his problem before God first; and then can be solved the problem in his body.

Learn to accept whatever lesson sickness may bring to you. For if you have dealings with God many of your problems will be resolved quickly. You will find out that often your illness is due to some sin or fault of yours. Upon confessing your sin and asking for forgiveness, you may expect healing from God. Or, should you have walked further with the Lord, you may discern that involved in this is the enemy's attack. Or the matter of God's discipline may be associated with your unhealthy state. God chastises with sickness so as to render you holier, softer or more yielding. As you deal with these problems before God you will be enabled to see the exact reason for your infirmity. Sometimes God may allow you to receive a little natural or medical help, but sometimes He may heal you instantaneously without such assistance.

We should see that healing is in God's hand. Learn to trust Him who heals. In the Old Testament God has a special name which is, "I am the Lord, your healer" (Ex. 15.26). Look to Him and He will be gracious to His own in this particular regard. . . .

### *The Way to Seek Healing*

How should men seek healing before God? Three sentences

in the Gospel of Mark are worth learning. I find them especially helpful, at least they are very effective for me. The first touches upon the power of the Lord; the second, the will of the Lord; and the third, the act of the Lord.

a) The Power of the Lord: "God can." "And Jesus asked his father, 'How long has he had this?' And he said, 'From childhood. And it has often cast him into the fire and into the water, to destroy him; but *if you can* do anything, have pity on us and help us.' And Jesus said to him, '*If you can*! All things are possible to him who believes'" (9.21–23). The Lord Jesus merely repeated the three words which the child's father had uttered. The father cried, "If you can, help us." The Lord responded, "If you can! Why, all things are possible to him who believes." The problem here is not "if you can" but rather "if you believe."

Is it not true that the first problem which arises with sickness is a doubt about God's power? Under a microscope the power of bacteria seems to be greater than the power of God. Very rarely does the Lord cut off others in the middle of their speaking, but here he appears as though He were angry. (May the Lord forgive me for phrasing it this way!) When He heard the child's father say "If you can, have pity on us and help us," He sharply reacted with "Why say if you can? All things are possible to him who believes. In sickness, the question is not whether I can or cannot but whether *you believe* or not."

The initial step for a child of God to take in sickess therefore is to raise up his head and say "Lord, you can!" You remember, do you not, the first instance of the Lord's healing of a paralytic? He asked the Pharisees, "Which is easier, to say to the paralytic, 'Your sins are forgiven,' or to say, 'Rise, take up your pallet and walk'?" (Mark 2.9) The Pharisees naturally thought it easier to say your sins are forgiven, for who could actually prove it is or is not so? But the Lord's words and their results showed them that He could heal sickness as well as forgive sins. He did not ask which was more difficult, but which was easier. For Him, both were equally easy. It was as easy for the Lord to bid the paralytic rise and walk as to forgive the latter's sins. For the Pharisees, both were as difficult.

b) The Will of the Lord: "God will." Yes, He indeed can, but how do I know if He wills? I do not know His will; perhaps He does not want to heal me. This is another story in Mark again. "And a leper came to him beseeching him, and kneeling said to to him, 'If you will, you can make me clean.' Moved with pity, he stretched out his hand and touched him, and said to him, 'I will; be clean'" (1.40–41).

However great the power of God is, if He has no wish to heal, His power shall not help me. The problem to be solved at the outset is: Can God?; the second is: Will God? There is no sickness as unclean as leprosy. It is so unclean that according to law whoever touches a leper becomes himself unclean. Yet the Lord Jesus touched the leper and said to him, "I will." If He would heal the leper, how much more wills He to cure *our* diseases. We can proclaim boldly, "God can" and "God will."

c) The Act of the Lord: "God has." One more thing must God do. "Verily I say unto you, Whosoever shall say unto this mountain, Be thou taken up and cast into the sea; and shall not doubt in his heart, but shall believe that what he saith cometh to pass; he shall have it. Therefore I say unto you, all things whatsoever ye pray and ask for, believe that ye receive [Gr. *received*] them, and ye shall have them" (11.23–24 ASV). What is faith? Faith believes God can, God will, and God has done it. If you believe you have received it, you shall have it. Should God give you His word, you can thank Him by saying, "God has healed me; He has already done it!" Many believers merely *expect* to be healed. Expectation regards things in the future, but faith deals with the past. If we really believe, we shall not wait for twenty or a hundred years, but shall rise up immediately and say, "Thank God, He has healed me. Thank God, I have received it. Thank God, I am clean! Thank God, I am well." A perfect faith can therefore proclaim God can, God will and God has done it.

Faith works with "is" and not "wish." Allow me to use a simple illustration. Suppose you preach the gospel and one professes that he has believed. Ask him whether he is saved, and should his answer be, I wish to be saved, then you know this reply is inadequate. Should he say, I will be saved, the answer is still incorrect. Even if he responds with, I think I shall definitely be saved, something is yet missing. But when he answers, I am saved, you know the flavor is right. If one believes, then he is saved. All faith deals with the past. To say I believe I shall be healed is not true faith. If he believes, he will thank God and say, I have received healing.

Lay hold of these three steps: God can, God will, God has. When man's faith touches the third stage, the sickness is over.

[*". . . the body is . . . for the Lord;*
*and the Lord for the body."—1 Cor. 6.13b*]

As far as our knowledge is concerned we already realize that our body is for the Lord; yet because of our self-will He is unable to fill us completely. But now we commit our all to Him that He may deal with us in whatever way He wishes. We present our bodies a living sacrifice; therefore we control neither our life nor our future. Now we truly understand what is meant by the body for the Lord. What worried us before cannot now shake us. The enemy may tempt us by reminding us that this way is too risky or that we are being too unmindful of ourselves; even so, we are not frightened as we used to be. One thing do we know: we belong to the Lord absolutely: nothing can therefore befall us without His knowledge and permission. Whatever attack may come is but an indication of His special purpose and His unfailing protection. Our bodies are no longer ours. Every nerve, cell, and organ has been handed over to Him. No more are we our own masters, hence we no longer are responsible. If the weather abruptly changes, this is His business. A sleepless night does not make us anxious. No matter in what unexpected way Satan assaults, we remember the battle is the Lord's and not ours. Then and there the life of God flows out through our bodies. At such an hour others might lose peace, grow despondent, become worried, and desperately seek some remedial measure; but we quietly exercise faith and live by God, for we know we henceforth live not by eating, drinking, sleeping, and so forth, but by the life of God. These things cannot hurt us.

Understanding now that the Lord is for his body, the Christian is able to appropriate all the riches of God for his needs. For every urgent requirement there is always His supply; his heart is accordingly at rest. He does not request more than what God has supplied, but neither is he satisifed with anything less than what He has promised. He refuses to use his own strength in any matter to help God ahead of His time. While worldly people are anxiously running for help because of the suffering and pain of the flesh, he can wait calmly for God's time and God's riches due to his union with Him. He holds not his life in his own hand but looks for the Father's care. What peace this is!

During this period the believer glorifies God in every respect. He takes whatever may happen as an opportunity to manifest His glory. He does not use his own ways and thus interfere with the glory which is due God. But when the Lord stretches out His arm to deliver, then is he ready to praise.

The aim of the child is no longer the blessing from the Father. God himself is far more precious than all His gifts. If healing would not express God then he does not want to be healed. Should we merely covet the Father's protection and supply, should we cry out only for deliverance from temptation, we already have fallen. God as our life is not a business proposition. Those who genuinely know Him do not beg for healing but always seek the Father. If health might lead him astray and take away from God's glory, he would rather not be healed. Believers continually should remember that whenever our motive is to covet God's gifts rather than God himself, we already are beginning to falter. Should a Christian live perfectly for the Lord he will not be anxious to seek help, blessing, or supply. He will instead commit himself unconditionally to God.

—TSM, III: 156-7, 183-6, 192-6, 211-2

# 29 The Blood

## *The Blood Is Primarily for God*

The Blood is for atonement and has to do first with our standing before God. We need forgiveness for the sins we have committed, lest we come under judgment; and they are forgiven, not because God overlooks what we have done but because He sees the Blood. The Blood is therefore not primarily for us but for God. If I want to understand the value of the Blood I must accept God's valuation of it, and if I do not know something of the value set upon the Blood by God I shall never know what its value is for me. It is only as the estimate that God puts upon the Blood of Christ is made known to me by His Holy Spirit that I come into the good of it myself and find how precious indeed the Blood is to me. But the first aspect of it is Godward. Throughout the Old and New Testaments the word "blood" is used in connection with the idea of atonement, I think over a hundred times, and throughout it is something for God.

In the Old Testament calendar there is one day that has a great bearing on the matter of our sins and that day is the Day of Atonement. Nothing explains this question of sins so clearly as the description of that day. In Leviticus 16 we find that on the Day of Atonement the blood was taken from the sin offering and brought into the Most Holy Place and there sprinkled before the Lord seven times. We must be very clear about this. On that day the sin offering was offered publicly in the court of the tabernacle. Everything was there in full view and could be seen by all. But the Lord commanded that no man should enter the tabernacle itself except the high priest. It was he alone who took the blood and, going into the Most Holy Place, sprinkled it there to make atonement before the Lord. Why? Because the high priest was a type of the Lord Jesus in His redemptive work (Heb. 9.11–12), and so, in figure, he was the one who did the work. None but he could even draw near to enter in. Moreover, connected with his going in there was but one act, namely, the presenting of the blood to God as something He had accepted, something in which He could find satisfaction. It was a transaction between the high priest and God in the Sanctuary, away from the eyes of the men who were to benefit by it. The Lord required that. The Blood is therefore, in the first place, not for ourselves but for Him.

Earlier even than this there is described in Exodus 12.13 the shedding of the blood of the passover lamb in Egypt for Israel's redemption. This is again, I think, one of the best types in the Old Testament of our redemption. The blood was put on the lintel and on the doorposts, whereas the meat, the flesh of the lamb, was eaten inside the house; and God said: "When I see the blood, I will pass over you." Here we have another illustration of the fact that the blood was not meant to be presented to man but to God, for the blood was put on the lintel and on the doorposts, where those feasting inside the house would not see it.

### *God Is Satisfied*

It is God's holiness, God's righteousness, which demands that a sinless life should be given for man. There is life in the Blood, and that Blood has to be poured out for me, for my sins. God is the One who requires it to be so. God is the One who demands that the Blood be presented, in order to satisfy His own righteousness, and it is He who says: "*When I see the blood,* I will pass over you." The Blood of Christ wholly satisfies God. . . .

### *The Believer's Access to God*

The Blood has satisfied God; it must satisfy us also. It has therefore a second value that is manward, in the cleansing of our conscience. When we come to the Epistle to the Hebrews we find that the Blood does this. We are to have "hearts sprinkled from an evil conscience" (Heb. 10.22).

This is most important. Look carefully at what it says. The writer does not tell us that the Blood of the Lord Jesus cleanses our hearts, and then stop there in his statement. We are wrong to connect the heart with the Blood in quite that way. It may show a misunderstanding of the sphere in which the Blood operates to pray, "Lord, cleanse my heart from sin by Thy Blood." The heart, God says, is "desperately sick" (Jer. 17.9), and He must do something more fundamental than cleanse it: He must give us a new one.

We do not wash and iron clothing that we are going to throw away. As we shall shortly see, the "flesh" is too bad to be cleansed; it must be crucified. The work of God within us must be something wholly new. "A new heart also will I give you, and a new spirit will I put within you" (Ezek. 36.26).

No, I do not find it stated that the Blood cleanses our hearts. Its work is not subjective in that way, but wholly objective, before God. True, the cleansing work of the Blood is seen here in Hebrews to have reference to the heart, but it is in relation to the conscience. "Having our hearts sprinkled from an evil conscience." What then is the meaning of this?

It means that there was something intervening between myself and God, as a result of which I had an evil conscience whenever I sought to approach Him. It was constantly reminding me of the barrier that stood between myself and Him. But now, through the operation of the precious Blood, something new has been effected before God which has removed that barrier, and God has made that fact known to me in His word. When that has been believed in and accepted, my conscience is at once cleared and my sense of guilt removed, and I have no more an evil conscience towards God. . . .

### *Overcoming the Accuser*

In view of what we have said we can now turn to face the enemy, for there is a further aspect of the Blood which is Satanward. Satan's most strategic activity in this day is as the accuser of the brethren (Rev. 12.10) and it is as this that our Lord confronts him with His special ministry as High Priest "through his own blood" (Heb. 9.12).

How then does the Blood operate against Satan? It does so by putting God on the side of man against him. The Fall brought about a state of affairs in man which gave Satan a footing within him, with the result that God was compelled to withdraw himself. Man is now outside the Garden—beyond reach of the glory of God (Rom. 3.23)—because he is inwardly estranged from God. Because of what man has done, there is that in him now which, until it is removed, renders God morally unable to defend him. But the Blood removes that barrier, and restores man to God and God to man. Man is in favor now, and because God is on his side he can face Satan without fear.

You remember that verse in John's first Epistle—and this is the translation of it I like best: "The blood of Jesus his Son cleanses us from *every* sin."* It is not exactly "all sin" in the general sense, but *every* sin, every item. What does it mean? Oh, it is a marvelous thing! God is in the light, and as we walk in the light with Him everything is exposed and open to that light, so that God can see it all—*and yet* the Blood is able to cleanse from every sin. What a cleansing! It is not that I have not a profound knowledge of myself, nor that God has not a perfect knowledge of me. It is not that I try to hide something, nor that God tries to overlook something. No, it is that He is in the light and I too am in the

*John 1.7: Marginal reading of New Translation by J. N. Darby.

light, and that *there* the precious Blood cleanses me from every sin. The Blood is enough for that! . . .

Since God, seeing all our sins in the light, can forgive them on the basis of the Blood, what ground of accusation has Satan? Satan may accuse us before Him, but, "If God is for us, who is against us?" (Rom. 8.31) God points him to the Blood of His dear Son. It is the sufficient answer against which Satan has no appeal. "Who shall lay anything to the charge of God's elect? It is God that justifieth; who is he that shall condemn? It is Christ Jesus that died, yea rather, that was raised from the dead, who is at the right hand of God, who also maketh intercession for us" (Rom. 8:33–34). Thus God answers his every challenge.

So here again our need is to recognize the absolute sufficiency of the precious Blood. "Christ having come a high priest . . . through his own blood, entered in once for all into the holy place, having obtained eternal redemption" (Heb. 9.11–12). He was Redeemer once. He has been High Priest and Advocate for nearly two thousand years. He stands there in the presence of God, and "he is the propitiation for our sins" (1 John 2.1–2). Note the words of Hebrew 9.14: "*How much more* shall the blood of Christ . . . cleanse your conscience." They underline the sufficiency of His ministry. *It is enough for God.*

—NCL 17–22, 26–8

### *The Blood the Basis for All Worship*

Many have the idea that they may come to God and worship Him because they have good works which are worthy of His praise. They cannot come and worship if they have not behaved themselves but have done things displeasing to God. Yet we need to understand that our conduct, whether good or bad, has no direct relationship to our approaching God: "Having therefore, brethren, boldness to enter into the holy place by the blood of Jesus" (Heb. 10.19). We are told in this verse that our coming to God is based on nothing else than the blood of the Lord Jesus.

Neither good works nor zeal nor spiritual experience qualifies us to approach God. The blood of the Lord Jesus alone enables us to draw near to Him. If anyone fails to see the blood of the Lord Jesus as being sufficient for him to come near to God, then may I speak most frankly that he has absolutely no possibility of approaching God. . . .

We know we are different from the children of Israel in worship, since all of us today may enter into the holiest of all and worship God because of the blood; but the children of Israel could not do so. The Old Testament or Covenant presents to us a picture of distance, for the congregation could not do anything by themselves. They could not worship directly. Even the slaying of cattle and sheep had to be done by the priests. They were separated from God; they could not draw near to Him. Not so, though, under the New Testament or Covenant. Each and every believer may come to worship in the holiest place. And no one may worship for other people. Strictly speaking, even our Lord Jesus does not worship for us. It is true that the Old Testament period divided the worshipers into three classes: the congregation, the priests, and the high priest. Only the high priest could enter the holiest of all once a year with the blood; none else could enter in. But today every one of us is like the high priest, because we all may enter directly into the holiest place. . . .

*The Blood Mentioned in Romans and Hebrews*

Romans speaks of the blood, and so does Hebrews; but what each of them says is different. Romans mentions the blood upon the mercy seat which deals with the one aspect of our sin being atoned for. Hebrews speaks of the blood before the veil which deals with the other aspect, that of drawing near to worship God. For the blood not only forgives and cleanses us of sin, it also leads us to approach God and worship Him. Some may still object and argue that they have not behaved well during the week, and therefore they dare not come to God with boldness. Then let me ask you, When will you be good enough to feel that there is nothing wrong with you so that you may come and worship with boldness? How long will you have to wait for such a day? When will your heart be able to burst forth with hallelujahs? According to your own requirements, you will not be able to worship until after you are raptured! Let us see that our worship is not determined by our works but by our trusting in the blood.

—FF 50, 52, 53–4

# 30 Forgiveness and Deliverance

There are four kinds of forgiveness in the Bible. For convenience sake, we shall give each a name: first, eternal forgiveness; second, borrowed forgiveness; third, communional forgiveness; and fourth, governmental forgiveness. In order to walk uprightly, we need to learn what God's governmental forgiveness is. Before we touch on this, however, let us first differentiate the four kinds of forgiveness.

### *Eternal Forgiveness*

We call the forgiveness we receive at the time we are saved eternal forgiveness. This is the forgiveness of which the Lord Jesus spoke when He said, "Repentance and remission of sins should be preached in his name unto all the nations, beginning from Jerusalem" (Luke 24.47). This is also what Romans 4.7 refers to: "Blessed are they whose iniquities are forgiven, and whose sins are covered."

We call this kind of forgiveness eternal forgiveness because once God forgives our sins, He forgives them forever. He casts our sins into the sea, into the depths of the sea, so that He no longer sees nor remembers them. Such is the forgiveness we receive at the time of salvation. For us who believe in the Lord Jesus, He forgives all our sins and takes away all our iniquities so that before God none are left. This is eternal forgiveness.

### *Borrowed Forgiveness*

Many times God himself says, "I forgive you!" Sometimes, though, He declares His forgiveness through the church: "God has forgiven your sins!" This kind of forgiveness we term borrowed forgiveness. "And when he had said this, he breathed on them, and saith unto them, Receive ye the Holy Spirit: whose soever sins ye forgive, they are forgiven unto them; whose soever sins ye retain, they are retained" (John 20.22–23). Here the Lord gives His Holy Spirit to the church so that she may represent Him on earth and be His vessel to forgive people's sins. Though we call this borrowed forgiveness, we need to exercise extreme care lest we fall into the error of the Roman Catholic Church. Notice what the Lord said. The forgiveness here is based on the Lord's breathing upon the church, saying, "Receive ye the Holy Spirit." The consequence of receiving the Holy Spirit is that the church knows whose sins are retained and whose are forgiven. Thus the church may declare whose sins are retained and whose sins are forgiven. Remember this: the church has such authority only because she herself is under the authority of the Holy Spirit. "Whose soever sins ye forgive, they are forgiven unto them; whose soever sins ye retain, they are retained"—these words come after "Receive ye the Holy Spirit." Borrowed forgiveness is God forgiving people's sins through the channel of the church. . . .

### *Communional Forgiveness*

What is communional forgiveness? "But if we walk in the light, as he is in the light, we have fellowship one with another, and the blood of Jesus his Son cleanseth us from all sin. If we say that we have no sin, we deceive ourselves, and the truth is not in us. If we confess our sins, he is faithful and righteous to forgive us our sins, and to cleanse us from all unrighteousness" (1 John 1.7–9). "My little children, these things write I unto you that ye may not sin. And if any man sin, we have an Advocate with the Father, Jesus Christ the righteous: and he is the propitiation for our sins; and not for ours only, but also for the whole world" (2.1–2). The forgiveness mentioned here is neither that which we received at the time of salvation nor that which the church extends to us. After we believe in the Lord and become God's children, we still may have need of God's forgiveness. We have mentioned this before as the forgiveness of the red heifer. Though we have received eternal forgiveness, we may weaken and once again sin before the Lord, thus interrupting our fellowship with God. So, once again we need forgiveness. . . .

### *Governmental Forgiveness*

There is still another kind of forgiveness which we call governmental forgiveness. This kind of forgiveness is seen in the following Bible passages: Matt. 9.2, 5–6; James 5.15 and Matt. 6.14–15, 18, 21–35.

What is God's governmental forgiveness? I am convinced that if I had known the government of God immediately following my salvation, I would have been spared many troubles and problems.

The parable of the girl may be continued here: formerly the mother always left the doors in the house open, including the cupboard door and the kitchen door. She never locked the cupboard in which she put food. But this time, when she came home, she discovered that some of the food in the cupboard had been eaten. Now that the mother knows what has happened, the girl is forced to confess her sin and ask for forgiveness. The mother forgives her and even kisses her. The incident is considered past and the fellowship is restored. However, next time the mother leaves the house, she locks all the doors. Her way of doing things has changed. Fellowship is one thing, but government is quite another.

What is government? Government is a way. God's government is God's way, God's administration. . . .

You, too, may sin against God, and at each confession of your sin God forgives you. This does not, however, hinder God from giving you new chastening. Since God has forgiven you, your fellowship with God may be restored. But God will change His way with you. It is important for us to know that God's disciplinary hand upon us is not easily moved, nor, once extended, is it easily removed. Unless God has full assurance that His children are all right, His governmental hand will not be removed. . . .

### *Humble Yourself under God's Mighty Hand*

Our God is the God of government. Sometimes when He is offended, He does not immediately move His governmental hand. He just lets you get by. But once He moves His governmental hand, there is nothing you can do except to humble yourself. There is no way for you to escape; He is not like man who will easily allow you to get away. To have your sin forgiven and your fellowship with God restored is quite easy. But you cannot remove the discipline God gives you in your environment—your home, your business, or your physical body. The only thing you can do is learn to subject yourself to the mighty hand of God. The humbler we are under His mighty hand and the less we resist, the easier it will be to have the governmental hand of God removed from us. If we are not submissive and patient, if we murmur and fret within, let me tell you, it will be harder for God's governmental hand to be removed. This is a most serious matter. Twenty years ago you did something according to your own idea. Today you meet the same thing again and you have yet to eat that fruit of your earlier action. That thing has come back and found you out. What should you do when this happens? You should bow your head, saying: "Lord, it is my fault!" You should humble yourself under God's hand and not resist. The more you resist, the heavier the hand of God. So I always say that you must subject yourself to the mighty hand of God. The more you resist God's governmental hand, the more things will happen to you. As soon as the governmental hand of God is upon you, you must humble yourself and gladly acknowledge that you deserve it, for the Lord cannot be wrong. You should be in subjection. You must not think of rebelling; you must not even murmur or fret. . . .

God's governmental hand is truly most serious. Let us be fearful, for we do not know when the disciplinary hand of God will come upon us. God may allow some to get by all the time. Or He may overlook rebellion ten times but on the eleventh time bring His hand down. Or His hand may come down the very first time. We have no way of knowing when His disciplinary hand will descend. God's government is not something we can control. Whatever He wishes, He does.

Because of this, brethren, we must first of all try our very best to learn to be obedient to the Lord. May God be merciful and gracious to you that you may not fall into the governmental hand of God. Howbeit, if you do fall into His governmental hand, do not resist or be rash. Do not attempt to run away, but hold on to the basic principle of subjection at any cost. You cannot naturally by yourself be submissive, but you can ask the Lord to make you so. Only by the mercy of the Lord can you get through. "O Lord, be merciful to me that I may get through!" If God's governmental hand has not fallen upon you, look persistently for His mercy. If it has already fallen, if He has allowed you to be sick or to have difficulties come upon you, remember well that you should never by your fleshly hand try to resist God's government. As soon as God's government falls on you, humble yourself at once under His mighty hand. You should say, "Lord, this is Your doing, this is Your arrangement; I gladly submit, I am willing to accept it." When God's governmental hand fell on Job (it could have been avoided), the more submissive Job was, the better his condition was; the more he boasted of his own righteousness, the worse his situation became.

Thank God, frequently God's governmental hand does not stay forever on a person. I personally believe that when God's governmental hand does fall on a person, sometimes the prayer of the church may easily remove that hand. This is what is so precious in James 5. There James tells us that the elders of the church may remove the governmental hand of God. He says: "And the prayer of faith shall save him that is sick, and the Lord shall raise him up; and if he have committed sins, it shall be forgiven him." So, when a brother finds that this is the way for him, the church may pray for him and help to remove God's governmental hand from him.

—LOA 1-2, 4, 6-7, 8, 14-5, 17-8

(a) God's eternal forgiveness. (This concerns eternal salvation.)

(b) Forgiveness through God's people. (This concerns the fellowship of God's children. We may also call this forgiveness as borrowed forgiveness or the forgiveness of the church.)

(c) Forgiveness for the restoring of fellowship. (This concerns one's communion with God.)

(d) Forgiveness with discipline. (This concerns the way of God with His children.)

(e) Forgiveness in the kingdom. (This concerns the forgiveness during the millennial kingdom.)

Now let us explain them separately. (a) *God's eternal forgiveness.* Eternal forgiveness is related to man's eternal salvation. Although such forgiveness is for eternity, it nevertheless is given to a sinner today. On what basis is such forgiveness given? "Apart from shedding of blood there is no remission" (Heb. 9.22). "This is my blood of the covenant, which is poured out for many unto remission of sins" (Matt. 26.28). These verses tell us that eternal forgiveness is based on the blood of the Lord Jesus. No matter how big or gross a sin is, it can be forgiven through His blood. Such forgiveness is not without price, since God cannot freely forgive; for "apart from shedding of blood there is no remission," says His word. In forgiving our sins He has not overlooked them, for He *has* condemned sin. He can only forgive us because He has judged our sins in the flesh of Christ. The Lord Jesus has died, shed His precious blood, and paid the price. And so God can be most righteous in forgiving us, for how can He not forgive us since we have a Savior who has died for us? . . .

(b) *Forgivness through God's people.* "Whose soever sins ye forgive, they are forgiven unto them; whose soever sins ye retain, they are retained" (John 20.23). . . .

. . . To what does the forgiveness mentioned in John 20.23 refer? It refers to the declaration made by the church after she has been instructed by the Holy Spirit and has known the forgiveness of God given to an individual. We need to notice that the verse reads "whose soever sins *ye* forgive," with the pronoun stated in the plural number, not "you" in the singular. It is corporate, not personal; the church, not individual. "Whose soever sins ye forgive" means to say that when the church declares whose sins are forgiven, the person or persons involved were already saved people to begin with. Suppose a person should come to the church and say, "I have heard the gospel and have believed. Please receive me in baptism and in the breaking of bread that I may be like the other disciples." For the brethren to receive him, they need to know that his sins are forgiven by God. If the brethren know they are forgiven and that he is already a child of God, they will declare that he is indeed a forgiven and saved person, and he is therefore received into the fellowship of the church. If the brethren are not sure within themselves and cannot testify for him, they are not able to receive him. The forgiveness of the church is based on the forgiveness of God. The church merely declares what *God* has already done. And through the church God announces what the condition of the person is before Him. . . .

(c) *Forgiveness for restoring fellowship.* "My little children, these things write I unto you that ye may not sin. And if any man sin, we have an Advocate with the Father, Jesus Christ the righteous: and he is the propitiation for our sins; and not for ours only, but also for the whole world" (1 John 2.1–2). "If we confess our sins, he is faithful and righteous to forgive us our sins, and to cleanse us from all unrighteousness" (1 John 1.9). . . .

. . . There is still the possibility of sinning after we are saved. As we sin, our fellowship with God is immediately cut. Such fellowship is not restored until our sins are forgiven. If we sin, we must confess our sins according to 1 John 1.9, acknowledging that we have done wrong in a certain matter and asking God to forgive us. By such confession our fellowship with Him will be restored. . . .

(d) *Forgiveness with discipline.* This pertains to God's way of dealing with His children. What is His dealing? It is His way, that is to say, it is the manner by which He will deal with people. Let us first read several passages in the Bible.

"With the merciful thou wilt show thyself merciful; with the perfect man thou wilt show thyself perfect; with the pure thou wilt show thyself pure; and with the perverse thou wilt show thyself froward" (2 Sam. 22.26–27). This is a description of God's way of dealing. He will deal with you in accordance with what you are. "Be not deceived; God is not mocked: for whatsoever a man soweth, that shall he also reap. For he that soweth unto his own flesh shall of the flesh reap corruption; but he that soweth unto the Spirit shall of the Spirit reap eternal life" (Gal. 6.7–8). These verses too show us the principle by which God deals with people. He who sows to the flesh shall of the flesh reap corruption; but he who sows to the Spirit shall of the Spirit reap eternal life. In our sinning, there is not only a crime committed before God, there is likewise a suffering which is an accompaniment or an aftermath of sin. The crime may be forgiven but the suffering cannot be avoided. . . .

(e) *Forgiveness in the kingdom.* Concerning the forgiveness in the kingdom we may read Matthew 18.21–35. . . .

. . . Concerning the church God speaks of grace; concerning the kingdom, He speaks of responsibility. As regards the church, we are told what the Lord has done and how He treats us; as regards the kingdom, we are shown how we are trained before God, how we live today, and what will be the judgment in the future. Here in Matthew 18 we are shown our responsibility, for this passage is concerned with the kingdom of heaven—with reigning for a thousand years—and not with the question of eternal salvation. . . .

We know that the daily life and work of a Christian on earth will be judged in the future. After the rapture all Christians will stand in judgment before the judgment seat of Christ. This is not to be a judging of the salvation of a Christian but the judging of his fitness for the kingdom and his position in the kingdom. Thus there are two perils in our standing before the judgment seat: first, we may be barred completely from the kingdom; or, second, we may receive a *low* position in the kingdom if we *are* allowed to enter. . . .

Since judgment is to begin at the house of God (1 Peter 4.17), how serious must be this judgment! And if so, who can pass this judgment? How must we expect God to be merciful to us at the judgment seat, for even there we need grace! This is exactly what Matthew 18 is talking about. It is true that God will judge us with absolute justice; nevertheless, there *is* forgiveness with Him, and His forgiveness is based on our forgiving others today. No matter how people may treat you, if you forgive five or ten persons who sin against you and you always forgive, then in that day God will treat you justly. Because you have forgiven others, it is most just for God to forgive you at the judgment seat. . . .

We need to be careful daily about two things: one is to examine ourselves lest we fall into the judgment of God; and the other is, that however much people may owe us, let us be merciful and forgiving so that we may receive God's forgiveness on that day.

—GD 165, 166, 167, 168, 169–70, 170–1, 174, 175, 176, 177, 178

New believers ought to know this aspect of the Lord's work, the aspect typified by the ashes of the red heifer [see Num. 19]. All the efficacy of redemption is embodied in the ashes, all the sins of the world are included. The blood was in these ashes. At any time thereafter, whenever one was defiled through touching an unclean thing, he had no need to slay another red heifer; he only needed to be sprinkled with "the water for impurity" containing the ashes of a red heifer. In other words, a believer today does not need the Lord to work for him a second time, since there is already provision for the cleansing of all his future defilements in our Lord's work of redemption. The Lord has already made full provision.

### *The Scriptural Meaning of the Ashes*

Perhaps some will ask what the ashes signify. Why must the red heifer be burned to ashes? Why should these ashes be collected?

The answer is that in the Bible ashes are used as a basic unit of matter. Ashes in the Bible are the last form of all things. Whether it be a cow or a horse or whatever it may be, it becomes ash when it is reduced to its final form. Ashes, therefore, are the final, irreducible unit. They are not only unchangeable but also incorruptible. They are not subject to rust or decay. They are most enduring. They are ultimate.

The redemptive work of the Lord as typified by the burning of the red heifer to ashes reveals a condition which is permanent and unchanged. What the Lord has done for us in His work of redemption can never be changed. It is most constant. Do not think the rocks on the mountain are enduring, for these can still be burned to ashes. Ashes, being the final form of all matter, are more constant than rocks. Likewise, the redemption which the Lord has provided for us is unchangeable, undefileable, and incorruptible. It is available to us at all times. The flesh, the skin, and the blood of the heifer are subject to corruption, but when they become ashes, they are beyond corruption. Our redemption is, therefore, eternally efficacious. Whenever we touch an unclean thing and are defiled, we need not ask the Lord to die once more for us. We have the incorruptible ashes and we have the living water of life. We know the ashes are ever effectual in cleansing us.

To put it another way: the ashes of the red heifer represent the finished work of the cross for today's use as well as for future need. We declare that the red heifer, once burned to ashes, is sufficient for all the needs of our lifetime. We thank God for the all-sufficiency of the redemption of the Lord Jesus. We come to see more and more that His death does indeed atone for all our sins.

### *Walk in the Light*

"But if we walk in the light, as he is in the light, we have fellowship with one another, and the blood of Jesus his Son cleanseth us from all sin" (1 John 1.7). What does the "light" here refer to? It has two possible meanings: one possibility is the light of holiness; the other possibility is the light of the gospel, that is, God revealed and manifested in the gospel.

Many would like the "light" here to refer to the light of holiness. Thus the first section of this verse might be paraphrased thus: "if we walk in holiness as God is in holiness." Such a rendering, however, would make what follows meaningless. It is quite evident that we have no need of the blood of Jesus, God's Son, to cleanse us from our sins if we are holy.

God has distinctly declared that He comes to save us and give us grace. If we are in this light as God is in the light of grace, the light of the gospel, then we can have fellowship one with another. By grace we come to God as He also comes to us in grace. Thus we have fellowship with God, and the blood of Jesus His Son cleanses us from all our sins. This truly is grace. . . .

Propitiation here is comparable to the ashes of the red heifer in Numbers 19. As we have mentioned, the provision found in Numbers 19 is for future use. Likewise, forgiveness of our sins, including those of the present and future, is based on the finished work of the cross. There is no need for a new cross, for the redemptive work of the cross is eternally efficacious.

New believers should clearly be exhorted not to sin. They ought not to sin and it is actually possible for them not to sin. But if they should unfortunately sin, let them remember that the blood of the Lord Jesus can still cleanse them from all their sins. He is their champion; He is the righteous One. The very fact that He is now with the Father guarantees the forgiveness of their sins.

Since this is so, do not linger in the shame of sin as if such suffering will bring in holiness. Do not think that to prolong the consciousness of sin is in any way an indication of holiness. If any man sin, the first thing to do is to go to God and confess, "I have sinned." This is judging oneself, calling sin by its right name. "If we confess our sins, He is faithful and righteous to forgive us our sins, and to cleanse us from all unrighteousness." If you do this, you will then see that God forgives you and that your fellowship with Him is immediately restored.

### *The Way to Restoration*

If a child of God should sin and continue in that sin without confession, he yet remains God's child and God is still his Father. Nevertheless, his fellowship with God will be lost. There is now a weakness in his conscience; he is unable to rise up before God. He may try to fellowship with God, but he will find it most painful and quite limited. It is just like a child who has done something wrong. Even though his mother may not know and may not scold him, he is still very uneasy at home. He finds it impossible to have sweet fellowship, for within him there is a sense of distance.

There is only one way to be restored. I must go to God and confess my sin. I believe that the Lord Jesus is my advocate and has taken care of all my sins. So here I am before God, humbly acknowledging my failure. I look to the Lord that hereafter I may not be so arrogant and careless. I have learned how prone I am to fall. I am no better than others. So I pray that God may be merciful to me, that I may continue on with the Lord step by step. Praise God, we do have an advocate with Him, One who does come alongside. . . .

The Lord expects you to treat others as He has treated you. Since He does not demand of you according to righteousness, He expects you not to demand righteousness of others. The Lord forgives your debt according to mercy. With what measure He has meted out to you, He wants you to mete out to others. He gives you in good measure, pressed down, shaken together and running over; He wishes you to do likewise. As He treats you, so should you treat your brother.

It is exceedingly ugly in the sight of God for the forgiven person to be unforgiving. Nothing can be uglier than for the one who was forgiven to be unforgiving, the one who received mercy to be merciless, and the one who was given grace to be graceless. We must learn before God to treat others as He has treated us. Let us be so humbled by what we have received that we treat others according to the same principle. . . .

I believe many of God's children have learned the lesson of forgiveness. Many, though, have forgotten what we should do after someone has sinned against us. According to Matthew 18.15–20, we must persuade or exhort our brother. We must not only forgive but we must persuade as well.

### *Tell Him*

"And if thy brother sin against thee" (v.15). It is quite common for God's children to sin against one another. Although such things may not happen too often, neither are they too scarce. The Lord shows us what we should do if anyone sins against us. "Go, show him his fault between thee and him alone." Should anyone sin against you, the first thing to do is to tell *him,* not to tell others. This is a word we should rightly understand. Show his fault to him when you and he are alone.

Therefore, when your brother sins against you, do not tell it to other brothers and sisters. Do not at this point go to the responsible brothers of the church either. The Lord has not even commanded you to tell God about it in prayer. New believers should be clear about this: when a brother sins against you, the first thing you should do is to go and tell him. I believe if the children of God kept this commandment of the Lord, many, perhaps half, of the problems in the church would be solved.

Today's difficulty is that soon after a brother has sinned against another brother, the matter becomes known to everyone, except to the one who has sinned. The offended brother has broadcast it everywhere. This indicates how weak he is, for it is only the weak who will tell tales. He is morally weak since he has not the strength to tell the offender. He can only backbite; he has not the courage to speak face to face. To broadcast and to spread rumors is a bad, unclean, sinful habit. We need to take care of our brother's fault, not tell others. The first person to be told ought to be the offender himself—no one else. If God's children learn this lesson well, the church will be delivered from many difficulties.

The Lord says, "Show him his fault." But how? The Lord does not suggest you write a letter but that you go to him. Talk to him when you and he are alone. This is the Lord's command. In dealing with personal sin, the two of you are sufficient; a third party is absolutely unnecessary.

Let us learn this lesson before God. We must control ourselves and never speak behind the back of the brother who has offended us. Nor should we speak in public against him. It is only when you and he are alone that you show him his fault. This requires the grace of God. When you speak, you are to show him his fault, not to talk about other things. To point out his fault is not an easy thing to do, but you have to do it. This is one of the lessons which the children of God must learn. Go to him and say,

"Brother, you hurt me by doing such a thing. It was wrong for you to do it. You have sinned."

If you feel the matter is so small that it does not require you to go and tell him, then it also does not warrant your telling anybody else. I have heard many complain that to follow this rule is very troublesome. Too many things happen daily for us to go and tell the offenders. Well, if you feel a matter is not important, only a small matter which need not be told to the offender, then I say it also need not be told to anybody else. How can you say it need not be told to the person himself yet you tell it to others? If it is necessary, tell the brother himself; otherwise, do not tell it at all. To do so is a sin.

### *Purpose: to Gain Your Brother*

God's children should learn to overlook offenses. But if an offense must be dealt with, deal with the offender directly. In such dealing, we need to remember this fundamental principle: "If he hear thee, thou hast gained thy brother" (v.15). This is the purpose of telling. The motive is not to lessen your difficulty nor to demand reparation from the offender. The purpose is to gain your brother.

Thus the problem is not how greatly I have suffered or even how far I can restore my brother. I go to persuade him because if he does not clear up this matter, he will have trouble with his prayer and fellowship with God.

If it is merely a matter of your hurt feelings, then it is too small a thing to require dealing. You need to see clearly before God as to which matters require your dealing with your brother and which do not. If it is only your hurt feelings, you may let it pass without telling your brother or anybody else. Whether or not it is more than that, no one knows better than you. Even the elders of the church do not know better. The responsibility is upon you. Some matters have great effect. There are many things which you can forget but there are certain matters which you should not. If your brother has sinned with the possibility that he will suffer loss, you must go to him and point out his fault when you and he are alone. That which cannot be casually dismissed has to be dealt with. How can he get by if there is something unforgiven between him and God?

God's children should learn to rid the church of problems, not to add problems to the church. We must seek to keep the oneness of the church. If you see a brother in a fault which creates a problem before the Lord, you know this is not a small matter. You feel this will hinder him from going on with the Lord. In such a case you should find an opportunity to speak to him when you two are alone. Tell him, "Brother, it was wrong for you to sin against me in this way. As a consequence, your way before God will be blocked. Your loss is great." If he hears you, the Lord says, "thou hast gained thy brother," for you have restored a soul.

The purpose of persuasion is to restore. It is not for reparation, nor for easing your feeling, but to restore your brother. Let me tell you, this passage in Scripture is one least obeyed by the children of God. What do we do instead? Some of us talk and broadcast the matter; some keep the thing in their hearts and refuse to forgive; some simply forgive and do nothing more. But none of these is what the Lord would have us do. . . .

### *The Inability of the Will to Overcome the Law*

Will is the inner power of man, while law is a natural power. Both are powers. I like to use an illustration to help people understand this matter of law. We know that the earth exerts a gravitational force. This force of gravity is a law. Why do we call it a law? Because it is always so. That which is not incidental is a law. That which is occasional is an historical accident, not a law.

Why is earth's gravitation a law? If I drop my handkerchief, it goes downward. It happens in Shanghai as well as in Foochow. Wherever the handkerchief is dropped, the same thing happens. Gravity pulls it down, so this is called the law of gravitation. Not only is gravity a force; it also is a law. If the handkerchief is only occasionally pulled to the earth, then this force could not be reckoned as a law. A law is something which always acts in the same way. If I throw my Bible upward, it will fall down. If I throw a chair up, it too will fall down. If I jump upward, I will also come down. No matter where or what, what goes up will come down. Then I realize that not only is there a gravitational force exerted by the earth, but there is also a law of gravity.

A law simply means it is always so. It permits no exception. If something happens once one way and another time a different way, it is a matter of history. But if something always happens the same way, it is a law. If a person commits a crime on the street, he will be taken into custody by the police. Should he commit this crime at home, he still will be taken into custody. Whoever murders, regardless of whom or where he murders, he will be taken by the police. This we call a law. A law applies to every person; there are no exceptions. If a man kills someone today, he is taken into custody by the police. But if he kills someone tomorrow and is not taken, kills again the day after tomorrow and is taken, then the matter of taking people into custody cannot be considered a law. A law needs to be consistent. It must be the same yesterday, today, and even tomorrow. The term "law" implies that it continues unchanged.

Every law has its natural power—something not manufactured by human effort. We may use the earth's gravitation as an example. Wherever I drop something, that thing gravitates downward. I do not need to press it down for there is a natural force which causes it to go down. Behind the law is the natural power.

What, then, is the will? Will is man's determination, man's decision. It speaks of what man decides or desires or wills. The exercise of the will is not without its power. If I decide to do a certain thing, I start out to do it. If I decide to walk, I walk; if I decide to eat, I eat. As a person I have a will, and my will produces a power.

However, the power of the will and the power of a law are different. While the power of the law is natural power, the power of the will is human. Gravitational force does not need the installation of some electrical appliance behind it in order to attract things downward; it acts naturally. If you light a lamp, the heat will naturally rush upward; this too is a law. When air is heated, it rises and expands; this is a law. In rising and expanding, it demonstrates a power, but this power is natural power. The power of the will, however, is something of man. Only that which is living has a will. Neither a chair nor a table has a will of its own. God has a will; man has a will. Only a living being has will. Though man's will does possess some power, it is nonetheless a human power. It is in direct contrast to the power of a law which is a natural power.

The question before us is: when the will and the law are in conflict, which will emerge as conqueror? Usually the will overcomes in the beginning, but the law conquers in the end. Man first overcomes, but the law eventually emerges as victor. For example: I am now holding up a Bible which weighs about half a pound. The force of earth's gravity is operating on this book and is trying its best to pull the Bible to the ground. So the law is working. But I as a person have a will. My hand is lifting the Bible and I will not allow it to fall. I succeed in holding it up; I have overcome. My will is stronger than the law.

Right now, at 8:17 in the evening, I have overcome. But wait till 9:17, and I will start to sigh that my hand will not listen to me. By tomorrow morning at 8:17, I will have to get a doctor to treat me! A law never tires, but my hand does. Man's power cannot overcome natural law. The law of gravitation continues to pull; it pulls without will or thought. I will not let the Bible fall; I forcibly hold onto it. Still the time will come when I can no longer hold on. When I cease to lift up the Bible, it will drop to the ground. The law works twenty-four hours a day, but I cannot.

Eventually the will of men will be defeated and the law will overcome. All of men's wills cannot conquer natural law. Human will may strenuously resist natural law and may at the beginning seem to overcome, but finally it will have to give in to the law. Do not despise the law of earth's gravitation. You are battling with it daily. All who are now in their graves, if able to speak, would have to concede that they are not as strong as the law. For decades you appear to be daily in ascendancy over gravity. You almost forget the great power of earth's gravity; you live as if there were no death. You are active from morning till night. But there will come a day when you too will be pulled down by the law of sin and death. At that moment, your activity will come to an end. There is nothing you can do; the law has conquered. Can you imagine a person who by force of will could hold onto a Bible so that it never falls? It is impossible. Sooner or later he has to yield; the law will come forth as conqueror.

In Romans 7 the subject is the contrast between law and will. Its theme is very simple, for it deals only with the conflict between will and law. At an earlier time, Paul was not conscious that sin is a law. Paul is the first one in the Bible to discover this truth. He is also first to use the term "law." People know that gravitation is a law, that heat expansion is also a law, but they do not know that sin is a law. At first even Paul did not know this; only after repeatedly sinning did he discover that there was a power in his body which gravitated him to sin. He did not sin purposely, but the power in his body pulled him to sin.

Sinning is more than historical; it is a law. When temptation comes, we try to resist, but before long we fail; this is our history of defeat. Again temptation comes and again we resist and fail. This happens the tenth time, the hundredth time, the millionth time. It is the same story: temptation comes, we resist; and before we realize it, we are defeated. As this occurs time after time, we begin to see that this is not just an historical fact. It has become a law. Sinning is a law. If one were to sin only once, he might consider it an historical event; however, we cannot say sinning is historical for it is not limited to once. It has become a law.

Temptation comes and I am defeated. I have no way to overcome. Each time it comes, I fail; thus I come to realize that my defeat is more than just defeat; it is the law of defeat in me. Defeat has become a law to me. Brethren, have you seen this? Paul saw it. In verse 21 he tells us his great revelation—a revelation about himself. He says, "I find then the law." This is the first time he realizes it that way. He senses a law. What is it? "That to me who would do good, evil is present." Whenever he wants to do good, he finds evil is present in him. This is the law. When I would do good, sin is present. Sin follows closely after good. Not just once, not just a thousand times, but it is always this way. I now understand it to be a law.

### *A Great Revelation*

It is not that I sin accidentally or occasionally; it is not that I sometimes sin and sometimes do not; sinning is a law to me, for I constantly sin. Because this occurs all the time, I know it is a law. Whenever I would do good, evil is present. When Paul's eyes were opened to this, he realized that all his own efforts were futile. What had he tried? He had tried to do good. He had thought his will could overcome sin, not knowing that no will can ever overcome sin. But as soon as he saw sin as a law, not just a conduct, he immediately conceded that to will was useless. The will could never conquer the law. This, indeed, was a great discovery, a very great revelation. . . .

### *The Way of Victory*

We know man is not delivered by exercising his will. When he is using his willpower, he is unable to trust God's way of deliverance. He has to wait for the day when he submits himself to God and confesses that he is utterly undone. Then he will pray, "Lord, I am not going to try again." Whenever one has no way but still thinks of finding a way, he will draw upon his will to help. It is only when he acknowledges he has no way and is not going to find a way that he forsakes calling upon his will for help. Then he will begin to see how to get real deliverance. Then he will read Romans 8.

Brothers and sisters, do not despise Romans 7. Many believers are unable to get out of that chapter. Romans 7 captures more Christians than any other passage in the Bible. Many Christians keep their address in Romans 7! That is where they may be found, for they dwell there. It is useless to preach Romans 8 alone. The question is not whether you know the teaching of Romans 8, but whether you have come out of Romans 7. Many preach on Romans 8 but are still buried in Romans 7. They are yet trying to deal with the law by the power of their will. They are still being defeated. Because they fail to see that sin is a law and that the will cannot overcome the law, they are imprisoned in Romans 7 and cannot enter Romans 8.

New believers should accept what the word of God says. If you have to wait to find out for yourself, you may have to commit many sins. Even after sinning repeatedly, your eyes still may not be opened. You will have to come to the point where you see that all your battles are futile. Paul said in Romans 7 that it is useless to battle, for who can overcome a law? Thus, at the start of Romans 8 he says, "There is therefore now no condemnation to them that are in Christ Jesus. For the law of the Spirit of life in Christ Jesus made me free from the law of sin and of death" (vv.1–2). You have seen that sin is a law. You have also seen that it is not possible for man's will to overcome that law. Where, then, is the way of victory, the way of deliverance?

The way of victory is here: "There is therefore now *no condemnation* to them that are in Christ Jesus." The word "condemnation" in the original Greek has two different usages, one legal and the other civil. If the word is used legally, it means "condemnation" as found in the English translation. But in its civil usage, the word means "disabling" or "handicap." According to the context of this passage of Scripture, probably the civil usage is clearer.

We are no longer disabled. Why? Because the Lord Jesus Christ has given us deliverance. It is something the Lord has done. But how does He do it? It is very simple, for it is explained by the second verse: "For the law of the Spirit of life in Christ Jesus made me free from the law of sin and of death." This is the way of victory. Can you alter Romans 8.2 and read it this way: "The Spirit of life in Christ Jesus made me free from sin and death"? I suppose ten Christians out of ten would read the verse this way. But what does it say? It says that "the *law* of the Spirit of life in Christ Jesus made me free from the *law* of sin and of death." Many have seen only the Spirit of life setting them free from sin and death, but have failed to see that it is the *law* of the Spirit of life which sets them free from the *law* of sin and of death.

To learn the lesson that sin and death is a law may take years. But even as it may take a great deal of time and resolution and failure to realize that sin is a law, so it may take years for many believers to discover that the Spirit of life is also a law. Sin has followed us for years and we have had a close association with it; yet we still do not know that it is a law. Likewise, we may have believed in the Lord for many, many years and have known the Holy Spirit in our lives, yet not known Him as a law.

It is a day of great discovery when our eyes are opened by the Lord to see that sin is a law. It is a day of even greater discovery when we are given the revelation that the Holy Spirit is also a law. Only a law can overcome another law. The will cannot overcome the law, but a higher law can overcome a lower law. We can never overcome the law of sin by our human will, but the law of the Spirit of life can set us free from the law of sin and of death.

We know that earth's gravity is a law which holds us. We know too that there is a thing called density. If the density of a thing is exceedingly low, such as in the case of hydrogen, then earth's gravitational force cannot hold it down. By pumping hydrogen into a balloon, we can make the balloon rise. The law of earth's gravitational force is a fixed law, but it only operates within a certain range or degree of density. If the density is too low, the law of gravity does not apply. Then another law takes over, even the law of buoyancy, which sends things upward. This upward surge needs no hand to push, no fan to stir. You just let go, and up it ascends. This law overcomes the other law. It is equally effortless. In a similar manner, the law of the Holy Spirit overcomes the law of sin.

Let us say it another way. To see sin as a law is a big thing, for it makes you decide against battling sin with your willpower. Likewise, seeing the law of the Holy Spirit in your life is another big crisis. Many seem to understand how the Spirit of life gives them life, but have yet to learn that the Holy Spirit in them, that is, the life which God has given them through Jesus Christ, is also a law. If you let this law operate, it will naturally deliver you from the law of sin and of death. When this law delivers you from the other law, it does not require an ounce of your strength. You need not make one resolution, spend any time, nor even lay hold of the Holy Spirit. . . .

To overcome sin does not require an ounce of strength, for it is the work of the law. There is one law which makes me sin without my effort, and there is another law which sets me free from sin—also without my labor. Only that which requires no exertion is true victory. I have nothing to do. Let me tell you, we now have nothing to do but to raise our heads and tell the Lord, "Nothing of me." What happened before was due to law; what is now happening is also due to law. The former law did a thorough work, for it made me sin continuously; this new law does an even better work because I am no longer handicapped by sin. The law of the Spirit of life has manifested itself; it is far superior to the law of sin and death.

If new believers can be brought to see this from the first day of their Christian life, they will then walk the road of deliverance. The Bible never uses the term "overcome sin"; it only uses the phrase "made free" or "delivered from sin." It is said here in Romans, "For the law of the Spirit of life in Christ Jesus made me free from the law of sin and of death." The law of the Spirit of life has pulled me out of the realm of the law of sin and death. The law of sin and death is still present, but I am no longer there for it to work upon. The earth's gravitational force is present, but if things have been removed to heaven, there is no object for it to act upon.

The law of the Spirit of life is in Christ Jesus and I am also now in Christ Jesus; therefore by this law I am made free from the law of sin and of death. "There is therefore now no disabling to them that are in Christ Jesus." The man in Romans 7 is labeled, "disabled." But this disabled person who is so weak and always sins is now, Paul says, no more disabled in Christ Jesus. How? By the law of the Spirit of life in Christ Jesus which has set him free from the law of sin and of death. Therefore, there is no more disabling. Do you see now how this problem of deliverance is completely solved?

—NI 9-11, 15-6, 50-1, 52-5, 91-6, 99-102, 103-4

*The Two Sides of Sin*

Whatever the Bible teaches is most amazing. Sin has its two sides just as the way God deals with man's sin is also two-sided. One side of sin is towards God; and the other side of sin is in us. The sin before God needs to be forgiven and washed by Him, while the sin within us must be overcome and delivered. As regards the sin before God, the Lord Jesus has borne our sins; as regards the sin within us, we must reckon ourselves as dead to it. For the sin before God, there is the washing of the *blood* of the Lord; for the sin in us, there is the deliverance of the *cross* of the Lord. The sin before God requires God's forbearance and forgiveness; the sin in us demands liberty and emancipation. . . .

*The Two Sides of Deliverance*

Just as sin has its two sides—before God and in man—so deliverance has its two sides too. Sin has its penalty and power, therefore salvation consists of two sides as well. Yet this is not two deliverances but two sides of *one* deliverance. The Lord saves us from the fear of penalty, the accusation of the conscience, and all agitations; at the same time, He delivers us from the power of sin. And thus His salvation is complete. He saves us from the penalty imposed by God and He delivers us from the power of sin in us.

How does the Lord die for us in order to affect these two sides of sin? The Bible tells us that he who sins must die. But the sinless Lord Jesus bore the penalty of death for us. He shed His blood to redeem us and to wash away all our sins before God. The blood of Christ has washed us. It is most amazing that the Bible never says that the blood of Christ washed our heart. Hebrews 9.14 observes this: "How much more shall the blood of Christ, who through the eternal Spirit offered himself without blemish unto God, cleanse your conscience from dead works to serve the living God?" Notice that it does not say the blood cleanses the heart, it only cleanses the conscience.

What is the conscience? It is that which accuses within us, telling us we are wrong, therefore deserving of death and perdition. The blood of Christ cleanses our conscience so that we are no longer being accused by it, thus securing peace. His blood causes us to know that although our sins are worthy of punishment, Christ has died for these sins and has fulfilled the righteousness of God. However, no one by the cleansing of the blood is transformed to be morally good and sin no more, thereby becoming free from sin. For the blood of Christ can only cleanse us before God and eliminate the accusation of the conscience; it does not wash our heart and make it so clean that sin no longer is hidden in us. The blood of the Lord is objective, not subjective, in its effect. It does not cleanse the heart; it cleanses the conscience.

Men are all defiled and corrupted. Through the blood of Christ, sins are forgiven and the *penalty* of sins is paid. But the Bible never tells us that the blood can eradicate the *power* of sin. This is that other side of which we spoke earlier. The word of God tells us, on the one side, of the blood of Christ and on the other side, of the cross of Christ. Blood speaks of death, and so, too, does the cross. Yet blood is related to penalty, for it deals with man's sins before God; but the cross deals with the power of sin within us. It is through the cross that our heart is purified and is made capable of overcoming sin.

Let us reiterate the difference between the cross and the blood. The blood of Christ takes away our sins before God, whereas the cross of Christ deals with the sin that is in us. Be aware, however, that the cross does not *crucify* the sin in us. Many advocates of holiness err here. The cross of Christ does not crucify sin. Nowhere in the Scripture can anyone find a verse saying that the cross crucifies sin. Then what *does* the cross crucify? The Lord was crucified on it. The Bible also says our old man was crucified there as well. It was not the powerful sin that was crucified, but it was the old man—who loved to be directed by sin—that was crucified. It was not the root of sin which was eradicated, but it was the old man—who was so intimate with the root of sin—that was crucified by the Lord. Let me tell you the good news today: that when Christ was crucified, not only He himself was crucified, but God also had the corrupted and defiled you and me crucified with Him. We *were* crucified with Him!

"Knowing this, that our old man was crucified with him, that the body of sin might be done away, that so we should no longer be in bondage to sin" (Rom. 6.6). Notice that what is said here is that the old man was crucified with Christ, not that sin was crucified with Him. Have you not heard people say that sin may be crucified or that the root of sin may be eradicated? Let us recognize that there is no such thing.

In this verse in Romans, we see three things: (1) the old man; (2) the body of sin—that is to say, the body that sins; and (3) sin. It also tells us of three important matters: (1) that our old man was crucified with Christ, (2) that the aim was that the body of sin might be done away, and (3) that the result would be that I should no longer be in bondage to sin. Thus, with the old man crucified, I should no longer sin nor will to sin. But sin itself will not have died, sin itself is yet alive.

Let me illustrate it as follows: Here are the three things: the old man, sin, and the body of sin. Sin is like a master, the old man is like a steward, and the body is like a puppet. Sin has no authority nor power to direct the body of sin to sin. As a master, sin directs the old man, and with the consent of the old man the body is made a puppet. As long as the old man is alive, it stands between the body at the outside and sin on the inside. When the inward sin tempts the old man and stirs up its lusts, the old man gives an order to the body to commit sin. The body is rather weak; it will do whatever it is made to do. It has no sovereignty of its own, nor can it do anything on its own. It does whatever the old man orders it to do. Now, though, the Lord comes to rescue us. He does not kill our body nor does He eradicate the root of sin; He instead has our old man crucified with Him.

Consequently, only two out of the three things mentioned in Romans 6.6 are left; the body is at the outside and sin is on the inside. But now, in the middle, a new person has taken over the position formerly held by the old man. So that today in order to induce the body to sin, the sin within must come to tempt the new man, trying to stir up lust; but the new man will not listen to it nor agree with its suggestion. Formerly the old man contemplated a love and desire for sin; but now the new man will have nothing to do with sin nor will it respond to its demand. And thus, the body is not able to practice sin.

Let us look at Romans 6.6 further. We know that sin is most corrupt in its nature, so we all hope to have it eradicated from our body. Nevertheless, we do not realize that the existence of the root of sin or the existence of the devil actually has nothing to do with whether or not we bear the fruit of holiness in our lives. What is actually at the bottom of it all is our old man. Each time we find ourselves tempted, stirred and committed to sin, it is all because our old man is alive. However, the Lord has already had our old man crucified with Him.

What is the aim of having the old man crucified? It is just this: "that the body of sin might be done away." In the original Greek, the word translated "done away" actually means "disemployed"; which signifies that without the old man, the body of sin is disabled from doing anything. Formerly the body of sin daily worked according to the order of the old man. Sinning appeared to be its profession. Apart from sinning, the body seems to have had nothing else to do because the old man loved sin too much; and hence, the body simply followed suit and became the body of sin. But now the old man has been dealt with by the Lord by it having been crucified with Him on the cross, and thus the body of sin has become unemployed. Formerly, when the old man was still alive, the body of sin daily sinned as though sinning was its profession, its job. Thank the Lord, the irrepressible old man, the old man of you and me, has been crucified! And the body of sin is now unemployed! Even though sin still exists and attempts to be master, yet you and I are no longer its bondman. In spite of its repeated efforts to cause the body to sin, the new man, under the dominion of the Holy Spirit, will not cooperate. Consequently, sin has now no way to cause the body to sin. The Bible shows us that the result of having the old man crucified and the body of sin unemployed is "that so we should no longer be in bondage to sin."

The old man is dead; therefore, we can overcome sin completely. The blood of Christ was shed to save us from our sins before God and to cleanse our conscience from accusation. It tells us that we are now no longer people of perdition but are those instead who have peace with God. However, if we only know this aspect of salvation, our daily living will still be miserable. Though we know our sins are forgiven, we yet continue to make sinning our profession. We still cannot overcome sin in our daily living, nor can we bear the fruit of holiness. We are forced to sin daily; we have no peace in our hearts; and our communion with God is frequently interrupted. We know we are saved and have eternal life, but such sinning daily deprives us of the joy of salvation. Thank God, though, that the salvation of the Lord is no half-way measure. The Lord sheds His blood to cleanse us from our sins, and His cross sets aside the old man and delivers us from the power of sin.

GG 52, 54–60

# 31 The Law and Its Deliverance

Romans 6 deals with freedom from sin. Roman 7 deals with freedom from the Law. In chapter 6 Paul has told us how we could be delivered from sin, and we concluded that this was all that was required. Chapter 7 now teaches that deliverance from sin is not enough, but that we also need to know deliverance from the Law. If we are not fully emancipated from the Law, we can never know full emancipation from sin. But what is the difference between deliverance from sin and deliverance from the Law? We all see the value of the former, but where, we wonder, is the need for the latter? For answer, we must first of all ask ourselves what the Law is, and what is its special value for us.

Romans 7 has a new lesson to teach us. It is found in the discovery that I am "in the flesh" (Rom. 7.5), that "I am carnal" (7.14), and that "in me, that is, in my flesh, dwelleth no good thing" (7.18). This goes beyond the question of sin, for it relates also to the matter of pleasing God. We are dealing here not with sin in its forms but with man in his carnal state. The latter includes the former, but it takes us a stage further, for it leads to the discovery that in this realm too we are totally impotent, and that "they that are in the flesh cannot please God" (Rom. 8.8). How then is this discovery made? It is made with the help of the Law. . . .

### *What the Law Teaches*

Many Christians find themselves suddenly launched into the

experience of Romans 7 and they do not understand why. They fancy Romans 6 is quite enough. Having grasped that, they think there can be no more question of failure, and then to their utmost surprise they find themselves right in the midst of Romans 7. What is the explanation?

First let us be quite clear that the death with Christ described in Romans 6 is fully adequate to cover all our need. It is the explanation of that death, with all that follows from it in chapter 6, that is as yet incomplete. We are still in ignorance of the truth set forth in chapter 7. For Romans 7 is given to us to explain and make real the statement in Romans 6.14, that: "Sin shall not have dominion over you: for ye are not under law, but under grace." The trouble is that we do not yet know deliverance from law. What, then, is the meaning of Law?

Grace means that God does something for me; law means that I do something for God. God has certain holy and righteous demands which He places upon me: that is law. Now if law means that God requires something of me for their fulfillment, then deliverance from law means that He no longer requires that from me, but himself provides it. Law implies that God requires me to do something for Him; deliverance from law implies that He exempts me from doing it, and that in grace He does it himself. *I* (where "I" is the "carnal" man of chapter 7.14) *need do nothing for God:* that is deliverance from law. The trouble in Romans 7 is that man in the flesh tried to do something for God. As soon as you try to please God in that way, then you place yourself under law, and the experience of Romans 7 begins to be yours. . . .

The more we try to keep the Law the more our weakness is manifest and the deeper we get into Romans 7, until it is clearly demonstrated to us that we are hopelessly weak. God knew it all along, but we did not, and so God had to bring us through painful experiences to a recognition of the fact. We need to have our weakness proved to ourselves beyond dispute. That is why God gave us the Law.

So we can say, reverently, that God never gave us the Law

to keep: He gave us the Law to break! He well knew that we could not keep it. We are so bad that He asks no favor and makes no demands. Never has any man succeeded in making himself acceptable to God by means of the Law. Nowhere in the New Testament are men of faith told that they are to keep the Law; but it does say that the Law was given so that there should be transgression. "The law came in . . . that the trespass might abound" (Rom. 5.20). The Law was given to make us law-breakers! No doubt I *am* a sinner in Adam; "Howbeit, I had not known sin, except through the law: . . . for apart from the law sin is dead . . . but when the commandment came, sin revived, and I died" (Rom. 7.7–9). The Law is that which exposes our true nature. Alas, we are so conceited, and think ourselves so strong, that God has to give us something to test us and prove how weak we are. At last we see it, and confess, "I am a sinner through and through, and of myself I can do nothing whatever to please a holy God."

No, the law was not given in the expectation that we would keep it. It was given in the full knowledge that we would break it; and when we have broken it so completely as to be convinced of our utter need, then the Law has served its purpose. It has been our schoolmaster to bring us to Christ, that in us He may himself fulfill it (Gal. 3.24).

### *Christ the End of the Law*

In Romans 6 we saw how God delivered us from sin: in Romans 7 we see how He delivers us from the Law. Chapter 6 shows us the way of deliverance from sin in the picture of a master and his slave; chapter 7 shows us the way of deliverance from the Law in the picture of two husbands and a wife. The relation between sin and the sinner is that of master to slave; the relation between the Law and the sinner is that of husband to wife. . . .

. . . The first husband is the Law; the second husband is

Christ; and you are the woman. The law requires much, but offers no help in the carrying out of its requirements. The Lord Jesus requires just as much, yea more (Matt. 5.21–48), but what He requires from us He himself carries out in us. The law makes demands and leaves us helpless to fulfill them; Christ makes demands, but He himself fulfills in us the very demands He makes. Little wonder that the woman desires to be freed from the first husband that she may marry that other Man! But her only hope of release is through the death of her first husband, and he holds on to life most tenaciously. Indeed there is not the least prospect of his passing away. "Till heaven and earth pass away, one jot or one tittle shall in no wise pass away from the law, till all things be accomplished" (Matt. 5.18).

The Law is going to continue for all eternity. If the Law will never pass away, then how can I ever be united to Christ? How can I marry a second husband if my first husband resolutely refuses to die? There is one way out. If *he* will not die, *I* can die, and if I die the marriage relationship is dissolved. And that is exactly God's way of deliverance from the Law. The most important point to note in this section of Romans 7 is the transition from verse 3 to verse 4. Verses 1 to 3 show that the husband should die, but in verse 4 we see that in fact it is the woman who dies. The Law does not pass away, but I pass away, and by death I am freed from the Law. Let us realize clearly that the Law can never pass away. *God's righteous demands remain for ever*, and if I live I must meet those demands; but if I die the Law has lost its claim upon me. It cannot follow me beyond the grave. . . .

### *I Thank God!*

Romans 6 deals with "the body of sin," Romans 7 with "the body of this death" (6.6; 7.24). In chapter 6 the whole question before us is sin; in chapter 7 the whole question before us is death. What is the difference between the body of sin and the body of death? In regard to sin (that is, to whatever displeases God) I have a body of sin—a body, that is to say, which is actively engaged in sin. But in regard to the Law of God (that is, to that which expresses the will of God) I have a body of death. My activity in regard to sin makes my body a body of sin; my failure in regard to God's will makes my body a body of death. In regard to all that is wicked, worldly and Satanic I am, in my nature, wholly positive; but in regard to all that pertains to holiness and heaven and God I am wholly negative. . . .

First let us ask ourselves, What is a law? Strictly speaking, a law is a generalization examined until it is proved that there is no exception. We might define it more simply as something which happens over and over again. Each time the thing happens it happens in the same way. We can illustrate this both from statutory and from natural law. For example, in Britain, if I drive a car on the right hand side of the road, the traffic police will stop me. Why? Because it is against the law of the land. If *you* do it you will be stopped too. Why? For the same reason that I would be stopped: it is against the law, and the law makes no exceptions. It is something which happens repeatedly and unfailingly. Or again, we all know what is meant by gravity. If I drop my handkerchief in London it falls to the ground. That is the effect of gravity. But the same is true if I drop it in New York or Hong Kong. No matter where I let it go, gravity operates, and it always produces the same results. Whenever the same conditions prevail the same effects are seen. There is thus a "law" of gravity.

Now what of the law of sin and death? If someone passes an unkind remark about me, at once something goes wrong inside me. That is not law; that is sin. But if, when different people pass unkind remarks, the same "something" goes wrong inside, then I discern a law within—a law of sin. Like the law of gravity, it is something constant. It always works the same way. And so too with the law of death. Death, we have said, is weakness produced to its limit. Weakness is "I cannot." Now if when I try to please God in this particular matter I find I cannot, and if when I try to please Him in that other thing I again find I cannot, then I discern a law at work. There is not only sin in me but a law of sin; there is not only death in me but a law of death. . . .

If we will let go of our own wills and trust Him, we shall not fall to the ground and break, but we shall fall into a *different law,* the law of the Spirit of life. For God has given us not only life but a law of life. And just as the law of gravity is a natural law and not the result of human legislation, so the law of life is a "natural" law, similar in principle to the law that keeps our heart beating or that controls the movements of our eyelids. There is no need for us to think about our eyes, or to decide that we must blink every so often to keep them cleansed; and still less do we bring our will to bear upon our heart-beat. Indeed, to do so might rather harm than help it. No, so long as it has life it works spontaneously. Our wills only interfere with the law of life. . . .

—NCL 152-3, 155-6, 158-62, 169-70, 185-6, 191

In order to know how to be delivered from the law, we must first understand the relationship between the law and us. The law is God's demands on our flesh. By the law God tells us what is right and what is wrong, what we should do and what we should not do, what is forbidden and what is commanded. Hence the law is God's demands on us. Or to phrase it another way, the law is God's demands on all who are in Adam. It is His commandments to all who are in Adam as to what they ought not to do. (The purpose or God's giving the law is to prove the corruption of the flesh which is beyond cure.) Let us remember that not only can God put us under the law, we too who are in Adam may also place ourselves under the law with a view to pleasing God. This means we may set up rules and regulations for ourselves to keep, by which we are saying: I ought not do this and I ought to do that. Besides the commandments given us by

God, we also lay down commandments for ourselves to keep, and they are as strict as God's. Consequently, we have demands on ourselves as well as God has demands on us. All this indicates that we still have hope in this man that is in Adam. We continue to expect him to strive to be better and more victorious. This, in sum, is our current situation: God puts us under the law, and we put ourselves under the law.

What is meant by being delivered from the law? It is to be totally disillusioned about yourself. Not only to be fully disappointed, but also to expect nothing anymore. Henceforth you no longer entertain any hope in yourself. This is a being delivered from the law. God, as it were, allows you to sin day after day in order to make you realize how corrupted and unclean, how unamendable and unconquering you really are, how unable you are to keep the law because you are beyond any help. He wants you to know why He has crucified you in Christ and with Christ. It is because you are corrupted beyond cure. When you finally see yourself helpless, as well as understand that God considers you hopeless, you will then stand on the ground which God has given you. God says you are corrupted to the core and there is absolutely no hope for you; you too say you are so corrupted and helpless that you can only sin, therefore you entertain no hope in yourself. Now this is a being delivered from the law. And what a great deliverance it truly is. *The one and only deliverance is a seeing yourself as being utterly hopeless. . . .*

Even though we know quite well in theory and in teaching that the old Adamic life is unamendable and beyond cure, yet strange to say, when it comes to experience, we still entertain hope in this Adamic life and try to amend and to improve it. Many of us are saying, I am surprised I could commit such a sin! May we be reminded that we should not be surprised at all. What sin will we *not* commit? We can commit any sin because the root of sin is in us. God crucified us because He saw we were, and still are, helpless and hopeless. So that when the Lord died, we too died. That God has crucified us reveals His estimate of us. Except for death or for being cast aside, we are not fit for anything.

How different is our own appraisal from God's. We always think we are able and that we can. We consider ourselves capable of victory, sanctification, and progress. But God expects nothing of these from us. He declares that from head to foot our whole being is full of sins and we are altogether useless. Apart from death there is no salvation. Today we should see this basic fact of how God looks at us and what He thinks we deserve. Whoever sees this first is blessed. . . .

To be delivered from the law is to be delivered from God's demand, which means that, having known the work of Christ as well as the life of Adam, we give up the idea of trying to please God. As long as there is in our heart the thought of seeking progress and pleasing God by our own effort, we are not delivered from the law nor are we exempt from sorrow and despair. Knowing that God does not expect anything from us is the only way not to despair.

We need to be delivered from the law; but how? It is only through death. Why is death capable of freeing us from the law. Because as long as we *live*, the law has its demand on us. A living person must not violate the law inasmuch as he will be prosecuted if he does. This is exactly what the apostle means by this statement: "For the woman that hath a husband is bound by law to the husband while he liveth" (Rom. 7.2). If the husband still lives, the law has its claim on the woman; but if he dies, the influence of the law ceases and it demands no more. Therefore, apart from death there is no other way to be liberated from the law. For if we live, the law will keep on demanding of us.

Let us go a step further and see how we die. "Wherefore, my brethren, ye also were made dead to the law through the body of Christ . . . " [v.4a]. Our death is through the body of Christ. As Christ himself died, so we died also. The time when Christ died is when we died. Since Christ has died, we too have died. This is not committing spiritual suicide, nor do we reckon ourselves as dead arbitrarily, attempting to hypnotize ourselves to death. No, it is because we have seen the accomplished fact of Christ on the cross. We therefore know that God has already included us in the death of Christ. When we see this, we cannot help but acknowledge ourselves as being dead.

There are two spiritual experiences in the world which are most amazing. One is seeing God's plan; that is to say, seeing what God has planned for you and what He designs you to be—to wit, God has sentenced you to death. The other amazing experience is seeing what God has done for you in Christ. These two spiritual facts are exceedingly great, that you can see what God has determined for you and also see how you are united in one with Christ, thus enjoying in Him all that He has accomplished. For instance, when Jesus Christ died on the cross you were there too, because God had included you in His death. And when His body was broken you too were broken. His crucifixion is your crucifixion, since you and Christ are one. For this reason we are careful about baptism. . . .

The way of deliverance lies not in a forced reckoning of ourselves as dead. Such teaching of forced reckoning is erroneous. What, then, is the correct way? It is reckoning ourselves as dead *in Christ.* Not that we die ourselves, but that we were made dead through the body of Christ. Since Christ has died, and we are united with Him, therefore we too have died. *The secret of victory is a never looking at ourselves outside of Christ.* This is what Christ means by the words "Abide in Me" found in John 15. It is never to look at ourselves outside of Christ. There is nothing good to be looked at outwardly, and these ugly sights cannot be improved either. If we want to look at ourselves we can only look at ourselves in the Lord. As soon as we look at the self outside of Christ we immediately fall. How often we forget the accomplished fact of Christ. We become angry with ourselves, saying, "How can I do this?" We always fail, we constantly fail. We bemoan ourselves and lose heart. Yet let us recognize the fact that all these things are done by the self that is outside of Christ. In Christ we are dead to the law. In case anyone among us has not known this deliverance, why not let that person look at himself in Christ today? In Christ God has had us crucified. He regards us as irreparable, hence there is no salvation except death. He has sentenced us to death and has also crucified us in Christ. We are now delivered from the claim of the law. We are free.

We must absolutely stand on these two facts. First, God sees that apart from death there is no other way to deliver us from the law. Second, God has already crucified us in Christ. The first speaks of God's plan, and the second, of God's work. The first is a decision, the second is an accomplishment. We have been broken into tiny fragments beyond the possibility of being made whole. Aside from death there is no salvation. Hence the foundation of redemption is in the cross. How we must accept this fact in our daily life so as to be delivered from the law. If we stand firm on this ground we will prosper. Of course you and I must confess and ask God for forgiveness when we fail. Nevertheless, we do not need to cast another look at the past since all our defeats and falls derive from the old Adamic life. Should we ask the Lord to give us strength so that we will not do it again, to men this looks excellent but to God this is unnecessary because we have died in Christ. Our history has ended, and therefore none of our decisions and desires count. How people always deem the making of a resolution to be the best thing in life, not knowing that it is like a reed which cannot withstand the enemy nor has any use before God.

We have seen how God has crucified us with Christ. But this alone is not sufficient. So we have the following word: ". . . that ye should be joined to another, even to him who was raised from the dead, that we might bring forth fruit unto God" [v.4b]—and thus we have not only the negative deliverance but also the positive joining, otherwise all will still be in vain. God has not only crucified us, He has also joined us—who have been delivered from the law—to Christ, who was raised from the dead. The one is a coming out, whereas the other is an entering in. The one is the *severance* of a relationship, while the other is the *establishing* of a relationship. It is a being delivered from the law on the one hand and a being joined to Christ on the other. And this latter is what we mean by resurrection. Resurrection is a being joined with Christ, yet not the joining of *one* but rather the joining of *many* to Christ. Resurrection is the bringing of many sons into glory. This is what is alluded to in John 12: "Except a grain of wheat fall into the earth and die, it abideth by itself alone; but if it die, it beareth much fruit" (v.24). Originally there is only one life; now this life enters into many grains. Originally there is but one grain of wheat; now it has multiplied to become many grains. Likewise, Christ through death distributes His life to all believers. Thus, there are two facts in Christ: one is that God has included us in the death of Christ, and therefore when Christ died, we too died; the other is that we are raised together with Christ from the dead, thus receiving His imparted life. These are what all regenerated persons possess and possess together.

We who are resurrected in Christ will bring forth fruit to the glory of God. Since God has given the life of Christ to us, we hereafter are able to live out Christ's life. Whatever be the grain of wheat that is sown, there shall be the thirty, the sixty or the hundred grains which grow out of it. If a person plants barley he will not get wheat or squash. What is sown is that which grows. There can be no change. If what is sown is wheat, all which grows out will be wheat. How can we live like Christ and bear fruit to glorify God as Christ did? In only one way: by letting Christ live in us and letting Him live out of us. Consequently, Christ not only died for us on the cross but He also lives for us within us. Who can make us live like Christ? None except the One who gives the life of Christ to us. As we have the life of Christ, we may bear fruit to the glory of God.

—GL 85-6, 87-8, 88-9, 90-1, 92-5

# 32 Righteousness

*The Lawfulness of Forgiveness*

God, then, has to propound a way by which He can forgive us and at the same time satisfy His own righteousness. He must be able to keep His law as He forgives us. This is called the grace of God. God's grace means that all the laws of God are still kept in tact and yet we may be saved. Salvation implies that men can be saved while simultaneously God remains righteous. We know that God will not only save us but will also save us righteously. He cannot do a work which is subject to criticism. He is not willing to have men saved that they then may criticize Him as having performed unrighteously. Not at all; God always works justly. In saving us, He saves most righteously. He leaves no ground for any to criticize. He leaves us speechless. Furthermore, He must save us in such a way that the devil's mouth too is shut. He cannot save us in such a way that the devil may accuse Him as being unrighteous. No, He cannot do that. He will so save that neither man nor the devil has anything to say against Him. And lastly, He must save us to the extent that He himself has no more to say. The salvation of God must not only look right in the eyes of men and of the adversary but in His own sight as well. For God to save us is not at all difficult, but to save *justly* is quite another matter. The Bible affirms that in saving men God has so worked that neither the saved nor the unsaved, neither the devil nor even God himself has any complaint. This is called salvation. Salvation is God saving people with His righteousness; and this is God's masterpiece. . . .

Our God, though desirous of saving us, cannot be unrighteous. He therefore gave us His Son that He might die for us on the cross. We have sinned, and hence we should be punished; but we have the cross to present to God. Before God granted us the cross, we would have had nothing to say if He had decided to punish us. But since He has given us the cross, He cannot but forgive our sins and accept us. Let us remember that upon our once having the cross, our salvation is based on the righteousness of God. *Without* the cross none can be saved, since God cannot be unrighteous. But *with* the cross, God has no way *not* to save us, because we are saved justly. The Lord Jesus has taken our punishment; therefore, the forgiveness of our sins is perfectly righteous. God cannot thoughtlessly forgive us; He forgives in accordance with His righteous procedure. . . .

*Christ Is Our Righteousness*

What, then, *is* our righteousness? This is a basic lesson which we Christians must learn thoroughly. We ought to know that in providing for our salvation God solved the problem of righteousness as well as that of sin. Through righteousness God has forgiven our sins, and He has also prepared for us a righteousness by which we can always come to Him. Forgiveness is like taking a bath; righteousness is like wearing a robe. Among men we are clothed that we may appear before them. So too, God clothes us with righteousness that we may live before Him; that is, that we may see Him. He has already cleansed our sins and given us a righteousness by which we may live in His presence.

What is our righteousness? The word of God tells us that our righteousness is Christ—the Lord Jesus himself. "But of [God] are ye in Christ Jesus, who was made unto us wisdom from God, and righteousness and sanctification, and redemption" (1 Cor.

1.30). From this rich verse we will lift out but one item and concentrate our attention upon it alone—namely, that God has made Christ our righteousness.

### *Not the Righteousness of Christ*

Before we discuss how Christ is our righteousness, we wish to explain briefly that the righteousness of Christ and Christ our righteousness are two totally distinct subjects. It is wrong to consider the righteousness of Christ as our righteousness. The righteousness of Christ cannot be our righteousness; it is Christ himself who is our righteousness.

The word found in 2 Peter 1.1—"the righteousness of our God and the Saviour Jesus Christ"—points to the righteousness which Christ himself possesses. If the Lord Jesus *himself* is not righteous, He is not qualified to be the Savior, and we have no way to be saved. This righteousness is purely for Christ himself, not for Him to give to us. The Bible never says the righteousness of the Lord Jesus saves us, because this righteousness is for the purpose of qualifying Him to be our Savior. His righteousness cannot be reckoned as our righteousness. His righteousness is that which He lives out while on earth. It is *His* personal standing before God. It is the righteousness of Christ's personal conduct. It has no way to be imparted to us. Christ's righteousness is what He himself has worked out. It is exclusively His and is absolutely unrelated to us. It is for this reason that the word of God never says we are "in Jesus." In being Jesus He is still the only begotten Son of God—He has not yet become the firstborn Son and hence we are not yet the many sons. We therefore have no part in Him.

Let us understand that our union with Christ begins at His cross, not at His incarnation. Until the time of the cross, all that Christ has is exclusively His own; He has not yet shared anything with us. If a grain of wheat falls into the ground and dies, it bears much fruit (many grains). Only since the Lord Jesus has died are we now those fruits, those many grains. Our union with Christ begins at His death, not at His birth. *Calvary* is where we are united with Him; at Bethlehem there is no such union. Before Calvary, we can only view His righteousness; we cannot share in it. The Bible from its beginning to its end tells us that we are not saved by the righteousness of Christ nor do we become righteous by His righteousness. Our becoming righteous before God is only because of Christ himself.

Some may ask, Does not the Bible tell us that God has given us the righteous robe of the Lord Jesus? But we would counter, Does God's word say that God will clothe us with the righteous robe of the Lord Jesus or that He will clothe us with the Lord Jesus as a righteous robe? In other words, are we clothed with the righteousness of the Lord Jesus or clothed with the Lord Jesus himself? In point of fact, we have never read in God's word that we are clothed with the righteousness of the Lord Jesus; we read instead that we are clothed with the Lord Jesus: "Put ye on the Lord Jesus Christ" (Rom. 13.14).

We see here a most wonderful and distinctive thing: our righteousness before God is not the earthly conduct of the Lord Jesus, our righteousness before Him is the Lord Jesus, a living person. Today we come to God because we are clothed with the Lord Jesus himself. The Lord Jesus is our righteousness; and this is not the righteousness which He has, but He himself as righteousness. Accordingly, since the Lord Jesus lives forever, we have righteousness before God at all times. We may come to Him with boldness at any time, for we have the Lord Jesus as our righteousness.

### *Christ Is Righteousness*

If our righteousness before God were our conduct we would be very unstable, because our conduct is sometimes good and sometimes bad; furthermore, our good conduct is always limited and can never meet the standard of God. Thank God, the righteousness we have before Him is not our conduct, but Christ; we are therefore immovable before Him. Today you may not be very strong and good. Satan will come and tempt you, saying,

"What are you, after all? God will not have such a person as you" But you can reply: "You have forgotten, Satan, that my righteousness before God is not my good conduct of yesterday nor is it my less good conduct of today; but my righteousness before Him is Christ. Christ has not changed today, so my righteousness remains unchanged." Should the garment we wear be of our own making, it would be dirty rags and we would be quite unable to meet God. But we are today clothed with Christ; hence we have boldness to see God. Oh! This is deliverance, this is emancipation, this is the foundation of Christian doctrine.

Suppose we imagine ourselves asking a brother who knows the word of God: "Will your righteousness ever fail?" He will answer, "No, never." "But will your conduct ever fail?" we may ask. He will say, "Certainly." Do you see that his righteousness will never fail, though his conduct may? His righteousness is not his conduct. If this were true, then when his conduct failed, his righteousness would fail too. Yet his righteousness is not his conduct, it is not that which is subject to failure; his righteousness is the Christ who never fails. And so our righteousness too never fails; it is as unfailing as Christ is. Now this may sound too bold, but it is the word of God. Our righteousness is Christ. Because He never fails, our righteousness never fails either.

Some may perhaps inquire, Does it then mean that our bad conduct does not matter? It definitely does matter. For the Bible shows us that a Christian has *two* garments: one is the Lord Jesus, for He is our robe, He is our righteousness; the other is the bright and pure fine linen of Revelation 19.8: "For the fine linen is the righteous acts of the saints." ("Righteous acts" is "righteousnesses" in the original, meaning the many acts of righteousness.) All the good conduct of a Christian—all his outward righteousnesses—come from grace as a result of the working of the Holy Spirit in him; they are not something which he has naturally. As we approach God we are not naked, because we are clothed with Christ who is our righteousness. However, as we appear before the judgment seat of Christ we must bring our own righteousness, that which is called the righteousnesses of the saints (see 2 Cor.

5.10, 1 Cor. 4.5). This present chapter deals exclusively with Christ our righteousness, not with the righteousnesses of the saints.

There is one name in the Old Testament which is very precious. It is "Jehovah our righteousness" (Jer. 23.6, 33.16). Jehovah is our righteousness, therefore our righteousness is not our conduct. May God open our eyes that we may see the gospel, even the foundation of the gospel. As we come to God, Christ—not our conduct—is our righteousness. The Lord is our righteousness. We come to Him through Christ. What else is as firm and immovable as this? . . .

We will now consider the third matter, which is found in 2 Corinthians 5.21: "Him who knew no sin he made to be sin on our behalf; that we might become the righteousness of God." We who sinned are saved because Christ was made sin for us. We who are saved through the work of Christ have now become the righteousness of God in Him. This is a direct complement to 1 Corinthians 1.30. There we see that "Christ became our righteousness"; here in 2 Corinthians we find that "we become the righteousness of God." Whoever acknowledges the One that was without sin and yet was made sin for us becomes himself the righteousness of God.

### *God's Redemption Reveals God's Righteousness*

We do not know how to say it, for it is truly most wonderful: we become the righteousness of God! The Bible tells us that our righteousness is Christ and God's righteousness is we ourselves. God has made Christ our righteousness, He has also made us His righteousness in Christ. What does it mean by our becoming the righteousness of God? It means that if anyone wants to learn and to see the righteousness of God, he need only find a Christian, for it is expressed in the life of a Christian. For this reason, a Christian is the righteousness of God.

Before we believe in the Lord we are blind to God's standards for righteousness and unrighteousness. But even after we become Christians, we may still be confused in identifying what is righteous and what is unrighteous. God will therefore not only save us but also teach us the lesson on righteousness. In His redemption He not only saves the unrighteous but He also instructs us as to what righteousness is. . . .

*Learn to Be Righteous*

Having come in by this way of righteousness, we are encouraged to learn a lesson; which is, that we Christians must learn to be righteous. We must not be loose in our daily walk. Since God has been so righteous in saving us, we must be righteous lest we stand as a contradiction to Him. Because of redemption, we as the saved manifest the righteousness of God; because of the teaching that is brought to us through redemption our lives must also manifest the righteousness of God.

We ought to live righteously. We should always remember that even in saving us God cannot be unrighteous. He cannot be unrighteous towards himself, for His nature is righteous and hence He cannot deny himself. Being the specimen of God's righteousness, how can we do anything unrighteous? Since the only one and true God needs to be righteous, ought we not to live justly on earth? . . .

Hence we must learn the principle of righteousness. What is righteousness? Righteousness means owing nothing to anybody: take not what is undeserved and give not what is improper. Let us reinforce this by stating that as God cannot be unrighteous towards himself so we who belong to Him ought not to be unrighteous. We should not owe any man anything. Whether we are good Christians who are making good progress depends a great deal on our understanding of, and feeling towards, righteousness when we first entered upon the Way. Many so-called Christians cause plenty of heartache to others because they never seem to have any sense of righteousness, are not even aware of what unrighteousness is. Some, upon having become Christians, have never once apologized or made any restitution. Is it because everything they had done or now do is right? If we do not acknowledge our faults, there can be only two possible explanations: either we are always right and never wrong, or else we will not confess our fault. May God be merciful to us that we may not deceive ourselves into thinking we have never done wrong; that we may not refuse—due to hardness of heart or a desire to save face—to acknowledge our fault.

—GL 7-8, 11, 19-24, 28-9, 30-1, 32-3

# 33 Discipline

"'My son, regard not lightly the chastening of the Lord, nor faint when thou art reproved of him; for whom the Lord loveth he chasteneth, and scourgeth every son whom he receiveth'" (Heb. 12.5–6). The apostle quotes from Proverbs, chapter 3. He says we must not despise the chastening of the Lord, nor should we faint under His reproof. Here he tells us there are two attitudes which believers need to maintain. When a person is in the process of passing through hardship, being under the chastening of the Lord, he may easily regard it lightly and let the chastisement of the Lord slip by. Or, when he is faced with the reproach of the Lord, the hand of the Lord being heavy upon him, he may faint, considering it too difficult to be a Christian. He expects to have a prosperous road in this life—to wear a white linen garment and walk leisurely on the golden street which leads to the pearly gate. He has never dreamed that to be a Christian means he will encounter so many troubles. Since he is not mentally prepared to be a Christian under such circumstances, he feels discouraged and thinks of quitting. But the book of Proverbs indicates that neither of these reactions is correct.

We should not despise the discipline of the Lord. If the Lord should chasten us, we need to be very serious about it. Whenever the Lord permits something to happen to us, He has His purpose behind it. He intends to use these happenings to edify us. All of His chastenings are to perfect us that we may be holier. He chastens us in order to make us partakers of His divine nature.

The aim of discipline is to educate and train our character. The Lord never scourges us without a cause. He always has His mind set upon beating and shaping us into a vessel, never desiring just to make His children suffer. To suffer for the sake of suffering is not His way. If He allows us to suffer, He always has a motive behind it, and that is, He wants us to have a part in His holiness [see v.10b]. This is the purpose of discipline. . .

*The Nature of Discipline*

"For whom the Lord loveth he chasteneth, and scourgeth every son whom he receiveth" (v. 6). This is quoted from Proverbs 3.12. It shows us the "why" of all chastenings.

God does not deal with everyone in the world. He only chastens those whom He loves. He chastens us because we are His beloved. He wants to make us into a suitable vessel. That is why He spends time on His children to chasten them. Chastisement, then, is love's arrangement. Love arranges these happenings. Love measures what we should meet. Love plans the details of our environment. We call this discipline because it always aims at the highest good and the ultimate intention of creation.

"And scourgeth every son whom he receiveth." Those who are chastened of the Lord are those who are assuredly accepted by God. To be scourged is not a sign of rejection, but rather the evidence of God's special approval. God does not deal with everyone; He just concentrates on dealing with those whom He loves, those who are accepted as His sons. . . .

After you become a Christian, you will see the hand of God leading you. Many prearranged things will happen to you. Scourgings will come too. Why the scourgings? Because whenever you are not walking in God's appointed way, you will be scourged and urged to turn from that direction back to the appointed road. Every child of God must be prepared to accept this disciplinary hand of God. Because you are His son, He chastens you. If you are not His beloved, He will not make the effort to discipline you. Thus, to be chastened and scourged is an indication that we are loved and accepted by God. Only Christians share in His chastening and scourging.

What we receive is not punishment but discipline. Punishment serves the purpose of repaying the wrong, but discipline has an educational purpose. Punishment deals only with the past —one is scourged because he has done wrong. Discipline has an eye toward the future though it also deals with past faults. Discipline, therefore, has these two elements—an educational purpose as training for the future. As soon as one comes to Christ and belongs to the Lord, he should be prepared to let God mold him into a vessel of honor. I can say with confidence that God wants to make every child of His glorify Him in some certain respect. All Christians shall glorify Him, but it will be in a different area for each one. Some glorify Him in one way, and some in another way. He is to be glorified in all kinds of situations that He may get a perfect glory. Each person glorifies God with his particular portion—something in his character that the Lord has formed in him. This is the outcome of the disciplinary hand of God upon him. For this reason, it is absolutely impossible for a child of God not to have God's hand upon him. . . .

How does God discipline us? Whatever God has led you through, whatever He has permitted you to endure—this is His discipline. Do not imagine that His discipline is something special. No, the discipline of God is found in that which you endure every day—a hard word, a bad face, a sharp tongue, discourteous treatment, an unreasonable criticism, an unexpected happening, various kinds of disgrace, irresponsibility on the part of family members—all the many pains and difficulties you meet, large or small. Sometimes you have to endure sicknesses, deprivations, distresses, and difficulties. All these are the discipline of God; what you endure, says the apostle, is God's discipline. . .

"God dealeth with you as with sons; for what son is there whom his father chasteneth not?" (v.7). All these chastenings come upon us because God treats us as His own sons. Do remember: discipline is God's favor, not His animosity. Many have the wrong idea that when they are disciplined they are being ill-treated by God. No, God treats us like sons. Is there any son whom the father does not discipline? In disciplining you, God is favoring you! Because you have become God's children, you are disciplined. He wants to bring you to the place of blessing and of glory. . . .

Discipline is shared by all the sons. You, too, are not an exception. If you are not a bastard but a son, then you will have to share in the discipline. The word of the apostle is very emphatic, "whereof all have been made partakers" [v.8]. As a son of God, do not hope for any different treatment. Discipline is shared by all God's sons. All who live today fare the same way as those who lived in the time of Peter and Paul. There is no exception whatever. How can you expect to travel a course which no child of God has ever traveled, a course void of God's discipline? Can a child of God be so foolish as to dream of a prosperous life and work without any discipline of God? You can easily see that such a one must be a bastard. Discipline, we now see, is a signal of being God's child, the evidence thereof. Lack of discipline reveals those who are bastards, those who do not belong to God's house. . . .

In sonship, we find discipline; and in discipline, we find subjection. Because we are sons, we will be disciplined; since we are disciplined, we must be in subjection. Remember, whatever God arranges in our environment is for the purpose of instructing and directing us in the straight path.

We must obey God. We must obey these two things He gives: first, His command; and second, His chastening. On the one hand, we obey God's word, obey His command, and obey all the precepts given us in the Bible. On the other hand, we subject ourselves to all God's arrangements in our environment; we are in subjection to all the discipline of God. Though our obedience to God's word may be sufficient, we often may yet be lacking in subjection to God's discipline. Since He has so ordered that such a thing should happen to you, you ought to be benefited by it and learn the lesson. God wants you to be benefited and to walk in the straight path. We must, therefore, learn not only to obey the Lord's command but also to obey the Lord's discipline. Although it costs us to obey the Lord's discipline, it nonetheless enables us to walk straightforwardly before God. . . .

### *The Purpose of Discipline*

"For they indeed for a few days chastened us as seemed good to them" (v.10a). When parents discipline their children, they reveal much deficiency, for they chasten according to their own thoughts. Consequently, the profit from such discipline is only a little. "But he for our profit, that we may be partakers of his holiness" (v.10b). The discipline of God neither issues from temper nor is it for punishment. All the discipline of God is educational; it is given for our profit. Scourging is not administered just for pain, but the pain is meant to produce some positive value. Pain has its purpose; it is not mere punishment for some fault. If one thinks in terms of punishment, it shows that his mind is yet under the bondage of law.

What is the profit? It is that we may be partakers of His holiness. This, indeed, is most glorious. Holiness is God's nature. We may say that holiness is God's character. It is for this reason that God uses all kinds of ways to chasten His children. From the very start of our Christian life, God chastens us with persistency. He has one purpose in mind, that is, He wants us to be partakers of His holy character.

Holiness in the Bible has various shades of meaning. For instance, the Bible teaches us that Christ is our righteousness and that we are sanctified in Christ; this gives us a different picture from what we have here in the book of Hebrews. Here, holiness is not something given but something fashioned. It fits in with the word "incorporated" which we have emphasized these many years. Holiness is that which God gradually works into us or slowly incorporates in us. Through His discipline, by His scourging, He daily incorporates His holiness in us. The aim of all these chastenings and works is to make us partakers of His holiness.

After each scourging, I learn and partake a little bit more of His holiness. Under His discipline, I come to see what holiness is. As I am constantly under His discipline, my character is gradually built up in holiness; that is, my character is transformed. Let me tell you, there is nothing greater than this work. I want you all to know that through discipline God's character is built in us. Each stroke of discipline has its value. We may derive fruit from every instance of discipline. I beseech God to be merciful to me that, whenever I am chastened, something more of holiness may be produced in me. May each chastening cause me to learn more of holiness and to incorporate in me more of His holiness. May holiness always be on the increase!

—LOA 26-7, 28-9, 30-1, 32, 33, 34, 35-6, 37-8

We may *delay* the growth of life of God's Son in us, but we have no way of *accelerating* it. Because of this, it is of utmost importance that we accept the ordering of God. His ordering is seen in the discipline of the Holy Spirit. "Are not two sparrows sold for a penny? and not one of them shall fall on the ground without your Father" (Matt. 10.29). "Are not five sparrows sold for two pence? and not one of them is forgotten in the sight of God" (Luke 12.6). Arithmetically speaking, two pence should buy four sparrows. There is here an extra sparrow which is casually added. Even this extra sparrow is not forgotten by the heavenly Father. How much more will we be cared for as children of God.

Therefore, let us not try our best to escape that which God has ordained. In escaping we miss the ordering of God, thus missing an opportunity to be expanded. The time for maturity will be prolonged, and the lesson will have to be relearned in order for us to be matured. It is like fulfilling the required amount of credits in school. If less credits are taken one year, more must be taken the next. Even after ten years, the required amount must be accumulated.

Accept the discipline of the Holy Spirit. Let Him enlarge your capacity. A believer will not be the same after he has suffered. If he is not expanded, he will become harder. For this reason, when he undergoes suffering, he should remember that maturity is the sum total of the disciplines of the Holy Spirit. We tend to see the maturity of a person but fail to see the accumulation of the discipline of the Holy Spirit in that person.

—GFB 87-8

The discipline of a member should never be a mere matter of business; rather should it be one of heart concern for the whole church. It is an abominable thing to see the disciplining of any child of God carried through in a trifling manner, as though it were a light thing; but it is no less abominable to see it carried through as a serious matter, if the seriousness is only that of a lawcourt. No discipline should be without grief and tears on the part of those who exercise it, nor can it ever be if they have recognized what the Church is. Paul wrote: "There is fornication *among you.*" He did not, in the first place, locate that sin in any individual believer; he located it in the church. And he wrote: "*Ye* are puffed up, and did not rather mourn" (1 Cor. 5.1-2). The sin was the sin of the whole Body, and the shame and the sorrow should not be just of one member but of the whole.

In Church discipline we need to see the oneness of the Body of Christ, but we need also to see not just the fact but also the potentiality of sin. I must first locate *in myself* the sin that is manifest in my brother, and not till I have judged it in myself dare I judge it in him. By the grace of God I may not have committed the same act, but I have within me the sin that provoked that act.

Discipline is always a remedial measure, and has as its object the recovery of the sinning brother. Even in the most extreme case the end in view is "that the spirit may be saved in the day of the Lord Jesus" (1 Cor. 5.3–5). Where God's children are concerned, there is mercy in all His judgment; and when we judge any of His children on His behalf, whether we do so as the whole church or as individual members, we should be full of mercy. Even though our outward act may have to be one of discipline, our inner attitude should be one of love.

After His resurrection, our Lord said to His disciples, "Receive ye the Holy Spirit," and added immediately, "Whose soever sins ye forgive, they are forgiven unto them; whose soever sins ye retain, they are retained" (John 20.22–23). Rome appropriated this falsely, and reacting against Rome, we repudiate it. But in doing so how much have we Protestants lost! And how much is God losing! For what belongs to the Church of God cannot be lightly thrown away. Though "the church" be but a handful of simple village believers gathering in a home, if they see themselves in Christ as an expression of His Body, and if, confessing before Him their weakness, they claim His wisdom and power, the Lord stands by that. "For where two or three are gathered together in my name, *there am I.*"

—WSM 137–8

Looking further still we find that the first half of the section [in Romans 1 to 8] deals generally speaking with the question of justification (see, for example, Romans 3.24–26; 4.5,25), while the second half has as its main topic the corresponding question of sanctification (see Rom. 6.19,22). When we know the precious truth of justification by faith we still know only half of the story. We still have only solved the problem of our standing before God. As we go on, God has something more to offer us, namely, the solution of the problem of our conduct, and the development of thought in these chapters serves to emphasize this. In each case the second step follows from the first, and if we know only the first, then we are still leading a sub-normal Christian life. How then can we live a normal Christian life? How do we enter upon it? We must, of course, initially have forgiveness of sins, we must have justification, we must have peace with God: these are our indispensable foundation. But with that basis truly established through our first act of faith in Christ, it is yet clear from the above that we must move on to something more.

So we see that objectively the Blood deals with *our sins.* The Lord Jesus has borne them on the Cross for us as our Substitute and has thereby obtained for us forgiveness, justification and reconciliation. But we must now go a step further in the plan of God to understand how he deals with *the sin principle in us.* The Blood can wash away my sins, but it cannot wash away my "old man." It needs the Cross to crucify me. The Blood deals with the *sins,* but the Cross must deal with the *sinner.*

You will scarcely find the word "sinner" in the first four chapters of Romans. This is because there the sinner himself is not mainly in view, but rather the sins he has committed. The word "sinner" first comes into prominence only in chapter 5, and it is important to notice how the sinner is there introduced. In that chapter a sinner is said to be a sinner because he is born a sinner; not because he has committed sins. The distinction is important. It is true that often, when a Gospel worker wants to convince a man in the street that he is a sinner, he will use the favorite verse Romans 3.23, where it says that "all have sinned"; but this use of the verse is not strictly justified by the Scriptures. Those who so use it are in danger of arguing the wrong way round, for the teaching of Romans is not that we are sinners because we commit sins, but that *we sin because we are sinners.* We are sinners by constitution rather than by action. As Romans 5.19 expresses it: "Through the one man's disobedience the many were made [or "constituted"] sinners."

How were we constituted sinners? By Adam's disobedience. We do not become sinners by what we have done but because of what Adam has done and has become. I speak English, but I am not thereby constituted an Englishman. I am in fact a Chinese. So chapter 3 draws our attention to what we have done—"all have sinned"—but it is nevertheless not because we have done it that we become sinners. . . .

At the beginning of our Christian life we are concerned with our doing, not with our being; we are distressed rather by what we have done than by what we are. We think that if only we could rectify certain things we should be good Christians, and we set out therefore to change our actions. But the result is not what we expected. We discover to our dismay that it is something more than just a case of trouble on the outside—that there is in fact more serious trouble on the inside. We try to please the Lord, but find something within that does not want to please Him. We try to be humble, but there is something in our very being that refuses to be humble. We try to be loving, but inside we feel most unloving. We smile and try to look very gracious, but inwardly we feel decidedly ungracious. The more we try to rectify matters on the outside the more we realize how deep-seated is the trouble. Then we come to the Lord and say, "Lord, I see it now! Not only what I have *done* is wrong; *I* am wrong."

The conclusion of Romans 5.19 is beginning to dawn upon us. We are sinners. We are members of a race of people who are constitutionally other than what God intended them to be. By the Fall, a fundamental change took place in the character of Adam whereby he became a sinner, one constitutionally unable to please God; and the family likeness which we all share is no merely superficial one but extends to our inward character also. We have been "constituted sinners." How did this come about? "By the disobedience of one," says the apostle. . . .

But here is our problem. We were born sinners; how then can we cut off our sinful heredity? Seeing that we were born in Adam, how can we get out of Adam? Let me say at once, the Blood cannot take us out of Adam. There is only one way. Since we came in by birth we must go out by death. To do away with our sinfulness we must do away with our life. Bondage to sin came by birth; deliverance from sin comes by death—and it is just this way of escape that God has provided. Death is the secret of emancipation. "We . . . died to sin" (Rom. 6.2).

But how can we die? Some of us have tried very hard to get rid of this sinful life, but we have found it most tenacious. What is the way out? It is not by trying to kill ourselves, but by recognizing that *God has dealt with us in Christ.* This is summed up in the apostle's next statement: "All we who were baptized into Christ Jesus were baptized into his death" (Rom. 6.3).

But if God has dealt with us "in Christ Jesus" then we have got to *be* in Him for this to become effective, and that now seems just as big a problem. How are we to "get into" Christ? Here again God comes to our help. We have in fact no way of getting in, but, what is more important, we need not try to get in, for we *are* in. What we could not do for ourselves, God has done for us. *He has put us into Christ.* Let me remind you of 1 Corinthians 1.30. I think that is one of the best verses of the whole New Testament: "Ye are in Christ." How? "Of him [that is, "of God"] are ye in Christ." Praise God! It is not left to us either to devise a way of entry or to work it out. We need not plan how to get in. God has planned it; and he has not only planned it but he has also performed it. "*Of him* are ye in Christ Jesus." We are in; therefore we need not try to get in. It is a divine act, and it is accomplished. . . .

The death of the Lord Jesus is inclusive. The resurrection of the Lord Jesus is alike inclusive. We have looked at the first chapter of 1 Corinthians to establish the fact that we are "in Christ Jesus." Now we will go to the end of the same letter to see something more of what this means. In 1 Corinthians 15.45–47 two remarkable names or titles are used of the Lord Jesus. He is spoken of there as "the last Adam" and He is spoken of too as "the second man." Scripture does not refer to Him as the second Adam but as "the last Adam"; nor does it refer to Him as the last Man, but as "the second man." The distinction is to be noted, for it enshrines a truth of great value.

As the last Adam, Christ is the sum total of humanity; as the second Man He is the Head of a new race. So we have here two unions, the one relating to His death and the other to his resurrection. In the first place His union with the race as "the last Adam" began historically at Bethlehem and ended at the cross and the tomb. In it He gathered up into himself all that was in Adam and took it to judgment and death. In the second place our union with Him as "the second man" begins in resurrection and ends in eternity—which is to say, it never ends—for, having in His death done away with the first man in whom God's purpose was frustrated, He rose again as Head of a new race of men, in whom that purpose will at length be fully realized.

When therefore the Lord Jesus was crucified on the cross,

He was crucified as the last Adam. All that was in the first Adam was gathered up and done away in Him. We were included there. As the last Adam He wiped out the old race; as the second Man He brings in the new race. It is in His resurrection that He stands forth as the second Man, and there too we are included. "For if we have become united with him by the likeness of his death, we shall be also by the likeness of his resurrection" (Rom. 6.5). We died in Him as the last Adam; we live in Him as the second Man. The Cross is thus the mighty act of God which translates us from Adam to Christ. . . .

The Cross was the means God used to bring to an end "the old things" by setting aside altogether our "old man," and the resurrection was the means He employed to impart to us all that was necessary for our life in that new world. "We were buried therefore with him through baptism into death: that like as Christ was raised from the dead through the glory of the Father, so we also might walk in newness of life" (Rom. 6.4).

The greatest negative in the universe is the Cross, for with it God wiped out everything that was not of himself: the greatest positive in the universe is the resurrection, for through it God brought into being all He will have in the new sphere. So the resurrection stands at the threshold of the new creation. It is a blessed thing to see that the Cross ends all that belongs to the first regime, and that the resurrection introduces all that pertains to the second. Everything that had its beginning before resurrection must be wiped out. Resurrection is God's new starting-point. . . .

But there is a further aspect of the Cross, namely, that implied in the expression "bearing his cross daily," which is before us now. The Cross has borne me; now I must bear it; and this bearing of the Cross is an inward thing. It is this that we mean when we speak of "the subjective working of the Cross." Moreover, it is a continuous process, a step by step following after Him. It is this which is now brought before us in relation to the soul, and as we have just said, with an emphasis here that is not quite the same as with the old man. We do not have here the "crucifixion" of the soul itself, in the sense that our natural gifts and faculties, our personality and our individuality, are to be put away altogether. Were it so it could hardly be said of us, as it is in Hebrews 10.39, that we are to "have faith unto the saving of the soul." (Compare 1 Peter 1.9; Luke 21.19.) No, we do not lose our souls in this sense, for to do so would be to lose our individual existence completely. The soul is still there with its natural endowments, but the Cross is brought to bear upon it to bring those natural endowments into death—to put the mark of *His* death upon them—and thereafter, as God may please, to give them back to us in glorious resurrection.

—NCL 33-5, 37-8, 42-3, 46-7, 88-9, 251

Although the Bible never teaches us to crucify ourselves for the sake of sin, it does tell us to bear the cross for the sake of self. Many times our Lord Jesus commanded us to deny ourselves, take up the cross and follow Him. This is because the way in which our Lord deals with our self is different from the way in which He deals with our sins on the cross. We know that the Lord Jesus did not bear in His body our sins until He was on the cross, but He denied himself throughout His entire life without His having waited to do so until He reached the cross. For this reason, a believer may overcome sin completely in a matter of a second, but he needs to deny self all his life.

The letter to the Galatians explains clearly the two-sided relationship of the flesh to the believer. It tells us on the one hand: "they that are of Christ Jesus have crucified the flesh with the passions and the lusts thereof" (5.24). This means that on the day a person belongs to Christ Jesus his flesh is crucified. Unless he is taught by the Holy Spirit, he may conclude that he has no more flesh because it *was* crucified. Yet the Scriptures tell us on the other hand to "walk by the spirit, and ye shall not fulfill the lust of the flesh. For the flesh lusteth against the Spirit, and the

Spirit against the flesh" (5.16–17). It is quite evident that a person who belongs to Christ Jesus and has the Holy Spirit indwelling him still has the flesh. He not only has the flesh, but also its power. Do these two passages contradict each other? Not at all. For verse 24 stresses the "sin" aspect of the flesh while verse 17 stresses the "self" aspect of the flesh. The cross of Christ deals with sin, and the Holy Spirit through the cross deals with the self. By the cross Christ delivers the believer from the power of sin so that sin reigns no more; by the Holy Spirit Christ dwells in the believer so that the latter may overcome his self. Overcoming sin is an accomplished fact; overcoming self is an affair being daily accomplished. . . .

What the flesh wants is total control, which is the very same desire of the spiritual life. The flesh wishes to put man permanently under it, whereas the spiritual life in man requires him to obey completely the Holy Spirit. The flesh and spiritual life are at odds at every point. The nature of the flesh is of the first man Adam, but that of the spiritual life is of the last Adam (Christ). The motive of the flesh is earthly, yet that of the spiritual is heavenly. The flesh makes self the center of all things, while the spiritual life centers all in Christ. Since these two are so radically different, it is no wonder that a believer finds a constant battle raging within him. The flesh tries to entice man to sin, but the spiritual life helps him to be righteous. A person who does not know the perfect salvation of Christ will experience much of this kind of battle after he is regenerated. . . .

God's purpose is not in reforming the flesh, but in destroying its vital center. In giving His life to man at the time of regeneration, God intends to use this life to destroy the self of the flesh. . . .

—SJ 124–5, 127, 128

"And he that doth not take his cross and follow after me, is *not worthy* of me" (Matt. 10.38). This verse sums up what has been said before—this is a cross! What is meant by taking the cross? The Lord has not said that he who does not take up his burden and follow after Him is not worthy of Him. No, He says that whoever does not take his cross and follow after Him is not worthy of Him. A burden is not a cross. Burden is something inescapable; the cross, however, is subject to personal choice and can therefore be avoided.

What the first cross in history was, so the countless smaller crosses will be which shall follow afterwards: just as the original cross was *chosen* by the Lord, so the crosses for today must also be *chosen* by us.

Some people assume that they are bearing the cross whenever they fall into some hardship or encounter some distress. This is not true, however, for these kinds of things may quite naturally happen to any person even if that person is not a believer. All the crosses one takes up must be *chosen* by oneself. Yet a person needs to guard himself against an error here, which is, that he must not create crosses for himself. We should *take* the cross, not *make* it.

It is therefore a great mistake to consider all which befalls us as constituting crosses for us to take. Whatever crosses we ourselves have created are not to be reckoned as crosses to take.

What then is a cross? It must be akin to what the Lord Jesus himself has said: "My Father, . . . thy will be done" (Matt. 26.42). The Lord asks His Father not to answer as He the Son wills, but as the Father wills. This is the cross. To take the cross is to *choose* the will which the Father has decided. May I say truthfully that if we do not *choose* the cross daily, we have no cross to take up. If the Lord had waited until the cross had come to Him on the earth, how would it have been possible for Him to have been the Lamb slain from before the foundation of the world? For had He not chosen the cross in heaven when He there and then "emptied himself, taking the form of a servant, being made in the likeness of man"? "And being found in fashion as a man, he humbled himself, becoming obedient even unto death, yea, the death of the cross" (Phil. 2.7–8). Our Lord truly *chose* the cross. "No one taketh it [my life] away from me," said Jesus, "but I lay it down of myself. I have power to lay it down, and I have power to take it again" (John 10.18). In accordance with the same principle, our cross must be something which *we ourselves choose.*

—SS 21-2

### *The Cross and the Body*

"Now in Christ Jesus ye . . . are made nigh by the blood of Christ. For he is our peace, who made both [Jew and Gentile] one . . . that he might create in himself of the twain one new man . . . and might reconcile them both in one body unto God through the cross" (see Eph. 2.11-22). What, we must ask ourselves, is this "one body," this "one new man"? What is this mystery of Christ that Paul has come to see?

In Romans 6.6 he has spoken of "our old man," by which he means everything that comes to us from "the first man, Adam"; and he sees this "old man" as having been nailed to the cross with Christ. In Colossians 3.11-12 he speaks of "the new man" as the sphere where now "there cannot be Greek and Jew . . . but Christ is all and in all." For our old man there was only crucifixion with Christ; in the new Man we are found in union with Him, risen and ascended. Between the one and the other towers the Cross as the only gateway into this fellowship with one another in Jesus Christ.

You ask me, what do I mean when I use the term "the Cross" in this way? I think it is best summed up in the words the crowd used of its Victim: "Away with him!" [John 19.15] Crucifixion, humanly speaking, is an end. The Cross of Christ is intended by God to be, first of all, the end of everything in man that has come under His sentence of death, for there it was that He took our place, and the judgment of God was fulfilled upon Him.

But the Cross has a further value for us, for it is there also that the Christian believer's self-sufficient and individualistic natural life is broken, as Jacob's strength and independence of nature were broken at Jabbok. There comes a day in God's dealings with each of us when we suffer in our souls that incapacitating wound, and ever afterwards "go halting." God never allows this to remain for us a mere theory. Alas, I must confess that for many years it *was* no more than theory to me. I myself had "preached the Cross" in this very sense, yet without knowing anything of it in my own experience—until one day I *saw* that it had been I, Nee To-sheng, who died there with Christ. "Away with him!" they had said, and in saying it they unwittingly echoed God's verdict upon *my* old man. And that sentence upon me was carried out *in Him.* This tremendous discovery affected me almost as greatly as did my first discovery of salvation. I tell you, it left me for seven whole months so humbled as to be quite unable to preach at all, whereas for long, I have to confess, preaching had been my consuming passion.

But if to see this somewhat negative aspect of the Cross can be so drastic an experience, it is not surprising that its positive aspect—the revelation to our hearts of the heavenly Body of Christ—has proved for many to be no less revolutionary. For it is like suddenly finding yourself in a place which you have hitherto known only by hearsay. And how different the reality proves! Reading a guide to London is no substitute for visiting that city. Nor can a book of recipes take the place of a spell of work in the kitchen. To know anything experimentally, we must sooner or later find ourselves personally involved in it.

Yes, there are certain fundamental experiences we must have, and this "seeing" of the Body of Christ, the heavenly Man, is one such. What is it? It is simply a discovery of values that, as I have said, lie on the resurrection side of the Cross. There, what has been for us already a way of release *from* our old selfish "natural life" in Adam becomes the gateway *into* the new, shared "everlasting life" in Christ. For unlike other Roman crucifixions, the Cross of Christ is not just an end; it is also a beginning. In His death and resurrection, our disunion gives way to oneness of life in Him.

God is not satisfied with single, separate Christians. When

we believed on the Lord and partook of Him we became members of His Body. Oh that God would cause this fact to break upon us! Do I seek spiritual experiences for myself? Do I make converts for my denomination? Or have I caught the wisdom of the one heavenly Man, and realized that God is seeking to bring men into that? When I do, salvation, deliverance, enduement with the Spirit, yes, everything in Christian experience will be seen from a new viewpoint, everything for me will be transformed

—WSM 68–70

Paul's message is the cross, and he himself is a crucified person. In the preaching of the cross, he adopts the way of the cross. A crucified person preaches the message of the cross in the spirit of the cross. How often what we preach is indeed the cross; but our attitude, our words and our feelings do not seem to bear witness to what we preach. Much preaching of the cross is not done in the spirit of the cross! Paul wrote to the Corinthian believers that he "came not with excellency of speech or of wisdom when proclaiming" to them "the testimony of God." The testimony of God here refers to the word of the cross. Paul did not use lofty words of wisdom in proclaiming the cross but came in the spirit of the cross: "My speech and my preaching were not in persuasive words of wisdom, but in demonstration of the Spirit and of power." Such is truly the spirit of the cross.

The cross is the wisdom of God, though to unbelieving men it is foolishness. When we proclaim the "foolish" message, we must assume the "foolish" way, adopt the "foolish" attitude, and use the "foolish" words. The victory of Paul lies in the fact that he is indeed a crucified person. He can therefore proclaim the cross with the attitude as well as the spirit of the cross. He who has not experienced crucifixion will not be filled with the spirit of the cross; and consequently he is not fit to proclaim the message of the cross.

Having seen the experience of Paul, does it not tell us tne

cause of our failure? The message we preach may be right, but let us examine ourselves in the light of the Lord, discerning whether we really are crucified men and women. With what kind of spirit, words and attitude do we preach the cross? Oh! May we deeply humble ourselves in the face of these questions so that God may be gracious to us and that others listening to us may receive life.

Failure of people to receive life must be the failure of the *preachers*! It is not that the word has lost its power; it is men who have failed. Men have hindered the outflowing of the life of God, and not that the word of God has lost its effectiveness. People who do not have the *experience* of the cross and hence lack the *spirit* of the cross are unable to impart the *life* of the cross to others. How can we give to other people what we ourselves do not have? Unless the cross becomes our life, we cannot impart that life to others. The failure of our work is due to the fact that we are eager to preach the cross without that cross being within us. He who truly knows how to preach must have first preached the word to himself. Otherwise the Holy Spirit will not work through him. . . .

Men and women who have not been crucified cannot, and are unfit to, proclaim the word of the cross. The cross we preach to others should first crucify us. The word we preach should first burn itself deeply into our life so that our life is the living message. The cross we proclaim ought not just be a message. We ought to let the cross live out of us daily. Then what we preach will be more than a message but a kind of life which we daily exhibit. Then we shall be able to impart this life to others as we preach. . . .

. . . The life of the cross is the life of the Lord Jesus. We must know our message in experience. The teaching which we know is solely a teaching until we allow it to work in our lives so that the teaching we know becomes a part of our experience and an integral element in our daily walk. Then the teaching is not mere doctrine but is the very stuff of our life—just as the food we have eaten has become flesh of our flesh and bone of our bones. We become a *living* teaching and a *living* word; and what we preach is no longer simply an idea which we know but is our real life. This is the meaning of being "doers of the word" according to the Biblical sense. . . .

In reading 2 Corinthians 4 we come to know the inner experience of this servant of the Lord. The secret to all Paul's works is found in this fragment: "So then death worketh in us, but life in you" (v.12). He died daily; he allowed the death of the cross to work deeply in him so that others might have life. Whoever does not know the death of the cross does not have the life of the cross for other people. Paul was willing to be in the place of death that others might receive life through him. Only the one who dies can give life. But how, Lord, to die?

What is the real meaning of this death? This death is more than death to sin, to self, and to the world. It is deeper than all these. This death is the spirit which our Lord Jesus exhibited when He was crucified on the cross. He does not die for His own sins, since He has none. Let us recognize that His cross declares His holiness. He is crucified wholly for the sake of *others*. Hence His death is due to His obedience to God's will. And such is the meaning of the death mentioned here. Thus we need to be delivered to death not only for our own sake that we may die to sin, self and the world, but also for the sake of obeying the Lord Jesus in enduring the hostility of sinners daily.

Yes, we ought to let the death of the Lord so work in us that we may have real experience of dying to self and arrive at the state of holiness. But we should equally let the Holy Spirit do a deeper work in us by the cross so as to cause us to live it out. We must know the *life* of the cross as well as its death. Having the death of the cross, we die to sin and the old Adamic walk; but having the life of the cross, we daily live in the spirit of the cross. This means that in our everyday walk we exhibit the Lamb-spirit of the Lord Jesus in suffering silently: "[Jesus] when he was reviled, reviled not again; when he suffered, threatened not; but committed himself to him that judgeth righteously" (1 Peter 2.23). This death is a step deeper than death to sin and self and the world. May the cross become our life! May we become a living cross! May we magnify the cross in all things! . . .

A death that can work must be a "working death"—the life of death, even the life of the cross. For the sake of the Lord Jesus, Paul is ready always to be delivered to death. Notwithstanding unpleasant words, high-handed attitudes, cruel persecution, or unjustified misunderstanding, he is quite willing to bear them all for the Lord's sake. Paul will not open his mouth when he is delivered to death. Like his Lord who could ask the Father to send twelve legions of angels to help Him, he will under no such circumstances adopt man's way to avoid these unpleasantries. He would rather have the "living death" of Jesus—the life and spirit of the cross—worked in him so as to show forth the spirit of the cross in all his dealings. He reckons the cross as all powerful, because it enables him to be willing for the sake of the Lord Jesus to be delivered to death and to suffer persecutions and hardships of the world. . . .

Every one of us has natural talent—some with more, others with less. After we have had some experience of the cross, we tend at first to depend on our natural gifts to proclaim the cross which we have newly experienced. How eagerly we expect our audience to adopt the same view and share in the same experience. Yet somehow they are so cold and unreceptive, falling short of our anticipation. We do not realize that we are rather new in our experience of the cross, and that our natural good talents need also to die with Christ. Are we ignorant of the fact that the cross must so work in us that not only should it be manifested in our lives but also be expressed in our works? But before we reach this more matured state, we usually look at our natural talent as harmless and very profitable in kingdom service. Hence why not use it? Not until we discover that the work done by relying on natural ability can only please men for a time but does not impart to their spirit the *actual* work of the Holy Spirit do we finally acknowledge how inadequate is our beautiful natural talent and how necessary it is that we seek for greater divine power. How many are those who proclaim the cross in their own power! . . .

Let us read another Scripture passage to help us understand what is the difference between depending on natural life and depending on supernatural life. "Verily, verily, I say unto you, Except a grain of wheat fall into the earth and die, it abideth by itself alone; but if it die, it beareth much fruit. He that loveth his life loseth it; and he that hateth his life in this world shall keep it unto life eternal" (John 12.24–25).

Here the Lord Jesus reveals the principle of fruit bearing: the grain of wheat which is sown must first *die* before it will bear much fruit. Hence death is the indispensable process for fruit bearing. The fact of the matter is, death *is* the only way to bear fruit. How we ask the Lord for greater power that we may bear more fruit; but the Lord tells us that we need to die, that we must have the experience of the cross if we desire the power of the Holy Spirit. Frequently in our attempt to achieve Pentecost we bypass Calvary, not realizing that without our being crucified and thus losing all belonging to the natural, the Holy Spirit cannot work with us to gain many people. Here is the spiritual principle: die, and *then* bear fruit.

The very nature of bearing fruit proves what we have stated before: the purpose of work is that people may receive life. This grain of wheat simply died, with the result that it produced many other grains. All these many grains now have life; but the source of the life they obtained was the *dead* grain of wheat. If we are truly dead, we will be the channels of God's life to transmit that life to other people. Hence this life is not a matter of vain terminology but has the power of God issuing forth from us to cause people to have life. . . .

But what does this phrase "fall into the earth and die" really mean? By reading the succeeding words which the Lord utters here, we may readily understand: "He that loveth his life loseth it; and he that hateth his life in this world shall keep it unto life eternal" (12.25). In the Greek original, two different words are used for the several times "life" is mentioned here. One Greek word *psuche* has reference to the soul life or natural life; the other word *zoe* signifies the spirit life or supernatural life. Hence what the Lord is actually saying here is: "He that loveth his soul life loseth the spirit life; and he that hateth his soul life in this world shall keep the spirit life unto eternity." To put it simply, we should deliver the soul life to death, just as the grain of wheat falls into the earth and dies; and then by our spirit life many grains will come forth and be kept to eternity. How we long to bear much fruit, yet we do not know how to let the soul life die and the spirit life live.

—MC 7-8, 10, 13, 18-9, 20-1, 24, 26-7, 28

# 35 Brokenness

Anyone who serves God will discover sooner or later that the great hindrance to his work is not others but himself. He will discover that his outward man and his inward man are not in harmony, for both are tending toward opposite directions. He will also sense the inability of his outward man to submit to the spirit's control, thus rendering him incapable of obeying God's highest commands. He will quickly detect that the greatest difficulty lies in his outward man, for it hinders him from using his spirit. . . .

## *The Inward Man and the Outward Man*

Notice how the Bible divides man into two parts: "For I delight in the law of God according to the inward man" (Rom. 7.22). Our inward man delights in the Law of God. ". . . To be strengthened with power by his Spirit in the inner man" (Eph. 3.16). And Paul also tells us, "But if indeed our outward man is consumed, yet the inward is renewed day by day" (2 Cor. 4.16).

When God comes to indwell us by His Spirit, life and power, He comes into our spirit which we are calling the inward man. Outside of this inward man is the soul wherein function our thoughts, emotions and will. The outermost man is our physical body. Thus we will speak of the inward man as the spirit, the outer man as the soul and the outermost man as the body. We must never forget that our inward man is the human spirit where God dwells, where His Spirit mingles with our spirit. Just as we are dressed in clothes, so our inward man "wears" an outward man: the spirit "wears" the soul. And similarly, the spirit and soul "wear" the body. It is quite evident that men are generally more conscious of the outer and outermost man, and they hardly recognize or understand their spirit at all.

We must know that he who can work for God is the one whose inward man can be released. The basic difficulty of a servant of God lies in the failure of the inward man to break through the outward man. Therefore we must recognize before God that the first difficulty to our work is not in others but in ourselves. Our spirit seems to be wrapped in a covering so that it cannot easily break forth. If we have never learned how to release our inward man by breaking through the outward man, we are not able to serve. Nothing can so hinder us as this outward man. Whether our works are fruitful or not depends upon whether our outward man has been broken by the Lord so that the inward man can pass through that brokenness and come forth. This is the basic problem. The Lord wants to break our outward man in order that the inward man may have a way out. When the inward man is released, both unbelievers and Christians will be blessed.

### *Nature Has Its Way of Breaking*

The Lord Jesus tells us in John 12, "Except the grain of wheat falling into the ground die, it abides alone; but if it die, it bears much fruit." Life is in the grain of wheat, but there is a shell, a very hard shell on the outside. As long as that shell is not split open, the wheat cannot sprout and grow. "Except the grain of wheat falling into the ground die . . . " What is this death? It is the cracking open of the shell through the working together of temperature, humidity, in the soil. Once the shell is split open, the wheat begins to grow. So the question here is not whether there is life within, but whether the outside shell is cracked open.

The Scripture continues by saying, "He that loves his life [Greek, *soul*] shall lose it, and he that hates his life [Greek, *soul*] in this world shall keep it to life eternal" (v.25). The Lord shows us here that the outer shell is our own life (our soul life), while the life within is the eternal life which He has given to us. To allow the inner life to come forth, it is imperative that the outward life be replaced. Should the outward remain unbroken, the inward would never be able to come forth. . . .

*The Alabaster Box Must Be Broken [Mark 14.3–9]*

The Bible tells of the pure spikenard. God purposely used this term "pure" in His word to show that it is truly spiritual. But if the alabaster box is not broken, the pure spikenard will not flow forth. Strange to say, many are still treasuring the alabaster box, thinking that its value exceeds that of the ointment. Many think that their outward man is more precious than their inward man. This becomes the problem in the church. One will treasure his cleverness, thinking he is quite important; another will treasure his own emotions, esteeming himself as an important person; others highly regard themselves, feeling they are better than others: their eloquence surpasses that of others, their quickness of action and exactness of judgment are superior, and so forth. However, we are not antique collectors; we are not vase admirers; we are those who desire to smell only the fragrance of the ointment. Without the breaking of the outward, the inward will not come forth. Thus individually we have no flowing out, but also the church does not have a living way. Why then should we hold ourselves as so precious, if our outward contains instead of releases the fragrance?

The Holy Spirit has not ceased working. One event after another, one thing after another, comes to us. Each disciplinary working of the Holy Spirit has but one purpose: to break our outward man so that our inward man may come through. Yet here is our difficulty: we fret over trifles, we murmur at small losses. The Lord is preparing a way to use us, yet scarcely has His hand touched us when we feel unhappy, even to the extent of quarreling with God and becoming negative in our attitude.

Since being saved, we have been touched many times in various ways by the Lord, all with the purpose of breaking our outward man. Whether we are conscious of it or not, the aim of the Lord is to break this outward man.

So the Treasure is in the earthen vessel, but if the earthen vessel is not broken, who can see the Treasure within? What is the final objective of the Lord's working in our lives? It is to break this earthen vessel, to break our alabaster box, to crack open our shell. The Lord longs to find a way to bless the world through those who belong to Him. Brokenness is the way of blessing, the way of fragrance, the way of fruitfulness, but it is also a path sprinkled with blood. Yes, there is blood from many wounds. When we offer ourselves to the Lord to be at His service, we cannot afford to be lenient, to spare ourselves. We must allow the Lord utterly to crack our outward man, so that He may find a way for His out-working. . . .

### *The Timing in Our Brokenness*

The Lord employs two different ways to break our outward man; one is gradual, the other, sudden. To some the Lord gives a sudden breaking followed by a gradual one. With others, the Lord arranges that they have constant daily trials, until one day He brings about large-scale breaking. If it is not the sudden first and then the gradual, then it is the gradual followed by the sudden. It would seem the Lord usually spends several years upon us before He can accomplish this work of breaking.

The timing is in His hand. We cannot shorten the time, though we certainly can prolong it. In some lives the Lord is able to accomplish this work after a few years of dealing; in others it is evident that after ten or twenty years the work is still unfinished. This is most serious! Nothing is more grievous than wasting God's time. How often the church is hindered! We can preach by using our mind, we can stir others by using our emotions; yet if we do not know how to use our spirit, the Spirit of

God cannot touch people through us. The loss is great, should we needlessly prolong the time.

Therefore, if we have never before wholly and intelligently consecrated ourselves to the Lord, let us do so now, saying: "Lord, for the future of the church, for the future of the gospel, for Thy way, and also for my own life, I offer myself without condition, without reservation, into Thy hands. Lord, I delight to offer myself unto Thee and am willing to let Thee have Thy full way through me."

### *The Meaning of the Cross*

Often we hear about the cross. Perhaps we are too familiar with the term. But what is the cross after all? When we really understand the cross we shall see it means the breaking of the outward man. The cross reduces the outward man to death; it splits open the human shell. The cross must break all that belongs to our outward man—our opinions, our ways, our cleverness, our self-love, our all. The way is clear, in fact crystal clear. . . .

### *Two Reasons for Not Being Broken*

Why is it that after many years of dealing some remain the same? Some individuals have a forceful will; some have strong emotions; and others have a strong mind. Since the Lord is able to break these, why is it that after many years some are still unchanged? We believe there are two main reasons.

First, many who live in darkness are not seeing the hand of God. While God is working, while God is breaking, they do not recognize it as being from Him. They are devoid of light, seeing only men opposing them. They imagine their environment is just too difficult, that circumstances are to blame. So they continue in darkness and despair.

May God give us a revelation to see what is from His hand, that we may kneel down and say to Him, "It is Thou; since it is Thou, I will accept." At least we must recognize *whose* hand it is that deals with us. It is not a human hand, nor our family's, not the brothers' and sisters' in the church, but God's. We need to learn how to kneel down and kiss the hand, love the hand that deals with us, even as Madame Guyon did. We must have this light to see that whatever the Lord has done, we accept and believe; the Lord can do no wrong.

Second, another great hindrance to the work of breaking the outer man is self-love. We must ask God to take away the heart of self-love. As He deals with us in response to our prayer, we should worship and say, "O Lord, if this be Thy hand, let me accept it from my heart." Let us remember that the one reason for all misunderstanding, all fretfulness, all discontent is, that we secretly love ourselves. Thus we plan a way whereby we can deliver ourselves. Many times problems arise due to our seeking a way of escape—an escape from the working of the cross.

He who has ascended the cross and refuses to drink the vinegar mingled with gall is the one who knows the Lord. Many go up to the cross rather reluctantly, still thinking of drinking vinegar mingled with gall to alleviate their pains. All who say, "The cup which the Father has given me, shall I not drink it?", will not drink the cup of vinegar mingled with gall. They can only drink of one cup, not two. Such as these are without any self-love. Self-love is a basic difficulty. May the Lord speak to us today that we may be able to pray: "O my God, I have seen that all things come from Thee. All my ways these five years, ten years, or twenty years, are of Thee. Thou hast so worked to attain Thy purpose, which is none other than that Thy life may be lived out through me. But I have been foolish. I did not see. I did many things to deliver myself, thus delaying Thy time. Today I see Thy hand. I am willing to offer myself to Thee. Once again I place myself in Thy hands." . . .

Each of us has much of the same Jacob nature in us. Our only hope is that the Lord may blaze a way out, breaking the outward man to such a degree that the inward man may come out and be seen. This is precious, and this is the way of those who serve the Lord. Only thus can we serve; only thus can we lead men to the Lord. All else is limited in its value. Doctrine does not have much use nor does theology. What is the use of mere mental knowledge of the Bible if the outward man remains unbroken? Only the person through whom God can come forth is useful.

After our outward man has been stricken, dealt with, and led through various trials, we have wounds upon us, thus allowing the spirit to emerge. We are afraid to meet some brothers and sisters whose whole being remains intact, never having been dealt with and changed. May God have mercy upon us in showing us clearly this way and in revealing to us that it is the only way. May He also show us that herein is seen the purpose of all His dealings with us in these few years, say ten or twenty. Thus let no one despise the Lord's dealings. May He truly reveal to us what is meant by the breaking of the outward man. Should the outward man remain whole, everything would be merely in our mind, utterly useless. Let us expect the Lord to deal with us thoroughly.

The breaking of the outward man is the basic experience of all who serve God. This must be accomplished before He can use us in an effective way.

When one is working for God, two possibilities may arise. First, it is possible that with the outward man unbroken, one's spirit may be inert and unable to function. If he is a clever person, his mind governs his work; if he is a compassionate person, the emotions control his actions. Such work may appear successful but cannot bring people to God. Second, his spirit may come forth clad in his own thoughts or emotions. The result is mixed and impure. Such work will bring men into mixed and impure experience. These two conditions weaken our service to God.

If we desire to work effectively, we must realize that basically "it is the Spirit which quickens." Sooner or later—if not on the first day of our salvation, then perhaps ten years after—we must recognize this fact. Many have to be brought to their wits' end to see the emptiness of their labor before they know how useless are their many thoughts, their varied emotions. No matter how many people you can attract with your thoughts or emotions, the result comes to nothing. Eventually we must confess: "It is the Spirit which quickens." The Spirit alone makes people live. Your best thought, your best emotion cannot make people live. Man can be brought into life only by the Spirit. Many serving the Lord come to see this fact only after passing through much sorrow and many failures. Finally the Lord's word becomes meaningful to them: *that which quickens is the Spirit.* When the spirit is released then sinners may be born anew and saints may be established. When life is communicated through the channel of the spirit, those who receive it are born anew. When life is supplied through the spirit to believers, it results in their being established. Without the Spirit, there can be no new birth and no establishment [see John 6.63]. . . .

### *The Dividing of the Outward and the Inward Man*

When the outward man is broken, outside things will be kept outside, and the inward man will live before God continuously. The trouble with many is that their outward man and inward man are joined together, so what influences the outward influences the inward. Through the merciful working of God the outward man and inward man must be separated. Then what affects the outward will not be able to reach the inward. Though the outward man may be engaged in conversation, the inward man is fellowshiping with God. The outward may be burdened with listening to the clatter of dishes, yet the inward abides in God. One is able to carry on activities, to contact the world with the outer man; nevertheless the inner man remains unaffected because he still lives before God. . . .

### *The Spirit's Use of a Broken Outward Man*

In His dealing with man, God's Spirit never bypasses man's

spirit. Nor can our spirit bypass the outer man. This is a most important principle to grasp. As the Holy Spirit does not pass over man's spirit in His working in man, no more does our spirit ignore the outward man and function directly. In order to touch other lives, our spirit must pass through the outward man. Hence, when the latter's strength is consumed by the many things in hand, God cannot do His work through us. There is no outlet for the human spirit nor for the Holy Spirit. The inward man cannot come forth because he is resisted and blocked by the outward man. That is why we have repeatedly suggested that this outward man must be broken. . . .

### *We Are His Instrumentality*

In diagnosing a case, a medical doctor has recourse to many medical instruments. This is not so with us. We have no thermometer nor x-ray, nor any other such device to help us discern man's spiritual condition. How, then, do we discern whether a brother is spiritually ill or determine the nature of his trouble? It is wonderful that God has designed us to be as "thermometers" for measuring. By His working in our lives, He would equip us to discern what "ails" a person. As the Lord's spiritual "doctors" we must have a thorough inward preparation. We must be deeply conscious of the weight of our responsibility.

Suppose the thermometer had never been invented. The doctor would have to determine whether his patient had a fever by the mere touch of his hand. His hand would serve as the thermometer. How sensitive and accurate his hand would need to be! In spiritual work, this is exactly the case.

We are the thermometers, the instrumentalities. We must undergo thorough training and strict discipline, for whatever is untouched in us will be left untouched in others. Moreover, we cannot help others to learn lessons which we ourselves have not learned before God. The more thorough our training, the greater will be our usefulness in God's work. Likewise, the more we spare ourselves—our pride, our narrowness, our happiness—the less our usefulness. If we have covered these things in ourselves, we cannot uncover them in others. A proud person cannot deal with another with the same condition; a hypocrite cannot touch the hypocrisy in another; nor can one who is loose in his life have a helpful effect on one who suffers the same difficulty. How well we know that if such is still in our nature we will not be able to condemn such particular sin in others; we in fact can hardly recognize it in others. A doctor may cure others without curing himself, but this can hardly be true in the spiritual realm. The worker is himself first a patient; he must be healed before he can heal others. What he has not seen he cannot show others. Where he has not trodden he cannot lead others. What he has not learned he cannot teach others.

We must see that we are the instruments prepared by God for knowing man. Hence we must be dependable, qualified to give an accurate diagnosis. So that my feelings may be reliable, I need to pray, "O Lord, do not let me go untouched, unbroken and unprepared." I must allow God to work in me what I have never dreamed of, so that I may become a prepared vessel whom He can use. A doctor would not use a defective thermometer. How much more serious it is for us to touch spiritual conditions than physical illnesses while still retaining our own thoughts, emotions, opinions and ways. If we still want to do this, and then suddenly want to do that, we are yet unstable. How can we be used when we are so undependable? We must pass through God's dealings or our efforts are vain. . . .

For the outward man to be broken, a full consecration is imperative. Yet we must understand that this crisis act alone will not solve our whole problem in service. Consecration is merely an expression of our willingness to be in the hands of God, and it can take place in just a few minutes. Do not think God can *finish* His dealings with us in this short time. Though we are willing to offer ourselves completely to God, we are just starting on the spiritual road. It is like entering the gate. After consecration, there must be the discipline of the Holy Spirit—this is the pathway. It takes consecration plus the discipline of the Holy Spirit to make us vessels fit for the Master's use. Without consecration, the Holy Spirit encounters difficulty in disciplining us. Yet consecration cannot serve as a substitute for His discipline.

Here then is a vital distinction: our consecration can only be according to the measure of our spiritual insight and understanding, but the Holy Spirit disciplines according to His own light. We really do not know how much our consecration involves. Our light is so limited that when it seems to us to be at its greatest, in God's view it is like pitch blackness. God's requirement so far exceeds what we can possibly consecrate—that is, in our limited light. The discipline of the Holy Spirit, on the other hand, is meted out to us according to our need as seen in God's own light. He knows our special need, and so by His Spirit He orders our circumstances in such a way as to bring about the breaking of the outward man. Notice how far the discipline of the Holy Spirit transcends our consecration.

Since the Holy Spirit works according to the light of God, His discipline is thorough and complete. We often wonder at the things which befall us, yet if left to ourselves we may be mistaken in our very best choice. The discipline He orders transcends our understanding. How often we are caught unprepared and conclude that surely such a drastic thing is not our need. Many times His discipline descends upon us suddenly without our having prior notice! We may insist we are living in "the light" but the Holy Spirit is dealing with us according to God's light. From the time we received Him, He has been ordering our circumstances for our profit according to His knowledge of us.

The working of the Holy Spirit in our lives has its positive as well as its negative side—that is to say, there is both a constructive and a destructive phase. After we are born again the Holy Spirit dwells in us, but our outward man so often deprives Him of His freedom. It is like trying to walk in a pair of ill-fitting new shoes. Because our outward and inward man are at variance with each other, God must employ whatever means He thinks effective in breaking down any stronghold over which our inward man has no control.

It is not by the supply of grace to the inward man that the Holy Spirit breaks the outward. Of course, God wants the inward man to be strong, but His method is to utilize external means to decrease our outward man. It would be well nigh impossible for the inward man to accomplish this, since these two are so different in nature that they can scarcely inflict any wound on each other. The nature of the outward man and that of external things are similar; and thus the former can be easily affected by the latter. External things can strike the outward man most painfully. So it is that God uses external things in dealing with our outward man.

—ROS 9, 10–1, 12–3, 14–5, 15–6, 17–8, 19–20, 27–8, 32–3, 40–2, 57–9

*The Treasure Is Manifested in Earthen Vessels*

In the mind of many people there is an ideal Christian. Please notice that this person is a figment of their imagination, not a creation of God. Such a Christian does not exist, nor does God want such a person. What we meet here are earthen vessels. What is special with these earthen vessels is that a treasure has been put into them, even as Paul once declared: "we have this treasure in earthen vessels" (2 Cor. 4.7a). This treasure overshadows each of these earthen vessels and is manifested through them. This, in a word, is true Christianity. This is what a Christian is. For here you see a man who fears but yet is brave, who is weak and yet he is strong: "Pressed on every side, yet not straitened; perplexed, yet not unto despair; pursued, yet not forsaken; smitten down, yet not destroyed" (2 Cor. 4.8–9). We see that he is weak, but yet he declares: "when I am weak, then am I strong" (2 Cor. 12.10b). He always bears in his body the dying of Jesus, yet he declares that the life also of Jesus is manifested in him. He endures "evil report and good report; [being viewed] as [a] deceiver, and yet true; as unknown, and yet well known; as dying, and behold, we live; as chastened, and not killed; as sorrowful, yet always rejoicing; as poor, yet making many rich; as having nothing, and yet possessing all things" (2 Cor. 6.8–10). Let me assert that this is what it is to be called a Christian—this, too, is Christianity.

What, then, is a Christian? A Christian is one in whose life there is a blending of paradoxes. What is Christianity? It is a life in which a mysterious spiritual paradox is present, and this paradox is given us by God himself. Some people imagine there is no earthen vessel but only the treasure. Other people confess nothing can be done to the earthen vessel. Human thoughts about this will generally fall within these two extremes. Either there is only the treasure which constitutes the ideal good, or there is but the earthen vessel which makes all things hopeless. But what we see before God is both the treasure and the earthen vessel. It is neither the annihilation of the earthen vessel nor the hopelessness of the earthen vessel. Rather, it is the treasure in earthen vessels. . . .

### *The Power of God Is Manifested in the Weakness of Man (2 Cor. 12.7–10)*

The apostle mentions a thorn in his flesh. I do not know what this thorn is, but I do know that this thorn weakens Paul. And for this situation he beseeches the Lord three times, expecting the thorn to be removed. But the Lord, in response to Paul's appeal, says to him: "My grace is sufficient for thee" (2 Cor. 7.9a). What the Lord means to say to the apostle is, that though this thorn weakens you, Paul, My power is made perfect in your weakness. How is the power of the Lord made perfect in the weak? His power covers or overshadows our weakness. Let me tell you that this is what Christianity is all about. Christianity is neither the elimination of weakness nor the power of the Lord alone. It is the Lord's power manifested in man's weakness. Christ does not create on earth a new species of mysterious angels. Christianity in its basic definition is the power of God manifested in the weakness of man.

Let me use an illustration here. Once I was afflicted with a very serious illness. Within two months I had three X-rays taken, and all three reports were very bad. I prayed, I believed, I also expected God to heal me. A few times my strength was increased. But I confessed I was annoyed before God because though I felt well, the root of the sickness was still there. I could have a relapse at any time. Why did God treat me like this? What was the use of temporary strength? I was tired of my sickness. One day I read this chapter in 2 Corinthians which said Paul besought the Lord thrice to remove the thorn but the Lord refused to do so. Instead He offered a further measure of His grace: "My grace is sufficient for thee." Due to the presence of the thorn, the Lord increased grace. For the sake of weakness, the Lord increased power. I saw that this is true Christianity. As I lay in bed, I asked God to give me clearer understanding. Within me came a thought. Here I was on a boat that needed ten feet of water by which to sail through the river. But there was a boulder that jutted up five feet above the riverbed. I asked God if He would remove the boulder for me that the boat might pass through. But then a question from God arose in my heart: which was better, to remove the boulder or to raise the water five feet more? My answer to this question of God's was that it would be far better to raise the water level five more feet. I must confess that thereafter many of my problems were resolved. I dare not say that I am no longer tempted, but thank God, from this incident I discovered that the Lord is able to supply us with additional grace. And this is Christianity. May I state it clearly that Christianity is not the removal of the boulder but the raising of five feet more of water. Are there difficulties? We do have difficulties. Are there trials? We all do have trials. Are there weaknesses? Indeed, we all do have our weaknesses. Nonetheless, let us ever be mindful that what the Lord does today is neither, negatively, to remove our problems or weaknesses nor, positively, to add us strength. All His powers are manifested in weakness, for the treasure [which is the Lord himself in resurrection life] is hidden in earthen vessels. . . .

*Man's Weakness Cannot Limit God's Power*

Finally, let me say that no matter how weak man is, it cannot limit God's power. For this we must especially thank God. What do we actually think? Is it not that if there is sorrow, there can be no joy; if tears, there can be no praise; if weakness, no power; if pressed, then we are straitened; if smitten, then we are destroyed, and if there be doubt, we no longer have faith. Let me protest loudly that this is just not so. For God is causing us to realize that man is to be an earthen vessel for the treasure. Man is but an earthen vessel with the treasure inside. Nothing in man can bury the treasure of God. So let us not be in despair at times of apparent desperation. Though we ourselves can do nothing, let that which is positive within us take over. The treasure will shine even brighter, better and more glorious. . . . God's treasure is able to be manifested in any earthen vessel. This is a spiritual paradox which Christians hold dear. It is in this spiritual paradox that we live. And it is also there that we learn to know God.

–TEV 68-9, 69-70, 73

# 36 | The World

"The earth" is the scene of this crisis and its tremendous outcome, and "this world" is, we may say, its point of collision. That point we shall make the theme of our study, and we will begin by looking at the New Testament ideas associated with the important Greek word *kosmos*. In the English versions this word, is, with a single exception shortly to be noticed, invariably translated as "the world." (The other Greek workd *aion*, also so translated, embodies the idea of time and should more aptly be rendered "the age.")

It is worth sparing time for a look at a New Testament Greek Lexicon such as Grimm's. This will show how wide is the range of meaning that *kosmos* has in Scripture. But first of all we glance back to its origins in classical Greek where we find it originally implied two things: first *a harmonious order or arrangement*, and secondly *embellishment or adornment.* This latter idea appears in the New Testament verb *kosmeo*, used with the meaning "to adorn," as of the temple with goodly stones or of a bride for her husband (Luke 21.5; Rev. 21.2). In 1 Peter 3.3, the exception just alluded to, *kosmos* is itself translated "adorning" in keeping with this same verb *kosmeo* in verse 5.

(1) When we turn from the classics to the New Testament writers we find that their uses of *kosmos* fall into three main groups. It is used first with the sense of the *material universe, the round world, this earth.* For example, Acts 17.14, "the God that made the world and all things therein"; Matt. 13.35 (and elsewhere), "the foun-

dation of the world"; John 1.10, "he was in the world, and the world was made by him"; Mark 16.15, "Go ye into all the world."

(2) The second usage of *kosmos* is twofold. It is used (a) for *the inhabitants of the world* in such phrases as John 1.10, "the world knew him not"; 3.16, "God so loved the world"; 12.19, "the world is gone after him"; 17.21, "that the world may believe." (b) An extension of this usage leads to the idea of *the whole race of men alienated from God and thus hostile to the cause of Christ.* For instance, Heb. 11.38, "Of whom the world was not worthy"; John 14.17, "whom the world cannot receive"; 14.27, "not as the world giveth, give I unto you"; 15.18, "If the world hateth you . . . "

(3) In the third place we find *kosmos* is used in Scripture for *worldly affairs: the whole circle of wordly goods, endowments, riches, advantages, pleasures, which though hollow and fleeting, stir our desire and seduce us from God, so that they are obstacles to the cause of Christ.* Examples are: 1 John 2.15, "the things that are in the world"; 3.17, "the world's goods"; Matt. 16.26, "if he shall gain the whole world, and forfeit his life"; 1 Cor. 7.31, "those that use the world, as not abusing it." This usage of *kosmos* applies not only to material but also to abstract things which have spiritual and moral (or immoral) values. E.g., 1 Cor. 2.12, "the spirit of the world"; 3.19, "the wisdom of this world"; 7.31, "the fashion of this world"; Titus 2.12, "worldly (adj. *kosmikos*) lusts"; 2 Peter 1.4, "the corruption that is in the world"; 2.20, "the defilements of the world"; 1 John 2.16–17, "all that is in the world, the lust . . . the vainglory . . . passeth away." The Christian is "to keep himself unspotted from the world" (James 1.27).

The Bible student will soon discover that, as the above paragraphs suggest, *kosmos,* is a favorite word of the apostle John, and it is he, in the main, who helps us forward now to a further conclusion.a

While it is true that these three definitions of "the world," as (1) the material earth or universe, (2) the people of the earth, and (3) the things of the earth, each contribute something to the whole picture, it will already be apparent that behind them all is something more. The classical idea of *orderly arrangement or organization* helps us to grasp what this is. Behind all that is tangible we meet something intangible, we meet a planned system; and in this system there is harmonious functioning, a perfect order.

Concerning this system there are two things to be emphasized. First, since the day when Adam opened the door for evil to enter God's creation, *the world order has shown itself to be hostile to God.* The world "knew not God" (1 Cor. 1.21), "hated" Christ (John 15.18) and "cannot receive" the Spirit of truth (14.17). "Its works are evil" (John 7.7) and "the friendship of the world is enmity with God" (James 4.4). Hence Jesus says, "My kingdom is not of this world" (John 18.36). He has "overcome the world" (16.33) and "the victory that hath overcome the world" is "our faith" in Him (1 John 5.4). For, as the verse of John 12 that heads this study affirms, the world is under judgment. God's attitude to it is uncompromising.

This is because, secondly, as the same verse makes clear, *there is a mind behind the system.* John writes repeatedly of "the prince of this world" (12.31; 14.30; 16.11). In his Epistle he describes him as "he that is in the world" (1 John 4.4) and matches against him the Spirit of truth who indwells believers. "The whole world," John says, "lieth in the evil one" (5.19). He is the rebellious *kosmokrator,* world ruler—a word which, however, appears only once, used in the plural of his lieutenants, the "world rulers of this darkness" (Eph. 6.12).

There is, then, an ordered system, "the world," which is governed from behind the scenes by a ruler, Satan. When in John 12.31 Jesus states that the sentence of judgment has been passed upon this world he does not mean that the material world or its inhabitants are judged. For them judgment is yet to come. What is there judged is that institution, that harmonious world order of which Satan himself is the originator and head. And ultimately, as Jesus' words make clear, it is he, "the prince of the world," who has been judged (16.11) and who is to be dethroned and "cast out" forever. . . .

Formerly we spoke much of sin and of the natural life. We

could readily see the spiritual issues there, but we little realized then what equally great spiritual issues are at stake when we touch the world. There is a spiritual force behind this world scene which, by means of "the things that are in the world," is seeking to enmesh men in its system. It is not merely against sin therefore that the saints of God need to be on their guard, but against the ruler of this world. God is building up His Church to its consummation in the universal reign of Christ. Simultaneously his rival is building up this world system to its vain climax in the reign of Antichrist. How watchful we need to be lest at any time we be found helping Satan in the construction of that ill-fated kingdom. When we are faced with alternatives and a choice of ways confronts us, the question is not: Is this good or evil? Is this helpful or hurtful? No, the question we must ask ourselves is: *Is it of this world, or of God?* For since there is only this one conflict in the universe, then whenever two conflicting courses lie open to us, the choice at issue is never a lesser one than: God . . . or Satan? . . .

Most of us would agree that to the apostle Paul was given a special revelation of the Church of God. In a similar way we feel that God gave to John a special understanding of the nature of the world. *Kosmos* is in fact peculiarly John's word. The other Gospels use it only fifteen times (Matthew nine, Mark and Luke three each) while Paul has it forty-seven times in eight letters. But John uses it 105 times in all, seventy-eight in his Gospel, twenty-four in his epistles and a further three in the Revelation.

In his first epistle John writes: "All that is in the world, the lust of the flesh, and the lust of the eyes, and the vainglory of life, is not of the Father, but is of the world" (2.16). In these words that so clearly reflect the temptation of Eve (Gen. 3.6) John defines the things of the world. All that can be included under lust or primitive desire, all that excites greedy ambition, and all that arouses in us the pride or glamor of life, all such things are part of the Satanic system. Perhaps we scarcely need stay here to consider further the first two of these, but let us look for a moment at the third. Everything that stirs pride in us is of the world. Prominence, wealth, achievement, these the world acclaims. Men are justly proud of success. Yet John labels all that brings this sense of success as "of the world."

Every success therefore that we experience (and I am not suggesting that we should be failures!) calls in us for an instant, humble confession of its inherent sinfulness, for whenever we meet success we have in some degree touched the world system. Whenever we sense complacency over some achievement we may know at once that we have touched the world. We may know, too, that we have brought ourselves under the judgment of God, for have we not already agreed that the whole world is under judgment? Now (and let us try to grasp this fact) those who realize this and confess their need are thereby safeguarded. . . .

Our deliverance from the world begins, not with our giving up this or that but with our seeing, as with God's eyes, that it is a world under sentence of death as in the figure with which we opened this chapter, "Fallen, fallen is Babylon the great!" (Rev. 18.2). Now a sentence of death is always passed, not on the dead but on the living. And in one sense the world is a living force today, relentlessly pursuing and seeking out its subjects. But while it is true that when sentence is pronounced death lies still in the future, it is nevertheless certain. A person under sentence of death *has* no future beyond the confines of a condemned cell. Likewise the world, being under sentence, has no future. The world system has not yet been "wound up," as we say, and terminated by God, but the winding up is a settled matter. It makes all the difference to us that we *see* this. Some folk seek deliverance from the world in asceticism, and like the Baptist, neither eat nor drink. That today is Buddhism, not Christianity. As Christians we both eat and drink, but we do so in the realization that eating and drinking belong to the world and, with it, are under the death sentence, so they have no grip upon us. . . .

At the end of his letter to the Galatians Paul states this very clearly. "Far be it from me to glory, save in the cross of our Lord Jesus Christ, through which the world hath been crucified unto me, and I unto the world" (6.14). Have you noticed something striking about this verse? In relation to the world it speaks of the two aspects of the work of the Cross already hinted at in our last chapter. "I have been crucified unto the world" is a statement which we find fairly easy to fit into our understanding of being crucified with Christ as defined in such passages as Romans 6. But here it specifically says too that "the world has been crucified to me." When God comes to you and me with the revelation of the finished work of Christ, He not only shows us ourselves there on the Cross. He shows us our world there too. If you and I cannot escape the judgment of the Cross, then neither can the world escape the judgment of the Cross. Have I really seen this? That is the question. When I see it, then I do not try to repudiate a world I love; I see that the Cross *has* repudiated it. I do not try to escape a world that clings to me; I see that by the Cross I *have* escaped. . . .

Far from seeking to avoid the world we need to see how privileged we are to have been placed there by God. "As thou didst send me into the world, even so send I them into the world." What a statement! The Church is Jesus' successor, a divine settlement planted here right in the midst of Satan's territory. It is something that Satan cannot abide, any more than he could abide Jesus himself, and yet it is something that he cannot by any means rid himself of. It is a colony of heaven, an alien intrusion on his territory, and one against which he is utterly powerless. "Children of God," Paul calls us, "in the midst of a crooked and perverse generation, among whom ye are seen as lights in the world" (Phil. 2.15). God has deliberately placed us in the *kosmos* to show it up for what it is. We are to expose to the divine light, for all men to see them, its God-defying rebelliousness on the one hand and its hollowness and emptiness on the other.

And our task does not stop there. We are to proclaim to men the good news that, if they will turn to it, that light of God in the face of Jesus Christ will set them free from the world's vain emptiness into the fullness that is His. It is this twofold mission of the Church that accounts for Satan's hatred. There is nothing that goads him so much as the Church's presence in the world. Nothing would please him more than to see its telltale light removed. The Church is a thorn in the side of God's adversary, a constant source of irritation and annoyance to him. We make a heap of trouble for Satan simply by *being* in the world. So why leave it?

"Go ye into all the world and preach the gospel" (Mark 16.15). This is the Christian's privilege. It is also his duty. Those who try to opt out of the world only demonstrate that they are still in some degree in bondage to its ways of thinking. We who are "not of it" have no reason at all to try to leave it, for *it is where we should be.*

So there is no need for us to give up our secular employments. Far from it, for they are our mission field. In this matter there are no secular considerations, only spiritual ones. We do not live our lives in separate compartments, as Christians in the Church and as secular beings the rest of the time. There is not a thing in our profession or in our employment that God intends should be dissociated from our life as His children. Everything we do, be it in field or highway, in shop, factory, kitchen, hospital or school, has spiritual value in terms of the kingdom of Christ. Everything is to be claimed for Him. Satan would much prefer to have no Christians in any of these places, for they are decidedly in his way there. He tries therefore to frighten us out of the world, and if he cannot do that, to get us involved in his world system, thinking in its terms, regulating our behavior by its standards. Either would be a triumph for him. But for us to be in the world, yet with all our hopes, all our interests and all our prospects out of the world, that is Satan's defeat and God's glory.

Of Jesus' presence in the world it is written that "the darkness overcame it not" (John 1.5 margin). Nowhere in Scripture does it tell us of sin that we are to "overcome" it, but it distinctly says we are to overcome the world. In relation to sin God's word speaks only of deliverance; it is in relation to the world that it speaks of victory.

We need deliverance from sin, because God never intended we should have any touch with it; but we do not need, nor should we seek, deliverance from the world, for it is in the purpose of God that we touch it. We are not delivered out of the world, but being born from above, we have victory over it. And we have that victory in the same sense, and with the same unfailing certainty, that light overcame darkness.

"This is the victory that hath overcome the world, even our faith. And who is he that overcometh the world, but he that believeth that Jesus is the Son of God?" (1 John 5.4–5). The key to victory is always our faith relationship with the victorious Son. "Be of good cheer," he said. "I have overcome the world" (John 16.33). Only Jesus could make such a claim; and He could do so because he could earlier affirm: "The prince of the world . . . hath nothing in me" (John 14.30). It was the first time that anyone on earth had said such a thing. He said it, and he overcame. And through His overcoming the prince of the world was cast out and Jesus began to draw men to himself.

And because He said it, we now dare say it too. Because of my new birth, because "whatsoever is begotten of God overcometh the world," I can be in the same world as my Lord was in, and in the same sense as He was I can be utterly apart from it, a lamp set on a lampstand, giving light to all who enter the house. "As he is, so are we in this world" (1 John 4.17). The Church glorifies God, not by getting out of the world but by radiating His light in it. Heaven is not the place to glorify God; it will be the place to praise Him. The place to glorify Him is here. . . .

"Take heed to yourselves, lest haply your hearts be overcharged with surfeiting, and drunkenness, and cares of this life, and that day come on you suddenly as a snare" (Luke 21.34). Note the term "life" in Jesus' words. In the Greek New Testament three words are commonly used for life: *zoe*, spiritual life; *psuche*, psychological life; and *bios*, biological life. The last is the word used here, appearing in its adjectival form, *biotikos*, "of this life." The Lord is warning us to beware lest we be unduly pressed with this life's cares, that is to say, with anxieties regarding quite ordinary matters such as food and dress which belong to our present existence on the earth. It was over just such a simple thing that Adam and Eve fell, and it will be due to just such simple matters that some Christians may overlook the heavenward call of God. For it is always a matter of where the heart is. We are exhorted not to let our hearts be "overcharged" or "laden" with these things to our loss. That is to say, we are not to carry a burden regarding them that would weigh us down. We are to be in a true sense detached in spirit from our goods in the house or in the field (Luke 17.31).

For let us realize who we are! We are the Church, the light of the world shining amid the darkness. As such let us live our lives down here. . . .

Every time you and I touch the world through the things of the world—and we must do so repeatedly—we should feel much as we would feel about taking morphine, for there are demons at the back of everything that belongs to the world. Just as I may, if seriously ill, be prescribed opium as a treatment, so also, because I am still in the world, I have to do business with the world, follow some trade or employment, earn my livelihood. But how much treatment with dangerous drugs I can safely take without falling a prey to the opium craving I do not know; and how many things I can buy, or how much money I can make, or how close can be my business or professional associations, without my becoming hooked, I likewise do not know. All I know is that there is a Satanic power behind every worldly thing. How vital therefore for every Christian to have a clear revelation of the spirit of the world in order to appreciate how real is the danger to which he is continually exposed! . . .

So a serious problem faces us here. As we have said, presumably there must be a limit. Presumably God has drawn somewhere a line of demarcation. Stay within the bounds of that line and we will be safe; cross it and grave danger threatens. But where does it lie? We have to eat and drink, to marry and bring up children, to trade and to toil. How do we do so and yet remain uncontaminated? How do we mingle freely with the men and women whom God so loved as to give His Son for them, and still keep ourselves unspotted from the world?

If our Lord had limited our buying and selling to so much a month, how simple that would be! The rules would be plain for any to follow. All who spent more than a certain amount per month would be worldly Christians, and all who spent less than that amount would be unworldly.

But since our Lord has stipulated no figure, we are cast on Him unceasingly. For what? I think the answer is very wonderful. Not to be tied by the rules, but that we may remain all the time within bounds of another kind: the bounds of His life. If our Lord had given us a set of rules and regulations to observe, then we could take great care to abide by these. In fact, however, our task is something far more simple and straightforward, namely, to abide in the Lord himself. Then we could keep the law. Now we need only keep in fellowship with Him. And the joy of it is that, provided we live in close touch with God, His Holy Spirit within our hearts will always tell us when we reach the limit! . . .

In any given instance there must be safe limits known to God beyond which we should not go. They are not marked out on the ground for us to see, but one thing is certain: He who is the Comforter will surely know them, even if perhaps Satan knows them too. Can we not trust Him? If at some point we are about to overstep them, can we not depend on Him at once to make us inwardly aware of the fact? . . .

Here at once it must be said that such a paradoxical life is a life that none but Christians *can* live. Perhaps the expression "as not having" affords us a clue. It reveals that the matter is an inner matter, a question of the heart's loyalty. In Christ there is an inner liberation to God, not merely an outward change of conduct. They have, and having, they rejoice in Ephesians 5; but they are not bound by what they possess, so that having not, they equally rejoice in 1 Corinthians 7. Notwithstanding all they "have," they are so truly delivered in spirit from the world's possessiveness that they can live "as not having" [see 1 Cor. 7.29ff.]. . . .

The essence of the world is money. Whenever you touch money you touch the world. The question arises, How can we take a thing which we know assuredly to be of the world, and yet not become involved with the world system? How can we handle and do business with money, that most worldly of worldly things, and not, in doing so, become implicated with Satan? Still more to the point, since nothing can be done today without paying for it, how is it possible for us to take money, that thing which is a supreme factor in building up the kingdom of Antichrist, and use it to build up the kingdom of Christ?

The widow who dropped her mite into the temple treasury did something so acceptable to the Lord that she received from Him special commendation. What in fact she did was just this: she took something out of the kingdom of Satan and contributed it to the kingdom of God. And Jesus approved. So how, let us ask ourselves, is such a transfer made? How is it possible to take money, which in its character is essentially unrighteous, and with it build up the kingdom of God? How can you make sure that all connection between the world and the money in your pocket has been severed? Do you dare to say that none of the money in your possession figures in Satan's books? . . .

Thus it is no easy matter to transfer money from the realm of Satan to the realm of God; it involves travail. To convert souls from Satan to God is in fact easier than to convert money from Satan to God. By the grace of God men and women may be won to Him whether or not we ourselves are devoted in any utter sense;

but this is not so with money. It takes great spiritual power to convert our shekels, which in their character are evil, into shekels of the sanctuary. Money needs converting as truly as men need converting; and the money can, I believe, be made anew (if in a rather different sense) as truly as souls can be made anew. But your bringing of an offering of money to the treasury will not in itself change the character of the money you offer. Unless your life goes out with your money it cannot be released from the kingdom of Satan and transferred to the kingdom of God. The spiritual value of your work for God will largely depend on whether or not the money you handle has been delivered from the world system. I ask you, Has it? Can you claim that there is no money in your hand that belongs to the world? Are you able to say now that your money is no longer a part of the *kosmos,* for it has all been converted? Are you willing to tell God: "I will convert all the money I earn by labor, and all the money I receive by gifts, that it all may be thine"? . . .

Here, then, is a vital question for each one of us to answer: Does the money I am touching today represent shekels of the sanctuary or the mammon of unrighteousness? Whenever I receive a dollar, or whenever I earn a dollar, let me make sure that that dollar is instantly converted from world currency into the currency of the sanctuary. Money can be our destruction, but money can also be our protection. Do not despise money; its value is too real for that. It can be of great account to the Lord. If you yourself come heart and soul out of the world, then you can, if God so wills it, bring many precious things out of the world with you. When the Israelites came out of Egypt they brought away much treasure with them. They spoiled the Egyptians, and the spoil they carried away with them went to construct the Tabernacle. Some too, we recall, went to construct a golden calf and was lost to God. But when God's people left Egypt the Tabernacle, at least in its materials, left Egypt with them. Egyptian gold, silver, copper, linen—all was converted and contributed to the sanctuary of God.

If you can find that reality in Old Testament times, how much higher still must be the standard set in the New! The New Testament key to all finance is that we hold nothing to ourselves. "Give, and it shall be given unto you," those were our Lord's words (Luke 6.38) and not, "Save and ye shall grow rich"! That is to say, the principle of divine increase is giving, not storage. God requires of every one of us proportionate and not just random giving. He desires, that is to say, giving that is not subject merely to the whim of the moment but that is the fruit of a definite covenant reached with him about the matter—and stuck to.

—LNW 10–4, 19–20, 49–55, 71–4, 80–1, 98–103, 119–24

Nonetheless, we must remember that to be redeemed by the blood is to be delivered from the world. Once redeemed, instantly we become pilgrims and sojourners on earth. This does not imply that we no longer live on earth; it simply means we are instantaneously separated from the world. Wherever there is redemption, there is separation. The blood divides the living and the dead; the blood separates God's children from the people of the world. The redeemed are no longer permanent residents of this world. . . .

We Christians must come out of the world as a system. To be separated from the world means to be separated from this world system in its moral connotation. It does not imply leaving the world as a place.

D. M. Panton has a well-spoken word concerning our walk in the wilderness. He says: in life, it is a way; in death, it is a tomb. No one can remain in this world too long, for it is only a way. It also serves as a grave when one dies. This should be our attitude towards the world. Every believer must be separated. In the eyes of the people of this world, we are but strangers and sojourners in the wilderness; they alone are the permanent residents of the world. .

### *Things Which the World Considers Unworthy of a Christian*

We must be separated from anything the world considers unworthy of a Christian. We start our Christian life before the world and the world sets up certain standards for Christians. If we cannot measure up to their standards, where will our testimony be? Of the things which we do, we should never permit non-believers to raise their eyebrows saying, "Do Christians do such things too?" Under such an accusation, our testimony before them is finished. . . .

### *Things Which Are Inconsistent to Our Relationship with the Lord*

Anything which is inconsistent to our relationship with the Lord must be rejected. Our Lord was humiliated on earth; can we seek for glory? He was crucified as a robber; can we court the favor of this world? He was slandered as possessed of a demon; can we look for praise from men that we are most clever and rational? Such conditions reveal the inconsistency of our relationship with the Lord. They make us different from the Lord, even contrary to Him. All the ways which He has gone we also must walk through. For this cause we must eradicate everything that is inconsistent to our relationship with the Lord. . .

### *Things Which Quench Spiritual Life*

Again we ask, "What is the world?" Each and everything which tends to quench our spiritual life before the Lord is the world. How impossible it is to tell new believers what things are permissible and what things are not permissible. If we tell them ten things, they have the eleventh thing to ask. But if they understand but one principle, they can apply it to numberless things. Whatsoever thing makes you lose zeal for prayer or for Bible reading or causes you to lose courage to testify is the world.

The world creates a kind of atmosphere which cools our love

to the Lord. It withers our spiritual life; it chills our zeal; it freezes our longing for God. Hence it must be rejected. . . .

*Social Affairs Which Hinder the Testimony*

Another thing to be mentioned is concerned with social relationships. Whatever social gatherings or feasts or good times together cause our lamp to be covered under a bushel are of the world. These should be rejected. How can Christians continue in social intercourse if they cannot confess that they are the Lord's and if they have to pretend to be polite by listening to and smiling with unbelievers? How can we suppress our inward feeling and put on a smiling face? How can we inwardly sense the world, yet show sympathy outwardly? How can we judge anything sinful, if we externally agree with it? Many of God's children have been gradually drawn back into the world because they failed to differentiate in their social life. . . .

*Things Which Weak Believers Condemn*

Whatever thing causes the conscience of weak believers to stumble is to be taken as the world. At the outset we mentioned things condemned by the world as unworthy of Christians; now we speak of things condemned by feeble Christians. Notice these are not things disapproved of by strong Christians; rather they are reprehended by weak Christians. As a matter of fact, these weak believers may not be correct in their judgment. What they disapprove of may be quite all right. Yet they have a weak conscience just as once we did. How can I stumble them in the things which they consider wrong? I must walk before them as without any offense. "All things are lawful for me; but not all things are expedient" (1 Cor. 6.12), says Paul. All things are lawful, for from our standpoint these things are not of the world; but to feeble Christians they are things of the world. Consequently, we must for their sake refrain from them.

—GC 19, 21–2, 24, 25–6, 28–9, 29–30, 30–1

# 37 Kingdom

The message John preached was as follows: "Repent ye; for the kingdom of the heavens is at hand" (original). Here, the word for "heaven" in the Greek is plural in number. This is therefore the kingdom of the heavens. This kingdom is wholly of God, and all the heavens participate in this kingdom. In the Gospel according to Matthew, this term "the kingdom of the heavens" is used thirty-three times. In the Old Testament, it is never used; nor is it used in other books of the New Testament, though there are similar ideas being conveyed. Consequently, this term "the kingdom of the heavens" occupies a special place here in Matthew.

What does "the kingdom of the heavens" mean? In Genesis 1.1 we read that "God created the heavens and the earth." The heavens and the earth belong to God. This is worthy of all attention. The heavens (in plural number) and the earth are God's. In Genesis 14.19–22 we read that God is the "possessor of heavens and earth" (Hebrew original). From Genesis to Chronicles, God's title is either "the Lord of the heavens and earth" or "the God of the heavens and earth." It was a title which men used at that time to address God. Why? Because up through the time of 2 Chronicles, God had a kingdom upon the earth (though never perfect). God had His chosen people. Hence He was not only the God of the heavens but also the God of the earth. But by the time of Ezra 1.2, His title was changed to "the God of heaven" because the nation of Israel had been destroyed and God had no habitation on earth any longer. He had no kingdom and no people on earth. So that He was thereafter called simply "the God of heaven." This was a noticeable change. It was ever afterwards used continuously by the prophets in exile (for example, see also Neh. 2.4,20). This was a Biblical fact.

In the New Testament we find that the term, "the kingdom of the heavens," suddenly makes its appearance. It cannot be found in the Old Testament, yet this is a continuation of the authority of the heavens spoken about in the Old Testament. Its scope is broader than the nation of Israel, and its nature is more heavenly and more of God. Daniel 2.44 is the only place in the Old Testament where the kingdom established by the God of the heavens is mentioned. It is a prophecy concerning this kingdom of the heavens. In the so-called Lord's Prayer, heavens and earth are mentioned together ("Thy kingdom come. Thy will be done, as in heaven, so on earth"—Matt. 6.10). This means God will regain the control of the earth. The kingdom of the heavens will come upon this earth, and the will of God shall prevail over it. At present God's will is done in the heavens, but it is hindered upon the earth.

The kingdom of the heavens means only one thing: the authority of the heavens shall be manifested on the earth. Do not view the kingdom of the heavens as mere history. For the fundamental aim of God is to gain this earth as He has gained in the heavens. Thus, disobedience becomes the greatest sin. In the Old Testament period, obedience was viewed as the most beautiful virtue. It far surpassed sacrifice (see 1 Sam. 15.22). It alone could bring the kingdom of God down to earth. Regardless how much you labor and toil, you are still a great failure if you do not obey in your heart. For the authority of the heavens is seen in our obedience, not in our works or sufferings or sacrifice. Man's rebellion may be manifested in disobeying God as well as in sinning. Wherever the authority of God is not, there the kingdom of God is absent.

Now John the Baptist came and proclaimed that "the kingdom of the heavens is at hand." This would clearly imply that God had not had His kingdom of the heavens during the Old Testament period. The Baptist declared it was near because in his words that were to follow, he also affirmed that the King was here. What did John the Baptist preach? And how should people get prepared for the kingdom of the heavens? There was nothing profound about it. It was simply to "repent." "Repent" means a change of mind. In the Greek the word speaks not of action but of an altogether different matter. This repentance is related to the baptism of John (the baptism of repentance is different from the baptism unto Christ). What does the baptism of repentance mean? John baptized in the river Jordan which signified death. In John's baptism, therefore, the children of Israel were put to death in Jordan.

Repentance is not linked to Christ, nor does the baptism of repentance join us to Christ. It merely indicates a change in our opinion concerning ourselves. The baptism is unto death. It declares that men ought to die. In receiving baptism, men confess their sins and acknowledge that the wages of sin is death. So that when the people came to John, they in essence confessed that they deserved death. If a person has not changed his thought and opinion about himself, he has not repented. Only by voluntarily taking the place of death and burial is repentance proven.

The kingdom of the heavens begins with John. Its first lesson—that of repentance—must be learned. May we learn the deeper lesson of the cross. May we by the grace of God review this lesson of repentance that we may have a new assessment of ourselves, reckoning ourselves as sinful and dead. . . .

We now need to move on to other considerations in this introductory section. First of all, we need to examine what exactly is the kingdom of the heavens as presented in the Sermon on the Mount. What is it in the Old Testament? What is it in Matthew 5–7 and what is it in Matthew 13? The kingdom of the heavens in chapters 5–7 seems to be very different from that in chapter 13. In the former, the kingdom of the heavens is crystal clear; but in the latter, it is extremely mixed. This constitutes a problem to many students of the Scriptures.

In the Old Testament—in Daniel 2.44 and 7.13-14—it makes clear that the heavens shall rule. The other prophets, such as Zechariah, Isaiah and David, also declare that God will set up a kingdom. The principal people of the kingdom will be the children of Israel; but there will also be those of the (sheep) nations (see Matt. 25.31ff.). All shall actually know Jehovah and worship God. Not only mankind will be blessed, even the beasts and other animals will be, too. This is the kingdom as prophesied in the Old Testament. It is clear that the kingdom of heaven spoken of in the Old Testament is not associated with the dispensation of the Church, nor is it the heaven or the New Jerusalem that Christians look forward to. So that it is neither for today's Christians nor is it the future heaven. It is another dispensation.

In the New Testament period our Lord succeeds John in declaring that "the kingdom of the heavens is at hand." What is the kingdom of the heavens? Matthew 3 indicates that John the Baptist proclaimed that "the kingdom of the heavens is at hand." Chapter 4 records that the Lord announces the same thing. By the time of chapter 5 the kingdom of the heavens has come. Yes, indeed, by the time of chapters 5-7, the kingdom has really come. Now the kingdom as prophesied in the Old Testament relates to the *environment* on earth in the future days. The kingdom as spoken of by the Lord and found in Matthew 5-7 refers to the *men* of the kingdom of the heavens who shall rule therein. And the kingdom spoken of in Matthew 13 applies to the *history* of the kingdom. All three point to the kingdom. A certain company of men come into being. Without them, this kingdom would never arrive. Thus the teaching in the Mount tells us what kind of persons these men are to be.

What the Lord therefore focuses on here is not environment, but people. Hence He subsequently said to Peter, "I will give unto thee the keys of the kingdom of heaven" (Matt. 16.19)—keys by which to open the door of the kingdom of the heavens, yet not to let out its environmental conditions but to let in the people. And we see later that the door was verily opened on the day of Pentecost, at which time the Jews came in. Furthermore, it was opened a second time at the house of Cornelius, with the Gentiles also being able to enter in. Moreover, in having cast out a demon, the Lord had declared: "then is the kingdom of God come upon you" (Matt. 12.28). So that where the Lord is, there is the kingdom of God. But Matthew 5–7 tells us that where a certain company of believers is, there, too, is the kingdom of the heavens. Wherever and whenever the believers become like the men described in the teaching on the Mount, there comes the kingdom of the heavens.

Let us not pay so much attention to the matter of environment that might induce us to think that the kingdom of the heavens will not have come until the right environment is present; for let us please understand that the kingdom represented by men is far more important than that signified by any kind of environment. It can consequently be stated that Matthew 5–7 informs us that when a very special and new company of believers comes into being, then and there the kingdom is present.

Matthew 13, on the other hand, speaks of another aspect of the kingdom. The seven parables therein show us what the kingdom is like. That is to say, when the kingdom of the heavens is preached on earth, these show us what are the *historical courses* it takes. It is very much the kingdom that is in view; only, it is its outward appearance. It is the Christianity that the world sees, the outward appearance of Christianity in this age.

Why does the Lord mention these lofty and deep standards to be found in Matthew 5–7? At the commencement of the teaching on the Mount, the emphasis is on what has already been alluded to above; namely, a certain company of persons whom the Lord is seeking to gain. The first seven beatitudes say "they" (persons); the last two use the word "ye." All such persons of the kingdom of the heavens possess certain dispositions. This in itself would indicate a difference between grace and law. (I personally do not like the fashion of some who label Matthew 5–7 as "the *law* of the kingdom of the heavens.") What is law? See Romans 5.20 and 6.14: "the law came in besides, that the trespass might abound; but where sin abounded, grace did abound more exceedingly"; "sin shall not have dominion over you: for ye are not under law, but under grace." The law is like trying to kindle fire in the water or like seeking gold in sand. The more you are incapable of doing, the more you are required to do. This is the law as given in the Scriptures. The law that the world speaks of is command. Yet the law of the Scriptures is not given to us to be kept, but given to us to be broken, that the inability of our natural self might be exposed and sin might be magnified.

How different, though, is the teaching on the Mount. The Son of God has come. He died, was buried and was resurrected. The Holy Spirit came upon Him as noted in Matthew 3. All His works subsequently done on earth are done on the ground of resurrection and the coming of the Holy Spirit. Although He was yet to die and to be resurrected and the Holy Spirit was yet to come on Pentecost, He has nonetheless already stood on such ground. (People who believe on Jesus as told of in John 3 have eternal life because He has already received the baptism of death before God, even though He has yet to die historically.) From God's viewpoint, the Lord has already stood on the ground of death, for He must indeed be baptized unto death to self in order to enter into His work for God. Now He has the Holy Spirit in Him and upon Him. And He now dares to give us—in the teaching on the Mount—such manner of strict command. For the heavier the demand, the greater the response of the divine life within. The life that our Lord has given us is inexhaustible. It is nothing surprising when we endure beyond our own endurance. God's demand never ends; it increases all the time; and yet the life within always carries us through. Therefore, whoever speaks of the Sermon on the Mount as constituting law knows nothing about either law or life. (Let us realize that a life lived according to the teaching on the Mount is a life lived under *grace,* not under *law.*)

Let us not despise the testing of the Lord. For through testing, the life within us is manifested. The greater the demands of God are upon this divine life, the greater is the manifestation of what is in this life. It is God who commands, but it is also God, by

His divine life within us, who keeps the commandment. God himself fulfills what He demands. And hence, the teaching of the Sermon on the Mount is not law. (What is given on Mount Sinai is indeed law, because it is something which we are not able to do.) When we believers go ahead to follow the teaching on the Mount found in Matthew 5–7, we unconsciously fulfill it. The impossibles become possibles. And precisely this is what it is to be a Christian, the daily showing forth of what is impossible in oneself. For this reason, Romans 6.14 says that this which we have in Matthew 5–7 is what is truly under grace: it is God who enables me to do what He commands, for I am no longer under the domination of sin nor under the law.

The teaching on the Mount creates for this world many individuals whom this world is not worthy to have. It is not enough for these persons just to have life. There also needs to be a demand upon this life; otherwise, this divine life will not be manifested. This life is able to meet every one of the challenges of the teaching on the Mount! Without such demand, the exceedingly great power of the Lord in us may not be expressed. But when there is this demand, and that demand is met in the lives of men, *then* there is truly Christianity. On the one hand there is testing, on the other hand there is the supply of Christ. And when both are present, there is Christianity, there is the kingdom of the heavens.

The Lord is out to get a company of men who will obtain and enjoy now the environment of the future kingdom. (The Greek word translated as "a people" in Acts 15.14 may also be rendered as "men.") This is the time that God is choosing men. What kind of men are they to be? Men according to Matthew 5–7. With respect to such men as these, they are now the kingdom; and in the future, they will reign in the kingdom to come. . . .

In the Scriptures the kingdom of the heavens is concurrently historical and geographical. The mistake of past Bible commentators has been to treat the kingdom of the heavens as purely historical. But today the course of history is less determinative in this matter of what the kingdom is than is geography. "If I by the Spirit of God cast out demons," declares the Lord Jesus, "then is the kingdom of God come upon you" (Matt. 12.28). This statement is geographical, not historical, in content. Wherever the Lord casts out demons, *there* is the kingdom of God. So that today it is more a matter of geography than of history.

—IM 28-30, 63-7, 103

There is a basic argument that can be given as to why the kingdom of heaven and the Messianic kingdom are greatly different: In Matthew 13.11 it is said that the kingdom of heaven is a mystery which was unknown by men but is now being revealed; moreover, 13.35 goes on to say about this kingdom that there are "utter[ed] things hidden from the foundation of the world"—all this showing that before its revelation no one knew anything about it. The Messianic kingdom, on the other hand, was known to Balaam, Isaiah, David, and the other prophets.

When does the kingdom of heaven begin? It begins with the sowing of wheat seed (Matt. 13.3), and thus the kingdom of heaven is parallel to this dispensation.

The passage found in Matthew 16.13-19 tells us that the Lord Jesus will build His church "upon this rock"—that is to say, upon the confession of Peter with respect to Him. In this same passage, "keys" in the phrase "the keys of the kingdom of heaven" is plural in number, and they are obviously used to open doors. Peter used these keys to open doors both on the day of Pentecost and in the house of Cornelius so as to bring in both the Jews and the Gentiles. And hence it can rightly be said that the church begins simultaneously with the kingdom of heaven.

The church is the believers' position, whereas the kingdom of heaven is their responsibility. The contrast between the two can be simply outlined as follows:

| *The Church* | *The Kingdom of Heaven* |
| --- | --- |
| Related to the Lord | Related to men |
| Pertains to the giving of life | Pertains to the receiving of disciples |
| Speaks of position and grace | Speaks of responsibility |

The word "heaven" is plural in the original. It is really "the kingdom of the heavens" in the verse. Why is it the kingdom of the heavens (plural), and not the kingdom of heaven (singular)? Let us see that when the word "heaven" is mentioned, people most often think of it in terms of location—that is to say, in heaven as a place; but "the kingdom of the heavens" is a phrase that conjures up the thought of authority and dominion, as for example when Daniel once declared that "the heavens do rule" (4.26). For we must note that before Christ died, and Satan being in the air, there never was any kingdom on earth that was under the rule of the heavens. The kingdom that is now being brought in by God is alone distinct from all the kingdoms on earth, in that it is a spiritual kingdom capable of communing with God. . . .

What is the "kingdom"? It points on the one hand to a spiritual state, such as is indicated in this statement: "The kingdom of God is not eating and drinking, but righteousness and peace and joy in the Holy Spirit" (Rom. 14.17); it points on the other hand to the future reign during the millennium. In the parable of the ten pounds (Luke 19.11–27), the idea of the kingdom includes both the spiritual living today and the future reward. Today's spiritual condition decides the reigning in the future. The "kingdom" to be sought here in Matthew 6 stresses a present spiritual condition, but even more so in the future.

The "righteousness" spoken of here is to be attained through seeking; thus it cannot have reference to justification or to the righteousness of God as is presented in the book of Romans. The righteousness in Matthew 5–7 exceeds the righteousness of the scribes and Pharisees. It is the righteousness specified in Matthew 6.1. Hence it denotes especially the Christian conduct presented in Matthew 5–7.

"Added" here means something given in addition to what you have already. Because you seek God's kingdom and His righteousness, you gain His kingdom and righteousness with a bonus of food and clothing. "To give" means there is nothing beforehand; "to add" means that something is already there. . . .

Let us review the things we have already seen previously concerning the kingdom of heaven. After the birth of Christ, there comes one who prepares the way for Him. His name is John, and he proclaims that the kingdom of heaven is at hand. The Lord, together with the apostles whom He sends forth, announce the same news. What does it mean? Later on, as noted in chapters 8 and 9, we see that the Lord heals the sick and casts out demons, and that all these are closely related to the nearness of the kingdom of heaven. Matthew 5–7 speaks of the nature of the kingdom of heaven: which is, that those who belong to this kingdom are absolutely righteous towards themselves, absolutely gracious towards others, and absolutely pure towards God. In Matthew 10 we learn that the Lord sends out His apostles. And in Matthew 11–12 we see that a great transition begins occurring, as though the kingdom of heaven is now being taken away from the Jews.

Now with regard to the kingdom of heaven found spoken of in Matthew 13, some interpreters have asserted that the mysteries of the kingdom of heaven are the kingdom of heaven in mystery. Such an assertion is logically unsound when it is held up against all the things which we have just seen: how that both John and the Lord as well as His disciples proclaim that the kingdom of heaven is at hand, how that the Lord then announces the nature or character of this kingdom, and how after He is rejected by the children of Israel He in the thirteenth chapter is found declaring only the outward boundary of this kingdom (what we see in this age being but the outward appearance). So that chapter 13 does not deal with the character or nature of the kingdom of heaven, for this has already been described in Matthew 5–7.

Some, on the other hand, contend that all who desire to enter the kingdom of heaven mentioned in chapter 13 must possess the character of the kingdom of heaven as laid down in chapters 5–7. This interpretation again is impossible to accept, since in chapter 13 we have presented the tares, the leaven, and so forth as being in the kingdom of heaven. So that this chapter presents to us nothing but the outward appearance of the kingdom of heaven.

The kingdom of heaven is not the millennial kingdom; it is the *reigning in* the millennial kingdom. Let us see that the kingdom of heaven has three different aspects.

(1) an outward appearance, boundary, or scope as is shown to us in Matthew 13;

(2) a spiritual reality, that is to say, a kind of spiritual conduct which is formed as a result of learning righteousness and grace progressively under the authority of God and which is elucidated for us in Matthew 5–7; and

(3) a reigning with Christ in the future millennial kingdom as revealed in the fact of our future reward as told to us in Matthew 5–7.

Accordingly, we must first of all enter into the sphere or boundary of this kingdom of heaven by being sons of the kingdom; then secondly, we need to have the kind of conduct described for us in Matthew 5–7—which is to have real spiritual conduct; and lastly, as a consequence we may reign with the Lord.

Today there are three different kinds of people:

(1) those who have entered within the sphere of the kingdom of heaven and yet are unsaved; these are represented by the tares.

(2) those who have been saved and are in the domain of the kingdom of heaven, yet they fail to keep the teaching of Matthew 5–7.

(3) those who are saved and also keep the teaching of Matthew 5–7; they truly overcome, and therefore in the future they shall reign with the Lord in the third stage or aspect of the kingdom of heaven.

### *A Comparison between the Kingdom of Heaven and the Kingdom of God*

The kingdom of heaven and the kingdom of God are distinguishable but are not separable. Let us consider in some detail these two descriptive phrases found in the Scriptures.

(1) With certain parables Matthew employs the statement "The kingdom of heaven is likened unto . . . "; but Luke uses the words "The kingdom of God is like . . . " for the *same* parables—thus indicating that the kingdom of heaven and the kingdom of God are one and the same. Both the kingdom of God and the kingdom of heaven in these parallel instances refer to the outward domain of the kingdom. On this level, it can be said that the outward appearances of both the kingdom of heaven and the kingdom of God are alike. Parables such as that of the leaven belong to this category.

(2) Yet the kingdom of heaven and the kingdom of God are not synonymous with respect to the second aspect of the kingdom of heaven, inasmuch as what is described in Matthew 5–7 speaks of actual overt behavior whereas "the kingdom of God is righteousness and peace and joy in the Holy Spirit" (Rom. 14.17). The one stresses spiritual conduct; the other, inner spiritual condition.

(3) Even so, in the third aspect the kingdom of heaven is again similar to the kingdom of God since both refer to the matter of reigning during the millennial period.

Though the kingdom of God and the kingdom of heaven are similar as regards the first aspect, the kingdom of God covers also the time of which the prophets in the Old Testament speak—for whenever the sovereignty of God is present, His domain is there at the same time. But this characteristic is not applicable to the kingdom of heaven.

With regard to the third aspect, it is true that the kingdom of God is the same as the kingdom of heaven in that both refer to ruling with Christ in the millennium; yet the kingdom of God extends further on into eternity since in eternity God also reigns—but by that time the kingdom of heaven will have passed away. With respect to the third aspect, therefore, the kingdom of God exists longer than the kingdom of heaven.

In a certain sense it can be said that the kingdom of God includes the kingdom of heaven, but not vice versa.

So far as the outward official history of the church on earth goes today, there can be said to be the Roman Catholic Church, the national churches, and the private churches. The Roman Catholic Church claims that the entire world is under her domain and that no national church is therefore allowed. The national church such as the Anglican Church asserts that every citizen of the nation belongs to the Church. But due to dissatisfaction with the national churches, there came into being the so-called private churches.

As regards the outward sphere, as long as people say they are Christians, no one can drive them out of the kingdom of heaven; for the Lord has not promised to weed out the tares today. At communion or the Lord's Table or the breaking of bread, however, the church may indeed weed out or separate the unsaved and the wicked from the saved ones. So that in the outward appearance of the kingdom of heaven, such as in a national church, unbelieving people may be included therein, but in the sphere of the believing assembly an unsaved person may be excluded from fellowship. This clarifies the two totally different spheres: that of the outward appearance of the kingdom of heaven and that of the church. Within the boundary of the outward appearance of the kingdom of heaven there may be tares; but within the church as the body of Christ there is only wheat but no tares. . . .

### *The Parable of the Hid Treasure (Matt. 13)*

v.44 "The kingdom of heaven is like unto a treasure hidden [past participle] in the field; which a man found [past tense], and hid [past]; and in his joy he goeth [present] and selleth [present] all that he hath [present], and buyeth [present] that field"—Most commentators interpret this parable in one of the following ways:

(1) The treasure is Christ, the field is the gospel. So Christ hides the gospel. The man is the sinner. He forsakes all to follow the Lord. But we would like to ask the following questions: (a) The gospel is to manifest Christ, how can it then be hidden instead? (b) Where in the Scriptures does "field" ever point to the gospel? (c) What can a sinner buy? (d) Is Christ an article of merchandise which costs something? (e) "Found" and "hid" here are totally at variance with the facts. (f) How do you hide the gospel? (g) If the gospel may be bought, it no longer is the gospel.

(2) The field is the Bible, the treasure is salvation, and the man is the sinner. Hence salvation is hidden in the Bible, and when man finds salvation he forsakes all to obtain it. Again, we would ask some questions and make some observations: (a) Does the Bible reveal or hide salvation? (b) Does man find salvation or is salvation preached to men? (c) Must one pay a price to know the Bible? (d) As a matter of fact, it does not require such a great price to purchase a Bible. (e) There is no guarantee that one would gain Christ after he has purchased a Bible anyway. (f) And why should anyone hide Christ after he has come to know Him? Why should he be afraid of being discovered by somebody else?

(3) The field is the world, the treasure is the church, and the man is Christ. Having seen the church, Christ forsakes all to buy her. Nevertheless, we would like to inquire into the following matters: (a) When and where did Christ discover the church while He was on earth? (b) Or if the treasure signifies the glory of the church, then while the Lord was on earth when did the church ever manifest her glory? (c) Or if the treasure speaks of sinners, the Lord met sinners everywhere he went and there was therefore no need to find them. (d) Why should Christ hide the sinners once He has found them?

Now if the above interpretations are faulty at various points, how then *should* we explain the parable of the treasure? Since the Lord has not himself explained it, we must interpret it by the use of other Scriptures. In 1 Chronicles 27.25 the word "treasures" is an expression for the glory of the kingdom of David. In Ecclesiastes the term "treasure" is used to show forth the abundance of Solomon's kingdom. The glory of a kingdom lies in its treasures. Even in the time of the Hebraic theocracy—that is to say, from Moses to the last of the judges—treasures represented glory. When the nation was strong, she kept her treasures; while she was weak, her treasures were taken as spoil.

"Field" is the world (see v.38). Why is the treasure hidden in the field? The glory of the kingdom of God has never been manifested on earth. Especially after the Jews were taken captive to Babylon, God was called the God of heaven. Men could not see that God actually ruled the universe. Even before the Captivity, the glory of God's kingdom was hidden to all eyes except to a relatively few. It was not unveiled appreciably until the time of John the Baptist, who began to proclaim that the kingdom of heaven was near. How long was the glory of the kingdom of heaven hidden? From the time of creation until John the Baptist (see Matt. 13.35, 25.34). Who had hidden the glory of the kingdom of heaven? God himself had (see Prov. 25.2, Rom. 11.33). The field is the world as explained in verse 38, else the Lord would certainly have said otherwise here. All this goes to show that in the future the kingdom of heaven will be connected with the world, for the kingdom of heaven shall one day be manifested on earth (see Zech. 14.5,9; and also Ps. 8.6-9—this latter Scripture being a psalm of the kingdom). The domain of the future kingdom of heaven shall be the earth (though its rule shall indeed be from heaven), for the world will not be destroyed until after the millennial kingdom is ended.

"Which a man found" –This refers to the work of Christ on earth. During the days of confusion in the world, there came one who cried in the wilderness, saying, "The kingdom of heaven is at hand"; and both the Lord and His disciples proclaimed the same message. The power (as manifested in healings and miracles) as well as the teaching of the kingdom of heaven were even then being made manifest (the word "found" in verse 44 actually means to have discovered without the necessity of earnest seeking). The Lord first discovered it; none before Him had even unearthed it. Therefore, the man here is Christ. Neither angels nor prophets could have disclosed it (see Heb. 2.5–8). And if the angels could not disclose it, who else but Christ could?

"And hid"—All actions which occurred before and including this one are cast in the past tense, indicating that the "hidden" and the "found" and the "hid" are all accomplished facts. The actions which follow in the verse are the things the Lord will do thereafter. But why is "hid" again mentioned? Because the Jews have rejected Christ and His kingdom (please recall that this rejection had already begun in the time of chapter 11 and is now fully manifested in the time of chapter 12). For this reason the glory of the kingdom of heaven is now hidden. Henceforth, the Lord does not perform many mighty works among the Jews (and if He does, He does so only for individuals). He also hides himself (see John 8.59, 12.36; Luke 4.30). And why does He hide? Because something is wrong (which points to the rejection of the Jews), and because there is now danger (which indicates the conspiracy of the Jews). He hides himself from the Jews as a nation, not from individuals or from His disciples. He may reject the nation of the Jews, but He never rejects any individual.

"In his joy"—For verses on the joy of the glory of the kingdom we must turn to Luke 10.17–20,21: the latter verse being the only place in the Gospels where the joy of the Lord is recorded.

"He goeth"—Christ goes to the cross at Jerusalem.

"And selleth all that he hath"—A price must be paid. It costs Christ His life. When the Lord came to this world, He had already forsaken the greater part of His possessions (yet not all). Soon at the cross, He is to sacrifice all, even His life.

"And buyeth that field"—Buy (see Acts 20.28, 2 Peter 2.1, Rev. 5.9 ). The purpose in buying is for the treasure in the field. The scope of the purchase is the world. According to 2 Peter 2.1, even the unsaved are also bought. Sin-offering is for believers, propitiation is for the whole world (1 John 2.2). God expects great things on earth, and so He purchases it. The future kingdom is connected with the earth, because the kingdom shall be on earth (see Rev. 11.15, Matt. 6.10). The Lord's heart is also upon the earth (see Matt. 6.21); therefore, He will come again to establish the kingdom of heaven on earth.

*The Parable of the Pearl*

vv.45–46 Most commentators chiefly interpret this parable in one of the following ways:

(1) The pearl is Christ (this interpretation has persisted from Luther to the present), the man is the believer. But how can Christ be bought? How can He be only a pearl of great price among many pearls?

(2) The pearl is the elite of the church, scattered throughout many churches. But men do not need to sell all in order to seek truth. Both the rich and poor may find the truth.

(3) The pearl is the righteousness of God (this was suggested a hundred years ago).

(4) The pearl is the church (this is partially correct).

How should this parable of the pearl be explained? The pearl stands for the beauty of the church. Such a beauty comes from life, not something manufactured by human effort. Pearls are found in the sea. As we have learned previously, the sea represents the Gentiles—the many peoples—while land represents the Jews. The mystery in Romans 11.25–26 is concerned with the Jews, but the mystery in Ephesians 3.4–6 is mainly concerned with the Gentiles. Treasure is either nationally- or family-owned, but a pearl is individually owned. Do take note of the following verses: Job 28.18 mg.; Matthew 7.6, 13.45–46; 1 Timothy 2.9; and Revelation 17.4, 18.12, 21.21. From such passages as these we may conclude that a pearl is for ornament, to give people beauty and satisfaction.

And the man in the parable is Christ. The Lord intends to obtain many pearls (finding pearls, in fact, is the work of Christ). He does not say He has not found any other pearls; He only states He has found a pearl of great price, for the beauty of the church surpasses all: "a glorious church, not having spot [no sin] or wrinkle [always fresh, never aging] or any such thing; but that it should be holy and without blemish" (Eph. 5.27). She is like the little child in Matthew 11.25. "One pearl of great price"—Note what the Bible says in 1 Corinthians: "Ye were bought with a price" (6.20). "Sold all" speaks of the Lord's death. The beauty of the church is the Lord's ornament. People will see this beauty and will praise the Lord.

The story of the making of a pearl is most interesting. Pearls are produced by certain mollusks in the sea which are rather ugly-looking. This signifies how the church comes from a most humble Christ. A smooth, lustrous, varicolored secretion, which is the very life of the mollusk, issues forth and surrounds a grain of sand or other foreign matter that finds its way into its shell. The mollusk must therefore be hurt if a pearl is ever to be formed. The roundness of the pearl depends on the tenderness of the mollusk. The more tender and sensitive the mollusk, the rounder the pearl. How soft and tender is our Christ. Now pearls are found in the sea. And the divers for them must search and kill the mollusks if they are to get any pearls. Unlike the preceding parable, the man in question (the merchant) must truly seek with effort for pearls. . . .

The kingdom of heaven: (1) whereas, on the one hand, the church is built by none other than the Lord himself (through regeneration, life, the Holy Spirit, and revelation from above) and not by flesh and blood—on the other hand, the kingdom of heaven is the realm in which we are called to be disciples; (2) in the kingdom of heaven, God causes us to enjoy our privileges as disciples; and (3) in the kingdom of heaven we are also to perform our duties and fulfill our responsibilities as disciples.

Here the Lord is telling Peter, "You shall bring people into the kingdom of heaven"—so that the keys mentioned here suggest the first step in the procedure of entering the kingdom of heaven, the first few things which help people to enter through the door. Peter used them in the events recorded in the book of Acts: (1) He had the key of witnessing—his preaching on the day of Pentecost (2.14ff.); (2) he also had the key of baptizing—his exhorting the people to be baptized into Christ (2.38–41; see also Rom. 6.3) that they might be obedient to the Lord and His command. Thus in Matthew 28.19, we have Christ's command to His disciples to "make disciples of all the nations" (the use of the first key) and this to be followed by "baptizing them" (the use of the second key). He who is not baptized can be in the church, but not in the kingdom of heaven (see Matt. 21.31–32). It is the Lord who adds to the church day by day those who are being saved (Acts 2.47 mg.; 16.5). Preachers can only bring people into the kingdom of heaven. The kingdom of heaven in its outward appearance can be likened to *the outer precincts* of the house of God which is the church. In these outer precincts one may find the tares, but in the true church these tares never exist.

The keys are not only given to Peter but also given to us. For please note that in Matthew 18.18 the Lord is recorded as giving the same promise again, but there the pronoun is "ye"—not just Peter but all who are in the church (see Matt. 18.19,20 where the church is brought into view). So, we too have these keys. With these keys we have the authority to bind (close) as well as to loose (open).

Since the keys which Peter has denote preaching and baptizing, naturally our keys are the same. Peter receives the keys first only because he confesses first.

"Loose"—We begin to preach the gospel and to baptize. "Bind"—Because the keys are in our hands we have the authority not to preach or not to baptize.

—KKH 20-1, 23, 64-5, 140-3, 161-6, 195-6

What is the meaning of the term "kingdom"? Surely it is the realm of a king. It is the sphere of his authority, his reign. So when Jesus comes into His kingdom, He comes into the place of power. Wherever the sovereignty of the Lord Jesus is recognized, there His kingdom is; and wherever that sovereignty is not recognized, there His kingdom has not yet come. If the kingdom of God is to be established on earth then men must be brought under the unquestioned rule of God. Man must bow to the absolute authority, dominon and sovereign rule of Jesus Christ. It is *His kingdom* that is to come. . . .

We know the incident well. Jesus was transfigured before them, presenting to their view in those moments the kingdom in its nature and essence—though not yet, of course, in its full scope—in the person of the King. Immediately Peter burst out with his spontaneous response. "Not knowing what he said," yet ever ready to say something, he proposed that they should build three tabernacles, one each for Jesus, Moses and Elijah.

### *The Father Intervenes*

Three tabernacles—not one! Do you see the import of Peter's brilliant suggestion? There were two very great men there with Jesus in the mount—great not alone for their own sakes but because of what they represented. There was Moses standing for the law, and there was Elijah for the prophets, and, in proposing to prolong the mountain-top experience, Peter would make provision for these two alongside the Lord. They would, of course, be in a subordinate position, but nevertheless they would have some standing beside Him and a position of authority to be reckoned with.

But in the *kingdom* you cannot do that! You cannot have more than one authority. You cannot have a multitude of voices. There can be only one Voice. It was to point this lesson that, "while he yet spake," the Father broke in with what amounted to a rebuke. Interrupting Peter, as though to say: "This is not the time for you to speak but to listen," He directed him to the One who alone has a right to speak in the kingdom. "This is my beloved Son, . . . hear ye him." In other words: "Everything in the kingdom hangs upon Jesus Christ speaking and upon your paying heed to His words." [See Matt. 17.1–8; cf. Mark 9.1–8.]

We said that Moses and Elijah represent the law and the

prophets. God's word makes it clear that now, with the coming of the kingdom, these were to give way before it. "The law and the prophets were until John: from that time the gospel of the kingdom of God is preached, and every man entereth violently into it" (Luke 16.16). In its very nature the kingdom supersedes them both. If there is still law, there is no kingdom; if there are still prophets there is no kingdom. The law and the prophets must yield to the kingdom of Jesus Christ; they cannot claim equal place with it. They must not usurp its authority. That is why Peter's speech was brought to a sudden conclusion by the intervention of God. His suggestion was set aside by a definite and deliberate utterance from heaven itself, for the whole basis of the kingdom was at stake, the very foundation of Christianity was involved. If the kingdom is to come, then Moses must give place to it, and so must Elijah. If you hold on to the law and the prophets you forfeit the kingdom, and if you have the kingdom you must let go the law and the prophets.

—WSM 19-20, 20-1

According to the Scriptures, the geographical factor of the kingdom of God exceeds its historical factor. "If I by the Spirit of God cast out demons," said the Lord Jesus, "then is the kingdom of God come upon you" (Matt. 12.28). Is this a historical problem? No, it is a geographical problem. Wherever the Son of God casts out demons by the Spirit of God, there is the kingdom of God. So during this period of time, the kingdom of God is more geographical than historical.

If our concept of the kingdom is always historical, we have then seen but one side of it, not the whole thing. In the Old Testament, the kingdom of the heavens is merely prophesied. With the coming of the Lord Jesus, John the Baptist first proclaims that the kingdom of the heavens is at hand; the same proclamation is made by the Lord Jesus himself later on. Why? Because here begins to appear the people of the kingdom of the heavens.

And when we come to Matthew 13, the kingdom of the heavens even begins to have an outward appearance on earth. Today wherever the children of God cast out demons by the Spirit of God, and destroy their work, there is to be found the kingdom of God. The Lord teaches us to pray "Thy kingdom come" because He anticipates the kingdom of God filling the earth.

"Thy kingdom come"! This is not only a *desire* of the church, it is also a *responsibility* of the church. The church ought to bring the kingdom of God to earth. In order to accomplish this task the church must be willing to pay any price, submitting herself to the restraint and control of heaven that she may be the outlet of heaven, letting through the authority of heaven onto earth. If the church is to bring in the kingdom of God she must not be ignorant of the devices of Satan (see 2 Cor. 2.11) and she needs to be clothed with the whole armor of God that she may be able to stand against the wiles of the devil (Eph. 6.11). For upon wherever the kingdom of God comes down, the demons will be driven out of that place. When the kingdom of God rules over the earth completely, Satan will be cast into the bottomless pit (see Rev. 20.1-3).

—PM 47-8

The Lord Jesus answered with one sentence, and in this one sentence is the crux of the whole problem. Let us too hold onto this word: "The things which are impossible with men are possible with God." It is quite clear that such a thing as abandoning all to enter into the kingdom of God is unheard of in this world. The Lord acknowledges this as humanly impossible. What was wrong with the young ruler was not his inability to sell all, but rather his sorrowful departure. God knows it is impossible for men to sell and distribute all to the poor. But when the young man sadly left, he seemed to conclude that this was also impossible with God. Of course it is wrong for me not to forsake my all, but does not the Lord know all about it? Therefore the Lord declares: what is impossible with men is possible with God. How can anyone get a camel through a needle's eye? Impossible. Similarly, people on this earth all love wealth and to ask them to sell all is to ask for the impossible. But if I go away with sorrow, then I am really wrong, for I have limited the power of God.

The young ruler could not abandon all, but God can do it. In other words, the Lord was prepared to give grace to the young man if he had only cried, "O Lord, I cannot abandon my wealth, but give me grace. What is impossible with me is possible with You. Enable me to do what I am unable to do. Lord, I just am too attached to my wealth to give it up and distribute it to the poor and then come and follow You, but You can make me to be what You want me to be." The mistake he made was to not pray, ask, and believe. He ought not to have sorrowfully departed. Man's failure is not due to his weakness, but to his not accepting God's strength. It is not in his inability but in not allowing God to enable him. He cannot do it, but why not let God deliver him? This is what the Lord stresses here. The things which are impossible with men are possible with God. Our Lord wanted to prove to the young ruler what God can do, but he, instead, went away with the conclusion that the thing was impossible to him. [See Luke 18.18–27.]

Let us therefore see that there is always a way for us. If we can gladly forsake all, as Peter did, then we should thank God for that. But if we feel hesitant, as the young ruler did, then there is yet a way open to us. We merely need to bow our heads and say to the Lord, "I cannot," and He will undertake for us.

—ALS 40-1

How, then, are we going to taste today the powers of the age to come? May God open our eyes to see how the Bible is full of absolute contrasts—out of sin into righteousness, out of death into life, out of sickness into health, out of darkness into light, out of the human into the divine, out of the natural into the spiritual, and so forth. Let us see that God has also delivered us out of this earth, but into what? Is it into heaven? No, the Bible does not say so. It says that we have been delivered out of this earth into the kingdom: our Father God has "delivered us out of the power of darkness, and translated us into the kingdom of the Son of his love" [Col. 1.13].

We need to remember that our ground, our home, our place is not here, but in the kingdom. We must stand into all the good of the kingdom now. Why is it that when we become Christians everything becomes difficult with relationships, business, and so forth? It is because God wants to show us that our place, our home, our country is no longer on this earth but in the kingdom. We must now live in the kingdom. Unless we are today using the powers God has given us against all the powers of the Enemy, against all the hosts of darkness in the thick of the spiritual battle—resisting, fighting and pressing the battle, we shall be utterly unprepared for the kingdom that is to come in fullness. Like a diver in the sea who has to live by the air from earth even though he is down below the earth, so we have to live down here by the air of the heavenly kingdom; otherwise we shall die. We are to bring the power of the heavenly kingdom to bear upon this earth now. We are not to allow any atmosphere or condition to be present in our home, our business, or in whatever place we are other than the righteousness, the perfection, the pure atmosphere and condition of the kingdom.

Yes, the kingdom is indeed future, but we are to bring it right into wherever we are and into whatever we do *now*. In and through and by the power of God—by the authority of God—which He has given us, we are to bring in the kingdom today wherever we are. "The kingdom of God," declares the Lord Jesus, "is in the midst of you" (Luke 17.21 mg.). Because the King is among us, therefore, wherever we are, there in fact is the kingdom. Yea, "the kingdom of God is within you," for Christ is there in us. Everything in our lives must be a kingdom matter; that is to say—it must be something taken from the kingdom and used now. Consequently, the question comes down to this: Are we taking kingdom power, kingdom blessings, kingdom gifts, kingdom fullness, kingdom position, kingdom viewpoint, kingdom attitude, kingdom everything—and possessing them and using them now? The kingdom is to be tasted now, both in its power, its rule, its glorious fullness, and so forth.

—GFB 65-7

# 38 Judgment

Ordinarily we do not like to hear the word "judgment" for it does not seem to connote any spiritual help and appears to be too negative. Yet aside from creation, God has not undertaken a work greater than judgment. The first thing He does is creation; but the last is judgment. Without judgment God's purpose of creation cannot be arrived at. So that in His plan His judgment is *con*structive, not *de*structive. Future judgment enables God to achieve His goal of creation. As we know, creation is to manifest God's purpose; but the devil, sin and the flesh soon thereafter came in. How, then, can His purpose ever be realized if there is no judgment?

Why is judgment necessary? Let us see that the very last work of God is judgment, after which He has no need to do anything else. On the seventh day God rested, for the work of creation was finished. After judgment the tabernacle of God, we are told, shall dwell among men forever (Rev. 21.3ff.). Whereas the work of creation does not insure that sin will never enter again, judgment guarantees that sin will forever be gone. While the work of creation fails to prevent the world from rebelling, judgment makes certain that hereafter there will be no more rebellion. God's judgment guarantees no more sin. Judgment has the power to drive away sin. So judgment has subjective uses in relation to us. At least in three areas God will accomplish His will through judgment:

(1) *Judgment glorifies God himself.* The judge is glorified accord-

ing to the judgment he gives. The way sin is judged expresses the kind of person handing down the judgment. The deeper the hate for sin, the severer the judgment. Hence God's judgment reveals what kind of God He is. Through judgment God sanctifies himself. . . .

(2) *Judgment exposes all hidden things, manifests the true character, and causes us to know ourselves.* People do not know themselves; they are deceived. One day God shall judge the world and manifest all the hidden things. He who will be the most surprised is each person's own self, for no one truly knows himself. Judgment will cause us to know our true character. Whatever has been hidden from us will be exposed on that day. Hence judgment is a great revelation, not only revealing God but also revealing what kind of person we are. "Yea, I judge not mine own self," said Paul; instead, he will wait "until the Lord come[s], who will both bring to light the hidden things of darkness, and make manifest the counsels of the hearts" (1 Cor. 4.3,5).

Only a fool would trust in himself. However great your revelation is and however much your dealing is, you should not become over-confident. Paul was a man of revelation, yet he dared not judge himself. Judgment is a great exposure. In hell, there will be all kinds of people except the proud (pride is the sin that Satan commits). For the proud can continue on till they reach the great white throne of judgment. But then and there they will not be able to be proud anymore. Hence Paul declares that every knee shall bow and every tongue shall confess that Jesus is the Lord. This sin of pride will not be continued. Sooner or later all shall know themselves. Though you may not confess Jesus as Lord today, one day you *will* confess Him as such. On that day you will be dethroned and will acknowledge yourself to be but dust.

(3) *Before God judgment has a great effect—that is to say, it puts an end to sin.* Whatever sin it may be, it ceases after its being judged. The world is so terrible for it is filled with all kinds of sin. Sin advances so rapidly that nothing seems to be able to stop it. Preaching the gospel is one way to stop sin, but more

people are being born into the world than are being saved into the kingdom. The number of people born in one day exceeds the number of souls being saved in one year. (It would almost appear as if the gospel, the cross, the church, the New Covenant have all failed; yet we know God does not use these but judgment to ultimately solve the problem of sin.) The entire problem of sin will be resolved in judgment. What the gospel cannot stop, judgment will. Whatever has not been terminated will be terminated by judgment. Judgment is God's great cleansing day. It is the day in which sin is finally ended in this world. It is by far the best day, for on that day God shall reign. God will come among men and judge and destroy all which men and the devil have done. He will bring in the new. The world which came into being in the day of Genesis shall be purified in the day of Revelation 20. It will be renewed, and God shall be satisfied. The church, however, must submit to God's judgment today.

"Zion shall be redeemed with judgment" (Darby's translation of Isaiah 1.27). Sin is Satan's challenge. It is unquestionably a difficult problem for God to solve. We often mistakenly deem redemption to be God's answer, but redemption is only part of the answer. The final response by God to sin is judgment. Our darkened thought considers judgment to be useless, because to us judgment is Hades, the lake of fire, suffering, and so forth. We fail to believe that in judgment lies God's power. Though judgment is destructive, it also possesses the greatest constructive power. Since God is willing to answer Satan's challenge with judgment, we are forced to conclude that it must be a very good answer. Whether we understand or not, judgment answers the challenge completely (for whatever God does is always perfect). Our mistake is, that every time we think of judgment we think of punishment; but God takes no delight in punishing men. Judgment has its other use besides punishment: "Jesus said, For judgment came I into this world" (John 9.39). . . .

With the enlightenment from God, man can no longer live in sin. Error is not corrected by argument but by judgment. Once the light of judgment shines everything is known. Ever since the garden of Eden, judgment has always destroyed sin, for its light consumes. One day all the world's sins will be destroyed. The last destruction of sin will occur at the judgment of the great white throne. Without question, judgment has tremendous power.

When we look at judgment we are compelled to recognize who God is. To know God as Father is one thing; to know Him as God is quite another. Through redemption we know the Father; through judgment we know God and worship Him. Sin seems to have compromised the glory of God. Who achieves the upper hand on the earth—the righteous or the unrighteous, the crooked or the honest? Today people may have many reasons to misunderstand God, but one day He will manifest His glory. For God is holy, righteous and terrible. Through judgment He will be recognized as God. Then men will know the terror of the Lord. "Knowing therefore the terror of the Lord," wrote Paul, "we persuade men" (2 Cor. 5.11 Darby). Today the terror of the Lord may be only a teaching to many, but one day the whole world will receive this great revelation. God will not permit sin to continue any further.

Yet we need not wait till that day to know this. There will indeed be burning before the judgment seat of Christ when all that can be burned shall be consumed. The lake of fire will indeed follow the judgment of the great white throne. But we can learn to let that light of judgment enlighten us *today.* Let the light be as bright today as it will be in that day. Let it shine more than once till we are smitten (how useless are mental knowledge and mere teaching here). May God have mercy upon us if we are *in*creased instead of being *de*creased. May He be merciful to us if we are not yet consumed. . . .

Therefore the cross is itself a judgment. Its enlightenment is not in any way less powerful than the enlightening of judgment. It is not behind judgment either in consuming sin or in glorifying God. Its power and work are as strong as those of the future judgment. When sin comes in, God uses judgment to solve it. Anything less than judgment cannot resolve the problem of sin. For this reason, the cross has the same intensity in its dealing with sin as the future judgment has. In the hearts of God's children the cross is living today. Let us now see how much our Lord has gone through for us. . . .

Justification by faith is cited in the book of Romans to show that God is just and righteous. Judgment proves how clear is God's righteousness. For righteousness is seen in judgment. We are saved because God has dealt with our sins. He does not overlook them. We are forgiven because God in Christ has paid it all. His forgiving us is wholly righteous. The cross will not be effective if its judgment is less intense than the future judgment. "For what the law could not do, in that it was weak through the flesh, God, sending his own Son in the likeness of sinful flesh and for sin, condemned sin in the flesh: that the ordinance of the law might be fulfilled in us" (Rom. 8.3–4). This is not only judgment but also condemnation. God has condemned sin in the flesh of our Lord in order that we might be delivered from the power of sin.

So that by the cross God has condemned sin to death through Christ Jesus. Through this light sin is condemned and consumed. This is the second thing which the Lord has done. For He was judged not only for sinners but also for sin. God has made Him who is sinless to be sin for us, and in His death sin died in Him forever. Thus the Lord said, " . . . of judgment, because the prince of this world hath been judged" (John 16.11).

The prince of this world is judged. How marvelous that in the death of our Lord the world was judged in its prince. Actually the cross was Satan's great gamble. He threw his all at the cross. There he gathered all the forces of nations, kings, people, and even death. He tried to put an end to Jesus' work once and forever. But our Lord arose from the dead and finished the devil off instead. Thus was the prince of this world judged. Hereafter all who have eternal life will declare that the satanic world is defeated. The hour the Lord's *heel* was crushed, Satan's *head* was crushed [see Gen. 3.15].

Hence the cross solves the problem of sins, and the power of sin, Satan and his world. The judgment of the cross today is just as powerful as the judgment of the future day. It has tremendous strength of burning as well as of enlightening.

In accepting the cross, it is not enough simply to accept God's love or forgiveness. The cross also stands for suffering, but it is not enough merely to accept it as suffering. The cross additionally means laying aside self and submitting to God, but still it is not enough to only accept it as that. No, the cross is equally a judgment by which God's aim is reached. It severely judges the sinners, the world, and the devil. Knowing the terror of the Lord we persuade men.

God does not expect His children to have their problems solved at the future judgment; He wants these resolved at the cross. For the people of the world, there remains a judgment wherein there is no salvation; but for God's children nothing should wait to be solved at the judgment seat of Christ, because God wants us to have everything cleared up at the cross. Therefore, our understanding of judgment must reach the depth of judgment....

Judgment will bring you to a point where nothing in you can resist God. Under His judgment, everything is withered and weakened. The cross is an experience whereby you must once be so enlightened by God that you are reduced to ashes. There must be a time when your self-confidence and pride are brought to an end. Then will there be resurrection out of the ashes....

The cross of Christ reveals the attitude of God toward sin. In dealing with the Lord Jesus, God deals with sin because our Lord was made sin for us. All that is contrary to God must be completely destroyed. Forgiving is grace, whereas hating is judgment. God cannot cheaply forgive, since He so greatly hates sin. Salvation must correspond with His holiness. Toward sin, the cross is God's judgment; towards us, it is His forgiveness. We receive grace on the one hand and are judged on the other hand. We are a people judged as well as favored....

When God executes judgment by enlightening you, you will

fall under the light. After your sin is judged by the light, that particular sin can never raise its head again. It is instead destroyed. The light that causes a person to judge his own sin is the light of judgment. No one can pass through God's light and live. For example, you cannot get rid of lying; but as the light of God shines, lying is eliminated. This is the work of God. It is the Lord who delivers. Some know how strong their natural life is, but they can do nothing about it. They may try to be humble before men. Yet only the light of judgment can break the power of death. They know, but this may only be a teaching to them. . . .

How often a person has something he cannot overcome. He may make resolutions and shed many tears, but strangely all to no avail. Yet one day the light of judgment shines upon him, he is made to see the terribleness of that thing, and as he confesses his sin, that sin is taken away from him; for how can he now confess and still have that sin remain in him? During enlightenment, the power of sin is destroyed.

You may worry about your being no good, but actually you have never seen how weak and bad you truly are. You say you are weak because you have heard the teaching. God speaks, but you hear only teaching. As a result you pursue after holiness, you even admire it, yet you can do nothing about it. Accordingly, ask God to enlighten you with His strong light, and then what bothers you will be removed. God works through His light. Commit yourself, therefore, into His hand, and let His terrible light fall upon you. And if you allow yourself to be judged *today,* you will not be judged *later.* . . .

Only God's children have the privilege of enjoying God's continual judgment. Those who are not God's children do not have this privilege: "when we are judged, we are chastened of the Lord, that we may not be condemned with the world" (1 Cor. 11.32). That we be judged is really grace and enjoyment; and as a consequence, we may not be condemned. Once in a while God will indeed judge the world to prevent it from becoming too corrupted. The Genesis flood, for example, was but a prevention. But in the lives of God's children, judgment is for the purpose of their being spared from future judgment. One day God will totally destroy the power of sin, but today He has it accomplished first in His children.

God enlightens as well as sets on fire. Today God's children do not lack power; they lack enlightenment. We may think it takes power to eliminate improper things. Yet who of us knows that that which takes away all which is opposed and contrary to God is *enlightenment* and not power? When God enlightens you and shows you the sinfulness of sin, that sin leaves you. It is withered and gone. For light brings in conviction, and more light generates the power to eliminate sin. Let us be willing to be enlightened of God. For when we are enlightened, sin cannot raise its head.

What, though, if we fail to see this light? Let us understand that the fire from God is for burning. If it does not burn away sin, then it will burn away the person. Light rejected will mean we incur chastening. Chastening is not God's second act, but it simply comes at the time when light is rejected. Discipline or chastening is a kind of judgment. He who accepts the judgment of light is saved, whereas he who rejects the light is disciplined. Chastening is God's judgment. It comes as the result of light being rejected. Not all unfortunate happenings are necessarily God's chastening, though many of them are. . . .

The degree of nearness to God decides the heaviness of chastening. Because they were God's house the children of Israel were judged many times. These instances but demonstrate God's work outwardly. Consider the priests of Israel. They must bear the sin against the sanctuary; they must bear the sin of their office. God could be lenient towards the *people* of Israel, but He was strict with their *priests.* An Israelite might bring a bullock and offer it as a sacrifice five months after he had sinned, but the priests in the holy temple must offer a sacrifice every day.

For the priest it was not a case of three times a year to offer up a sacrifice. If the priest did not continually offer it up, he would die instantly. God could let the ordinary people go, but He would not allow the priests to do so.

We Christians today are God's house, we are all the temple of the living God. Just as the Lord required of the children of Israel long ago, so He requires of us. Either the light burns away sin or we receive chastening. We are judged because we are the temple of God. It is not easy to be a Christian, because he cannot resign or escape. A Christian is one who is to disregard his own feeling. The life of God as well as the Spirit of God is in him. Other people may live carelessly, but you and I cannot so live. The least contradiction will make us uneasy. And such is vital Christianity. Light reproves, and God judges to the extent that some may be weak, and some may even die. . . .

Judgment is God's answer to death, for He uses it to get rid of sin. The cross is redemption, but it is also judgment. We should accept the cross. The house of God is constantly under His light of judgment. There is the altar in God's temple. The temple of God is able to stand because all must pass through the altar (the altar serves as a type of the judgment of the cross). Judgment is manifested daily in God's house. No one can live in His house without being judged. As long as God's temple exists, there ought to be enlightening. The purpose of God's enlightening judgment is to keep His children in full harmony with His holiness.

I would like to mention still another aspect of judgment (the Hebrew word *mishpat* can be translated ordinance or judgment). It is the keeping of the judgments of God. God has declared that we should keep His judgments. If we know them, we should also keep them. . . . God's judgments are God's laws. As laws express His high wills, so His judgments manifest His mind. Hence we must keep His judgments in the church as much as we keep His laws. Judgment reveals the mind of God concerning a particular matter. Though it may happen in another's life, nevertheless I too must keep it. The judgment of God, therefore, becomes our law.

God's judgment is God's great enlightening which causes us to know our fault, know the sinfulness of sin, and know ourselves. There is unity in God's enlightenment, judgment, and condemnation. Some say the experience of Kadesh-barnea is but an historical fact; there is no command, hence it has nothing to do with us. Yet God considers it to be a judgment—which we must learn to keep. God will do the same thing today because His attitude toward sin has not changed.

All the past judgments are our judgments. God's judgment upon Moses for striking the rock twice for water, for example, is nothing less than a judgment meant for us to keep. If the same incident were to happen today, God would do the very same thing. Likewise, both the incidents of Uzzah and that of Korah with his band of 250 people were matters of God's judgment. And God's judgments remain forever. Thus do we realize what is meant by keeping the judgments of God. What God did among His people in the past, He will do the same in the church today [see 2 Sam. 6 and Num. 16]. . . .

Today the house of the Lord is the sphere of God's judgment. He judges through His church. He not only judges in the church but also judges through the church. In the outer court the light is natural; in the holy place it is artificial, man-made light; but in the holiest of all there is neither natural nor artificial light; there is only the light of the glory of God. Only in the holiest of all will you see God's light. Consequently, the condemnation in the holiest is more severe than in any other place. If there is sin, it needs to be exposed to the light of the holiest.

Formerly the tabernacle was inanimate material, now it is living. God's light is in the sanctuary. The church today is the sanctuary where God's light is manifested. Though many times God will enlighten directly, many more times He will enlighten through the church. God gives light to men through the church. Hence judgment is not only in *God's* hand, it is also in the hand of the *church.*

In 1 Corinthians 5 it is said that we do not judge those outside but we do judge those who are within the church. The light in the sanctuary is to enlighten the sanctuary. So God's light will shine and judge when people in the church fail to see. The posture of 1 Corinthians 5 is not a sitting on the legal bench judging those who are beneath. It is rather the expression of the mourning of the church. For in the church there is no judge yet there is judgment. The judgment of the church is therefore neither positional nor authoritative. It ought instead to be that which brings forth repentance and sorrow.

The sinner in question in 1 Corinthians 5 had not been excommunicated, and the church had grown boastful and was without any sorrow. Yet the judgment of the church should result in humility and mourning. Had there been the light of judgment present, the church in Corinth would have prostrated herself before God for the sin in her midst and risen up to cast out the sin. The church cannot judge until light shines in her. She is not to be authoritative but mournful. She must judge herself first; she herself must repent, and *then* exercise discipline. Otherwise, excommunication becomes something legalistic. . . .

Let us understand that all the judgments of God are related to the anger of God. Yet God never loses His temper. Such anger is the strength of His judgment. Love is God's positive strength; patience is God's waiting strength; whereas anger is His destroying strength. Anger destroys all that is contrary to God. So far as the Lord is concerned, His love, patience and anger are tremendously great. When God becomes angry, sin is destroyed. So is it with the judgment of the church. As long as *God* forbears a matter, you have absolutely no way to rightly judge that matter. Only at the moment when God's light comes and exposes its wickedness will you have the anger of God placed in you (but without losing your temper). Then you can invite your brother to come and be reproved of you.

It is more difficult to reprove than to comfort. Love is what you should show daily; but anger is rather unusual. When you first perceive the wickedness of sin, you have no strength to judge.

Only as light shines does the anger of God become your strength to judge. A weak person may scold but cannot reprove. To reprove and to scold are quite different actions. Losing one's temper is a losing of one's self-control; but anger is what God has added in. In anger there should be the power of self-control. In the case of Peter and Ananias, Peter did not lose his temper while talking severely with Ananias. His words were most rational. This was the anger of judgment. The first step in any judgment of the church is to reprove; the last step is to excommunicate.

When God's judgment is executed in the church, then besides repentance there will be one of two other consequences: (1) all communications are interrupted; the person will be looked upon as one of the gentiles; he cannot pray or have his prayer answered. (2) there may be physical punishment. The light of judgment in the church is serious. If it does not result in (1), it will end up with (2). Either there will be no communication or there will be death. Both are very serious. All who live before God should avoid such consequences. . . .

Why must the church judge? It is not because there may be a lack of brotherly love, but because of the need to maintain the glory of God. . . .

—SJ 4–5, 6–10, 13–4, 17, 18–20, 20, 24, 25–6, 27, 30–1, 34–5, 39–40, 47–8, 50–1, 51

# 39 Rapture

In order to understand Matthew 24 and 25, it is essential to have a clear knowledge of the subject of rapture. For it is one of the most important matters in this last hour. Unfortunately it is greatly misunderstood by many.

Rapture is the same as the word "receive" found in John 14.1–3. It does not signify the idea of "climbing up" to heaven but of the Lord receiving us to heaven. Hence rapture is a specific term used to denote His receiving us at His soon return.

There are different views on rapture among believers. Some say (1) that the whole body of the saved will be raptured before the Great Tribulation; others believe (2) that the whole body of the saved must go through the Great Tribulation before they are raptured; while still others feel (3) that a part of the saved will be raptured before the Great Tribulation and a part of them will be raptured after the Great Tribulation. There are mainly these three schools of interpretation on the subject; yet merely because any one of them is different from the one you hold to does not give you any warrant to denounce the different view as heresy. It is wrong to withhold fellowship simply for this reason.

Well-known believers are found in all three schools. Of the first school mentioned, names can be cited such as J. N. Darby, William Kelly (C. H. Spurgeon once said that Kelly's brain was as large as the universe), R. A. Torrey (who later changed to a post-tribulation rapture view), Phillips Brooks, James Gray, Arno C. Gaebelein, J. A. Seiss, C. I. Scofield, and so forth.

Of the second school, there could be listed such names as George Muller (who first believed in pre-tribulation rapture), A. J. Gordon of Boston, A. B. Simpson, W. J. Erdman, W. G. Moorehead, Henry Frost of Canada, James Wright, Benjamin Newton, and so on.

And as to the third school, we have names such as Hudson Taylor, Robert Chapman, Robert Govett (Spurgeon praised his writings as having light a century ahead of his time and as being full of gold), G.H. Pember, D.M. Panton (the "prince of prophecy") and others.

None of the three schools can completely ignore the others, yet only one is correct. Let us therefore examine them with fairness, having the attitude of a judge and not that of a lawyer.

I. Reasons given by the first school—that is to say, by the adherents of a pre-tribulation rapture—are presented in the following paragraphs.

A. 1 Thessalonians 1.10 "The wrath to come"—This is the Great Tribulation. Since the Lord Jesus will deliver us from the wrath to come, we must be raptured *before* the Great Tribulation. Also, 1 Thessalonians 5.9 "For God appointed us not unto wrath"—Once again this "wrath" has reference to the Great Tribulation.

Let me say, though, that such an interpretation of "wrath" here as being the Great Tribulation is incorrect. How do we know that this wrath must necessarily be the wrath in the Great Tribulation? And even if it were granted that it is, such an interpretation of this word "wrath" would still be unreasonable because the Great Tribulation, on the one hand, is God's punishment and wrath coming upon the unbelievers, and on the other hand is Satan's attack and wrath descending on the believers. When Satan assaults the believers, the latter enter into the experience of the Great Tribulation but do not come under the wrath of God.

B. Jeremiah 30.6–7 "The time of Jacob's trouble"—The Great Tribulation is only for the Jews, not for the Gentiles or for the church. Since the church is not the Jews, we therefore will not go through the Great Tribulation. See also Daniel 12.1.

If there were only these two passages in the entire Bible which speak of the Great Tribulation, then the Great Tribulation would indeed be exclusively for the Jews. But we can read other passages in the Bible, such as Revelation 3 which speaks of "the hour of trial, that hour which is to come upon the whole world, to try them that dwell upon the earth" (v.10). The prophecies of Jeremiah and Daniel were directed toward the Jews, and hence they used such words as "Jacob" and "thy people" quite logically.

C. Revelation 4.1–4 Interpreters of this first school consider Revelation 2 and 3 as depicting the age of the church; 4.1 as referring to the rapture of the church; 4.4 (with the 24 elders) as representing the glorified church after the rapture; and chapters 5 and 6 as having reference to the beginning of the Great Tribulation.

But 4.1 is not spoken to the whole church. It is only spoken to John. "Come up hither" is an accomplished fact in the personal experience of John on the isle of Patmos. Otherwise, Philip's experience as recorded in Acts 8.29 might also be taken as signifying the rapture of the whole church.

As regards the 24 elders, it is rather absurd to deem them as signifying the glorified church, for the following reasons:

(1) 24 is not the number of the church; only seven or multiples of seven are, such as the seven churches in Asia.

(2) Nowhere in the Scriptures does "elder" ever represent the church. There are elders in the church and among the Jews, but not all believers are elders. God first created the angels, then He chose the Jews, and finally gave grace to the church. How can the church bear the title of elders?

(3) In Revelation 4 and 5 we learn that the elders sit on thrones with crowns of gold on their heads, whereas Christ is standing there. Can the church receive glory before Christ is glorified? Thrones and crowns are symbols of kingship.

(4) The elders are clothed with white garments. Some sug-

gest that these garments speak of Christ our righteousness for His blood has washed them white. Yet nowhere in the Scriptures is there mention made that the garments of the elders are washed with the blood. *Our* robes need to be washed with blood because we have sinned; but the 24 elders have never sinned.

(5) The elders never experience redemption. In chapter 4 we observe that they sing the song of creation. And we see in chapter 5 that though they sing the song of redemption they sing not of themselves but of men who are purchased by the blood of the Lamb. "And madest them to be . . . " (v.10)—The word "them" here refers to the church. Now if it is the church who sings, would she use "them"?

(6) Revelation 4 deals with the universe and not with the church, the nations, or the Jews. And hence we may say that these are the elders of the universe. The church is not an elder of the universe.

(7) Revelation 5.8. The church cannot bring people's prayers to God.

(8) Revelation 7.13 If John also represents the church, it would then be the church asking the church.

(9) John calls one of the elders "My lord" (7.14), thus indicating that his position is lower than the elders. If the 24 elders represent the church, then John who is among the first in the church, should be the elder of the elders.

(10) The number 24 should be taken literally, not symbolically. Since one of the elders speaks to John, how can one twenty-fourth of the church talk to John? The number is fixed, and hence the elders are fixed. These 24 elders are archangels who rule the universe. Even under Satan in his domain there are principalities and authorities.

D. 1 Thessalonians 4.16–17 Do not these verses speak of rapture? Obviously they do, yet they do not specify what time. They deal with the *fact* of rapture, not with the *time* of rapture. Thus, they can not be used to prove pre-tribulation rapture.

E. 1 Corinthians 15.50–52 Whether dead or living, all

will be raptured. Yet, again, it presents the fact of rapture without specifying a time sequence that would indicate a pre-tribulation rapture. On the contrary, it can be used to prove a post-tribulation rapture. "At the last trump" is a descriptive phrase that is equal to the seventh trumpet cited in Revelation 11.15. Some people advance the theory that according to Roman custom the trumpets are sounded three times. But the Holy Spirit follows no Roman law.

F. Luke 21.36 The Lord distinctly promises that the church may escape the Great Tribulation and "stand before the Son of man"—This no doubt refers to rapture. Nevertheless, there is a condition involved. Not for all who are simply born again, but for those born-again ones who watch and pray. "That ye may prevail"—If you watch and pray, you may prevail. Hence the promise is given to those who do these things. Does everyone in the whole church watch and pray? Let us pay attention to this.

G. Revelation 3.10 This is reckoned as being the strongest argument, yet it too is a promise with a condition. It therefore cannot be taken as evidence for the pre-tribulation rapture of the entire church. What is meant by "the word of my patience"? Today people revile Him and curse Him, but the Lord neither punishes them nor smites them with lightning and thunder. Such is the patience of Christ in this age. Today we are patient together with Christ. We do not resist. But does every Christian keep the word of His patience in this manner? If so, the whole church would indeed be raptured. If this verse can be used indiscriminately to prove the rapture of the whole church before the Great Tribulation, then people can with equal justification forget the condition "whosoever believeth on him" and erroneously claim that all men are saved.

Furthermore, the promise of the Lord here is addressed to the church in Philadelphia, not to the whole church. If the church in Philadelphia can represent the whole church, then we may surmise that the entire church will be raptured before the Great Tribulation. Yet at that time there were actually these seven churches in Asia Minor, and the promise of the Lord was given to but one of these seven. Accordingly, the church in Philadelphia cannot represent the complete church; or else the overcomers in the other six churches mentioned will not be raptured.

II. This first school has not only no scriptural evidence but bases too much of its arguments merely on assumptions. For such a weighty problem like rapture, it should certainly not be decided on mere assumptions. Its assumptions are as follows.

A. Revelation 1–3 speaks of the church. After chapter 3 the church is no longer mentioned, so that she must have already been raptured by the time of chapter 4ff. (in the kingdom age, all will be righteousness and majesty; there will not be the patience of Christ). If chapters 1–3 refer to this age, chapters 4–19 will be the time of the Great Tribulation, in which the church has no part. This kind of argument is called the argument from silence.

However, we cannot say that from chapters 4 through 19 the church is never touched upon. Even though the word "church" is not used, many other descriptions employed do indeed fit the church, such as "didst purchase unto God with thy blood men of every tribe, and tongue, and people, and nation" (5.10), "the saints" (17.6), and "the armies which are in heaven" (19.14). Unquestionably the word "church" is not used, but who can say that those in view in the above examples do not belong to the church?

Furthermore, "the things which must shortly come to pass" (including the Great Tribulation) are shown to "his servants" (22.6), and "these things" (including the Great Tribulation) are testified "for the churches" (22.16). These things will not be written if they are not relevant to the church and to the believers.

B. After the church is raptured, there will still be very many on earth who shall be saved. These are the saints who come out of the Great Tribulation (see Rev. 7.9–17). They are saved during the Great Tribulation. There is a weakness in such assumptions by this first school which it must recognize; otherwise its adherents will be unable to round out their theory.

Let us understand, however, that the "great multitude, which no man could number" (7.9) must exceed the number of 200 millions ("twice ten thousand times ten thousand") which is the biggest among many numbers cited in the book of Revelation (9.16). Taking today's population at about 2 billions,* there will still be 1.5 billions after one fourth are killed (Rev. 6.8). Such a numberless multitude who "come out of the great tribulation" mentioned in the Revelation 7 passage must therefore have reference to those overcoming saints who come out of the great tribulation experienced by all believers throughout the twenty centuries of church history.

C. Before the Great Tribulation, the Holy Spirit returns to heaven. Since the church is with the Holy Spirit, it may be assumed that the whole church is raptured before the Great Tribulation. The basis for this assumption is 2 Thessalonians 2.6–7 where the phrase "one that restraineth" is made to refer to the Holy Spirit.

Yet "one that restraineth" cannot be the Holy Spirit, for the subsequent clause—"until he be taken out of the way"—is not the proper terminology to be used in speaking about the Holy Spirit. The Third Person of the Trinity has many different names, such as the Spirit, the Spirit of glory, the Spirit of revelation, etc; and the word "Spirit" is usually present—and even though in one instance the word "Comforter" is used alone, yet from the next clause which follows ("even the Spirit of truth") it is evident that this has clear reference to the Holy Spirit (John 14.16–17). Never do the Scriptures say the Holy Spirit is "he that restrains"; moreover, how can the Holy Spirit be said to "be taken out of the way"? Furthermore, where does the Bible announce that the Holy Spirit is absent during the Great Tribulation? And how can there be the so-called believers of the Great Tribulation if the

*That is, in the early 1930's; but the world population for 1976 was estimated at about 4.3 billion. —*Translator*

Holy Spirit is not present? For no one is saved without the Holy Spirit. He who is born of the Spirit is spirit.

Moreover, this matter of the Holy Spirit's presence during the Great Tribulation is clearly shown in Revelation 5: "and seven eyes, which are the seven Spirits of God, sent forth into all the earth" (v.6). The time of the Great Tribulation is the time of the latter rain (see Acts 2.15–21, Joel 2.28–31). The prophecy of Joel was not completely fulfilled on the day of Pentecost. For on that day there were no "wonders in the heaven and in the earth: blood, and fire, and pillars of smoke"; nor was "the sun . . . turned into darkness, and the moon into blood" (Joel 2.30–31). All of these five wonders will be fulfilled around and in the time of the Great Tribulation: blood (first trumpet), fire (first and second trumpets), smoke (fifth trumpet), sun and moon (sixth seal). Pentecost is only a miniature, a foretaste. Peter does not say: "It is fulfilled"; he merely says that "this is that" (Acts 2.16). As a matter of fact, the Holy Spirit is going to do greater work during the time of the Great Tribulation. If there will not be the Holy Spirit present, how can the saints ever endure during the Great Tribulation?

D. The disciples in the four Gospels are Jews. It is to them, that is to say, to the Jews, that the Lord exhorts to watch and pray. Since we Christians will be raptured anyway, there is no need for us to be exhorted to watch and pray. We go to the Epistles for our inspiration. However, the disciples are Christians, and they too are in the church. Are not the disciples called Christians (Acts 11.26; cf. Matt. 28.19)?

E. Adherents of this first school of interpretation do not regard much of the four Gospels and the Acts as written for Gentile believers. C.I. Scofield, for example, maintained that the so-called Sermon on the Mount is exclusively for the Jews. They forget, though, the words in Matthew 28.20 ("teaching them to observe all things whatsoever I commanded you") and in John 14.26 ("and bring to your remembrance all that I said unto you"). They base all their teachings on the words of the apostle Paul, whereas they should remember what Paul himself said in Colossians 3: "Let the word of Christ dwell in you richly" (v.16).

F. "This gospel of the kingdom shall be preached in the whole world . . . ; and then shall the end come" (Matt. 24.14). They suggest that the gospel of the kingdom is different from the gospel of grace and that the gospel of the kingdom is only preached during the time when the Lord was on earth and immediately before the Great Tribulation. Since we are saved by the gospel of grace, it is their contention that the gospel of grace need not be preached to the whole world before we are raptured. Thus, the gospel of the kingdom will only be preached again ten or twenty years before the Tribulation.

Yet the gospel of the kingdom is the gospel of the kingdom of God, and the gospel of grace is the gospel of the grace of God. According to Acts 20.24–25, "the gospel of the grace of God" spoken of in verse 24 is none other than "the preaching" of "the kingdom" mentioned in verse 25. Also, please note from Acts 1 that the Lord after His resurrection spoke to the disciples "the things concerning the kingdom of God" (v.3).

G. They view the work of Christ on earth as fulfilling the ministry towards the circumcised, thus showing a definite Jewish background; and therefore whatever is commanded in the Gospels is not for us Christians but is for the Jews.

Let me say in response, however, that the dispensation of Grace also begins with Christ. Please read the following passages: (1) Matthew 11.13–14 and Luke 16.16—where the phrase "from that time" in Luke means from the time of Christ; (2) Acts 10.36–37 and 13.25–27—where we see that "the word of this salvation" (13.26) begins to be preached at the time of John the Baptist; (3) Mark 1.1–15 and John 1.1–15—from which we learn that "the gospel of Jesus Christ" (Mark 1.1) commences with John the Baptist; (4) Luke 4.17–21—which verses describe the gospel of grace in a number of ways and concludes by recording the Lord Jesus as saying: "Today hath this scripture been fulfilled" (v.21); (5) John 4.23—wherein the phrase "and now is" indicates that during the dispensation of Grace those who worship God worship Him in spirit and truth (whereas under the dispensation of Law, men apprehended God in the flesh and according to rituals); and (6) John 5.24–25—which verses tell us that what is included in the phrase "and now is" is the gospel of grace.

III. The Bible has sufficient evidence to prove that the church passes through the Great Tribulation. The following are some of the evidences.

A. 2 Thessalonians 2.1–9. Please read this passage very carefully. Verse 1 gives the topic of this passage—namely, the coming of Christ and rapture. Since the rapture spoken of here is a being gathered in the air, there is already a hint as to its being after tribulation. In verse 2, the word "spirit" signifies another spirit, not the Holy Spirit; the term "word" means rumor; "us" refers to Paul, Silvanus and Timothy; and "the day of the Lord" is the day of the coming of Christ and rapture. In those days there were people who deluded the Thessalonian believers by saying that the day of the Lord had already come and that they had been left behind. Yet verse 3 shows that this day will not arrive until after the following two signs: (1) that before rapture, there will appear the man of sin, the son of perdition, who is the Anti-Christ; and (2) that there will first come the falling away, which is apostasy. When will the man of sin be revealed? It will naturally be at the Great Tribulation. So that rapture will be after this Tribulation. At least part of the church must go through the Great Tribulation.

B. 1 Corinthians 15.50–55; 1 Thessalonians 4.16–17. The first passage dwells on resurrection and change; the second deals with resurrection and rapture. These two are parallel passages. All students of the Bible agree that the events in both passages happen at the same time. Is there any intimation as to the actual time for these events? Indeed, there is. "At the last trump" indicates that the time must be after the Tribulation. The first school of interpretation insists that the blowing of the last trumpet occurs before the Tribulation, but its adherents have not a single Scripture verse to support their view. The last trumpet is sounded after the Tribulation; it is the last of the seven trumpets mentioned in the book of Revelation. How absurd it would be if after the *last* trumpet had been sounded there would still remain seven more trumpets to be heard! It would be like having had the *last* son born, only to be followed by seven more sons.

Someone contends that the "trump" here is the trump of the church, not that of the Tribulation. Where, then, is there recorded in the Scriptures anything said about the *first* trump of the church? Still others say that Paul merely borrows from the Roman military custom, that as soon as the last trumpet is blown the entire army marches away. Yet the Scriptures have not adopted this Roman military practice. This "trump" is the trump of God, not of the church. Without a doubt it is the last of the seven trumpets cited in the book of Revelation. Furthermore, according to Revelation 10.7, at the sounding of the seventh trumpet the mystery of God is finished—which mystery is the church.

C. Other evidences are these:

(1) Matthew 24.3, 13.40, 28.20: "the end of the world"—The word "world" is *aion* in Greek, which means "age"—that is to say, the end of this age. Chronologically, the Great Tribulation falls in this age. If rapture is to occur before the Tribulation, there will be a gap of three years and a half.

(2) 1 Corinthians 15.25; cf. Acts 2.35: "till he hath put all his enemies under his feet"—This is factual after the Tribulation.

(3) 1 Timothy 6.14: "that thou keep the commandment, without spot, without reproach, until the appearing of our Lord Jesus Christ"—The appearing of the Lord Jesus Christ will occur after the Tribulation. If He is to come to the air before the Tribulation, would there be any need for waiting, watching, and keeping?

IV. Though there are evidences in the Bible on a post-tribulation rapture of believers, this still does not imply that the *whole* body of believers will be raptured after the Tribulation. And hence this second school of interpretation has its errors too. For the Bible clearly indicates to us that some believers are raptured before the Tribulation. Here are some of the reasons for this view.

A. Were the *entire* body of believers to be raptured after the Tribulation, there would again be no need for us to watch and wait and be prepared. Knowing that the Lord would not come before the end of the three and a half years' period, we could live evilly up to three years five months and twenty-nine days. Yet such a concept violates the very principle of the Scriptures.

B. Were *all* of us believers to be raptured after the Great Tribulation, then our waiting would not be a waiting for Christ but for the Antichrist, since the latter must come first.

C. The church would lose her hope—"Looking for the blessed hope and appearing of the glory of the great God and our Savior Jesus Christ" (Titus 2.13)—for included in this hope is the blessing of escaping the Tribulation.

D. The second school of interpretation does not accept the idea of a secret rapture; yet its followers forget the word, "Behold, I come as a thief" (Rev. 16.15). A thief comes secretly, is never preceded by a band, and always steals the best.

E. This second school views the twelve disciples as being purely Christians in direct contrast with the view of the first school which considers these twelve as being merely Jews. As a matter of fact, however, these twelve disciples are Christians as well as representatives of the Jewish remnant. For example, in Matthew 10.5–6 and 23.3 we see that all have a Jewish background, a fact which is thus inapplicable to Christians.

F. There is a failure in this second school to distinguish between rapture and the appearing of the Lord. There is a difference between Christ coming *for* the saints and Christ coming *with* the saints. That which Enoch prophesied, as recorded in Jude, points to the coming of the Lord "with his holy myriads" (see Jude 14–15 mg.) when His feet step down on the Mount of Olives. So does the prophecy which is given in Revelation: "Behold, he cometh with the clouds; and every eye shall see him, and they that pierced him; and all the tribes of the earth shall mourn over him. Even so, Amen" (1.7). In taking the historical view, the second school of interpretation regards that part of Revelation up to chapter 17 as having already been fulfilled, with only the part from chapter 17 onward waiting to be fulfilled. (This is exactly opposite to the futuristic view taken by the first school of interpretation which deems only chapters 1–3 as having already been fulfilled, with the rest remaining to be so.) If the book of Revelation only records primarily things of the past, then how can the average child of God ever understand it? It would require doctors of philosophy and learned historians to comprehend it! Furthermore, it would no longer be revelation either!

V. As we have come to see, the first school lacks scriptural evidences while the second school, though it possesses many proofs, nevertheless has many errors too. What, then, does the Bible actually teach? Let us consider the following observations.

A. Revelation 3.10 "The hour of trial, that hour which is to come upon the whole world"—This is the Great Tribulation. This verse tells us that a certain class of people may escape the Great Tribulation, even those who keep the word of the patience of Christ. Instantly it tears apart the arguments of the second school of interpretation as well as those of the first. Although Philadelphia represents the true church in the dispensation of Grace, it is nonetheless only one of the seven local churches in Asia at that time. Thus it shows that only a relatively small number of people (one seventh) may be raptured before the Tribulation. Furthermore, pre-tribulation rapture is not based purely on our being born again as children of God, but is dependent on one other condition, which is, our keeping the word of the patience of Christ. Do all believers today keep the word of the patience of Christ? Obviously not. It is therefore evident that not the *whole* body of believers will be raptured before the Tribulation.

The second school contends, however, that this passage of Scripture does not refer to pre-tribulation rapture, for it speaks of keeping—that God will "keep" them safely through the Great Tribulation: just as, for example, when an entire house is caught on fire, one room may be left untouched; or for example, when the land of Egypt came under the plague, the land of Goshen where the children of Israel dwelt in Egypt went unscathed (see Ex. 9.26, 10.23). Such an explanation is erroneous because (1) the "keeping" in view here is not a keeping *through* but a keeping *from*. In the Greek text, after the word "keep" in this verse there is the word *ek* which means "out of" (as in the word *ekklesia* which means "the called out ones"). Here, therefore, *ek* signifies a being kept out of the Tribulation. And (2) "Because thou didst keep the word of my patience, I also will keep thee from the hour of trial" (3.10a)—As we have seen, the trial which is to come upon the whole world is the Great Tribulation; but notice that it is not a keeping from the *trial* but a keeping from the *hour* of the trial. In order to be kept out of the hour of trial, we must *leave the world*. There are only two ways for God to keep us out: death and rapture. And hence part of the living will be raptured before the Tribulation.

B. Luke 21.36 also proves that not the entire church but only a part of it will be raptured before the Tribulation. The accounts of Luke 21 and Matthew 24 are quite alike, except that Matthew stresses more the coming of Christ and the Tribulation while Luke focuses more on the destruction of Jerusalem and the Tribulation. Hence there is the famous question asked in Matthew (24.3), and there are also more parables recorded in Matthew's account than in Luke's. In 70 A.D. Jerusalem experienced a terrible destruction, and at the end she will experience a great tribulation. The record in Luke can be outlined as follows: 21.8–9—the things before the end; 10–19—believers will suffer; 20–28—how Jerusalem will be destroyed (verse 28 seems to suggest that the saints will all pass through the Tribulation); 29–33 —a parable guaranteeing the certainty of these things to come; and 34–36—Were it not for this passage, it might be inferred that the whole body of believers would surely be raptured after the Tribulation: yet verse 34 has a change in tone from the preceding verses, verse 35 shows that the things mentioned earlier concern the whole inhabited world, and verse 36 presents the condition for escaping the Great Tribulation—which is to watch and pray.

How are believers to escape all these coming things and to stand before the Son of man? Naturally by being raptured. Death is not a blessing: we do not pray and expect death. The condition here for rapture is to watch and pray. Hence here, not all the regenerated may be raptured. Pray always. What to pray for? Pray that we may escape all these things which shall come to pass. "That ye may prevail" (or, "ye may be accounted worthy" AV). It is not a question of grace, but rather a matter of worthiness. How about worthiness? God cannot receive you to the place where you have no desire to go. Some people may consider heaven as too tasteless a place in which to live as may be indicated by these words: "Lest haply your hearts be overcharged with surfeiting, and drunkenness, and cares of this life" (v.34). If a balloon is tied, it cannot ascend. In sum, Luke 21.36 shatters the arguments of both the first and second schools of interpretation.

The second school may still raise other arguments, such as (1) that rapture is not dependent on conduct—yet in reply it should be asked whether anyone thinks a carnal believer lying on a bed of fornication will be raptured? Or (2) that the phrase "all these things" does not refer to the Great Tribulation but to the surfeiting, drunkenness, and cares of this life cited in verse 34. In reply, it should be noted that verse 36 reads, "all these things *that shall come to pass*"—whereas "surfeiting, and drunkenness, and cares of this life" pertain to the things *which are present now.* And therefore, "watch ye" means to not be deceived by such activities.

C. Other proofs as follows:

(1) By reading Matthew 24.42 together with 1 Thessalonians 5.2,4, it is evident *that there are at least two raptures:* for note that the first passage suggests rapture before the Tribulation because one must be watchful since he does not know when his Lord will come; while the second passage suggests rapture after the Tribulation because one knows when the day of the Lord shall come.

(2) The places to be raptured towards are also different. Whereas Revelation 7.15 mentions to "the throne of God" and Luke 21.36 mentions "to stand before the Son of man," 1 Thessalonians 4.17 says that it is to "the air"—Such distinctions would thus indicate that the entire body of believers is not raptured all at one time.

(3) Mark 13 states, "But of that day or that hour knoweth no one, not even the angels in heaven, neither the Son, but the Father" (v.32). So that the day of the coming of Christ is unknown. But 1 Thessalonians 4 declares that "the Lord himself shall descend from heaven, with a shout, with the voice of the archangel, and with the trump of God" (v.16). From this second passage we know that the appearing of Christ is after the sounding of the seventh trumpet. And hence the first passage relates to pre-tribulation rapture while the second relates to post-tribulation rapture.

VI. Questions raised against separate rapture, and answers thereto, are submitted below.

A. Some people say that the rapture of the church cannot be divided because the body of Christ cannot be divided. It should be noted in reply, however, that the body is a figure of speech which signifies one life. If the body is taken literally, then there is already division today because the Lord is now in heaven, Paul has already died, we remain living on earth, and some believers are yet to be born.

B. Others object that rapture is part of redemption, that

since redemption is according to grace, rapture cannot be based on the concept of worthiness. In reply, it needs to be pointed out that while the act of changing (see 1 Cor. 15.51–52) is indeed according to grace, the act of being taken (rapture) is according to works.

C. Some observers ask, Is it not rather cruel to take away hope from the church? To which we must answer that in the Scriptures there is no such false hope given; and therefore it is better to alert people to this fact.

D. 1 Corinthians 15.23, say some, only mentions "they that are Christ's" and that nothing is said about works. But let us be aware that this verse does not speak of rapture, it speaks of resurrection.

E. Since the dead will not go through the Great Tribulation, would it not be unfair to the living for them to go through it? Will not the righteous God be unjust in this regard? In response, let me say that we do need to be concerned; for during the millennium each and every believer (including all believers who died prior to the Great Tribulation) will receive, as a consequence of appearing before Christ's judgment seat, the things done in the body while alive, according to what he has done whether it be good or bad (2 Cor. 5.10).

F. Since in 1 Corinthians 15.50–52 ("We all shall not sleep, but we shall all be changed") "all" is the word used, surely this signifies the whole body. Yes, the "all" here does indeed refer to the entire body, but it does not have reference *to the same time.* For example, we all will die, but certainly not all of us will do so in one day.

G. There is a distinction made in the Bible between wheat and tares, some say, but no difference made between wheat and wheat; consequently, all wheat must be raptured. In reply, it should be noted that the times of ripening for wheat are not the same. Thus there are the firstfruits and the later harvest.

H. Some argue that according to 1 Thessalonians 4.15

the living "shall in no wise precede them who are fallen asleep"—The dead are resurrected at the seventh trumpet; and so timewise, rapture occurs after the Tribulation. Now if there is a first rapture, it will have to take place before the resurrection of the dead. But since this verse distinctly says "shall in no wise," how then can rapture take place twice? Let me say in reply that it is most precious and significant to find in both verse 15 and verse 17 the qualifying clauses "we that are alive, that are left"—Now to be alive is obviously to be left on earth; why, then, is there this apparent unnecessary repetition? Because it implies that there are people who though alive yet have already gone ahead (that is, raptured) and therefore are no longer left on earth. Would Paul enlist himself among this class of people who are alive and are left? Not at all. He uses the word "we" only because he is speaking at that moment of writing. And the proof of this is that since Paul no longer lives today, he cannot be numbered among those who are left on earth.

Our summary conclusion to all this is that the third school of interpretation seems to be the correct one—that is to say, that one group of believers will be raptured before the Tribulation while another group of believers will go through the Tribulation and be raptured afterwards.

Concerning the second coming ("What shall be the sign of thy coming?"), we need to distinguish three Greek words (1) *parousia,* (2) *apokalupsis,* and (3) *epiphaneia.*.

The term used by the disciples in asking the Lord about His "coming" is the Greek word *parousia* which should be translated "presence"—it is used in the Scriptures 24 times. Besides the seven times wherein it applies to man (1 Cor. 16.17; 2 Cor. 7.6,7; 10.10; Phil. 1.26, 2.12; and 2 Thess. 2.9), the remaining 17 occasions refer to the Lord (Matt. 24.3,27,37,39; 1 Cor. 15.23; 1 Thess. 2.19, 3.13, 4.15, 5.23; 2 Thess. 2.1,8; James 5.7,8; 2 Peter 1.16; 3.4,12; and 1 John 2.28).

The word *apokalupsis* (meaning "uncovering" or "revelation") appears in the Scriptures in the following places: 1 Peter 1.7,13;

4.13; 1 Corinthians 1.7; and 2 Thessalonians 1.7. "Revelation" is given to help people to understand.

The term *epiphaneia* (meaning "appearing") is used in the Bible in: 1 Timothy 6.14; 2 Timothy 1.10, 4.1,8; Titus 2.13; and 2 Thessalonians 2.8 where this Greek term is translated as "manifestation" in English. The "appearing" is for the purpose of causing people to see.

The word "coming" in Matthew 24.3 is *parousia* ("presence"). Why does the Holy Spirit choose to use this particular term? Possibly because this matter of our Lord's coming is a rather complicated event and the Greek term *parousia* carries within its meaning a very broad scope.

The *parousia* (or "presence") of the Lord commences with the first rapture to the throne. "Be patient therefore, brethren, until the *parousia* of the Lord" (James 5.7). "Be ye also patient; establish your hearts: for the *parousia* of the Lord is at hand" (5.8). As we have noted earlier, all who have kept the word of the patience of Christ shall participate in the first rapture (Rev. 3.10).

Look further at 2 Peter 3.4, where the question raised is: "Where is the promise of his *parousia*?"

Then 1 Thessalonians speaks (1) of a standing before the Lord Jesus Christ at His *parousia* (2.19), (2) of the time of the *parousia* of the Lord with all His saints (3.13), (3) of how we shall all be caught up and meet the Lord in the air at His *parousia* (4.15–17), and (4) of having our spirit and soul and body preserved entire without blame at the *parousia* of our Lord Jesus Christ (5.23).

What are the things which transpire during the time of *parousia*? All who are Christ's shall be resurrected (1 Cor. 15.23). *The parousia* of the Lord is where the believers will gather together with Him (2 Thess. 2.1). In His *parousia*, He will deal with the Antichrist (2 Thess. 2.8). The lawless one will also have his own *parousia* (2 Thess. 2.9). If we abide in Christ we may have boldness and not be ashamed before Him at His *parousia* (1 John 2.28).

We deduce from these Scripture passages that *parousia* includes the throne and the air. Time-wise, it begins with the first rapture and ends with the appearing of Christ and His saints on earth. Thus *parousia* actually stands between the church and the kingdom. It comprises (1) the first rapture to the throne, (2) tribulation and the Great Tribulation, (3) the Lord descending to the air, (4) the general rapture of believers to the air, and (5) the appearing of Christ with His saints on earth. Perhaps the following diagram and the explanatory text which follows can make it clearer.

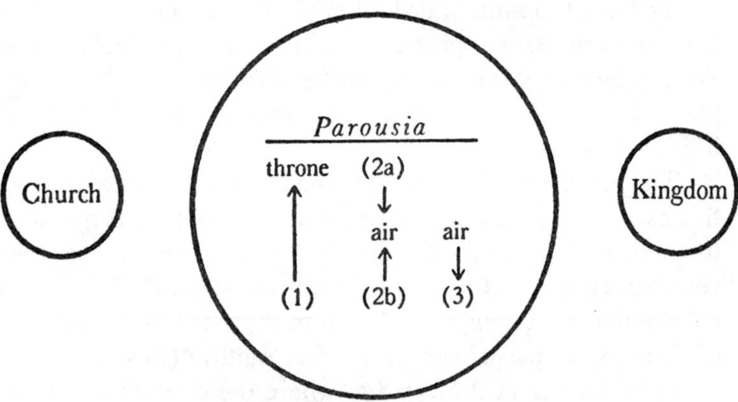


During *parousia* there are three periods which coincide with three locations: (see large center circle above): At the beginning of *parousia* (1) the overcoming believers are raptured to the throne (Matt. 24.37,40–41). After some time (2a) the Lord descends from heaven to the air (1 Thess. 4.15–17, 1 Cor. 15.23)—(please remember that the throne is presently in heaven—Rev. 4.1–2). Meanwhile (2b) the dead in Christ shall rise, and those believers who are alive and left on the earth from the previous rapture (to the throne) shall, together with the risen dead in Christ, be caught up to the air. There they shall experience *parousia* with the Lord. And finally, *parousia* ends (3) with the appearing of the Lord with His saints from the air to the earth. He will bring to nought the Antichrist by the exploded glory of His *parousia* (2 Thess. 2.8–9).

What should be the attitude of believers toward *parousia*? Wait patiently (James 5.7–8); have the heart established unblamable in holiness (1 Thess. 3.13); and have one's spirit, soul, and body preserved entire without blame (1 Thess. 5.23).

What will happen to the believers in *parousia*? Each man's work shall be judged (1 Thess. 2.19, 1 John 2.28, 1 Cor. 3.12,15. . . .

24.40–41 "One is taken, and one is left" —Why do we have these two verses? We know that all who belonged to Noah entered the ark and were therefore saved from the impending flood. According to strict typology, then, is not this to be interpreted that all the saints will be raptured together? Let us see that the Lord purposely adds the words of these two verses here lest we greatly misunderstand. Although it is true that as the days of Noah were, so shall be the coming of the Son of man, there is nevertheless this one exception which our Lord tries to explain here.

There are three different views on the men or women mentioned in verses 40 and 41: (1) they all refer to the Jews at that time; (2) the ones taken point to the regenerated, while the ones left point to the unsaved; or (3) both the taken and the left are Christians.

Let us first examine closely interpretations (1) and (3): According to (1) we must assume that the ones taken are the Jew who will be punished while the ones left will be those Jews who will enjoy the blessing of the kingdom on earth. But according to (3), we need to postulate just the opposite—that the taken are the saved who will enjoy the blessing of glory while the left are the saved who will go through the Great Tribulation on earth. Before we can settle on view (1) or view (3), we should investigate the words "taken" and "left" as to their meaning. If "taken" means good, then view (3) is more applicable since the rapture of Christians is a blessed thing. On the other hand, if "taken" means bad, then view (1) is more likely because these Jews will not be left on earth to enjoy the blessing of the kingdom.

The word "taken" is *paralambano* in Greek. Besides being translated "to receive" as its basic meaning, it can also denote the idea of "to take to (or with) oneself" —In the New Testament this word is used 52 times, most of which instances convey a good meaning. John 14.3 ("and will receive you unto myself") is the only instance wherein our Lord speaks directly on rapture. Three times He took Peter, John and James along with Him (see Mark 5.35–43, Matt. 17.1 and 26.37). There, "paralambano" on all three occasions connotes a good idea. In John 1.11 ("they that were his own received him not"), the meaning will be good if people receive the Lord. The word "received" in Colossians 2.6, "received" in 1 Thessalonians 4.1, "received" in 2.13, "receiving" in Hebrews 12.28, "take" and "took" in Matthew 2.13–14, "took" in Acts 15.39, "took" in 16.33, and "took" in 23.18—all are *paralambano* and all suggest something good. Even in the Old Testament, the equivalent Hebrew word for "took" (*laqach*) in Genesis 5.24 refers to rapture; and the same Hebrew word for "fetched" (*laqach*) in 1 Samuel 10.23 means something good.

Though the word "left" has also its favorable implication such as in Genesis 32.8, Numbers 26.65 and Isaiah 24.6, yet it can be used in both the good and the bad sense. The question is decided by the identity of the one who leaves them behind. If they are left behind by the devil, nothing is better. But if they are left behind by the Lord, can anything be worse? It is woe to those who are taken by the devil, but blessed are those who are taken by the Lord.

However, the meaning of a word is not in itself decisive enough for making a judgment. We have to consider its context. According to Matthew 24.19, those who are left behind because they cannot flee are in bad trouble. Then, too, verses 42 and 43 tell us that the Lord shall come as a thief; what He steals away must therefore be the best. Even in the parable of the ten virgins in Matthew 25, the virgins who are taken inside are the wise, while the virgins who are left outside are the foolish.

Of course, whether taken or left, all the men and women spoken of here in 24.40–41 are saved—so that the ones left cannot be viewed as being unsaved because of the following reasons:

(1) "Watch therefore" (v.42). The word "therefore" connects with the preceding verses 40 and 41. Since you are saved and have life, you are expected to watch. Those who lack the Lord's

life cannot watch. The determining factor in rapture is not a being saved or unsaved but is a case of one's works after regeneration. To say that all the regenerated will be raptured *together* is a serious mistake.

(2) "Your Lord cometh" (v.42). The unsaved do not have the relationship of servant and master with the Lord. Man may misuse this word, but the Lord never will. The unsaved person may consider himself to be a servant of the Lord, but the Lord will not carelessly use such a term as "your Lord" here.

(3) "The thief was coming" (v.43). If a thief comes to steal apples, he will take the ripe ones and leave the unripened ones behind. Thus it is not a difference in kind but one of degree.

(4) The five foolish in the parable of the virgins told of in chapter 25 are not false virgins. They are real, except that they are not wise as are the five wise virgins. The wise ones spare no effort to carry oil in the vessels whereas the foolish are too lazy to make such a provision. Nevertheless, both the wise and the foolish are virgins, and they all go forth to meet the bridegroom.

(5) Judging from typology, those who are left can be the saved as well as those who are taken. Both Enoch (who was raptured) and Noah (who entered the ark) were saved. Yet both Abraham (the intercessor) and Lot (who passed through tribulation) were saved too. But Elijah (the taken) and Elisha (the left) were saved. The disciples whom the Lord in His ascension left behind were all saved ones. Both Philip (the one taken away) and the eunuch (the one left behind) were saved.

We conclude, therefore, that the "taken" and the "left" in verses 40 and 41 are all saved.

v.42 Joining verses 40 and 41 with verse 42, one may readily see that the real issue lies in "watch" or "not watch"; otherwise the Lord cannot employ the word "therefore" nor can He exhort us to be watchful. If the condition for early rapture is regeneration and not watchfulness and proper works after regeneration, then there would be no reason for the Lord to enjoin us to watch. For in this verse He merely charges us to be watchful, with nothing being said about repentance, faith, or regeneration. Thus, both the taken and the left mentioned in verses 40–42 are saved ones. Surely our Lord will not advise the unregenerated to watch.

What is the significance of the word "watch"? Some people have suggested that this matter of watching concerns only the Jews, while we Christians need only to wait. Yet we know that the Jews will themselves have to pass through "Jacob's trouble": there is no way for them to escape the wrath of God. And hence they cannot avoid the Great Tribulation simply because they are watchful. But with the church, watchfulness is most useful. The meaning of watching is not to be careless. How prone Christians are to be overly self-confident. Watchfulness is the very opposite of carelessness. He who sleeps must be so confident in himself that he reckons nothing is going to happen, whereas the watchful person puts no trust in his flesh at all. The self-confident one is prone to fall, for to boast that "I am different from yesterday" opens the way to failure. Only the person who deeply senses his own inadequacy will be watchful. To watch is to be careful, guarding daily against the possibility of a fall. Whoever considers himself as unable to fall will not be vigilant.

We need to see from all this that if all believers were to be raptured together, what would be the need for our Lord to warn us to watch? Moreover, if we knew the time of His coming, we again would have no need to watch. But since the Lord has not told us the hour, let us ever be watchful and on guard.

—KKH 271–89, 298–300, 332–6

# 40 | Overcomers

### *God Looks for Overcomers*

Now whenever the church fails, God finds a few in the church—called to be overcomers—that they might bear the responsibility which the church as a whole ought to but fails to bear. He chooses a company of the faithful few to represent the church in the demonstration of the victory of Christ. He has His overcomers in all the seven periods of the church (as represented by the seven churches described in Revelation chapters 2 and 3). This overcomer line is never cut. The overcomers are not some special class. They are simply a group of people who conform to the *original* plan of God.

### *The Principle of Overcomers*

The way God works, as illustrated in His Holy Scriptures, is to find a few as a nucleus in order to reach the many. This was true in the patriarchal age. At that time God chose people individually: those such as Abel, Enoch, Noah, and Abraham. Later on through Abraham (the few) God reaches the whole nation of Israel (the many)—that is to say, God reaches the dispensation of the law through the patriarchal age. Then from the dispensation of the law (the nation of Israel) God reaches to the dispensation of grace (the church out of all nations); and likewise from the dispensation of grace He will reach to the dispensation of the kingdom (the entire world), and from the dispensation of the kingdom to the new heaven and the new earth (the new creation), for the kingdom is the prologue to the new heaven and the new earth. So then, the principle of God's operation is from the few to the many.

". . . the Head, from whom all the body, being supplied and knit together through the joints and bands, increaseth with the increase of God" (Col. 2.19). The joints are for supplying, while the bands are for knitting. The Head holds the body together through these joints and bands. And these joints and bands are the overcomers. . . .

### *The Work of the Overcomers*

In examining the principle of the overcomers we must notice two things: (1) that whenever the whole body fails, God will choose relatively few to stand for the whole body; and (2) that God calls these few to carry out His command so that through them He may later reach the many. . . .

### *How to Become an Overcomer: the Case of Gideon*

(1) *Recognize one's own littleness*—that is, know oneself. It is relatively easy to be humble before God; but to be humble before men or to esteem others as more excellent than oneself is extremely difficult. To say I am the least is comparatively easy, but to confess that I am the least in my father's house is not easy. To acknowledge that my father's house is the poorest is not too hard, yet to admit that my father's house is the poorest in Manasseh is most humiliating. He whose face shines and is unconscious of it, though others can see the light of his countenance, is an overcomer. All who look at mirrors in an attempt to see the light on their faces are definitely not overcomers. Although David was anointed, he looked upon himself as a dead dog (1 Sam. 24.14). Overcomers are those who have the reality of, yet not the name of, overcomers.

(2) *See the heavenly vision*—that is, see the Lord. No one without

vision is able to serve. With vision, one can press on to reach the goal even though he is beset by difficulties. Having the word of the Lord, one may with certainty sail on to the other shore. The feet of a worker are steadied by the vision he has seen.

(3) *Be not disobedient to the vision*—but respond to the calling of the Lord with sacrifice. One should offer his insignificant self to God and leave himself in God's hand. Judging one's own self as being either great or small without committing all in God's hand is equally useless. All the living sacrifices according to God's will are accepted by God. Overcomers are called of God. Have you heard the call for overcomers that is found in Revelation chapters 2 and 3? And have you answered the call?

(4) *Break down idols*—which is to say, maintain an outward testimony. A heart already consecrated needs to break down the idols without, in order to bear the testimony. One should pay attention to his own person, his family, and his contacts. Whatever strives to be equal with God must be broken down. He who sees God knows what an idol is. Having seen the angel of the Lord—that is to say, the Lord himself, one discerns the things outside the Lord as idols. A sight of the angel of the Lord reveals the wood (the Asherah) as not being God (Judges 6.22–27). The sacrifice on the rock is for a personal purpose, whereas the sacrifice on the altar is for corporate use.

After these four steps have been taken, the Holy Spirit will fall on the person. The filling of the Holy Spirit is not the result of asking for power; when one stands on the right ground, he shall receive the outpoured Spirit.

—GP 55–6, 60, 68–9

# 41 Reward

### *Salvation and Reward*

We have now seen that the book of Revelation is a book of righteousness. Yet for us to appreciate its righteous effects, we need to distinguish salvation from reward. The word of God presents a clear distinction between these two. What God has parted, let not men join together. Let us consider this matter carefully and see the contrast between them.

Salvation is that which is *given freely.* It is not earned by means of man's works. For it is God who gives *grace* to us, and not on the basis of our *merit.*

"Ho, every one that thirsteth [points to the sinner], come ye to the waters [points to God's salvation], and he that hath no money [points to works or righteous deeds]; come ye, buy, and eat [means all sinners may believe and be saved]; yea, come, buy wine and milk [means the joy of salvation] without money and without price [points to the fact that there is no need of good deeds, since it does not depend on one's goodness]" (Is. 55.1).

"The *gift* of God" (John 4.10).

"The *free gift* of God is eternal life" (Rom. 6.23).

"By grace have ye been saved through *faith;* and that not of yourselves, it is the *gift* of God; not of works, that no man should glory" (Eph. 2.8–9).

"Not by works done in righteousness, which we did ourselves, but according to his *mercy* he saved us" (Titus 3.5).

"He that will, let him take the water of life *freely*" (Rev. 22.17).

Through these verses which have been quoted and many other Scripture passages not quoted, it is proven beyond any doubt that we receive our salvation *freely* and not by our works or righteous acts; we are saved by the *grace* of God, the free gift of God. All we do is to believe. For the work of salvation is wholly done for us by the Lord Jesus. His death on the cross has accomplished our salvation. For us now to be saved and to gain eternal life, there is no need for us to perform more works or to add more merits but simply to *believe* and *receive.* This is because none of our good works is acceptable to God. Throughout the entire New Testament there are about 150 instances of such sayings as these: believe and be saved, believe and have eternal life, believe and be justified. Just as soon as we believe, we are saved, receive eternal life, and are justified. This is all freely given: "... the witness is this, that God *gave* unto us eternal life, and this life is in his Son. He that hath the Son hath the life; he that hath not the Son of God hath not the life" (1 John 5.11-12). All who accept the Lord Jesus as Savior by faith have eternal life according to the word of God. Truly, "he that *believeth* on the Son hath eternal life" (John 3.36). *Believe* and you have!

Reward, though, is a different matter. It is not something freely received; it must be obtained through *good works.* It is given according to the works of each *saint.* Let us look at the following Scriptures.

"My *reward* is with me, to render to each man *according as his work is*" (Rev. 22.12). Note that this word is spoken to the Church (see v.16).

"Each shall receive his own *reward according to his own labor*" (1 Cor. 3.8).

"Whatsoever ye *do,* work heartily, as *unto* the Lord, and not unto men; knowing that from the Lord ye shall receive the recompense of the inheritance ... For he that *doeth* wrong shall *receive* again for the wrong that he hath done" (Col. 3.23-25).

"Now to him that *worketh, the reward* is not reckoned as of grace" (Rom. 4.4).

There are many more Scriptures which could be quoted, but

these above are sufficient to prove that *reward is not freely received.* According to the teaching of the Bible, reward is added to the believer's good works. As insignificant as is a cup of cold water (Matt. 10.42), or as hidden as is the counsel of the heart (1 Cor. 4.5) or as humble as is one's service (Mark 10.43) or as unknown as is the suffering for the Lord's sake (Luke 6.22)—all such deeds or attitudes may still have the opportunity of being rewarded (cf. Luke 6.23).

According to the Bible, the goal which is set before a person is twofold: when we are yet *sinners,* our goal is *salvation;* after we are saved and become *believers* our goal is *reward.* For salvation is provided for sinners, whereas reward is provided for believers. Men ought to receive salvation first and then pursue after reward. The perishing should receive salvation; and the saved should win reward. By reading 1 Corinthians 9.24–27 and Philippians 3.12–14, we can readily see that some *believers* fail to obtain *reward.* For in these two passages, Paul is talking about reward and not about salvation. He well knows that he is saved. In his other epistles, he frequently expresses himself as one who has received grace. But in these two passages, he tells us of what he is seeking after having been saved and that is, reward. At this moment he dare not say for sure that he has achieved the reward, he instead is still pursuing. Sinners ought to seek for salvation, while believers ought to seek after reward.

However corrupted a sinner may be, if he is willing to believe the Lord Jesus as Savior, he shall be instantly saved. Once saved and regenerated, he should seek to develop this new life in him and to serve the Lord faithfully so that he may obtain the reward. He is saved through the work of *Christ;* he is rewarded by his *own* works. He is saved through *faith;* he is rewarded by *works.* God is willing to save an undeserving sinner, but He will not reward an undeserving believer. Before anyone believes in the Lord, if he is willing to acknowledge himself as a sinner, come to the Lord Jesus and believe in His substitutionary death on the cross, he is saved and eternal blessing is guaranteed to him. But according to the Scriptures, after he is saved he is placed by God on the race course of life that he may run. If he wins, he shall be rewarded. If he loses, he will not be rewarded. Yet he *will not lose eternal life because of his defeat.* For salvation is eternal. Here we find the most balanced teaching, the perfect truth. Unfortunately, many people only know salvation. They are content with merely being saved and do not care about the reward.

How sad that people have mixed up salvation with reward. They reckon salvation is most difficult, requiring their supreme efforts of self-discipline to attain it. But this is not the teaching of the Bible. The Scriptures consider salvation to be that which is most easy to come by, for the Lord Jesus by His own initiative has already accomplished everything for us. But the Scriptures regard reward as that which is somewhat harder to obtain because it depends upon the works which we by *our* initiative accomplish through Christ.

Let us illustrate the matter in this way. Suppose a certain rich man opens a free school. All who attend are free from all charges since this rich man pays for all their expenses. But those who achieve excellence in learning shall receive a special reward. Accordingly, salvation can be likened to entering this free school. All who are willing to come to the Lord Jesus are saved because He himself has paid the cost of salvation. It is very easy to become a student in this free school since it costs nothing. It is enough just to *come.* In like manner, then, salvation is most easy. One need not do anything except *believe.* But for one who is now enrolled as a student, to obtain the reward is not that easy; he must *work* hard. Similarly, it is not so easy for a believer to win the divine reward; he must have *good* works.

Let not any reader think that it is enough to be saved and not seek the reward as well. To every truly born-again person, the Lord is calling that one to pursue after spiritual excellence—to win the reward. And it should be a natural thing for him to pursue and win. Yet not for his personal benefit, but to gain the Lord's heart and pleasure. For whoever is rewarded by the Lord has delighted His heart. Just as a sinner should be saved, so a believer should be rewarded also. Reward to a believer is as important as salvation to a sinner. If a saint fails to achieve the reward, it does not mean that he has sacrificed his profit, it only indicates that his life is not holy and his labor is not faithful and that he has not manifested the Lord Jesus Christ during his pilgrim days.

Recent teachings have swung towards two extremes. Some reckon salvation to be so difficult that it demands people to do a great deal. Thus they nullify the substitutionary death and the work of redemption of our Lord Jesus. Such teaching puts the entire responsibility on man and overlooks what the Bible says about our being saved by *grace* through faith. Some others think that since all is of grace, then all who believe in the Lord Jesus will not only be saved but also be rewarded with glory and rule in the future with the Lord Jesus. And hence, they lay the entire responsibility on God and neglect what is observed in the Scriptures that some believers—though they be saved—will suffer loss, yet as through fire (1 Cor. 3.15).

Yet there is a most balanced teaching here. Before a sinner believes, the Lord bears His responsibility; after the sinner believes, he must bear the responsibility himself. The work of salvation is totally done by the Lord for him, so it is enough just to believe. But this matter of reward depends wholly on the believer's works, and therefore to believe alone is not adequate. As a sinner cannot be saved by good works, so a saint cannot be rewarded by only believing. Salvation is based on faith; reward is judged by works. Without faith, there is no salvation; without works, there is no reward. If we carefully study the New Testament, we shall perceive how clearly God separates salvation and reward. Salvation is for sinners, but reward is for saints. Both are divinely ordered: sinners should be saved and saints should be rewarded. Overlooking either of them will incur great loss. Let us therefore not mix salvation and reward together.

What is salvation? It is to not perish but to have eternal life. This is what we all know. Yet this does not decide our positions in glory since those are in fact determined by rewards. What is reward? From the Scriptures we can see that reward is to reign with Christ during the millennial kingdom. Every believer has eternal life; but not every believer will be rewarded by being given the right to reign with Christ. The kingdom of the heavens in the Gospel according to Matthew points to the *heavenly part* of the millennial kingdom—that is to say, it points to our reigning with Christ. Every careful reader of the Gospel can see the difference between eternal life and the kingdom of the heavens. To have eternal life requires only faith, but to gain the kingdom of the heavens demands violence to oneself (see Matt. 11.12). So that to be saved is to have eternal life, while to be rewarded is to enter into the kingdom of the heavens.

Let us all press on towards the goal. May God enable us to forsake everything for His sake in order that we may win His reward. To be saved is something now and instantaneous, because it is recorded in God's word that he who believes has eternal life (see the Gospel according to John). Reward is something in the future, for the Scripture says that when the Lord shall come, "then shall each man have his praise from God" (1 Cor. 4.5). Salvation is now, reward is then. Let us not mix them up, because there is a great difference in the principles which govern salvation and reward. Salvation shows the *grace* of God because He does not recompense us according to our sins but rather saves us who believe in the Lord Jesus. Reward expresses the *righteousness* of God because He recompenses the saints according to their good works. Whoever serves Him faithfully shall receive reward.

Let us never forget that our God is not just gracious, nor is He only righteous; His character bespeaks *both* grace and righteousness. Saving sinners is His act of grace; rewarding saints is his act of righteousness. We earlier observed that the book of Revelation expresses the righteousness of God. Knowing the difference between salvation and reward is essential to our understanding of this book. Otherwise it will be difficult to explain the righteous dealing of God with the saints which is delineated in its pages.

Through John God reveals the word of eternal life. In his Gospel, he shows the way to eternal life. In his epistles, he describes the manifestations of eternal life. But in the book of Revelation, he discloses the judgment of the saved. And hence the last book of the Bible touches very little on the matter of the salvation of believers but rather strongly on the question of their reward. Its pages speak of righteousness, and reward is God's righteous act. By reading chapters 2 and 3 we come to see not the matter of salvation but that of the Christian life, believers' works, and their victory. Such knowledge will help us to grasp hold of not only these two chapters but of the rest of the book as well.

—ATR 39–47

# 42 Spiritual Warfare

*Identify the Enemy*

The most important thing before us now is to identify the enemy. We should know for sure who is our adversary, who it is that causes us much suffering. How frequently we account our sufferings to be from men. But the Bible tells us that "our wrestling is not against flesh and blood, but against the principalities, against the powers, against the world-rulers of this darkness, against the spiritual hosts of wickedness in the heavenly places" (Eph. 6.12). Hence every time we suffer from the hand of man, we need to remember that behind flesh and blood Satan and his powers of darkness can very well be there directing everything. We should have the necessary spiritual insight to discern the work of God from the maneuver of Satan at the back of everything. We should distinguish what is natural and what is supernatural. We should be so inwardly exercised as to gain knowledge of the spiritual realm so that none of Satan's hidden work can escape our observation.

Such being the case, shall we not recognize that what we usually consider to be incidental and natural happenings may involve the works of the enemy behind the scenes? We shall readily see that Satan is really trying to frustrate us at every turn and oppress us in all things. What a pity we have suffered so much from him in the past without knowing that it was he who made us suffer. Now part of the most urgent work of ours today is to generate a heart of hatred towards Satan for his cruelty. We do not need to be fearful lest our enmity towards Satan becomes too deep. Before there is the possibility of our overcoming we must maintain in our heart a hostile attitude towards him, no longer willing to subject ourselves to his oppression. We ought to understand that what we have suffered at Satan's hands is a real grievance which must be avenged. He has no right to harass us, yet he does it anyway. This is indeed an injustice, a grievance which cannot remain unavenged. . . .

Satan has a work, which is attacking the children of God. His attack may not come suddenly; oftentimes, it comes gradually and slowly. Daniel 7.25 mentions how Satan shall wear out the saints of the Most High. Satan has in fact a plan against the saints of the Most High, which is to wear them out. Hence let us clearly recognize that the work of Satan in the lives of God's children is frequently not very noticeable, since his work is slowly to wear them down.

What is the meaning of the phrase, "wear out"? It has in it the idea of reducing a little this minute, then reducing a little further the next minute. Reduce a little today and reduce a little more tomorrow. Thus the wearing out is almost imperceptible; nevertheless, it *is* a reducing. The wearing down is scarcely an activity of which one is conscious, yet the end result is that there is nothing left. Hence this principle of Satan's working in the lives of God's children is to wear them out until they are worn down completely. He will wear you out a little today and then a little more the next day. He will make you suffer a small amount now and a little more later. You may think this to be something insignificant, nevertheless Satan knows that the consequence of such wearing away is to wear the saint out completely.

For this reason, the Bible indicates that "the love of the many shall wax cold" (Matt. 24.12), which means a *gradually* growing cold. It also mentions how a certain maid, having a spirit of divination, cried out after Paul and his colleagues for *many days* (see Acts 16.17–18). Moreover, the Scriptures record that when Felix hoped that Paul would give him money, he sent for Paul the *oftener* and communed with him (Acts 24.26). And the Old Testament also describes how Delilah pressed Samson *daily* with her word and so urged him continually that his soul was vexed unto death (Judges 16.16). Such is how Satan gradually, and for many days, will frequently wear out the children of God. "The evil day" spoken of in Ephesians 6.13 refers to the wearing-out tactics of Satan. We must ask God to open our eyes that we may discern how Satan would wear us out and how we should combat his wearing-out tactic.

### *Wearing Out the Physical Body*

Especially with respect to the human body, we may easily see how the enemy wears out the children of God. Two examples come to mind: the smiting of Job's body (Job 2.7–8) and the thorn in Paul's flesh (2 Cor. 12.7). These are classic cases of Satan's wearing out men's bodies. Quite a few Christians experience sickness and the weakening of their body after they are saved, whereas formerly they were rather healthy. Should the Lord open our eyes we will perceive that there is one who is scheming against the children of God all the time, and that one is Satan. Along this same line, we ought to point out how many of the Lord's servants, before they went forth to preach the gospel, were in good health, but that after they went out to work for the Lord their health failed in a short period of three to five years. This is the enemy wearing out the saints of the Most High. He makes the child of God eat a little less today and sleep a little less tomorrow. He causes him to feel a little tired today and a little more tired tomorrow. By thus adding a little at a time, a believer's health can finally become entirely shaken. Such is the work of Satan.

### *Wearing Out Man's Heart*

Not only does he work on the body, Satan also works in the human heart. Upon first believing in the Lord you may feel very happy, joyful and peaceful. But if you are not watchful—being ignorant of what the enemy can do—you will find yourself one day mysteriously uncomfortable. You feel somewhat restless today, somewhat unhappy tomorrow, and somewhat depressed the day after. Little by little, your peace is completely lost, your joy totally gone. This is the way the devil wears you down to a state of fatigue and despair.

### *Wearing Out the Spiritual Life*

Satan also wears out your spiritual life. He will take away your prayer life little by little, and cause you to trust God less and less and yourself more and more, a little at a time. He will make you feel somewhat cleverer than before. Step by step you are misled to rely more on your own gift, and step by step your heart is enticed away from the Lord. Now were Satan to strike the children of God with great force at one time, they would know how to resist the enemy since they would immediately recognize his work. What is so wickedly subtle about Satan, though, is that he does not strike with one grand stroke; instead, he will employ the tactic of wearing out the saints over an extended period of time, thus causing God's children to lose out and to backslide a little at a time. He uses this method of gradualism to wear down the people of God.

### *Wearing Out Our Time*

Satan will also wear out our time. Felix often sent for Paul and communed with him. After two years of conversation with the powerful and gifted apostle, he was still unsaved. This is the enemy's device to wear people out. Today, Paul is invited to talk without any result; tomorrow he is again invited to talk, with still no result; and the day afterwards he is once more invited to talk, and again, without any result. Paul was inveigled to engage in "resultless" work for two whole years. How the enemy wears out man's time and energy!

If the children of God do not discern Satan's wiles they can easily fall into his trap. How we must redeem our time and make every hour count. We must resist Satan from wearing out our time and must withstand him from causing us to do works that will have no results. . . .

*Must Detest the Wearing Out Work of Satan*

When Paul was preaching in Macedonia he met a certain maid having a spirit of divination. She followed after him and cried out, saying, "These men are servants of the Most High God, who proclaim unto you the way of salvation." And this she did for many days until Paul was so sorely troubled that he turned and declared to the spirit, "I charge thee in the name of Jesus Christ to come out of her." And the evil spirit came out that very moment (see Acts 16.16–18). In the spiritual realm we need to have such detestation as Paul exhibited here. We are not to detest men but must detest the evil spirits. Paul, for sure, loathed the evil spirit but not the maid. He commanded the spirit to come out of her. In the affair, he treated the maid as a third person. Let us have Paul's kind of detestation whenever the devil is wearing men down.

If you really know how Satan tries to wear you out, you will ask God to give you this sense of detestation—which is, to loathe Satan and be angry with him! Many know how to lose their temper on men but strangely enough do not know how to hurl their temper on Satan. When they are annoyed by people they will be thrown into a fit of temper, yet they are not aware of how the enemy is wearing them down. Day after day Paul was being worn down by Satan until he was so exasperated that he opened his mouth to resist the evil spirit, and thus the spirit left the maid. Hence do not keep silent all the time. Let there be voice raised in resistance. If God's children would grow angry and open their mouths to oppose Satan, all would be well. If people will become angry with the devil we will shout Hallelujah, How wonderful! How very pitiful are some, who are so weak that they allow the enemy to wear them down all the time. Children of God should be angry at Satan and should detest him. By being angry and showing abhorrence they cease experiencing the wearing down of the enemy.

How frequently as you are being worn down by Satan you keep silent, patiently enduring and quietly suffering until you feel so disgusted within yourself and become so angry that you declare: "I oppose this, I will not have it!" Just by saying this, just by being infuriated about it, you are delivered and the wearing out process ends. God's children should therefore rise up to repudiate and reprove the enemy. Some people fail to get relieved because they still have "strength" to endure. A person who keeps on enduring Satanic wear and tear, allowing the devil to waste away his energy, his joy and his spiritual life, has fallen into the wile of the enemy. Let us be clear, of course, that we should not be angry at the people who are used by Satan; on the contrary, we ought to be patient with them, even loving them. But we must oppose and resist the hidden conspiracy of Satan. If we withstand what he does, we will soon be freed.

The power to resist the evil one comes from discerning his pressure. A number of believers, when they are manipulated and assaulted, do withstand and resist him; yet they find no strength in themselves. This is because they fail to see Satan's pressure. Though they resist, they do not seem to have the strength to raise their voice against the enemy. Whether or not you can resist him depends on how much you detest him. If you are not quite annoyed at him, your words to him will vanish into the air. But if you are really exasperated, you become angry at him. This anger becomes your power. As you open your mouth you cause him to flee.

Such a detestation comes from revelation. Because you perceive how the devil keeps on wearing you down, you resist him. The moment you see this, Satan knows his tactic is discovered and his hope is lost. May God truly have mercy upon us that we may recognize the wearing-out work of Satan. Let us realize that if we patiently endure, the work of Satan will most certainly continue; but if we are outraged, he will immediately leave us alone. Let us understand that all means of resistance are of no avail except we speak out to resist, and then we shall see that Satan is forced to retreat. If one day we recognize what Satan is doing—that he does plan everything—we shall rise up boldly and declare: "I reject it; I oppose it!" And as God gives us such a resistance, it instantly becomes effective.

In conclusion, we ought to read Ephesians 6.13, in which Paul writes that we, "having done all" ought "to stand"; we must stand, and not allow Satan to continue wearing us down. We should ask the Lord to open our eyes to see what wearing-out work Satan is performing on the children of God. May we rise up to resist and to speak against the enemy. May we declare: "I resist, I oppose, I do not accept such wearing down." If we reject and resist whatever wearing-down tactic Satan may use upon us, we shall witness the salvation of the Lord and the deliverance from Satan's wearing-out strategem.

Such a word needs the covering of the blood. May God cover us with the blood.

—LUP 56-7, 79-83, 84-7

According to God's thought the Church has been placed on a war-footing. Everything ought to be in relation to this. If the Church is not a militant Church, it is not a Church at all. For God only recognizes a militant Church. If we are still bound by the earth, by ourselves or by the devil, it is because we do not see our enemy. Let it be known that we have three enemies: the world, the flesh and the devil. Just as our God is a Triune God, so our enemy is also three-in-one.

How do we recognize the enemy? Which one do we first overcome—the world, the flesh or the devil? (1) According to experience, *the world* is the first to be overcome. This is the lowest plane of victory. If we are touched by the spirit of the world in our life and work, then we are out of the battle. In order to be overcomers, what we must overcome is not only the *things* of the world but also the *spirit* of the world. In overcoming the world we maintain our proper relationship with the Father.

(2) *The flesh.* The world is outward, but Satan has planted something *in* us. You can have a clear break with the world, but you will find that there is something following you everywhere. You cannot get away from it. In the very best thing you do, you will find that you yourself are in everything. God has to take many years to deal with us till He can show us *ourselves* in His light, and then we shall be properly weakened. Light results in the flesh not being able to rise up in the same way as before, because now it has no strength left. Only after this dealing can we know the third enemy, Satan.

(3) *The devil.* Because he is a spirit, only those who have been set free from the flesh can—in their spirit—know the battle in the spirit realm. Those who are in the flesh only know what the flesh is. Hence all who have not been delivered from the world and the flesh are fuzzy towards Satan. In the Letter to the Ephesians we find that it is only in the sixth and final chapter that warfare is mentioned. Just as explained in the earlier chapters of Ephesians, the first two issues—the world and the flesh—have to be solved in our lives before we get to the third—the devil. . . .

You can never truly know spiritual warfare until you are in the heavenlies. If you are bound to the earth, you may know warfare, but it will only touch the realm of the flesh. Ephesians 1–2 shows what our position is. Ephesians 6 shows that our foes are in the heavenlies. This is why we need to be seated *there.* The intervening chapters say nothing of the heavenlies (except in 3.10).

—WG 47–9, 52

> Be sober, be watchful: your adversary the devil, as a roaring lion, walketh about, seeking whom he may devour: whom withstand stedfast in your faith, knowing that the same sufferings are accomplished in your brethren who are in the world. (1 Peter. 5.8–9)
>
> That no advantage may be gained over us by Satan: for we are not ignorant of his devices. (2 Cor. 2.11)

These two scriptural passages indicate to us how full of evil devices Satan is. His basic work is to camouflage whatever he does so that people will not know it is his doing! He even fashions himself into an angel of light (2 Cor. 11.14). All his works are done under the cover of deceit. When he speaks a lie, he speaks of his own: for he is a liar and he always lies (John 8.44). Of all that he has ever done, he has never willingly and openly acknowledged anything as his work. If he were to make a public report of his works, probably nobody would want them; everyone would probably resist them. For this reason, he always disguises his work in a multitude of ways.

### *The Work of Satan*

Satan's works are manifold. In order for a Christian to walk well before God, he must learn how to resist Satan. In order to do that, he must discern what is the work of Satan. According to the judgment of the Bible, many so-called natural things are actually Satanic works. From a human point of view we may consider something to be incidental, natural, or circumstantial, but the Bible distinctly labels it as the work of the devil. If we are to follow a straight course, God's children must not be ignorant of the devices of Satan—how full of wiles he is, how pretentious and deceptive. We should recognize him in order to resist him.

#### 1. The Work of Satan in the Human Mind

Let us now mention a few of Satan's devices so that we may resist him and overcome him before the Lord.

"For the weapons of our warfare are not of the flesh, but mighty before God to the casting down of strongholds; casting down imaginations, and every high thing that is exalted against the knowledge of God, and bringing every thought into captivity to the obedience of Christ" (2 Cor. 10.4–5). Satan surrounds man with strongholds so as to prevent him from obeying Christ. The special field of his work is found in man's mind or thought life. Oftentimes man is bombarded with speculations or imaginations which are adverse to the obedience of Christ. Paul says the weapons of our warfare against these are not of the flesh. These imaginations must first be destroyed before we can bring our thoughts into captivity to the obedience of Christ.

The sphere of Satan's operation is in man's thought life. He will inject a thought, an imagination, which appears to be your own. Under this deception, you accept it and use it as if it were yours, though in actuality it is his.

Do remember that many things in the life of a Christian begin with speculations or imaginations. Many sins are first committed in the imagination of the mind. Many unpleasantnesses among brothers and sisters arise from these fancies.

Then there are those sudden thoughts. Sometimes a thought will flash into one's mind that a certain brother is wrong. Many of God's children do not recognize such thoughts as the work of Satan. A person may consider such a thought as his own and take it as true, thinking that the brother really is wrong. And yet, this is not true. It is Satan who has put the thought into his mind. How is he to resist the devil? He must say, "I do not want this thought. I return it to you, Satan." Should he accept it, it will become his own thought. It is Satan's at the start, but it will become his if he keeps it.

Christians need to know what Satanic temptation is. Satanic temptation enters mainly, if not exclusively, in the form of thought. When Satan tempts people, he does not attach a label saying, "This is Satanic temptation!" If people knew it was of Satan they would resist it. No, he sneaks in stealthily without causing a ripple. All his temptations are formulated so as not to easily arouse the Christians. He does not want them to suspect him; he would rather have them sleep on. So he surreptitiously injects a thought into their mind. Once they accept it, it has become a foothold for him.

This is why the children of God must learn how to resist inordinate thoughts. However, they also should be careful lest they become overly attentive. Any excess in this respect will cause further confusion of the thoughts, causing them to fall further into the wiles of the enemy. If one is concentrating on his thoughts, his eyes will not be focusing on the Lord. We must, indeed, resist improper thoughts, yet we should not be wholly occupied with our thoughts.

I would like to cry aloud that over these years I have seen two extremes: some people exercise no restraint in their thoughts, others are totally taken up with dealing with their thoughts. The latter are just as deceived by Satan as the former. Further, they are likely candidates for a nervous breakdown. So we need to maintain the right balance. We should not allow Satan to tempt us by injecting his thoughts; neither should we be engrossed in how to deal with our thoughts. If we are constantly taken up with dealing with our thoughts, then we have fallen into Satan's temptation, for, instead of having our eyes on the Lord, they are on our thoughts.

Satanic thoughts can be quite easily withstood. There is a saying frequently quoted by many servants of the Lord that goes, "You cannot forbid a bird to fly over your head, but you certainly can forbid it to make a nest in your hair." Do remember, then, that though you cannot prohibit many thoughts from passing through your mind, you can prohibit them from nesting in you. As a thought flashes through you, you may thrust it away by simply saying, "I do not want it. I will not accept it. I reject it." Then you will see that it is thrown out.

Many of God's children have great difficulty with their thoughts. They cannot easily control them. Of the many letters I have received over these past years, the one question most frequently asked is, "How can I control my thoughts?" Some confess that they find it especially difficult to control their thoughts during their prayer time. At this point there is something I would like to say briefly. "Finally, brethren, whatsoever things are true, whatsoever things are honorable, whatsoever things are just, whatsoever things are pure, whatsoever things are lovely, whatsoever things are of good report; if there be any virtue, and if there be any praise, think on these things" (Phil. 4.8), the Bible tells us. Think on these things! God's children should learn to engage their thoughts in positive thinking. The more they use their mind positively, the less their thoughts will be out of control. Many are not able to control their thoughts because they do not think; they are passive in their thought life. This gives Satan the opportunity to insert some of his many ready-made thoughts into their minds.

Satan will not find it so easy to inject his thought into your mind if you learn to use your mind for thinking on things spiritual, good, righteous, holy, peaceful, and lovable. When your mind is positively engaged and your thoughts are not idle, Satan has no opportunity. But if a Christian's mind is unoccupied and idle, then that passive, ungirded mind of his is open to Satanic infiltration.

Because of this, God's children ought to exercise their minds as they exercise their bodies. This will prevent the intrusion of Satanic thoughts. Learn to recognize what thoughts are unclean, divisive, and slanderous, and then learn to resist them as soon as they are discovered to be of the enemy. Many thoughts are distinctly Satanic and therefore can be easily rejected. Some thoughts, though, are quite subtle and therefore not so easily repudiated. Nonetheless, we must learn to resist all of them.

Satan is neither omniscient nor omnipresent. He is, however, acquainted with many things, for through his evil spirits—the sinful angels—he has spread an intelligence network throughout the earth. When we are idle, Satan easily puts something that is known to him, but not to us, into our thought. He injects the intelligence that his secret service has obtained into our thoughts. He makes us fancy something, imagine something, and thus thrusts his intelligence into our mind. As soon as we ponder it and accept it, it becomes real to us. God's children, therefore, must reject all communications from Satan, even if such communications do shed light on things. We should refuse to know anything that does not come to our knowledge by revelation received through prayer.

A child of God must not be curious or nosy. If he is not, he will escape many Satanic thoughts. If he is, Satan will supply him endlessly with some of the many things he knows. The Christian at first may think that such knowledge is beneficial. However, if he continues to accept these thoughts, he will soon become a pawn in Satan's hand. Satan will employ the Christian's mind to do his work. It is for this reason that one must resist all causeless thoughts. Whenever a thought about another brother's fault flashes into one's mind, if it comes from the thought of the mind and not from the consciousness of the Spirit, it should be rejected. If it is accepted, it will eventually become a personal conviction. One who thinks a brother has done him wrong will soon reckon it to be real. Consequently, he will break fellowship with his brother.

Unless these sudden thoughts are cut off at the beginning, they will get out of hand afterward. When Satanic temptations first invade the mind, they are relatively easy to deal with; but once they become "facts" in the mind, they are most difficult to get rid of. For this reason we must deal with thoughts. We must reject all unclean thoughts lest we sin. We must actively use our mind so as not to live a loose and dissipated life. Under God's light, we shall see that many sins come through receiving temptations in the thought life.

Let me reiterate: after a thought is first resisted the matter is considered closed. When the thought comes the second time, it should be ignored. In other words, when a thought first comes to you, resist it by faith, believing that it has fled away. Should it present itself the second time, it comes as a lie, not the truth. Therefore, you must reckon it as false and declare that you have already resisted it. Take this position until the thought flees. If you acknowledge the returned thought as true, you shall soon find it so attached to you that you can hardly throw it off. Many defeats may be attributed to this error. If you resist the devil, he will flee from you. This is the word of the Lord and it is totally trustworthy. Whatever Satan says is undependable. The Lord says, "Resist the devil, and he will flee from you" (James 4.7). Therefore, that which comes back again must be a fake and should be totally discredited.

Why are the minds of so many Christians confused? It is because they are always resisting. "Resist the devil, and he will flee from you," says the Bible. Resist him once, and he will flee. You ought to believe that he has fled away. You do not need to resist him many times. Simply believe that he has fled, for this is in accordance with God's word. Whatever then comes back is not true. You can well afford to ignore it, and, if you do, it will soon disappear. It lurks just outside the door, trying to peep in; if you reckon it as true, it will immediately step in. So, the basic principle is: resist the first time, ignore the second time. If a second time indeed comes, you do not even need to resist; all that is necessary is to not pay the slightest attention. To resist the second time is to discredit the first resistance; to resist the third time is to refute the first and the second resistances, and so on. Each new resistance means one more distrust of your former resistance. Because you do not believe what the Lord has said, "Resist the devil, and he will flee from you," you resist to the hundredth time. You will be occupied with resisting from dawn to dusk. The more you think, the more confused you become. The more you use your mind, the more severely you suffer. Therefore, do not resist foolishly. Simply believe that once resisted the devil will flee.

### 2. The Work of Satan on Man's Body

Satan sometimes works upon the human mind and sometimes on man's body. Many sicknesses are not real sicknesses, but are actually Satanic works. Sometimes illnesses are manifestly Satanic attacks. . . .

Many sicknesses are indeed physical ailments, but many are the results of Satanic attacks on the body. God's children need to learn how to resist this latter kind.

Sometimes you cannot understand why you are sick. You have not been careless; so far as you know there has been no possibility of contagion for this particular sickness in your immediate environment. Yet you are sick. You are suddenly incapacitated when you have something of God's work or some spiritual thing to do. This sickness is not ordinary since it cannot be attributed to any natural cause. Furthermore, you became sick just at the time when you had some spiritual work to fulfill. With your eyes closed you can almost judge that this sickness is due to Satanic assault.

This kind of sickness will disappear if you resist it before the Lord, saying, "Lord, I do not accept this sickness, for it comes from the enemy!" Most amazing, you will find that it goes away as suddenly as it came. Neither its coming nor its going can be attributed to any natural cause. It leaves under rebuke. . . .

Satan desires not only a believer's sickness but even his death. Being a murderer from the beginning, he conspires to bring about the premature death of many, especially of God's children. Therefore, before God we must resist Satan's murderous design. We need to resist him not only as a devil but also as a murderer. Too many of the children of God have the mistaken notion that it would be good if they died. No, such a thought comes from the enemy, for he is always plotting against human life. We can see his evil intention to murder in his insidious attack on Job.

Do not accept the thought of death. It comes from Satan. Perhaps a sudden thought flashes into your mind to put yourself into a dangerous position while you are walking on the street, riding in a boat, or boarding an airplane. You are tempted to accept that thought of possible death. No, learn to reject it and resist it. At no time should you allow Satan to put such a thought into your mind. . . .

You should not turn your back on Satan, for this will mean *you* are running away instead of *him* running away from you! You should face him and let him turn *his* back. If you are facing his back, it means he is running. But if you turn back from facing him, you are defeated. Declare that you will not commit suicide. If you do this, then you are facing him, and he will have to run away. If you tremble for fear you will kill yourself, then you are the one who is running away. If you are afraid of him, you are finished! . . .

### 3. The Accusation of Satan in the Conscience

Satan not only attacks the mind and the body but also the conscience. This attack is what we call accusation. It causes great distress to the Christian who feels himself at fault and thus unable to rise up before God.

Accusation may weaken one's whole being. Many dare not resist for fear that it may be the reproof of the Holy Spirit. They cannot distinguish Satanic accusation from the reproach of the Holy Spirit. Hence they accept Satan's accusation as the Holy Spirit's reproach. Consequently, their lives are wasted under accusation. Do remember that Satanic accusation may cripple the most spiritual and most useful person and reduce him to nought. A weakened conscience weakens the entire person.

What is the difference between a conscience under accusation and the reproach of the Holy Spirit? It is extremely important that we know the difference. Satan's accusation is never clear and sharp, whereas the revelation from God distinctly places your sin before you. Far from being distinct, Satan's accusation is that which is continually mumbling. It is said in Proverbs that "the contentions of a wife are a continuous dropping" (Prov. 19.13). Satanic accusation also operates somewhat like that. It comes down in two or three drops at a time, instead of a pouring out of the whole bucket of water at once. Satan's accusation babbles long like a talkative and dissatisfied woman. Her nature is such that she will not speak out clearly but she will murmur incessantly so as to leave you with a guilty feeling. So is Satanic accusation. It never comes out boldly but rather mumbles along till you feel greatly distressed. When the Holy Spirit comes, though, He enlightens you with a great light so that you distinctly see your fault.

Furthermore, Satanic accusation lacks positive purpose. It does not edify you but, instead, causes you to suffer. It mumbles till it affects you and so overwhelms you that you are no longer able to stand up before God. The purpose of the reproach of the Holy Spirit, however, is to strengthen you, not to weaken you.

The more you are reproved, the easier for you to rise up before God. Satanic accusation produces the opposite effect: the more you are accused, the more you are weakened. Hence the reproach of the Holy Spirit is positive in nature. He so reproves that you have to go to the Lord and learn your lesson. Satanic accusation is quite different. It keeps accusing you until you have been crushed and become useless. Remember, therefore, whenever there is a mumbling that accuses you of fault and so overwhelms you that you cannot even pray or confess or draw nigh to God, then you are definitely under Satanic accusation and must resist.

Furthermore, the results of Satanic accusation are very different from the results of the reproach of the Holy Spirit. If it is the reproach of the Holy Spirit, you will have joy, and at the very least, peace within you after you have confessed your sin. At the time you are reproved, you do suffer agony; but as soon as you confess your sin before God, you enjoy peace in your heart. Sometimes you will be filled with joy, for the heavy burden has been lifted. With Satanic accusation it is not so. Even at the time of prayer and confession, you are still bothered by his mumbling. He will insinuate that you are sinful and useless, that your confession before God is of no avail, that you will be just as weak after asking for forgiveness as you were before. These are sure signs that the accusation is of Satan; it is not the reproach of the Holy Spirit.

We should understand that the primary fields of Satanic operation are not only in the mind and in the body but also in the conscience. He tries to weaken our conscience. Be careful, then, not to fall into his snare! Do keep it well in mind that through the blood of the Lord our conscience may be purified. No sin in the world is so great that the blood cannot cleanse it. Satan, though, will attempt to weaken our conscience to such an extent that we wonder if the blood of our Lord is able to cleanse us. We feel as though we could never be forgiven. This is indeed a Satanic accusation, a lie of the devil.

Satanic accusations need never be confessed. I have found this out after many years of searching. We may wish to play it safe, and hence we confess and ask the Lord's blood to cleanse us. Let me tell you, if once you ask for the cleansing of the precious blood, then you will also have to do the same thing the second time Satan comes to bother you. And so this will go on endlessly. I have met quite a few brothers and sisters who are afflicted in just such a way as this. You can only advise them not to confess. Instead, they should say to the Lord, "Lord, pardon me for not confessing! If I actually have sinned, I still will not confess, for confession carries little meaning these days. It may be Satan's accusation, so I will not even confess." . . .

4. Satan's Assault through Environment

We have paid special attention these days to the matter of the discipline of the Holy Spirit. We have noticed how the Holy Spirit so arranges all our circumstances that, even as the word of God tells us, our hairs are all numbered (Matt. 10.30). Our hairs are not only counted as to their total number but also each is identified by its own number. God knows today when you comb your hair not only how many hairs but also which hairs have fallen!

God's ordering of our environment is clear and detailed. He has looked into all our affairs. Everything is in His hands. Yet, at the same time, Satan has asked God's permission to attack us through our environment. This is something we need to know about.

The story of Job in the Old Testament is the most prominent example. Satan was allowed not only to afflict Job's body with boils, but also to cause his house to fall, his sheep and cattle to be taken away, and his children to die. He sent down fire, wind, and enemies. All these were performed by Satan.

For another example, what did the Lord say about Peter's fall? "Behold, Satan asked to have you, that he might sift you as wheat" (Luke 22.31). Thus we see that though our environment is all arranged by God, yet many attacks may come from Satan. While the Lord Jesus was sleeping in the boat, there arose a great tempest in the sea. Peter and John were certainly not cowards. Yet, as fishermen, they judged by their experience and knew those waves would cause certain disaster. That was why they awoke the Lord Jesus, saying, "Save, Lord; we perish" (Matt. 8.25). The Lord knew, though, that on the other side of the sea in the country of the Gadarenes there were demons to be cast out and that these demons were now trying to drown Him in the sea. So, at the Lord's rebuke, the wind and the sea calmed down. Ordinarily the wind and the sea are not subject to rebuke because they do not possess personality. But here the Lord rebuked them, for Satan was behind, and Satan *is* subject to rebuke.

Whenever Satan attacks us in our environment, there are two things for us to consider. The passage we read in 1 Peter 5, referring especially to our environment, gives these two sides. It first states, "Humble yourselves therefore under the mighty hand of God" (v.6). Then it continues with, "Whom withstand" (v.9).

Whenever God's children encounter unreasonable attacks or causeless perils in their environment, they should on the one hand maintain before God such an attitude as, "Lord, I humble myself under Your mighty hand! I do yield to whatever You have sent me!" They must not utter any word of insubordination; instead they should learn to submit to their environment. Even if it is a Satanic attack, it nonetheless has been permitted by God and hence must be accepted. On the other hand, though, they should resist Satan by declaring, "Whatever the Lord does, I accept; but whatever Satan does, I categorically oppose. I resist everything that has befallen me through Satan!" Let me assure you, if the attack has been Satan's work, it will fade away by your resisting it.

Alas, many of God's children neither submit to the discipline of the Holy Spirit nor resist Satan's attack in their environment. This really is a problem today—no submission on the one hand, and no resistance on the other hand. . . .

### *How to Resist the Devil*

We need, then, to learn how to resist the devil. What are the various ways of resistance?

## 1. Fear Not

Whenever Satan works against God's children, he must first secure some ground in them. Ephesians exhorts us, "Neither give place to the devil" (4.27). Without a foothold, Satan cannot operate. Hence, his first tempting of us will be in order to secure a ground; his next will be an assault on us from the ground he has already secured. Our victory lies in not giving him any ground from the very beginning. One very large ground, perhaps the very largest, that he seeks is fear. Satan's characteristically customary work is to instill fear in the mind of God's children, a foreboding that something is going to happen.

Let us note the words of Job: "For the thing which I fear cometh upon me, and that which I am afraid of cometh unto me" (3.25). What this verse reveals to us is of tremendous significance. Before these terrible things happened to him, Job already had had some apprehension. He was fearful lest his children would die; he was afraid that he might lose all his property. Satan's first job is to plant this fear in man. If the fear is accepted, things will soon happen; if it is rejected, nothing will come of it. Satan has to obtain one's consent before he can operate. If this consent is withheld, he cannot work, for man is created with a free will. Without man's consent, Satan can neither tempt him to sin nor attack him at will. So, in the case of Job, Satan first implanted a tiny little thought of fear in Job. Having once accepted the thought, it made Job tremble.

"Fear is Satan's calling card," said Miss Margaret E. Barber. And whenever you accept his calling card, you receive a visit from him. If you reject his calling card, you drive him away. Fear him, and he comes; fear not, and he is kept away. Therefore, refuse to be afraid! Perhaps one *will* eventually kill himself if he is obsessed by the thought of cutting his throat while shaving. How often men have thoughts of fear in them, fearful lest this or that thing happen. This is especially true of nervous people. But remember, these thoughts come from Satan and must be resisted.

To the question of what is meant by resistance, an elderly

person once replied, "To resist means to say, 'Thank you, but I do not want it,' when something is offered to you." Whatever is offered you, you always answer, "No, thanks!" Though Satan may present you with this or that thing, your reaction is a simple refusal. Such an attitude is enough; it is all that is needed to defeat his purpose. Let us learn this lesson today: resist every thought of fear. Fear not, for fear will bring to you the very thing you are afraid of. May I remind you that no child of God should be fearful of Satan because Satan cannot overcome us. Although he *is* quite powerful, we have in us One who is greater than he. This is an unchangeable fact, "because greater is he that is in you than he that is in the world" (1 John 4.4). Therefore, never accept fear. He who accepts fear is a fool. Has not the Bible clearly taught that, by resisting Satan, he will flee? What place does he have in us except to retreat!

### 2. Know the Truth

The second condition of resistance is to know the truth. "Ye shall know the truth, and the truth shall make you free" (John 8.32).

What is truth? Truth is the reality of a thing. When Satan tempts or frightens or attacks people, he always comes in stealthily. He never lets you know he is there. He will not proclaim aloud that he has arrived, for that would arouse your suspicion. He lies, he counterfeits. He never does anything in the light. But if you know what the reality of the thing is, it will set you free. In other words, if you know something is of Satan, you are freed. The difficulty for many children of God is their unawareness of the enemy. They may say with their mouths that it is Satan's attack, yet they do not sense it deep down in their spirits. Though their lips pronounce it to be the work of Satan, their spirits are not as clear. But the day they see the truth, really knowing that this is Satan's work, they are instantly set free.

The power of Satan lies in his deception. If he cannot deceive, he loses his power. Hence, seeing is resisting; seeing makes resistance easy. When you are surrounded with perils in your environment, you cannot overcome if you only feel that these *may* be Satanic attacks. You need to know *for sure* that these are of Satan, and then it is easy for you to withstand. To deal with Satan takes more than opposing, for it is difficult to fight against his falsehoods. But when you meet him, you need to recognize him as such; then resist, and he will flee from you. . . .

### 3. Resist in Faith

Resistance must be done in faith. We must believe that the Lord has been manifested to destroy the work of the devil, that the blood of the Lord has overcome the attack of Satan, that the resurrection of the Lord has put Satan to shame, and that the ascension of the Lord transcends the power of Satan.

#### BELIEVE THE LORD HAS BEEN MANIFESTED TO DESTROY THE WORK OF THE DEVIL

The Son of God has manifested himself! He has come to this earth! While here, He cast out every demon He met; He overcame every temptation from Satan. Indeed, "To this end was the Son of God manifested, that he might destroy the works of the devil" (1 John 3.8). Let us, then, believe that wherever the Lord Jesus goes, whenever He is manifested, the work of the devil cannot exist, for it is totally destroyed.

#### BELIEVE THE BLOOD OF THE LORD HAS OVERCOME THE ATTACK OF SATAN

How do Christians overcome? "Because of the blood of the Lamb" (Rev. 12.11). Through the death of the Lord Jesus, we are united with God into one. The primary objective of Satanic attack is to separate us from God. As long as we are one with God, Satan has absolutely no way to injure us. What, then, separates us from God? Sin alone separates us, but the blood of Jesus, God's Son, cleanses us from all our sins.

Revelation 12.11 tells us that the brethren overcame Satan

because of the blood of the Lamb. With the cleansing of the blood of the Lord Jesus, we are made one with God. When we have the consciousness of sin upon our conscience, we are instantly separated from Him. As soon as the consciousness of sin comes upon us, the devil begins his attack. Without such consciousness he has no way to launch his assault. Thank God, the blood of the Lamb has overcome Satan. Today even the feeblest of God's children can overcome Satan, for every one of us has the blood.

You may not have many other things, but the blood you definitely do have. Through the blood of the Lord Jesus, you quite naturally declare that all your sins have been cleansed. Today God is your God. If God is for you, who can be against you? With your God by your side, the devil cannot attack you. The reason why he is able to accuse and attack is because he has first implanted a consciousness of sin in us. But the blood has placed you on God's side, so Satan cannot do anything with you.

Remember well that once the conscience is purified from the consciousness of sins, Satan can no longer stage his attack. The blood of the Lamb overcomes him. Is it not an amazing thing that whenever man comes before God he senses his unworthiness, but when he confronts Satan he feels guilty? Such a guilty feeling makes him susceptible to the hand of the enemy. So he needs at that moment to declare, "I am sinful; that is why you attack me. But through the blood of the Lamb I overcome you. The Lord Jesus has died for me; His blood has been shed. What can you do to me?" Let us therefore believe. Believe that the Lord was manifested to destroy the works of the devil. Believe that the Lord's death has spelled destruction to Satan's attack.

### BELIEVE THE RESURRECTION OF THE LORD HAS PUT SATAN TO SHAME

On the cross our Lord disarmed principalities and powers, making a show of them openly (Col. 9.15). Through death, He brought to nought him that had the power of death, that is, the devil (Heb. 2.14). By His death and resurrection He has utterly destroyed Satan. How did the Lord Jesus put Satan to shame?

By shaking off all the works of Satan when He rose from the dead.

What is resurrection? It is a realm beyond the touch of death. Every living thing in the world is within the touch of death. Men die, animals and plants die. All living things are subject to death. There is no exception, for death has spread like a net over this entire world. It has entered into every living thing. But here is a Man who came out of death, for death could not retain Him. He has entered into a realm beyond the touch of death and this realm is called resurrection.

The life we receive at the time of new birth is this resurrection life, for the Lord regenerates us by His resurrection. This new life in us has no relationship whatever to Satan. It is absolutely beyond the reach of Satan; furthermore, it is indestructible (see Heb. 7.16 mg.). Satan did all he could at the cross, but he was completely routed and put to shame by the Lord. So we have in us a life which all the powers of Satan cannot defeat.

Always remember that Satan's attack on us can never be greater than his attack on our Lord on the cross. There he poured forth all that he had accumulated since the creation of man of wrath, cunning devices, plans, and strategy—and all for one purpose: to destroy life. But all his plans and devices were of no avail. He was defeated, and ever after he is the defeated foe. The Bible affirms that his head is bruised.

We must show brothers and sisters that there is no reason for a Christian to be afraid of Satan. By the resurrection life in us, we shall overcome. Satan is fully aware that he can do absolutely nothing to this resurrection life. His days of victory are gone! His head is broken! So his prime effort now is to prolong his days, for he has already given up the hope of victory. Resurrection life is beyond his touch. It is absolutely transcendent over the power of Satan. Therefore, let us not be afraid. Let us resist him not because he is so fierce but because this is the will of God.

### BELIEVE THE ASCENSION OF THE LORD HAS TRANSCENDED THE POWER OF SATAN

We should believe in ascension as well as in resurrection. The

Bible shows us that when the Lord Jesus ascended to heaven, He was made to sit at the right hand of God the Heavenly Father, far above all rule, and authority, and power, and dominion, so that He might be head over all things to the Church (Eph. 1.20–22). The Lord has transcended all things and is now seated at the Father's right hand. By reading Ephesians 2 we see that we too were raised up with Him and were made to sit with Him in the heavenly places (Eph. 2.6).

Let us therefore observe this: that it is not the Lord Jesus alone whose manifestation destroys the works of the devil, whose cross and resurrection and ascension disarm Satan and his power, and who has transcended all things; all the children of God share in this transcendency of the Lord. Even the weakest members are far above all evil rule and authority and power and dominion.

The point of conflict between us and Satan lies not in the struggle to win, but rather in strife to avoid defeat. These two are vastly different. Many of God's children have a mistaken concept of war with Satan. They wrongly think that they must fight in order to win. Such an idea reveals a lack of understanding of what the gospel is. No Christian is able to fight to win. We fight because we have won. The Lord Jesus has already defeated Satan. Satan has totally lost his ground. Satan's battle today is to recover, ours is to retain. We do not fight in order to occupy; we protect what we have already occupied.

The question, then, is not victory, for Satan is already defeated. The Lord has overcome! The Church has overcome! The conflict between the Church and Satan is to protect the Lord's victory, not to win it. Our aim is not to wrestle victory from Satan but rather to keep victory from being robbed.

We should always triumph in the cross of our Lord. We should proclaim, "Satan, you are a defeated foe!" We must always remind him of this fact. When you resist Satan, believe this fact that he is a defeated foe. We do not withstand him because of his fierceness. Not at all. I must tell you that such an understanding is a complete distortion. It will only bring in confusion. No, we stand before Satan and declare to him: "You are already defeated! You are finished. I am now in the heavenly places. I defy you and I resist you."

I hope brothers and sisters understand what is meant by resisting. Satan is a defeated foe; he is a fugitive, a prisoner who should have been totally eliminated on the cross of our Lord. Today is only the day of his escape. When the kingdom comes, he shall be completely destroyed. So today he does not tempt in open warfare; rather, he hides outside the door behind the wall to sneak in with his temptation. He does everything secretly. When that happens, do not forget that you represent the Lord God and that Satan is but a fugitive tempting you outside the wall, not inside the room. You need not be afraid of him nor resist him as though he were part of the regular army. You should announce to him, "You are completely defeated! You were done for at the cross! You ought to have been eliminated, but were not; hence your coming today is not permitted!"

The Bible states clearly that if you withstand, Satan will flee from you. He is a fugitive today, trying to deceive you at the door. You should tell him who he is; then he will run away. If you think of him as already being in your home, then you will certainly be disturbed. He comes only to deceive and to try you. If he cannot succeed, he will flee from you.

—LOA 45–52, 53, 55–6, 56, 57–60, 61–3, 63–6, 67–72

*"Finally, be strong in the Lord, and in the strength of his might. Put on the whole armor of God, that ye may be able to stand against the wiles of the devil. . . . That ye may be able to withstand in the evil day, and, having done all, to stand. Stand therefore, having girded your loins . . . having put on the breastplate . . . having shod your feet . . . taking up the shield . . . and the helmet . . . and the sword . . . praying . . . and watching" (6.10,11,13–18).*

Christian experience begins with sitting and leads to walking, but it does not end with these. Every Christian must learn also to stand. Each one of us must be prepared for the conflict.

We must know how to sit with Christ in heavenly places and we must know how to walk worthy of Him down here, but we must also know how to stand before the foe. This matter of conflict now comes before us in the third section of Ephesians (6.10–20). It is what Paul calls "our wrestling with wicked spirits."

But let us first remind ourselves once again of the order in which Ephesians presents us with these things. It is: "sit . . . walk . . . stand." For no Christian can hope to enter the warfare of the ages without learning first to rest in Christ and in what he has done, and then, through the strength of the Holy Spirit within, to follow him in a practical, holy life here on earth. If he is deficient in either of these he will find that all the talk about spiritual warfare remains only talk; he will never know its reality. Satan can afford to ignore him for he does not count for anything. Yet the very same Christian can be made strong "in the Lord, and in the strength of his might" by knowing the values first of His exaltation and then of His indwelling (compare 6.10 with 1.19 and 3.16). It is with these two lessons well and truly learned that he comes to appreciate the third principle of the Christian life now summed up in the word "Stand."

God has an archenemy, and under his power are countless demons and fallen angels seeking to overrun the world with evil and to exclude God from His own kingdom. This is the meaning of verse 12. It is an explanation of things taking place around us. *We* see only "flesh and blood" ranged against us—that is to say, a world system of hostile kings and rulers, sinners and evil men. No, says Paul, our wrestling is not against these, "but against the principalities, against the powers, against the world-rulers of this darkness, against the spiritual hosts of wickedness in the heavenly places"—in short against the wiles of the devil himself. Two thrones are at war. God is claiming the earth for His dominion, and Satan is seeking to usurp the authority of God. The Church is called to displace Satan from his present realm and to make Christ Head over all. What are we doing about it?

I want now to deal with this matter of our warfare first in general terms in relation to our personal Christian lives and then in a more special sense in relation to the work of the Lord entrusted to us. There are many direct assaults of Satan upon God's children. Of course we must not attribute to the devil those troubles that are the result of our own breach of divine laws. We should, by now, know how to put these right. But there are physical attacks upon the saints, attacks of the evil one upon their bodies and minds, of which we must take serious account. Surely, too, there are few of us who do not know something of the enemy's assaults upon our spiritual life. Are we going to let these pass unchallenged?

We have our position with the Lord in the heavenlies, and we are learning how to walk with Him before the world; but how are we to acquit ourselves in the presence of the adversary—His adversary and ours? God's word is "Stand!" "Put on the whole armor of God that you may be able to stand against the wiles of the devil." The Greek verb "stand" with its following preposition "against" in verse 11 really means "hold your ground." There is a precious truth hidden in that command of God. It is not a command to invade a foreign territory. Warfare, in modern parlance, would imply a command to "march." Armies march into other countries to occupy and to subdue. God has not told us to do this. We are not to march but to stand. The word "stand" implies that the ground disputed by the enemy is really God's, and therefore ours. We need not struggle to gain a foothold on it.

Nearly all the weapons of our warfare described in Ephesians are purely defensive. Even the sword can be used as well for defense as for offense. The difference between defensive and offensive warfare is this, that in the former I have got the ground and only seek to keep it, whereas in the latter I have not got the ground and am fighting in order to get it. And that is precisely the difference between the warfare waged by the Lord Jesus and the warfare waged by us. His was offensive; ours is, in essence, defensive. He warred against Satan in order to gain the victory. Through the Cross He carried that warfare to the very threshold of Hell itself, to lead forth thence His captivity captive (4.8–9). Today we war against Satan only to maintain and consolidate the victory which Christ has already gained. By the resurrection God proclaimed His Son victor over the whole realm of darkness, and the ground Christ won He has given to us. We do not need to fight to obtain it. We only need to hold it against all challengers.

Our task is one of holding, not of attacking. It is a matter not of advance but of sphere, the sphere of Christ. In the person of Jesus Christ, God has already conquered, He has given us His victory to *hold.* Within the sphere of Christ the enemy's defeat is already a fact, and the Church has been put there to keep him defeated. Satan is one who must do the counterattacking in his efforts to dislodge us from that sphere. For our part we need not struggle to occupy ground that is already ours. In Christ we *are* conquerors—nay, "more than conquerors" (Rom. 8.37). In Him, therefore, we *stand.* Thus today we do not fight *for* victory; we fight *from* victory. We do not fight in order to win but because in Christ we have already won. Overcomers are those who rest in the victory already given to them by their God. . . .

Satan's primary object is not to get us to sin, but simply to make it easy for us to do so by getting us off the ground of perfect triumph onto which the Lord has brought us. Through the avenue of the head or of the heart, through our intellect or our feelings, he assaults our rest in Christ or our walk in the Spirit. But for every point of his attack defensive armor is provided, the helmet and the breastplate, the girdle and the shoes, while over all is the shield of faith to turn aside his fiery darts. Faith says: Christ is exalted. Faith says: We are saved by His grace. Faith says: We have access through Him. Faith says: He indwells us by His Spirit (see 1.20; 2.8; 3.12,17).

Because victory is His, therefore it is ours. If only we will not try to gain the victory but simply to maintain it, then we shall see the enemy utterly routed. We must not ask the Lord to enable *us* to overcome the enemy, nor even look to *Him* to overcome, but praise Him because He has already done so; He *is* victor. It is all a matter of faith in Him. If we believe the Lord, we shall not pray so much but rather we shall praise Him more.

The simpler and clearer our faith in Him, the less we shall pray in such situations and the more we shall praise. . . .

## *In His Name*

But this is not all. Ephesians 6 is concerned with more than the personal side of our warfare. It has to do, too, with the work of God entrusted to us—the utterance of the mystery of the gospel of which Paul has already had much to say (see 3.1–13). For this it arms us now with the sword of the Word and its companion weapon, prayer.

*"Take . . . the sword of the Spirit, which is the word of God: with all prayer and supplication praying at all seasons in the Spirit, and watching thereunto in all perseverance and supplication for all the saints, and on my behalf, that utterance may be given unto me in opening my mouth, to make known with boldness the mystery of the gospel, for which I am an ambassador in chains; that in it I may speak boldly, as I ought to speak" (6.17–20).*

I want to say something more about this warfare in its relation to our work for God, for here we may encounter a difficulty. It is true, on the one hand, that our Lord Jesus is seated "far above all rule, and authority," and that all things have been put "in subjection under his feet" (1.21–22). Clearly it is in the light of this completed victory that we are to "give thanks always for all things *in the name of Jesus Christ"* (5.20). Yet on the other hand we have to admit that we do not yet see all things subject to Him. There are still, as Paul says, hosts of wicked spirits in the heavenly places, dark, evil powers behind this world's rulers, occupying territory that is rightly His. How far are we correct in calling this a defensive warfare? We do not want to be falsely presumptive. When, therefore, and under what conditions are we justified in occupying territory that is outwardly the enemy's and holding it in the name of the Lord Jesus?

Let us "take . . . the word of God" to help us here. What does it tell us about prayer and action "in the name"? Consider first the following two passages: "Verily I say unto you, What things soever ye shall bind on earth shall be bound in heaven: and what things soever ye shall loose on earth shall be loosed in heaven. Again I say unto you, that if two of you shall agree on earth as touching anything that they shall ask, it shall be done for them . . . For where two or three are gathered together in my name, there am I . . . " (Matt. 18.18–20). "In that day ye shall ask me nothing. Verily, verily, I say unto you, If ye shall ask anything of the Father, he will give it you in my name. Hitherto have ye asked nothing in my name: ask, and ye shall receive, that your joy may be fulfilled. . . . In that day ye shall ask in my name" (John 16.23,24,26).

None can be saved without knowing the name of Jesus, and none can be effectively used of God without knowing the authority of that name. The apostle Paul makes it clear that the "name" to which Jesus alludes in the above passages is not simply the name by which He was known while here among men. To be sure, it is that very self-same name of His humanity, but it is that name invested now with the title and authority given to Him by God after He had become obedient to death (Phil. 2.6–10). It is the outcome of His sufferings, the name of His exaltation and glory; and today it is in *that* "name which is above every name" that we gather and that we ask of God.

This distinction is made not by Paul alone but already by Jesus himself in the second passage quoted above: "Hitherto ye have asked nothing . . . In that day ye shall ask" (verses 24,26). For disciples "that day" will differ greatly from the "now" of verse 22. Something they do not have now they will receive then, and having received it they will use it. That something is the authority that goes with His name.

Our eyes must be opened to see the mighty change wrought by the ascension. The name of Jesus certainly establishes the identity of the One in the throne with the Carpenter of Nazareth, but it goes further than that. It represents now the power and dominion given to Him by God, a power and a dominion before which every knee in heaven and earth and beneath the earth must bow. Even the Jewish leaders recognized that there could be this kind of significance in a mere name, when they inquired of the disciples concerning the healing of the lame man: "By what power, or in what name, have ye done this?" (Acts 4.7)

Today the name tells us that God has committed all authority to His Son, so that in the very name itself there is power. But further, we must note in Scripture the recurring expression "*in* the name" — that is to say, the use to which the apostles in fact put that name. It is not only that he *has* such a name, but that we are to *use* it. In three passages in His last discourse the Lord Jesus repeats the words "ask in my name" (see John 14.13–14; 15.16; 16.23–26). He has placed that authority in our hands for us to use. Not only is it His, but it is "given among men" (Acts 4.12). If we do not know our part in it we suffer great loss.

The power of His name operates in three directions. In our preaching it is effective to the salvation of men (Acts 4.10–12) through the remission of their sins, and through their cleansing, justification, and santification to God (Luke 24:47; Acts 10.43; 1 Cor. 6.11). In our warfare it is mighty against the Satanic powers, to bind and bring them into subjection (Mark 16.17; Luke 10.17–19; Acts 16.18). And as we have already seen, in our asking it is effective towards God, for twice we are told: "Whatsoever ye shall ask . . . "; and twice: "If ye shall ask anything . . . " (John 14.13–14; 15.16, 16.23). Faced with these challenging words, well might we reverently say: "Lord, your courage is very great!"

—SWS 51-5, 56, 57-61

# 43 Prophecy

*The Interpretations of "Revelation"*

The interpretation of the book of Revelation is a point of contention among commentators. Generally speaking, there are three different schools of interpretation; namely, (1) the Praeterists, (2) the Historical Interpreters, and (3) the Futurists. The Praeterists hold that the whole, or by far the greater part, of the prophecy has been fulfilled in the past struggle between the Church and Rome, with the victory of the Church as the final outcome. Such an interpretation is too abstract and is objected to by orthodox commentators.

The Historical Interpreters hold that the prophecy embraces the whole history of the Church, it showing how the evil forces of the world fight against the Church. This interpretation was very popular during the time of the Reformation and was still strongly advocated in the nineteenth century. Especially with the rise of Napoleon, this view had been recognized as the final interpretation. Among the Protestants, people who hold this view consider the Pope and the Roman Church to be the Antichrist and the beast. Martin Luther himself took this view. But the Roman Catholic commentators took the opposite view and reckoned that Protestantism was the Antichrist. They even claimed to have found the number 666 in the name of Martin Luther. Many of God's people at the end of the eighteenth and at the beginning of the nineteenth centuries held that Napoleon fulfilled the personage mentioned in Revelation 13. And many of the numbers in the book were arbitrarily taken to be a fixed period of prophecy; for example, the number of three years and a half was considered to represent the tribulation in their own current history.

The Futurists maintain that the greater part of the prophecy has yet to be fulfilled in the future. Commencing from chapter 4 onwards, not even a letter has yet been fulfilled. Chapters 2 and 3 speak of the Church. Only after the Church period has been completed can anything from chapter 4 on be fulfilled. Chapters 6–19 refer to events that will happen at the time of the last seven of Daniel's seventy sevens. And even Daniel's last seven cannot commence until Church history has been completed. This interpretation is the most satisfactory one for it coincides most with the prophecies to be found in other passages of the Bible. Nevertheless, we have no intention to strive after an opinion! Indeed, may the Lord ever keep us from it. What we desire is His truth. May His Spirit lead us into all truths and enable us to understand God's word.

It is unavoidable that there be much argument over the interpretation of Revelation among these three schools. But our aim, as we have already made clear, is to know what *God* wants us to know, not to strive in defense of any human school of opinion. Hence we will not present all the arguments either pro or con. Though these may be welcomed by some people, they are not edifying.

A few words, however, do need to be said to demonstrate that there is fallibility in both the Praeterists and the Historical Interpreters. The Praeterists hold the view of the Rationalistic teachers. No one in the Church of the first few centuries believed it. For it limited the horizon of John to seeing only the Roman persecution of Christians. It reduces the prophecy to allegorical value only, and it merely predicts the defeat of the Romans. The Historical Interpeters, on the other hand, blunt the most solemn warnings of the Holy Bible directed towards the people at the end of this age, so that they cannot know what the wrath of God is to be. Let us therefore be clear as to what the Bible actually teaches.

In 1 Corinthians 10.32 Paul divides mankind into three main categories; namely, Jews, Gentiles, and the Church of God. During the time of the Old Testament there was no Church for it was established by the Lord only in the New Testament period. Since the book of Revelation is the last one in the Bible and by that position it sums up the entire Scriptures, it naturally ought to show us how these three categories of people eventually end up. The Praeterists, though, hold that Revelation relates only to the past history of the struggle of the Church. The Historical Interpreters, too, limit the prophecy to the experience of the Church after the time of John. Both embrace the Church and overlook the Jews and the Gentiles. Such a view is too lopsided and makes the revelation of God in the Bible imperfect. For according to their interpretations we would be left in the dark as to the future end of both the Jews and the Gentiles. Yet we ought to expect to see in this last Bible book (1) the course the Church will travel along on earth and her future glory, (2) the protection of the Jewish remnant by the Lord through the Great Tribulation and their receiving the promised blessings of God as prophesied by the prophets, and (3) the judgment of the Gentiles who sin and disbelieve as well as the joy of those Gentiles who come to the Lord.

I will not argue which interpretation is right and which is wrong. There must of course be a true interpretation which agrees with all the prophecies in the Old and New Testaments and which profits us spiritually. Where can we find this true interpretation? Any answer is in the book itself. What this book of Revelation tells us is most trustworthy. We need not spend very much time in researching the interpretations and ideas of the different schools. We can even disregard such terms as the Praeterists or the Futurists. The best way is to search the Scriptures directly. For I believe that in the pages of Revelation itself our Lord Jesus Christ has given us the key to its own interpretation.

### *The Key to Interpreting "Revelation"*

In each book of the Bible there is a key verse, by which that book can be opened. And hence we would hope to find the key verse in Revelation so as to give us the outline of this book too. Where is this verse? The Lord Jesus himself commanded John to write this book; so let us see how John received the commission: "Write therefore the things which thou sawest, and the things which are, and the things which shall come to pass hereafter" (1.19). The Lord directed John to write down three main elements: first, the things "which [John] saw"; second, "the things which are"; and third, "the things which shall come to pass hereafter." And John wrote accordingly. At the time he was about to write, he had already seen a vision; therefore, the first thing for him to write was a record of the vision he had just seen. John then continued to set down "the things which are" and concluded with "the things which shall come to pass hereafter." And thus, this one verse of Scripture alludes to the things of the past, the present, and the future.

### *Three Main Divisions of "Revelation"*

Taking this as the key, then, the book of Revelation must be divided into three main parts. With twenty-two chapters in the book, how are the three divisions made? Before we touch upon the first and the second divisions, let us begin by looking at the third. There is a verse in chapter 4 which plainly indicates that the third division commences at that chapter: "After these things," said John, "I saw, and behold, a door opened in heaven, and the first voice that I heard, a voice as of a trumpet speaking with me, one saying, Come up hither, and I will show thee the things which must come to pass hereafter" (4.1). "The things which must come to pass hereafter" must be the things after the first three chapters. Revelation 1.19 indicates that the third division speaks of "the things which shall come to pass hereafter," and the things which John saw from chapter 4 onward are in fact "the things which must come to pass hereafter." It is thus evident that his third division of Revelation commences at chapter 4 (and since the book has only three divisions, the third division must be from chapter 4 through chapter 22). This leaves only the first three chapters for covering the first and the second divisions of the book.

Revelation chapter 1 is concerned with that which John saw. Verse 11 says "What thou seest, write in a book," and in verse 19 John is ordered to "write therefore the things which thou sawest." In between the time of these two verses John saw the vision, which constitutes the things which he saw. The first division of the book is therefore chapter 1. Since we have learned that the whole book by its own description is to be divided into three main divisions, and since we learned also that the first division is chapter 1 and the third division is from chapter 4 to the book's end, it can reasonably be concluded that the second main division of the book must be chapters 2 and 3. In those chapters we will find "the things which are," which are the things concerning the Church.

John lived in the Church age, and therefore the Church is recognized as "the things which are." Chapters 2 and 3 give the prophetic history of the Church from its beginning to its end. It commences with Ephesians forsaking the first love (2.4) and finishes with the Laodiceans being spewed out of the Lord's mouth (3.16). The entire history of the Church is thus being delineated by these seven local churches. Since "the things which shall come to pass hereafter" follow upon "the things which thou sawest, and the things which are," the matters recorded from chapter 4 onward must wait till Church history is concluded before they can be fulfilled. Although today the end is indeed approaching, we must acknowledge that the Church still exists on earth, and hence her time is not yet entirely fulfilled.

This is the teaching of the Scriptures. Revelation 1.19 is in fact the key which unlocks the mystery surrounding the book. And from this verse we have now obtained a true interpretation. . . .

*The Year-Day Theory*

Recently the study of prophecy had earned for itself a bad reputation among believers because of the so-called year-day theory. According to this theory, many numbers of days in the Scriptures are computed as though a day were a year, thus fostering predictions as to the precise date for the second coming of the Lord Jesus Christ—an exercise of the mind which is plainly contradictory to the Lord's announcement: for no one knows the date of His return, not even Jesus himself. Then, too, some commentators on Revelation have twisted God's word in ways that are meant to fit in with this year-day theory. We have no intention to argue about this theory; we only desire to point out a right understanding of the "days" that are mentioned in the Bible.

The advocates of the year-day theory base their conception on Numbers 14.34 and Ezekiel 4.6. Let us first examine Numbers: "After the number of the days in which ye spied out the land, even forty days, for every day a year, shall ye bear your iniquities, even forty years, and ye shall know my alienation." Here we are told that due to their unbelief, the children of Israel were disciplined by God for forty years, a year for every day they had spied out the land. But this does not apply equally to other "days" mentioned in Scripture, and certainly not to the "days" found in Revelation. As to Ezekiel: "And again, when thou hast accomplished these, thou shalt lie on thy right side, and shall bear the iniquity of the house of Judah: forty days, each day for a year, have I appointed it unto thee." Here we see that God commanded Ezekiel to lie down in a certain position as a response to the iniquity of Judah. This has nothing to do with the other "days" found in the Bible.

Let us look at a few more passages.

(1) "And yet seven days, and I will cause it to rain upon the earth forty days and forty nights" (Gen. 7.4). Did God wait for seven years and then have the rain fall for forty years? No, for the record goes on to explain as follows: "And it came to pass after the seven days, that the waters of the flood were upon the

earth. . . . And the rain was upon the earth forty days and forty nights" (vv.10,12). Here, a day is not a year.

(2) "Joseph said unto him, This is the interpretation of it: the three branches are three days; within yet three days shall Pharaoh lift up thy head" (Gen. 40.12–13). Was it that after three years the chief butler was released from prison? Not at all: "And it came to pass the third day . . . [that] he restored the chief butler unto his butlership again" (vv.20,21).

(3) "Then said Jehovah unto Moses, Behold, I will rain bread from heaven for you; and the people shall go out and gather a day's portion every day . . . And it shall come to pass on the sixth day . . . [that] it shall be twice as much as they gather daily" (Ex. 16.4–5). The children of Israel went out to gather manna every day, not once a year.

(4) God gave meat to the children of Israel to eat for "a whole month" (Num. 11.19–20). They did not eat meat for thirty years.

(5) "Within three days ye are to cross this Jordan" (Joshua 1.11). What actually happened afterwards? Did the children of Israel cross over Jordan after three years? No, they crossed after three days.

(6) "For as Jonah was three days and three nights in the belly of the whale; so shall the Son of man be three days and three nights in the heart of the earth" (Matt. 12.40). Was the Lord Jesus in the heart of the earth for three years? We know from the biblical record that He was there for only three days and three nights.

From this evidence, therefore, we can easily conclude that the year-day theory is erroneous. If some of the "days" appearing in the book of Revelation are to be taken as years, then the rest of the "days" found therein should also be treated as years. And in that case, the three and a half years of the Great Tribulation would have to be calculated as a thousand two hundred and sixty years; and the millennial kingdom would have to be extended out to three hundred and sixty thousand years. Obviously, we know that such calculations as these cannot be true.

May we therefore trust the Holy Spirit to guide us correctly as we read the word of God. Let us not seize upon strange ideas like this. Even though the Bible is most wonderful, it is not to be explained in any quaint or bizarre way. We ought to learn to be more obedient to God in our thought. And then we will not be likely to misinterpret His word. . . .

*A Brief Summary Concerning the Things to Come*

It might be helpful to conclude with a brief summary of the end-time events. The first thing to come is the rapture of the overcoming believers. All who have the cross wrought deeply in their lives will be raptured. But those who are saved and yet mix with the world and compromise with sins will remain on earth and pass through the Great Tribulation. Only the victorious and watchful saints are ready to be received (the rest of the saved believers will go through the Great Tribulation and be received at the sounding of the seventh trumpet). All this pertains to Christians.

During that time the Roman Empire will be revived, and a very strong person shall be her emperor. He will be given certain powers by Satan in order to perform signs and lying wonders. He will call himself Christ and steal the hearts of many Jews. At that period, the Jews have already returned to their native land, but most of them are unbelievers. They shall rebuild the temple and restore their former worship and sacrifices. Out of fear towards outside powers, they will make a pact with the Antichrist for seven years in order to receive his protection. No doubt, there will still be a remnant who believe in the word of God and oppose the name of the false Messiah.

In the midst of these seven years, there will come forth a sign in heaven, for the red dragon (Satan) will be cast down from heaven to the earth. He will be filled with hatred towards the saints of God—those Jews who bear witness for God. He will stir the heart of the Antichrist—the Roman Emperor—to oppose those Jews.

But just as Satan persecutes those who belong to God, so God will punish those who belong to Satan. The "trumpets" and the "bowls" spoken of in the book of Revelation shall be the manifestations of God's wrath towards the Antichrist and the inhabitants of the earth. In punishing the world, God will still expect them to repent, but the world will persist in evil and will not repent.

Through the power of Satan, the Antichrist will break his covenant, cause all sacrifices and offerings to cease, and will set up the idol image—that wing of abomination—for people to worship. The false prophet will come forth to persuade people to worship the image. As soon as the image is set up, the remnant will immediately flee to the wilderness. Although Satan will use every means to destroy them, God shall take care of them during the three and a half years.

Having no outlet for his wrath, Satan shall turn to persecute those Christian believers who have not previously been raptured. Many will be martyred. But at the sounding of the seventh trumpet, the believers who remain on earth shall also be raptured because they will have learned obedience through sufferings and will have now been perfected.

Then will the Antichrist gather together all nations to come and attack the Jews (the war of Armageddon). The Jews will flee from the city (see Zech. 14). This will happen at the conclusion of the last seven mentioned in Daniel, when the Lord Jesus will come from heaven with His saints and His feet will touch the Mount of Olives. He will save the children of Israel and destroy the nations which war against Him. Then shall commence the millennial kingdom.

Such is a general outline of the book of Revelation. However, those who believe in the Lord and have been *faithful, watching, ready, overcoming,* and *praying* will have already been raptured to heaven before these things shall come upon the world. There will be no need for them to go through the Great Tribulation. Therefore, we need to have the spirit of rapture now. We must have the experience of rapture in spirit before we can find it fulfilled in body. Our spirit should go to heaven first, and then our body will follow suit. May we not be entangled in the things of this world so that we may go when the time comes. The "powers of the age to come" (cf. Heb. 6.5) should be manifested in the lives of the saints today. But, alas, many today seem to fall short.

Lord, will You be gracious? Lead us and keep us that we may seek the truth, that we may have the light of the future to illumine our current course, that we may let the future judgment seat of Christ induce us to judge ourselves at present, and that we may taste the future joy now so as to strengthen our communion with the Spirit of the Lord today. Let us not study this most blessed book as though it were a kind of mental examination, but may the study of it radically change our lives and works. Amen.

—ATR 25-31, 75-8, 112-6

## REV. 4.4 "THE TWENTY-FOUR ELDERS"

The common interpretation of the 24 elders as given by most commentators is that they point to the entire glorious church. But do these commentators have sufficient proof for offering this interpretation? Recently some of them have quoted 4.4, saying that these elders have thrones and therefore they reign as kings; they also point out that in 5.8 these elders are shown as having harps and golden bowls full of incense, and hence they are priests. And does not 1 Peter 2.9 state that believers are "a royal priesthood"? Since these 24 elders are both kings and priests, surely, they conclude, these elders represent the glorious church.

According to this interpretation, therefore, the entire church must be raptured together and thus it does not go through the tribulation. But how, then, will 3.10 be explained? Furthermore, there are ten other reasons why the 24 elders do not represent one glorious church.

(1) The name of elder is not the name of the church. If the elders here point to the church, it will be almost like saying that the entire church is made up of elders. According to historical fact, God first chooses the angels (Is. 14.12; Eze. 28.11-19), then the Jews (Gen. 12.1-3), and thirdly the church (for it is formed in the time of Acts 2). Not only the church cannot be reckoned

as elders, even the Jews are not to be considered as elders (the election mentioned in Ephesians 1.4 refers to the eternal purpose of God, and hence is quite different from the elect angels as mentioned in 1 Timothy 5.21).

(2) The number of the elders is not the number of the church. The church's number in the Scriptures is seven or multiples of seven, but 24 is not such a multiple.

(3) The church cannot have the throne and the crown before the Lord Jesus has His. The one who sits on the throne as seen in 4.2 is God the Father (the Lamb is standing, according to 5.6). The 24 elders also sit on thrones, and they all wear crowns of gold as described in 4.4. If they represent the church, how can it be that the church sits while the Lamb stands? According to this interpretation, in 5.6 the church is already crowned. Yet please note that the Lord Jesus will not be King until the time of chapter 20 is reached! How can the church receive glory in advance of the Lord? Moreover, after 19.4 there is no more trace of the 24 elders. If these elders do indeed represent the entire church, what has happened to the glorious church thereafter?

(4) The white garments which the elders wear are not said to be cleansed by the precious blood; however, in another place (7.14) the white garments are said to have been washed and made white in the blood of the Lamb. The white garments here show that the elders are without sin.

(5) The song these elders sing is not that of redemption since the song in 4.11 tells of the creation of God. They thus know only God's creation; they have no personal knowledge of God's redemption. Though they do sing a new song as mentioned in 5.9–10, this is because the Lord has redeemed "them" — not these elders, but men of every tribe and tongue and people and nation.

(6) All the phenomena in chapter 4 stand for the state of the universe. Besides the throne and the seven Spirits, there are the four living creatures and the 24 elders; none else is mentioned. This indicates that these elders are the elders of the universe. Can we possibly say that the church is the eldest in the universe?

(7) To carry prayers to God as is shown in 5.8 is not the ac-

tion of the church. Even though the church is commanded in the Scriptures to pray for others, God has not asked her to bring others' prayers to Him. The church does not have this power. Many commentators agree that the angel spoken of in 8.3–4 refers to the Lord. Whether or not it is the Lord, it can at least be said that the task of carrying prayers to God is done by angels. Thus, bringing prayers of the saints to God as mentioned in 5.8 must be a task done by the angels.

(8) Never once do the 24 elders identify themselves as the church. The "them" in 5.10 is a reference to the church by these elders. If the "them" were indeed an expression of self-identification, the elders should have instead said "us." What the elders do say clearly distinguishes them from the church. The 24 elders cannot represent the entire church. There are three classes of people in view in 7.13–17, namely: (1) elders, (2) John, and (3) those arrayed in white robes. Should the 24 elders be an allusion to *part* of the church, it would still make some sense for the elders to ask John, "Who are they, and whence came they [those in white robes]?" But if the 24 elders mean the entire church, it would be absurd for the entire church to ask concerning part of the church.

(9) John addresses one of the elders as "my lord" (7.13–17), thus showing the superior position of the elder over John. Otherwise how could the elder permit John to call him "my lord"? (cf. 22.8–9)

(10) The demeanor of the 24 elders before God is most peculiar. They have never been hungry and thirsty like the church nor have they ever shed any tears. They are not afraid of God, neither do they possess any sense of sin. They are strangers to the experience of being redeemed. All these points prove that they are not the redeemed church.

Who, then, are these elders? Let us assume that they are the kings and priests among the angels, that they are the elders of the universe (that is to say, they rule over the angels and the universe in God's service). The evidences for such a conclusion are as follows.

(1) Since they sit on thrones and wear crowns of gold, they must be kings.

(2) They wear white garments which are the garments of the priests (see Ex. 28; Lev. 6.10, 16.4). They have harps, sing songs, and hold golden bowls of incense—all these are evidences of their priesthood.

(3) The reason they are the priests among the angels is because they are the elders of the universe. In chapters 4 and 5 God is God, the Lord is the Lamb, the Holy Spirit is the seven Spirits, the four living creatures represent the animate creation, and the 24 elders are the elders of the universe since they are the oldest among created things.

(4) Besides the angels, who are entitled to sit on thrones and wear golden crowns ahead of the Lord Jesus? God had originally appointed angels to govern the universe. But one of the archangels fell and turned himself into Satan, there thus coming into existence the satanic kingdom. As to those angels who had not followed Satan in rebellion, God still assigns them the rule over the universe. Now just as Michael is the chief prince over the nation of Israel (Dan. 10.13), even so, all of us who are redeemed have our guardian angels (Acts 12.15; Matt. 18.10; Heb. 1.14). The 24 elders sit while the seven angels who blow the trumpets stand before God (8.2). They are now in charge of the universe. When they see people getting saved they are not jealous at all; rather, they praise God for it. They will govern the universe until the kingdom shall come; and then they will resign their appointments and there will be the transfer of the government of the universe to men (Rev.11.16–18; Heb. 2.5–8). This is why there is no mentioning of the 24 elders after 19.4.

(5) The number of the 24 elders is the number of the priesthood. At the time of David the priesthood was divided into 24 courses (1 Chron. 24.7–18). The duty of the priesthood is to bring the prayers of the saints to God. The harps are for singing, and the golden bowls are for prayers. . . .

REV. 4.7-8 THE FOUR LIVING CREATURES

Some observers maintain that since the 24 elders represent the church, the four living creatures also stand for the church. But we do not think the book of Revelation is primarily a book of symbols. Whatever is not symbolic should be explained literally. If the 24 elders speak of the church, then how should the other numbers in the book be interpreted? Such an interpretation not only will be most difficult but also will impair the value of this book. Consequently, the four living creatures are not symbolic but are rather the representatives of the created things. As the 24 elders are representative of the angelic beings, so the four living creatures are representative of the living things on earth. . . .

Now of the four living creatures both the calf and man are clean, whereas the lion and the eagle are unclean. Yet all of them stand before God without any differentiation between clean and unclean. The lion and the eagle are fierce while man and calf are mild-mannered. But because all are redeemed, all of them can dwell together in peace. . . .

These people [mentioned in Rev. 7.4–8] who are sealed with the seal of the living God are:

a) the Jews who will rule with Christ on earth in the future (though not as kings). Twelve thousand is the resultant number of the multiples of 12, it being 12 x $10^3$. This number represents the eternal perfection of God's government.

b) the suffering Jews who make up part of the little brother mentioned in Matthew 25.

c) the Jewish counterpart of those who endure to the end as spoken of in Matthew 24.

d) the Jews upon whom the Holy Spirit will be poured out in the coming day (the former rain has already been poured out—Acts 2, but the latter rain is yet to be poured forth—Joel 2.28–29). The blood and fire mentioned in Joel 2.30 coincide with the phenomena of the first trumpet; the pillars of smoke agree with the fifth trumpet. Thus the second outpouring of the

Holy Spirit will occur between the sixth seal and the fifth trumpet.

And e) those Jews who receive the New Covenant when the Lord Jesus shall establish His New Covenant with Israel on earth (Jer. 31.31–34). . . .

In the Old Testament record there is only one woman who had an encounter with the serpent, and she is Eve of Genesis 3. Now in the New Testament there is also one woman who had a skirmish with the serpent, and she is this woman of Revelation 12. This shows the unity of the Bible. Here God purposely mentions that the great dragon is the old serpent, thus distinguishing it as the one, same and only old serpent. Likewise, this woman will also be the same woman as in the Garden. Moreover, as there are sun, moon and stars mentioned in Genesis 1, so there are sun, moon and stars spoken of here. As there is the serpent in Genesis 3, so the serpent is present here. As the seed of the woman is mentioned in Genesis 3, so the seed of the woman is also shown here. And as travail in birth is predicted in Genesis 3, so travail in birth is presented here. By studying these two passages of the Scriptures together we may conclude that this woman is none other than the woman who has been foreordained in the eternal purpose of God and who will experience such things as these at the last days. Hence we may say that the woman mentioned in Genesis 2 reveals the eternal will of God; the woman seen in Ephesians 5 unveils the position and future of the church; the woman spoken of in Revelation 12 discloses that which will happen at the last days; and there is yet a woman who will declare what is going to be in eternity.

When this woman appears in the vision now before us, the Bible describes her as "arrayed with the sun, and the moon under her feet, and upon her head a crown of twelve stars"—And these descriptions have their dispensational meanings:

(1) This woman is arrayed with the sun—the sun points to the Lord Jesus. Since the woman is arrayed with the sun, this indicates that the sun shines at its brightest hour upon the woman. In this dispensation God is manifesting himself through her. This

is her relationship with Christ and with the dispensation of grace.

(2) This woman has the moon under her feet—the word "under" does not imply "tread upon"; in the Greek the word simply means a lying under her feet. The light of the moon is not self-producing but is reflective. Things in the dispensation of law only reflect the things in the dispensation of grace, for the law is but a shadow. The holy temple, the ark, the incense and the shew-bread, the sacrifices which the priests offer, and even the blood of the bullocks and lambs—all these are types. The moon being under the woman's feet shows how the things of the law are subjected to her, that is to say, they belong to her. So that this description tells of the woman's relationship with the dispensation of law.

(3) This woman wears upon her head a crown of twelve stars—the distinguished personages who figured during the dispensation of the patriarchs may be counted from Abraham up to the birth of the twelve tribes of Israel. Wearing such a crown of twelve stars shows the relationship between this woman and the dispensation of the patriarchs.

From the above observations we can understand that this woman is related not only to the dispensation of grace but also to the dispensations of law and of the patriarchs, although here her relationship with the dispensation of grace is most intimate. And hence representationally this woman includes in herself the people found in the dispensations of the patriarchs and of law as well as in the dispensation of grace. . . .

Verse 5 [of Rev. 12] "And she was delivered of a son, a man child, who is to rule all the nations with a rod of iron: and her child was caught up unto God, and unto his throne"—In order to know the relationship between this man child and the woman, please read Galatians—"But the Jerusalem that is above is free, which is our mother" (4.26). Read also the last clause in the next verse: "For more are the children of the desolate than of her that hath the husband" (v.27). The Jerusalem above is the New Jerusalem, which is the woman whom God has prepared to have in eternity to come. She is none other than Eve in creation, the body of Christ in the dispensation of grace, this woman whom we see at the close of the dispensation of grace, and the New Jerusalem God will have in the eternity to come. A having many children does not suggest that the mother is separated from the children; rather does it mean that the one is divided into many, yet the many are combined into one. By adding up these many children you have the mother. It is not a case of a mother with five children making six, but a case of the five children making up the one mother. Each child is a part of the mother, who imparts a little of herself to each child. They seem as though they are begotten of her, yet actually they are but her own self. Thus the mother is not one who stands alongside her children but is the sum total of many children that are in view. This is a very special principle.

In chapter 12 the man child whom the woman delivers is subject to the same principle. This being a vision, it is symbolic in character. The word "delivered" here does not imply the idea of the child coming out and being separated from the woman, it instead implies that within the woman there is such a man child. In other words, a class of people is included in this woman. All the people of God are ordained to have a share in the eternal purpose and plan of God. Due to their failure in taking up responsibility, however, God chooses from among them a number of people. The people whom God has chosen from the many form the man child. The mother represents the whole, the man child represents the remnant. This man child is the "brethren" mentioned in verse 10. He is not one person but is a considerable number of people—a composite of many; though in comparison with the mother, this man child is only a minority. Nevertheless, in spite of their smallness in number as compared to the whole body, the plan and purpose of God is upon them.

"And she was delivered of a son, a man child, who is to rule all the nations with a rod of iron" (v.5). Three times in the book of Revelation is this ruling with an iron rod mentioned. The first time is in 2.26–27: "And he that overcometh, and he that keepeth my works unto the end, to him will I give authority over the nations: and he shall rule them with a rod of iron"—This most distinctly points to the overcomers in the church. The last time is in 19.15: "And out of his mouth proceedeth a sharp sword, that with it he should smite the nations: and he shall rule them with a rod of iron"—This is in reference to the Lord Jesus.

Now then, to whom does this verse in 12.5 refer? If it is not applicable to the overcomers in the church it must have reference to the Lord Jesus. Yet can it mean the Lord Jesus here? It is highly improbable (though not absolutely impossible, since later on we will observe that the Lord Jesus is also included). Why is it not probable? Because as soon as the man child is born he is caught up to the throne of God. It thus indicates that the man child cannot be Christ since the Lord Jesus when on the earth lived for over 33 years, died, and was raised from the dead before He ascended. Hence we believe this man child signifies the overcomers in the church. He represents a part of the church, that part which overcomes. Nonetheless, the man child also *includes* the Lord Jesus since He is the first overcomer and all other overcomers are included in Him. . . .

REV. 14.1–5 "THE FIRST FRUITS"

14.1 Is Mount Zion in heaven or on earth? It is the heavenly Jerusalem, not the earthly one, because (1) the Mount Zion on earth is at that time in the hands of the Gentiles (11.2); (2) it is clearly stated in 14.4 that "these were purchased from among men," thus implying that they no longer stand on the earthly Mount Zion during that moment; (3) by joining the last two clauses of 14.4 with Exodus 23.19 we learn that the first fruits are not left in the field since as soon as they are ripened they are to be brought to the house of God (see also Ex. 34.26), and since the 144,000 are the first fruits they cannot be left in the field—which speaks of the world (Matt. 13.38)—but are placed instead on the Mount Zion in heaven which is the New Jerusalem; (4) 14.3 says "they sing . . . before the throne, and before the four living creatures and the elders"—thus all these are in heaven and not on the earth; (5) the people referred to in 14.1–5 are the first fruits while those alluded to in 14.14–16 are the harvest, so if the harvesting is unto the air, can the first fruits be gathered elsewhere except to heaven? and (6) there is, moreover, no reason to suggest it as being the Mount Zion on earth since the Lord Jesus will come to the earth only by the time of chapter 19.

Who are the 144,000? The 144,000 cited in Revelation 7.4 and 144,000 spoken of here in 14.1 are two different classes of people, contrasted as follows:

(1) The people of 7.4 are the chosen among the children of Israel, while those of 14.1 are purchased from among men.

(2) The seals received by them are not the same. The one spoken of in 7.2 is "the seal of the living God," which is Old Testament terminology. The seal alluded to in 14.1 bears the name of the Lamb and the name of the Father, and such names are related to the church. Hence these people must come from the church.

(3) The people told about in 7.3 are called "the servants of our God," but those in view in 14.1 are the children of God (this conclusion is deduced from the name of the Father).

(4) Throughout the entire book of Revelation the Lord calls God as Father each time. And He always says it in connection with the church (1.6, 2.27, 3.5, 3.21). The Lord never uses it in connection with Israel.

(5) The people spoken of in 14.1ff. are associated with the Lamb (standing with the Lamb, having the name of the Lamb, following the Lamb, and being the first fruits unto the Lamb). In chapter 7 the Lord is seen as another angel; and this, as we have seen, is a returning to His Old Testament position.

(6) The song they sing is described in 14.3 as a new song, whereas the song the people mentioned in 7.4 sing is but an old song.

(7) The people in view in 14.4 are virgins, but with Israel virginity is to be bewailed. (According to Ex. 23.26, Deut. 7.14, 1 Sam. 2.5, and Ps. 113.9, to bear children is considered a blessing while to be barren is deemed a curse. In Judges 11.38–39 the

daughter of Jephthah is said to have bewailed her virginity for two months.)

(8) The articles preceding both of the 144,000 numbers cited in 14.1 and 7.4 are indefinite, and are therefore general and not specific. Thus these 144,000 numbers constitute two different classes.

14.1 The group of 144,000 here is a special class of people in the church; they are not all the people of the church. And the reasons for this conclusion are as follows:

(1) Since the 144,000 figure in 7.4 is taken literally, the number here should also be reckoned as literal.

(2) This group being the first fruits (14.4), it cannot be said that the entire church makes up the first fruits.

(3) There is no such fact that the people in the entire church keep their virginity.

(4) Prior to the arrival of the Great Tribulation (for it is before the voices of the three angels are heard, 14.6–11), these people are already raptured to Mount Zion.

(5) 14.5 tells of the exceptional features of these people, concerning which it cannot be said that all the born-again ones possess such characteristics.

Consequently, the 144,000 standing on Mount Zion are the best of the overcomers of the church; that is to say, this group of 144,000 is representative of the totality of the overcomers. . . .

21.10 "And he carried me away in the Spirit to a mountain great and high" — If we wish to see the eternal vision of God we need to be brought by God to a great and high mountain. Unless we stand on a spiritual high mountain we cannot see anything. Those who live on the plain will not be able to see the New Jerusalem — the finality of God's work.

"The holy city Jerusalem, coming down out of heaven from God" —The wife of the Lamb whom John saw was the holy city Jerusalem. The description of the city is allegorical. By its description we are told of the corporate body which God from eternity has purposed to obtain.

This is a city which comes out of heaven from God. God pays attention not only to where this corporate man will go but from whence he comes out as well. Not only the destiny but also the source. The wife of the Lamb comes out of heaven, not from earth. God does not show us here the man who has a past history of sin but is now saved by grace. This does not mean, of course, that we do not have a history of sin, therefore needing neither repentance nor salvation. This passage of Scripture simply reveals to us that portion which comes out of God, which is the glorious church of Ephesians 5 that is to be presented to Christ.

One characteristic of this new Jerusalem is holiness. Among Christians, some look for greatness, some look for holiness. The former is the principle of Babylon, whereas the latter is the principle of New Jerusalem. What is holiness? We may say that only God is holy; therefore, all that comes out of God is holy: "For both he that sanctifieth and they that are sanctified are all of one" (Heb. 2.11).

21.11 "Having the glory of God . . . a jasper stone"—The God on the throne whom John saw was like a jasper stone (see 4.3). In other words, jasper means the God who is seen. The God whom we know as we stand before His throne is like jasper stone. Our knowledge of God today here on earth is at best termed "darkly" or "in a riddle" (1 Cor. 13.12 mg.); but in the city which has the glory of God like a jasper stone we shall then see Him as He is—"clear as crystal" (v.11).

21.12-14 "Having twelve gates, . . . and names written thereon, which are the names of the twelve tribes of the children of Israel: . . . And the wall of the city had twelve foundations, and on them twelve names of the twelve apostles of the Lamb"—Whom does this corporate man include? Having the twelve names of the tribes of Israel on its gates and the twelve names of the apostles on its foundations, this city includes all the Old and the

New Testament saints. At the time of the new heaven and the new earth, all who have the life of God are to be included in the New Jerusalem.

21.15–17 "And he that spake with me had for a measure a golden reed to measure . . . the wall thereof"—Besides the glory of God, the next thing mentioned is the wall of the city. Separation—as depicted here by a wall—is an important principle in Christian living. Lack of separation devaluates the Christian's worth. A line must be drawn between what is spiritual and what is carnal. New Jerusalem has its boundary, its wall of separation. From this we learn that whatever is of Babylon must be rejected and whatever is of God must be protected. Building a city wall is not an easy task; it is greatly hated by Satan. For example, when Nehemiah returned to Jerusalem to build the city wall, he was opposed vehemently by Sanballat and Tobiah. Consequently, with one hand he held his weapon and with the other hand he built. Let us ask God to teach us how to take up spiritual weapons against the spiritual hosts of wickedness in the heavenlies and how at the same time to maintain the principle of separation.

Having the names of the twelve apostles on the foundations means that everything in the city is based on the principle of the kingdom of God as proclaimed by the apostles. "Being built upon the foundation of the apostles and prophets" (Eph. 2.20) simply means that the revelation which the apostles received from the Lord is the foundation of New Jerusalem.

Why are the names of the twelve tribes of Israel written on the doors? The answer is supplied by the words of the Lord Jesus himself, who declared that "salvation is from the Jews" (John 4.22).

The Bible employs gold to represent all that is of God. To measure with a golden reed suggests that this city is measurable by God's standard, for it meets His standard.

"And the city lieth foursquare, . . . the length and the breadth and the height thereof are equal"—In the Scriptures we find that only the holiest of all things in the temple and the New Jerusalem are in perfect cubes. This is thus to imply that in the new heaven and the new earth the New Jerusalem will be the holiest of all to God.

"According to the measure of a man, that is, of an angel"—Why at that time is the measure of a man equal to the measure of an angel? In resurrection, men shall be equal to the angels (Luke 20.36). In other words, all that is in the city is on resurrection ground. That which cannot be bound and retained by death is called resurrection. Whatever comes out of us will be finished at the cross; that which is of God cannot be touched by death.

21.18–21 "And the city was pure gold, like unto pure glass"—One special feature of New Jerusalem is that the gold therein is pure. Everything is wholly of God; there is not a speck of mixture. Whatever is not of God is dross. No one can say to God that he has something in himself to give to Him. What God wants is nothing but pure gold.

"The foundations of the wall of the city were adorned with all manner of precious stones"—There is a basic difference between gold and precious stone. The first is a single chemical element, but the second is a compound. Gold is directly created by God, whereas precious stone is the result of the fusing together of several elements under the earth after they have gone through extremely high temperature accompanied by pressure. In other words, what the precious stone represents is not that which God gives directly to man, rather it stands for the refining work which the Holy Spirit has done in man. The life which God gives to us is gold, the life which God forges in us is precious stone. God does not stop with merely imparting the life of Christ to us; He goes on to incorporate or work into us that life in us.

"And the twelve gates were twelve pearls"—Pearl is formed by the secretion of a mollusk in the sea after it is wounded by a grain of sand or other foreign matter. Hence pearl signifies that life which comes out of death. It represents the life which the Lord Jesus Christ has released in His death on the non-atoning side.

"And the street of the city was pure gold, as it were transparent glass"—A street is a place for fellowship. Inasmuch as the street of the city is pure gold, all who walk on it will never have their feet defiled. Today all who are bathed still need to wash their feet continually (John 13.10) in order to maintain their fellowship with God. For as long as we walk on this earth we cannot help but be contaminated by the dust of the earth, thus affecting our fellowship with God. But the day shall come when nothing will defile us nor hinder our fellowship with God. In eternity nothing defiles us, therefore our whole life shall be holy.

"As it were transparent glass"—Today many situations are opaque, but in the future everything shall be transparent before God. If that is the case, then we must begin to learn even today to be true and transparent, not attempting to pretend to be what we are not.

—CLJ 57-61, 62-3, 64, 83-4, 130-2, 134-7, 153-5, 230-4

## 44 The Study of God's Word

One thing, then, is of supreme importance: in studying the Bible, the man as well as the method needs to be right. Indeed, only the right man may fully utilize the proper method. Study method is unquestionably quite significant; without it one cannot master his study. Yet the man himself must first be transformed before he is able to study well. Those who believe that only a few are able to understand the Bible are as mistaken in their thinking as are those who consider all as being qualified to know it. For the truth really is that neither few nor all but only one class of people may actually study the Bible. Unless we belong to this class of people we will not be able to study the Scriptures too well. We therefore ought to realize that the man stands ahead of the method. If the man is not right, not one method will work; but if he *is* right, all these good methods may be used. We sincerely regard method as necessary; yet we will never rank it first; *the man himself must be primary.*

### *Three Prerequisites*

A. SPIRITUAL.

*"The Words That I Have Spoken. . . Are Spirit"*

The Lord Jesus once said: "The words that I have spoken unto you are spirit" (John 6.63). And hence the words of the Bible are not words only, nor are they mere letter, they are also spirit. We should not forget what our Lord has declared: "God is spirit: and they that worship him must worship in spirit" (John 4.24 margin). He is telling us there of a basic principle, which is, unless man exercises his spirit he is unable to touch God; for God being Spirit, we cannot worship Him except in the spirit. If we engage anything other than the spirit, we shall altogether fail to worship. We cannot worship Him with our mind, nor our emotion, nor our will. "Will-worship" (Col. 2.23) is of no value whatsoever. Because God is Spirit, He must be worshiped in spirit. This same fundamental principle governs in our Lord's later statement, recorded in John 6: "The words that I have spoken . . . are spirit." Since the Lord's words are spirit, they must be read in the spirit. In other words, spiritual things can be touched by the spirit alone.

This Bible which we have is more than words printed on paper. So far as its nature is concerned, it is spirit. Hence all who intend to read this book need to *use their spirit.* There is no other way to read it. Of course, the spirit we refer to here points to the spirit of the regenerated person. For the sake of convenience, let us for the time being call it "the regenerated spirit." Since not everyone has this regenerated spirit, neither can everyone understand the Bible. Only those who have this regenerated spirit are able to study the Scriptures. The spirit is to be used in reading the Bible as well as in worshiping God. Without this spirit none may know God nor know the Bible. . . .

As a rule, after a person becomes a Christian he should know spiritual things. Yet why is it that many brothers and sisters still do not know? This is due to the fact that though they possess a regenerated spirit, they are not necessarily spiritual men. In 1 Corinthians 2 and 3 Paul lays stress on the "spiritual" rather than on the "spirit." John's emphasis is on "spirit" whereas Paul's is on "spiritual." Man needs not only to possess this spirit but needs also to be possessed by this spirit. It is absolutely necessary to have the spirit; there is no other way. But having the spirit he must live under its principle, walk according to the spirit, and be a spiritual man; otherwise it is still of no avail. . . .

B. CONSECRATED.

*Heart Must Be Open*

The Bible is the word of God. It is full of God's light. This light is to enlighten all whose hearts are open to Him. "But we all, with unveiled face beholding as in a mirror the glory of the Lord" (2 Cor. 3.18). Beholding the Lord with unveiled face is a basic condition to being enlightened by glory. If anyone approaches the Lord with veiled face, how can he expect the glory of the Lord to shine on him? God's light shines only on those who are open to Him. Unless one is open to God, he has no way of obtaining His light. The problem lies in his being closed to God. His spirit, his heart, his will, and his mind are all closed to Him, and hence he will not have the light of the Bible to shine on him. . . .

The question may be asked, What exactly is meant by being open to God? This openness must come from a consecration which is unconditional and without reservation. To be open to God is not a temporary attitude; it is a permanent characteristic before Him. It is not occasional, it is continuous. If one's consecration to God is perfect and absolute, his attitude towards God will naturally be unreserved and nowhere in him is he closed to God. Any indication of closure only points to the imperfection of one's consecration. All darkness comes from closure, and all closure comes from lack of consecration. Wherever consecration is lacking there is a place of reservation. Where one is unable to yield to God, there he must defend himself; and in that area he has no way to the truth of the Bible. For when he comes to that area, he will only circle around and around it. Simply stated, then, darkness arises out of closure, and closure stems from lack of consecration. . . .

*Obedience Must Be Persistent*

According to our obedience will God give the revelation of the truth of the Bible to us. The measure of our obedience before

God determines the amount of light we receive. If we obey God persistently, we will see continuously. Without consecration, there can be no seeing; without persistent obedience, there will be no increase in seeing. Should our consecration be less absolute, our enlightenment will also be less complete; if our consecration is too general, our enlightenment cannot be any more specific. So that the basic problem lies in consecration. He who does not know consecration has no way to know the Bible. In order to see continuously, the consecrated must have not only that basic consecration once made but also a persistent obedience. The degree of enlightenment depends on one's obedience after consecration. To see fully demands perfect obedience.

Let us pay special attention to the word of the Lord Jesus: "If any man willeth to do his will, he shall know of the teaching, whether it is of God, or whether I speak from myself" (John 7.17). If any man wills to do the will of God, he shall know. In other words, obedience is the condition for knowing. *Willingness to do the will of God is the condition for knowing God's teaching.* It is completely impossible to know God's teaching without intending to do God's will. To know God's teaching requires the willingness to do His will. To will is a matter of attitude. God likes us to have this attitude of obedience. When it is present in us, God's teaching will become clear to us. Instead of always asking what the Bible teaches, let us ask if we are willing to hear the word of the Lord. The problem lies with our attitude, not with the teaching of the Scriptures. Whether or not the Bible will become manifest hinges largely on our attitude, while God is responsible for His teaching. If our attitude is right God will immediately reveal His word to us. And another instant obedience with another right attitude, and we shall have another revelation of God. With right attitude comes revelation; with obedience to that revelation comes more right attitude and further revelation. . . .

C. EXERCISED.

"Solid food is for fullgrown men, even those who by reason of use have their senses exercised to discern good and evil" (Heb.

5.14). "By reason of use" may also be translated "on account of habit" (Darby). In order to receive God's word one condition must be fulfilled. What is this condition? Solid food is for fullgrown men. Why is this so? Because they have developed the habit of consuming solid food. The fullgrown are able to take in solid food on account of the habit of having their senses exercised to discern good and evil. "Experience of the word of righteousness" in the preceding verse (v.13) means skillful in the word of God on account of habitual use. The word "use" or "habit" is an industrial term in Greek. It means "skillful." Among workers, some are new hands while some are skillful hands. The latter are those who have become skillful through a certain period of training. To be skillful in the word of righteousness means to be well trained in the word of God. For a person to understand God's word he needs to develop that skillful habit.

The Bible exposes its readers. Certain kinds of people read certain things out of the Scriptures. If you wish to ascertain a person's character and habit you need only ask him to read a chapter from the Bible and see what he gets out of it. A man of curiosity will read curious things out of the Bible. A man with a big brain will find the Bible full of reasons. A man who does not think will see only the letters in each verse. How true it is that a person's character and habit can be revealed in the way he reads the Scriptures. Now if these traits are not dealt with, they will lead the person astray and make his reading of the Bible fruitless.

What kind of character and habit is required for studying the Bible well?

(1) *Must not be subjective.* It is required of all readers of the Bible to be objective. No subjective person can study the Bible well, for he is not apt to learn. Speak to an objective person once and he understands. Speak to a subjective person thrice and he still does not understand. Many people do not hear and understand because they are too subjective, not because their brains are inferior. Since they live wholly in their own thoughts, they are unable to hear other people's words. Being already filled with

their own opinion and ideas, how can they take in another's words? If they are thinking of water and people talk to them of hill, they will reckon it as the water of the hill. Can such people who fail to hear another's words hear the word of God? If they are not able to understand earthly things, how can they be expected to comprehend spiritual things? . . .

(2) *Must not be careless.* The Bible must not be read carelessly since it is a most accurate book, exact to its very last jot and tittle. The word of God will slip away through the least negligence. Just as a subjective person will miss God's word, so will a careless person lose its lesson too. Let us be careful. The more a person knows God's word, the more careful he becomes. To a thoughtless person, the Bible he reads turns casual. By listening to the way a brother reads the Bible, you can readily judge whether he is a careful or careless person. It is a very bad habit indeed to misread some important word or words in a verse or passage. Due to the bad habit of inaccuracy, we often are inexact in the knowledge of the Bible. How easily God's word may be taken in error if we are slightly careless. . . .

(3) *Must not be curious.* We should seek for accuracy, yet we must not be curious. The word of God is exact, but we are not to search it with a curious heart. If we do, we will miss its spiritual value. The Bible is a spiritual book, therefore it needs to be understood with the spirit. Should the intention of our search for its accuracy be the satisfaction of the urge of curiosity instead of the pursuit of spirituality, we have gone the wrong way. How pitiful it is that many look always for strange things in the Bible. For example, people spend much time trying to prove that the tree of the knowledge of good and evil is the vine. Such study of the Word is futile. Recognizing that it is a spiritual book, we need to touch life, spirit, and the Lord in it. By seeing spiritual things we see also the exactness of its letter, because all things spiritual are accurate. We will go astray in our search if we do

not approach it from the standpoint of seeking for spiritual things. . . .

These above-mentioned matters of subjectivity, carelessness, and curiosity are the common ills of man. We need to have these defects corrected before God so that we may become objective, accurate and incurious. Such traits are not formed in one or two days; they become habitual only after persistent self-discipline (or better said, Spirit-discipline). Whenever we take up the Scriptures to read, let us do so objectively, accurately, and incuriously. And when our nature and habit are duly corrected, we will then be able to study the Bible well.

### *Three Penetrations*

In order to study the Bible well we must also penetrate into three things of the Holy Spirit. Especially in the study of the New Testament, these three things are quite manifest.

*First.* The Holy Spirit desires us to enter into His thought. To understand the word of the Holy Spirit our thought must merge with the Holy Spirit's thought. This is particularly important in the understanding of the New Testament.

*Second.* The Holy Spirit inserts many basic facts within the Bible for us to enter into. If we fail to get into these facts we have no other way to know God's word. Particularly in the four Gospels and the Acts, the Holy Spirit wishes us to penetrate into those prevailing facts.

*And third.* The Holy Spirit wants us to enter into the spirit of what has been written. In many places we need to not only penetrate into the thought but into the spirit of that thought as well; not only the fact, but the spirit of that fact too. This is evident in the Gospels, the Acts, and the Epistles. . . .

We must learn to touch the spirit of the Bible with our spirit. With a view to training our spirit the Holy Spirit orders our environments. Let us recognize that the discipline of the Holy Spirit is the primary and very best training of our life. Such training is in His hand, not in ours. He disciplines us intermittently, with one exercise following another, until our spirit is brought to the proper state. Our spirit is being dealt with in a variety of ways and at different moments: here a blow and there some joy; here a little patience and there something forsaken; and thus are we led to a condition not unlike that condition we read about in a particular passage of the Bible. Our spirit has been trained to such a degree of suitability that even though the meaning of the word has not increased, the inward understanding seems to be clear and thorough. When we speak of it we know what we are talking about, for we have become quite clear as to what it is. We are not only clear in meaning or in word, we are clear in spirit. It is consequently deeper than word and meaning. Our spirit is being brought by the Spirit of God into a oneness with the spirit of His word.

So with regard to this matter of touching the spirit of the word of the Bible, it is not a question of method but a question of the man being dealt with. If our spirit has not been brought into oneness with the spirit of the writer of the Bible, we can at most be teachers but cannot at all be prophets. The most we touch will be teachings or doctrines but not the spirit. Unless we are dealt with by God and are disciplined, we will be reading the Bible as though behind a veil. No matter how we read, we will be far off. Our spirit must be strictly dealt with by God.

During the first few years of our studying God's word, we may indeed be able to comprehend a few doctrines and understand a few facts. But to touch the spirit is not as easy a matter because our spirit is not yet prepared and remains unusable. It takes considerable time—at least a few years—for our spirit to be adjusted properly, being stricken and broken so as to be conformed to the particular state or condition called for by any particular Scripture passage. As a matter of fact, it requires a considerable period of time for our spirit to be brought into oneness with the spirit of the Bible. To enter into its spirit man's wisdom is absolutely no help. Human wisdom may aid us in grasping the word quicker, but it cannot assist us in touching the spirit behind the word. No matter how strong is our imagination and our power of comprehension, these are unable to get us into the spirit of the word. It requires the Holy Spirit to bring us into harmony with the spirit of the word.

—YS 11-2, 13-4, 20, 23, 24-5, 30-1, 32-3, 35, 40-1, 41-4, 76-8

### *How the Living Word Divides*

"For the word of God is living and operative, and sharper than any two-edged sword, and penetrating to the division of soul and spirit, both of joints and marrow, and a discerner of the thoughts and intents of the heart. And there is not a creature unapparent before him; but all things are naked and laid bare to his eyes, with whom we have to do" (Heb. 4.12-13).

The first thing to be noticed is that the word of God is living. His word is sure to be living when we see it. For if we do not find it living, we simply have failed to see God's word. We may have read over the words of the Bible, but if we do not touch something living, we do not see God's word.

John 3.16 says: "For God so loved the world, that he gave his only begotten Son, that whosoever believes on him may not perish, but have life eternal." Consider how one hears such a word; he kneels down and prays: "Lord, I thank Thee and praise Thee, for Thou hast loved me and saved me!" We immediately know this man has touched the word of God, for His word has become living to him. Another man may sit by his side, listening to the very same words but not actually hear the word of God. There is no living response from him. We can draw but one conclusion: since God's word is living, he who listens and does not live has not heard the word of God.

Not only is the word of God living; it is also operative. "Living" points to its nature, while "operative" applies to its ability to fulfill the work on man. God's word cannot return void; it will prevail and accomplish its purpose. It is not mere word, but word that will so operate as to produce results.

What then does God's word do for us? It penetrates and divides. It is sharper than any two-edged sword. Its sharpness is demonstrated in the "penetrating to the division of soul and spirit, both of joints and marrow." Note the analogy here: the two-edged sword against joints and marrow, and the word of God against soul and spirit. Joints and marrow are embedded deeply in the human body. To separate the joints is to cut across the bones; to divide the marrow is to crack the bones. Only two things are harder to be divided than the joints and marrow: the soul and spirit. No sword, however sharp, can divide them. Similarly, we are wholly unable to distinguish between what is soul and what is spirit. Yet the Scripture tells us how the living word of God can do the job, for it is sharper than any two-edged sword. God's word is living, operative, and able to penetrate and divide. It is the soul and spirit of man which are thus penetrated and divided.

Perhaps someone may raise this question: "It doesn't seem that the word of God has done anything special in me. I have often heard God's words and even received revelation, but I do not know what penetrating is, nor do I understand this dividing. As far as I can tell, I am a stranger to both these processes."

How does the Bible answer this question for us? It says "penetrating to the division of soul and spirit, both of joints and marrow," but it also goes on to say that it is "a discerner of the thoughts and intents of the heart." "Thoughts" refers to what we deliberate in our heart and "intents" has reference to our motives. Thus the word of God is able to discern both what we think and what motivates the thinking.

Too often we can easily identify what comes from the outward man. We quite glibly confess, "This was soulish, for it came from self." But we do not really "see" what the soul or self is. Then one day God's mercy comes to us, His light shines upon us and His voice announces to us with severity and solemnity: "What you frequently refer to as your self *is* your self! You have talked lightly and easily about the flesh. You must 'see' how God hates this and will not allow such to continue."

Before this "seeing" we have been able to talk jokingly about the flesh; but once we are stricken with light we shall confess: "Ah, this is it! This is what I have talked about." Thus we have more than an intellectual dividing. It is the word of God that comes upon us to point out to us what we conceive and purpose in our heart. We receive a twofold enlightenment: how our thoughts originate from the flesh, and how our intentions are entirely selfish.

—ROS 67-9

### *The Word of God and the Spirit of God*

The word of God and the Spirit of God are inseparable. God gives His word to us by giving us the Bible, but at the same time He adds a condition: men must receive His word in the power of His Spirit. God backs up His word by His Spirit; He proves His word with His Spirit. He uses His Spirit to preserve His word so that no one will fall short. Whoever contacts God's word without contacting the Holy Spirit will not see the power of God's word. For without the Spirit of God the word of God becomes dead letter.

"Now the natural man receiveth not the things of the Spirit of God: for they are foolishness unto him" (1 Cor. 2.14a). To an unbeliever who searches the Scriptures by his own wisdom the Bible is as good as dead. This does not imply that the Bible is not the word of God, nor that God's word has no power. It simply means that without the Holy Spirit the Bible in the experience of that unbeliever is merely a dead and powerless book.

The word of God remains the same. For some people, however, it becomes life, whereas for others it is only letter. What is the reason for such a difference? None other than because the first class of persons receives the word of God in the power of the Holy Spirit while the second class tries to understand the same word in the wisdom of their mind.

The word of God is powerful and has life. Yet when a person receives it solely with the mind, he will not experience the power and life of God's word. Whatever truth is accepted simply with the mind becomes a mere thought for that person. Such truth has no effectiveness in his walk. He cannot depend upon it in time of need. Though he may know the argument, the fact or the procedure, he will not be able to obtain the power therein. For him in his life, the truth is not truth but only empty teaching, because he cannot demonstrate its truthfulness.

For a believer to know whether he has received the word of God in the power of the Holy Spirit, he need only ask if he finds the word powerful in his life when he receives it; because God sends the Holy Spirit to prove to the believer the truthfulness of His word. Consequently, if the word of God fails to be proven, it is due to the fact that the power of the Spirit is lacking in it.

The danger today is that believers hear God's word, read the Bible or seek the truth with only the wisdom of the mind. God joins His word and His Spirit together, but men will either separate His word from His Spirit or His Spirit from His word. The peril of these two extremes is equally as great in either direction. For in separating the word of God from the Spirit of God, what the person obtains will be mere idea or an ideal. And in separating the Spirit of God from the word of God, what that person becomes will be an oddity. More people fall into the trap of the first extreme than into the trap of the second.

Many people read the Bible as though perusing a scientific book. It is as if, with a good mind, some good instruction and good effort, they can understand the Bible. Such kind of research may enable a person to know something of Biblical history and doctrine, but it will not help him to experience the power of God's word. We must be brought by the Lord to the place where we will depend on His Spirit in the reading of His word. We will then understand His truth in His power. The Holy Spirit alone is able to apply the word of God with its life and power to a believer's walk. Accepting the truth merely in the power of the mind will not enable him to realize this life and power in his daily experience.

—MC 73-6

# 45 The Ministry of God's Word

## *Three Kinds of Ministry*

"But we will devote ourselves . . . to the ministry of the word" (Acts 6.4). The *matter* of serving people with God's word is called the ministry of the word; the *person* who so serves is called a minister. "Ministry" points to the matter, while "minister" speaks of the person. The ministry of the word occupies an important place in the work of God. There are definite principles to be learned by those who preach the word of God and serve people with God's word.

From the Old Testament time to the New, God always is found speaking. He spoke in the Old Testament days; He spoke while the Lord Jesus was on earth; and He continues to speak in the New Testament church. We learn from the Bible that God has a prime work to perform on earth, which is, to utter His own word. If the word of God is taken away, then almost nothing is left of God's work. No word, no work. When the word is eliminated, the work is reduced to near zero. We must therefore recognize the place of God's word in His work. Once the word is removed the work of God ceases immediately, for God operates through His word; He treats His word as His work. The work of God is filled with His word.

How does God utter His word? This is a very special and quite remarkable method: God's word is spoken through the mouth of man. Not only is there the word in the Bible; there is also the minister of the word. Were God to speak directly by himself, He would have no need for the minister of the word. Since His word is delivered by man, the minister of the word becomes a real concern. How very significant is man, therefore, in the work of God. God employs no way other than man to deliver His word. God is in need of a special class of people to be the ministers of His word.

Briefly stated, one can find throughout the whole Bible three different kinds of people whom God uses to preach the word. In the Old Testament God's word is spread by the prophets; hence we have the ministry of the prophets. Once again, at the time of the earthly pilgrimage of the Lord Jesus, God's word became flesh; and thus we have the ministry of the Lord Jesus. And finally, in the New Testament God's word is propagated by the apostles; with the result that we have the ministry of the apostles.

### *The Old Testament Ministers of the Word: the Prophets*

In the Old Testament God chose the prophets as the men to speak His word. These many prophets spoke according to the visions they received. Even a person such as Balaam could speak for God, for Balaam was a prophet; his prophecies were some of the greater ones in the Old Testament. The way by which the Old Testament prophets could serve as ministers of God's word was through the word of God coming to them. Balaam, for example, prophesied as the Spirit of God came upon him. He spoke in spite of himself. God set aside his feeling and his thought and gave him revelation. The word of God came to him irrespective of his condition. He neither added his own opinion nor mingled his own feeling or thought in with God's word. In other words, God merely employed the man's mouth to utter His word. This is typical of the Old Testament ministers of the word. The Holy Spirit gave the word to a particular individual and so controlled that person that there could be no error in God's word as propagated by him. Though God used the person, there was little, if any, human element involved in this type of revelation. Man merely spoke the word of God without adding anything to it.

Nevertheless, in the Old Testament we do find people such as Moses, David, Isaiah, and Jeremiah whom God employed as mouthpieces in a way which was more advanced than that of Balaam and other prophets. The words which Moses wrote were mainly what God had commanded him. As the Lord spoke, so spoke Moses. Isaiah recorded vision after vision which the Lord had shown him. In this respect these prophets functioned under the same principle as Balaam. But in another respect Moses and Isaiah were quite different from Balaam. For we know that whenever Balaam himself came forward, his personal feeling was so wrong that he was condemned before God. While under revelation, Balaam spoke the word of God; but as soon as he spoke by himself, he manifested sin, error and darkness. This was not true of Moses. Though he largely spoke according to what God commanded, yet there were times before God when he spoke as he felt. During these occasions he was not looked upon as doing anything wrong; instead, his word was recognized as also being God's word. This shows that Moses was more used by God than was Balaam. The same is true of Isaiah. Most of his prophecies came directly from the visions he received from God, but sometimes he himself began to speak. David and Jeremiah expressed their own feelings before God even more than Moses and Isaiah. All of these prophets approached the way of the later New Testament ministers; even so, they acted mostly under the same principles as the rest of the Old Testament prophets. They spoke when the word of God came to them.

### *The Minister of the Word in the Gospels: the Lord Jesus*

When the Lord Jesus came to the earth, the Word became flesh (John 1.14). The Lord Jesus himself is the word of God. He clothed himself with flesh and became a man in the flesh. Whatever He did and said were all God's word. His ministry was the ministry of God's word. The way God's word was spread through the Lord Jesus is totally different from that through the Old Testament prophets. Earlier God merely engaged man's voice to propagate His word. Even John the Baptist, the last of the prophets, was but a voice in the wilderness. The word of God simply used his voice.

Not so with the Lord Jesus. He is the Word become flesh. The very Person is the word of God. In the Old Testament the word came upon man. The word and the man were two separate entities. The former was simply spoken by the latter's voice. Although with Moses and David it was somewhat different, the basic principle of the Old Testament was that God merely engaged the human voice. In incarnation, however, the word of God was clothed with a human body; God's word became man. It was no longer the word coming to man, nor was it God's word using the human voice. The word instead was dressed in man; therefore it had human feeling, thought and opinion, though it remained God's word.

If man's opinion had entered into God's word during the Old Testament period, that word would have ceased to be the word of God. For in the instant that human feeling, thought or opinion is mixed in with God's word, the latter turns imperfect, impure, and unclean. It is the ruination of God's word. To maintain the purity of His word, nothing of man's opinion, thought and feeling may be mingled in. When the word of God was voiced by Balaam it became a prophecy. But if Balaam had attempted to add his own feeling and idea to it, it would have immediately ceased to be God's word, for the nature of the word would have been changed. This fairly well sums up the Old Testament situation.

With the Lord Jesus, however, God's word used not only man's voice but his thought, feeling and opinion as well. His human thought was God's thought; so too were his feeling and opinion God's. This is the ministry of the word which God was able to obtain in the Lord Jesus. How vastly unalike it was from the Old Testament way. God did not want His word to be merely word; He wished it to be like a person. He delighted in having His word become flesh. This is one of the greatest mysteries in the New Testament. It was God's desire that His word should carry human feeling, thought, and idea through a personality. It was this kind of ministry which the Lord Jesus possessed.

In the Lord Jesus God's word was not objective, but rather, subjective. It possessed human feeling, thought, and idea; yet it remained God's word. In this do we find a great principle of the Bible: that it is possible for the word of God to be unimpaired by man's feeling. The presence of human feeling does not necessarily ruin God's word; it does so only when such feeling is inadequate.

Herein lies a tremendous problem. The great principle is that human elements must not be of such a nature as to hinder God's word. In the life of the Lord Jesus who is the Word become flesh the thought of His flesh is the thought of God. Naturally speaking, the thought of the flesh is only man's thought; but in incarnation the word became flesh in a Man, so that this Man's thought is fully adequate. When it is blended with God's word it fulfills rather than spoils the word of God. The word of God in the Lord Jesus rises higher than the Old Testament word. "You have heard," spoke Jesus one day, "that the ancients were told" thus and so (Matt. 5.21). This tells us that the Lord God spoke to Moses, giving His revelation to His servant. Yet the Lord Jesus proceeded further with, "But I say to you . . . " (v.22). We find here that Jesus himself was speaking on earth, using His own thought and His own idea. And in so speaking, far from overturning God's authority, He fulfilled it. He did not overthrow God's word, but raised it to a height beyond that of the Old Testament.

The characteristic of the Lord Jesus as the minister of God's word lies in the fulfilling of God's word. Not only is there a voice, there is likewise feeling and thought emanating from a sinless person. God's word in the Lord Jesus is no longer a revelation; it has become a Person. It not only engages a Man's voice but is the Person of the Lord Jesus himself. The word of God has taken up personality. It is united with man's word. And when that Man speaks, God speaks. How glorious is this union! When Jesus of Nazareth speaks, God speaks! None has ever spoken like Jesus of Nazareth, nor will any ever afterward speak like Him. He knows absolutely no sin. He is the Holy One of God, and He is wholly of God. The word of God is upon Him because He is the Word become flesh. He is God's word. What He says is said by God. In Him the word of God is absolutely subjective, for He is God's word.

In the Old Testament we can find certain prophets who spoke the word for God, but in the Gospels we can point to the Lord Jesus and say, this Man *is* God's word. In the first instance we are only able to testify that when the prophet opened his mouth the word of God came forth. As to the Lord Jesus, though, we can refer to Him as the word of God. His feeling was the feeling of God's word, and His thought, the thought of God's word. When he opened His mouth there was God's word; even when He shut His mouth, God's word was still there, for as a Person He is the word of God.

Through our Lord Jesus the word was advanced from revelation to personality. Upon the Old Testament prophets the word of God came as revelation, but in the Lord Jesus it was personified. In the Old Testament the word and the person were two separate entities. Although the word was using him, the man remained a man. At the coming of the Lord Jesus, the word of God became flesh. This fleshly Man was God's word. What He spoke was the word of God. To Him revelation was unnecessary, for He himself was the word. There was no need to have the word of God come to Him from outside before He could speak God's word. For was not *His* word the word of God already? He did not need anything extra, because He himself was God's word. In Him God's word was unaffected and unrestricted by man. The word He spoke was the pure word of God. Jesus was a man; even so, the word of God never suffered because of Him. Indeed, God's word found its fullest expression through Him. This is the ministry of Jesus of Nazareth.

### *The Ministers of the Word in the New Testament: the Apostles*

The ministry of the word in the Old Testament is entirely

objective, whereas that of the Lord Jesus is absolutely subjective. Beginning with the apostles, however, the ministry of the word follows the nature of that of the Lord Jesus together with the addition of Old Testament revelation. The difference between the ministry of the word in the New Testament and the ministry of the Lord Jesus is as follows: in the Lord Jesus it is the Word become flesh, that is, first the word, then the flesh to fit the word. His consciousness, feelings, and thoughts are harmonious with God's word. However, in the New Testament ministry of the word we have the flesh first; in order to make it a minister of the word, this flesh must be transformed according to the requirements of God's word. The feeling, thought, and idea of the flesh must undergo a change that it may be suitable to God's word. Hence, this New Testament ministry is different from both the Old Testament ministry and the ministry of the Lord Jesus. That of the Lord Jesus is wholly subjective, for the word is Himself. The New Testament ministry is that of the Lord Jesus added to that of the Old Testament prophets. The word of God comes to man as revelation along with that man's feeling, thought and idea. It is consequently God's revelation plus human elements.

Those who are chosen in the New Testament are not holy as is the Lord Jesus, who alone is the Holy One of God with no impurity, whose word is the word of God. God must not only put His word in these New Testament ministers but must deal with them as well. He needs to raise them to the level He demands. He will use their thoughts, feelings and characteristics, but these have to be dealt with first. So God deals with these New Testament ministers in respect to their experiences, words, feelings, cleverness, opinion, characteristics and other areas, in order that His word might be communicated through them. The word of God is not just imparted through a human voice but is also manifested in deed through these various areas of the man. God takes pleasure in putting His word in man and then in letting it be exhibited through man. The Lord Jesus is the Word become flesh; the New Testament ministers have their flesh wrought upon for the sake of conveying the word of God.

### *Human Element in Revelation*

It is a mistake to assume that there is no human element in God's revelation or that the first necessarily destroys the second. The revelation of God does indeed contain the human element, for God's word is manifested in it. Even with respect to Old Testament prophetic ministry, however small a place the human element occupies, we cannot say there is absolutely none of it present, since the word of God at least needs to be uttered by man's mouth. In incarnation, the Word has become flesh, and so the entire human element of Christ is now the word of God. Today God desires that His word, delivered through New Testament ministers, should be blended with human elements.

In carefully perusing the New Testament we discover that certain words are constantly employed by Paul which were never employed by Peter or John or Matthew. Likewise, Luke has his favorite words, and so has Mark. In their writings, each maintains his peculiarity. The Gospel of Matthew is different from that of Mark, Mark from Luke, and Luke from John. Paul's writings have their own definite tone; Peter's are in another strain. But the Gospel of John and John's Epistles share the same subject and are continuous in nature. For instance, the Gospel of John commences with "In the beginning . . . ," and his First Epistle opens with "What was from the beginning . . . " One refers to the very beginning, the other starts from that beginning and proceeds onward. And his Revelation joins these two together, using the same style of writing.

Pursuing this matter further, we find that each writer of the Bible possesses his own idiosyncrasies. As a physician Luke invokes certain medical terms with which to describe various sicknesses, while the other three Evangelists employ common words. Again, because the Book of Acts is also written by Luke, medical words once more appear. Each Gospel possesses its special phraseology and has its particular topics. In Mark, "immediately" is frequently found; in Matthew, "the kingdom of heaven"; in

Luke, "the kingdom of God." On each book the writer leaves his indelible mark; yet all are the word of God.

The New Testament is full of human elements; still, it is God's word. Each writer maintains his emphasis, uses his special phrases, and retains his characteristics. Through these, God's word is delivered without suffering any loss. Having man's marks and possessing human chacteristics, but nonetheless remaining God's word—such is the New Testament ministry. God's word is entrusted to man and is conveyed through that man's elements. God does not turn man into a tape recorder—first recording every word and subsequently sending them out verbatim. He does not wish it so. Since the Lord Jesus has already come and the Holy Spirit has now entered into the believing man, God will work in man until his human elements do not damage God's word. This is the basis of New Testament ministry. The Holy Spirit so operates in man, so controls and disciplines him, that the latter's own elements can exist without impairing God's word; on the contrary, they fulfill it. Were no human element involved, man would become a tape recorder. Today the human element is in God's word, and the word is fulfilled by man.

Do we know why Paul does not stress that all believers must speak in tongues in the meeting? Yet are not tongues a gift of God? The explanation is because, in the speaking in tongues, man's thought is not involved. In other words, human thought is not included. This makes it more like the Old Testament ministry than that of the New, because this is God putting unknown tongues on the lips of man. God's emphasis in New Testament ministry is in bringing into play the human element in the word. Under the discipline, control and work of the Holy Spirit, all human elements can be properly engaged by God. The word of God is to be released through man. It is God's word, yet it also involves human elements.

Let us use an illustration. Suppose a musician is capable of playing piano, organ, and violin. He may perform the same music on different instruments. Since each musical instrument possesses its unique characteristics, the sounds are distinctly unique. The various characteristics of these musical instruments help to express the feeling of the music. The ministries of the New Testament word somewhat resemble these musical instruments. Some are like pianos, others like organs or violins. The same music played produces a distinct sound according to the different instruments employed. From one minister the word of God comes through with his particular human element; from another there is a different sort of human element. Each and every one of those who are used by God has his own human element implanted in the word. Under the discipline, government and education of the Holy Spirit, this personal element of man no longer hinders the coming forth of God's word but on the contrary renders its manifestation more glorious.

In view of the fact that God's word is to pass through man using human elements, it is obvious that the elements of all those who have not been dealt with by God are unusable. If the personal element is questionable before God, His word cannot come through that person. He is unsuitable; he cannot be a minister of God's word. In the Old Testament God once spoke through an ass, but today the New Testament ministry is quite different. In New Testament times God's word comes through the human element; as a consequence the Lord must be strict in selecting His instrument. We cannot propagate God's word like a tape recorder. God desires to change us. If we are not up to His standard, we are not usable.

To be one who delivers God's word we must be pruned and refined. God has to lay aside those whose human makeup contains many uncleannesses, fleshly things, and matters condemned by God. Others He has to bypass because they have never been broken before God, or their thoughts are not straightforward, or their lives are undisciplined, their necks stiff, their emotions untamed, or they have a controversy with God. Even if these individuals receive God's word, they are not able to deliver it for it is blocked within them. Should they force themselves to preach, the word is ineffective. Hence man's condition before God is a basic problem for New Testament ministers.

Today God wishes His word to be uttered like man's word. It is truly God's word, yet it is also man's word. Which verse in the entire New Testament is not spoken by man? A characteristic maintained from the beginning to the end of the New Testament is that all words spoken by men are *human* to the nth degree, yet also *divine* to the nth degree, being purely the word of God. This is the New Testament ministry of the word.

"For out of much affliction and anguish of heart I wrote to you with many tears," said Paul (2 Cor. 2.4). Paul here is ministering God's word to the Corinthians. He wrote under much affliction. He wrote with many tears. Here was one whose whole being was involved in the word. What he wrote was full of human feeling. The word of God in him made him suffer and caused him to shed many tears. When he wrote, his human element was mingled with God's word and magnified it. He was not void of feeling or thought. His was not like one speaking in tongues with the word coming in and going out without so much as touching the thoughts of the heart. He wrote with his inward being full of thought and feeling. As the word of God came forth, word after word, he was in much affliction and with many tears. This represents the New Testament minister of the word.

Since God's word is to pass through man, his characteristics, idiosyncrasies, tone, and experiences before God may all be manifested in the word. The degree of discipline he has received from the Lord and the measure of trial he has undergone may likewise be disclosed in the word. A minister of the New Testament word may, without any error, add his personal element to the word of God which comes to him. After years of learning before the Lord, he may be brought to a place where he can be freely used by Him as a channel of the word. Should that which man puts into the word be flesh or something of the natural man, the word of God will be adulterated as it passes through man.

God's word contains human elements; only then will it come forth as the perfect word of God. Never misconstrue God's word to be merely one commandment or ten commandments. The Bible demonstrates to us clearly that it possesses a human flavor.

God gives His word to man and lets the latter speak. If man's condition is right, God puts him into the word too. The basic law of God's speaking is: "the Word became flesh" (John 1.14). It is God's desire today that there be not only His word but that His word become flesh. This does not suggest that God's word is lowered to be man's word; it simply means that His word has the flavor of humanity without the least sacrificing of its purity. Truly it is God's word, yet it is in addition man's word; man's word indeed, but God's word too. In New Testament ministry men propagate God's word. We find this in Acts, in Corinthians, in Timothy, in Titus, in Philemon, and so forth. God's word is unveiled through man's word and is magnified through the human element. It is man who is speaking; nonetheless, God recognizes it as His own word.

How very great, then, is the responsibility of those who preach God's word! If the man is wrong and mingles his own unclean things in with the word, he defiles the word of God, greatly damaging it. The fundamental problem in preaching rests not on how much one knows of the Bible, for the mere knowledge of doctrine is of little avail. Knowledge may be wholly objective; it can be delivered without being personally involved. As ministers, though, we can never be like the Lord Jesus who is the Word become flesh; still, the word of God is deposited in our flesh and is to be released through this flesh. This flesh must therefore be wrought upon by God. We need to be daily disciplined. Any defect in us will defile the word and destroy its power.

Do not think that just anybody can preach the word of God. We know of only one kind of person who may preach it—those who have been dealt with by God. The greatest difficulty we confront in preaching the word is not whether the subject is proper or the phraseology correct, but whether the man is right. If the *man* is wrong, all which emanates from him is likewise wrong. May God show us the true way of the ministry of the word. Preaching is not as simple as we usually regard it. It is to serve God's people with God's word. Only when the word is not adversely affected by us can people hear the pure word of God.

We know the stories of Paul, Peter, Matthew, Mark, Luke, John and many other servants of the Lord. They blend their personal elements with God's word, yet we do not touch blood or flesh through them; instead we sense that the word of God is all the more glorified. How marvelous it is—God's word is man's word, and man's word is God's word. . . .

The distinctive feature of God's word is that it includes many, many human elements. His word is not spoken abstractly, it is instead uttered through man. It is manifested through the many affairs of men. Hence it is simple, easily heard, and easily understood. Whenever God speaks, men are able to hear, for the word of God is not only spoken by God but is also comprehensible to men. It is both supernatural and natural, divine and human. Through the lives of various men we may see the words of God and understand the words He is speaking.

In the book of Acts we find very little preaching. Its narrative is preeminently concerned with the works the apostles performed under the leading of the Holy Spirit. We behold what Peter was like, and that is the word of God. We see also what Paul did, and again it is God's word. We notice the beginning of the church in Jerusalem, in Samaria, and also in Antioch; these are not only histories but the word of God as well. Men work out the word of God in history; they speak God's word in history too. In history the Holy Spirit reveals God's word through the lives of men. The word of God is full of human element. Such is the peculiar feature of the Bible. The Bible is not a collection of devotional articles; it is men performing or living out the word of God.

The governing principle of the Bible is the Word becoming flesh. For those who do not know the meaning of incarnation, it is extremely hard for them to understand what the word of God is. God's word is neither abstract nor spiritual to such an extent that it eliminates all human savor. It is not so elevated that it is beyond human sight or touch. "In the beginning was the Word, and the Word was with God," opens John's Gospel; but he goes on to add that "the Word became flesh and dwelt among us, full of grace and truth" (John 1.1,14). This is the word of God. The Word dwells among men. The basic principle which controls the ministry of the word is the principle of the Word becoming flesh. Consequently, although it is most heavenly, nevertheless it is not in heaven but on earth. Though intensely heavenly, the word is definitely manifested through men. Heavenly, yet it can be seen and touched by men. This is the testimony of the apostle in 1 John, where he declares: "What was from the beginning, what we have heard, what we have seen with our eyes, what we beheld and our hands handled concerning the Word of life" (1.1).

To use another example: We at one time did not know what holiness is. But today holiness is no longer an abstraction, for in the life of the Lord Jesus we have seen holiness, how it lives and walks among men. By seeing the Lord Jesus we know what holiness is. Holiness, as it were, has become flesh. Similarly, we did not know patience, but in the Lord Jesus we have seen patience. God is love, yet we were ignorant of how He loves. Now we have beheld this love in Jesus of Nazareth. We misunderstood spirituality, thinking a spiritual person should neither smile nor cry and should be totally devoid of any feeling; now, in the person of Jesus of Nazareth we comprehend what spirituality in actual fact is.

We do not know the holiness of God, but we can comprehend the holiness of the Lord Jesus. So it is with God's love, patience, glory, or spiritual nature. All need to be understood in the Lord Jesus. This is the meaning of the Word becoming flesh. Holiness, love, patience, glory, or spirituality must all become flesh. As we touch *this* flesh, we touch God. The love of Jesus is God's love, the glory of Jesus is God's glory, and so forth. If something is merely in God, we are unable to apprehend it; but we shall know it when we see the Lord Jesus.

Hence the Word becoming flesh is the basic principle. It governs all the dealings of God with men, and it regulates the communion between the two. Though the word had not yet become flesh in the Old Testament, God was pushing in that direction. Today the incarnated Word has already ascended to heaven, nonetheless God is still working according to this principle. God at this present moment is not an abstract God, One who is intangible and who hides himself. Not so; He has become flesh, He has come. How gladly do we proclaim to the world that God has already come. In the Old Testament it seems as if God were yet to come, for "He made darkness his hiding place, his pavilion round about him" (Ps. 18.11). In our day, however, God is in the light; He reveals himself in that light for us to see. When He hid himself in darkness, none could see Him; but in these latter days He is seen in the light. God has come forth. He has come in the Person of His Son, Jesus Christ.

### *The Delivery of the Word*

Since the word of God is full of the human element, its delivery must be by human beings. God does not enlist a tape recorder, thunder and lightning, or angels to proclaim His word; rather, He uses man to propagate it, and not as a machine but as an integral part of the word. He does not ask men to merely send out the voice He gives, for His word needs to pass through man's spirit, thought, feeling and understanding until it becomes that man's word. Only then may it be delivered. This is called the ministry of the word. Receiving with one hand and handing out with the other hand is not considered to be the ministry of the word. If so, it would be similar to a sound machine. No, God does not want us to announce His word mechanically. He puts His word in us that we may meditate on it, feel after it, be afflicted by it, or rejoice in it, before the word is released by us.

"On the last day, the great day of the feast, Jesus stood and cried out, saying, 'If any man is thirsty, let him come to me and drink'" (John 7.37). If I am thirsty I can come to the Lord Jesus and drink. But His proclamation continues with, "He who believes in me, as the Scripture said, 'From his innermost being shall flow rivers of living water'" (v.38). When I am thirsty I may go to the Lord Jesus and drink of Him. But if I meet others in need, do I simply pour out a cupful to them? No, the Lord indicates that whoever drinks of Him shall find the water in the deepest part of his being, and that out of his *depths* the living water shall flow. This constitutes the ministry of the word. The word of God first enters a person, then out of his depths it flows to others. Such a turning becomes the ministry of the word. It does not depend on how many Scripture verses we can recite to others, nor on how many sermons we can give; rather is it the turning of the living water deep down within us. Such a process demands a costly price. Sometimes the living water fails to flow out after it has flowed in; at other moments it ceases to be living after it has entered in; and at still other times it may issue forth with many of the impure things of the heart. Under all these circumstances the ministry of the word is arrested.

Thus the ministry of the word is not the mere delivery of sermons we memorize. We must allow the word to come to us, to drill and to grind us, until it flows out with—yes, our personal elements in it—and yet not spoiled or corrupted in the least. The Lord wishes to use us as a channel of living water. The very depth of our being is the channel. For the living water to flow freely from us we must be right before God; otherwise we will hinder His word. True preaching never brings in cleverness or eloquence. It depends on whether we perfect or corrupt the word of God as it passes through us and mingles with our personal makeup. The great problem is that many living waters cease to be living after they flow through men! How extremely necessary, therefore, is the discipline of the Holy Spirit in our lives. Should anyone fail to see the necessity of having himself dealt with by God, fail to see how his habits, temperament and life need to be pruned and refined, he is of no use to the word of God.

How very far from the truth it would be if you should accept eloquence and cleverness as the prerequisites of a minister of the word! The word of God comes to you. You are satisfied as it passes through you, yet you are at the same time being tried, drilled, ground, and dealt with by the word. You undergo much affliction, pay some costly price, till gradually you begin to be clear in regard to that word. In this manner God's word is being increased in you. Word after word and line upon line is knit and woven into you. The time arrives for its delivery. It issues forth not only with words but also with the spirit. The water remains pure, being wholly of God. Your words do not lessen but rather increase the perfectness of the word. You do not diminish, but instead add to, its holiness. You, as a person, have come forth; so also has the living water. You are speaking, but God is speaking too. This, then, is the ministry of the word.

In the ministry of the word two streams instead of one seem to flow, and they flow together. It is the consequence of the working of the Holy Spirit within us as well as His disciplining us through the arrangement of our environment. We become channels of living water only after the Holy Spirit has succeeded in breaking and grinding us down. Our outward man needs this breaking by God. It needs drastic and thorough dealings. Whereupon our spirit may begin to breathe freely—the Holy Spirit being freed within us—and the word of God may commence to flow from us. The word of God and ourselves are consequently like two streams merging and flowing together.

Never forget what the ministry of the word is. It is the outflowing of the Spirit of God in man as well as in the word. One part of it consists of God's word and the other part of man's ministry. The word of God comes to man, who adds in his ministry, and then the two flow out together. God's word is not delivered if it is just the word without the human ministry. . . .

Having been set apart as a minister of God's word from our mother's womb, none of us can afford to be foolish before God. Each must know what the Lord has arranged for him. A person's environment, family, profession: each of these human matters has God's arrangement in it. God never intends to destroy these human aspects. He does not want us to be spoiled—to be pretentious and unnatural. He desires us to be innocent people, though at the same time He will work to break down our outward man. That about you which is the human element is something established by the Spirit of God; but you as a person, that is, your natural skill, your natural life with its thought, will and emotion, must assuredly be broken down by God. The breaking of the outward man does not at all imply that God also rejects our human elements. . . .

The main trouble in the church is the lack of ministers of the word. It is not the rarity of God's word nor the infrequency of vision and light, but the scarcity of those who can be used by the Lord. God wants the spirits of the prophets to be subject to the prophets [see 1 Cor. 14.32]. What kind of a prophet can command the subjection of his own spirit? Can the spirit of the prophet be subject to him who is licentious, self-willed, heady, or excessively emotional? He who has no mark of the cross in his spirit and who remains wild and proud after many strokes by the Lord is disqualified. Is vision infrequent? Is light scanty? Or is the word rare? Not at all! The sad fact is, usable prophets are what are scarce.

The distinctive feature of Paul is that he was suitable and faithful. How can God trust His word to those who are unfit? How would you deliver the word if it were given to you? Would you speak by yourself? What if your thought were not right, your emotion not fitting, your intention not pure, or your opinion not correct? You know that if your spirit is not right, what is released will similarly not be right, even though you do say the right word. How much the word of God has suffered in the hands of men! . . .

When we spoke earlier about the ministry of God's word, we did not assert that there could be God's word outside of the Bible. As we categorically deny that beyond the sixty-six books of the Bible someone could write a sixty-seventh book, we equally reject the notion that men today can receive revelation not found in the Bible or can possess ministry additional to what the Bible permits. We firmly believe God's word is in the Old Testament and His word is in the New Testament; we do not intend to add anything to the Bible. Even so, we additionally understand that not all who are familiar with the Bible can preach God's word. It is therefore necessary for every minister of God's word to know what the word of God is. The lack of such knowledge precludes him from being God's minister.

The whole Bible contains sixty-six books, written by approximately forty persons. Each of the writers has his own peculiarities, style, and phraseology; each possesses his personal feeling, thought, and individual traits. When the word of God came to these writers, God used their personal human elements. Some were used more while some were used less. But all have been used by God, and all have received revelation. The word of God is a symphony and the writers are like the musical instruments. There are many and various musical instruments in an orchestra, each emitting its own sound; but when they play together they render harmonious music. We can still distinguish the sound of the piano, violin, trumpet, clarinet, or flute. Yet what we hear is not a jarring discord but a symphonic blending. Each of the instruments has its individual characteristics, yet all play the same musical score. If they each were playing independent musical numbers there then would be the jarring notes and the unbearable sounds. The same is true of the ministers of the word. Each has his personal characteristics; nonetheless, all speak the word of God.

From beginning to end the Bible maintains an organic unity. It is not a chaotic compilation. Though each minister says a little, they all nevertheless come together into an organic oneness. Many are those who speak—almost forty in number—but the Word is one. There is absolutely no confusion, nor are they unreconcilable bits and pieces. Many instruments, but one music. Something extra added in would hurt our ear and make us sense that something is wrong. God's word is one. There can be different voices but no jolting notes. Not because one knows how to make some sound can he justifiably stand up and deliver God's word. The word of God is an organic unit. The ministry of the word in the present is one with that of the past. Nothing foreign can be added. God's word is the Lord Jesus himself; it is livingly and organically one. No one can mix anything else into it; any addition would be confusion and disturbance and impairment to the word of God.

There are thirty-nine books in the Old Testament. Chronologically the book of Job may have been the first one written, but the five books of Moses stand at the very beginning of the compilation. Let us grasp a very significant point here—that all who wrote after Moses did not write independently, but wrote according to what had been written before. Moses wrote his Pentateuch independently, yet Joshua set down his book on the foundation of the Pentateuch. In other words, Joshua's ministry of the word of God was not an independent one; he became a minister according to what he knew of the Pentateuch. So was it with the one who wrote the Books of Samuel; he too based his ministry on the five books of Moses. This is to say, therefore, that aside from Moses—who was called of God to write independently—all those who followed became ministers of God's word according to the word already given. Every book in the Old Testament was composed in this fashion. The writers are various, yet they all write on the basis of the previous writings. Every minister of the word after Moses speaks in accordance with the words already uttered. The word of God is one; no one can speak what he wants to; those who follow must speak according to the words given by their predecessors.

We now come to the New Testament. Except for the mystery of the Gentiles and the Jews forming one body, as unfolded in the Letter to the Ephesians, nothing is new; all else can be found in the Old Testament. Any revelation of truth can be located in the Old Testament, even that of the new heavens and the new earth. There is a certain edition of the Bible which capitalizes all of the many Old Testament quotations in the New Testament. It becomes quite evident that many words used in the New Testament were already seen in the Old. Many are direct quotations, and many more repeat what the Old Testament had already expressed. There are more than a thousand five hundred places in the New Testament which are quotations of Old Testament words. Let us remember that the ministry of the New Testament word is based upon God's word in the Old Testament; they were not independently spoken. Hence if anyone should stand up today and claim to have received an independent revelation, we would know for sure that it was undependable.

No one today can have God's word extraneous to the Bible; even the New Testament cannot exist alone, nor can the words of Paul. You cannot cut the Old Testament away and retain much of the New Testament; neither can you excise the four Gospels and keep the letters of Paul. We must see that all the later words follow those previously uttered. The words spoken later arose from light in the former words; they were not isolatedly spoken. Should another word ever come forth independently, it is heresy and not God's word. All the ministries in the Bible are interdependent; none possesses an unconnected revelation totally unrelated to the others and entirely disconnected. Even the twenty-seven books of the New Testament are based on those of the Old Testament. The subsequent ministers received what was handed down to them by their predecessors. . . .

Therefore, all who wish to speak for God today must receive His word from the Old and New Testaments; they are not to obtain anything from outside the Bible. This is a most important axiom: just as the ministers of old were not independent, neither are today's ministers of the word to be independent. Each one must depend on what God has already said. None are able to secure any revelation outside of the scope of the Bible. . . .

Today's ministers of the word must know what God has said in the Old Testament as well as in the New. It is evident that those ministers of the word who wrote the New Testament were familiar with the Old Testament. Today's ministers must be well acquainted with both. By knowing the words of our predecessors we are able to utter what harmonizes with these two Testaments. We will not speak independently. God does not put an additional word in our mouths; He only gives us new light on what He has already spoken in the Old and New Testaments that we may stand before men and deliver His word. . . .

We stress that a minister of the word needs to be familiar with the Bible. If we do not hear what God has spoken in the past we have no way to obtain revelation. Revelation is born out of previous revelation, never isolatedly given. First God puts His revelation in the word said before, then God's Spirit enlightens that word and enlarges the revelation. Thus the process continues. This is the way of revelation. It is not a light given in isolation, but is a light which comes from within the word and increases in brightness as time goes on. This is God's revelation. Without past revelation God's light has no ground in which to operate. God's revelation today cannot be given in the same way as at the very first. When He revealed to the first man He spoke without there being any previous background on man's part. In the advanced word of today, however, He speaks only on the basis of what He has already said. All His subsequent revelations are derived from the first one. . . .

Now we wish to proceed further to see that the words these ministers speak are not only rooted in God's former words but are also interpreted by Him. The ministry of the word requires God's interpretation as well as God's written word. His former words alone are not sufficient. One who has laid hold of God's speaking in the past is not necessarily thereby qualified to deliver God's word. He who is familiar with the Old Testament is not automatically enabled to write the New Testament; neither is one who is well versed in the New Testament necessarily competent as a minister of today's word. Upon the basis of God's recorded word there needs to be God's interpretation. God must explain His own past word to His minister; otherwise there can be no ministry. . . .

As those in the New Testament had the ministry of the word, we today must have such ministry. Should we desire to be ministers of God's word we must diligently read the recorded word of God, and not merely with our head but looking to the Spirit of the Lord to reveal to us what characterizes His word that we may take of the facts and receive the interpretation. When a minister of the word speaks, he must speak from background. Never speak without foundation, nor consider familiarity with God's past words as sufficient. Always seek for the Holy Spirit's interpretation. . . .

The Bible is a wonderful book. Its special characteristic rests in the fact that it speaks with human words, yet is truly God's word. Though written by human hands, it is nevertheless recognized as having been written by God's hand too. Its many terms, phrases and statements are all God-breathed. The original for "inspired by God" (2 Tim. 3.16) is "God-breathed." The Bible is God-breathed, as "men moved by the Holy Spirit spoke from God" (2 Peter 1.21). When God was creating heaven and earth, He formed man of dust of the ground; but man was not a living soul until God breathed the breath of life into him. Though the Bible was written by human hands and spoken from human mouths, even so, God breathed on it and made it a living book. It became a living word spoken by the living God. This is the meaning of inspiration in the Bible.

There are human elements and men's words in the Bible. Many, in reading it, touch these elements and words, but they so often miss what God intends to say through them. The distinctiveness of this Book is its dual feature: on the one hand the Bible has its outer shell—the physical part of the Bible—similar to that part of man which is made of dust; on the other hand it has its spiritual part, that which is in the Holy Spirit, what is God-breathed and God-spoken. The outer shell is something which comes from man's memory (hence it can be memorized by man), from the human mouth (hence can be heard by man's ears), which is written in human language (it may be apprehended by man's understanding), and was also spoken by man as doctrine or teaching (it can thus be remembered, understood and propagated by more people). This, however, is the outer shell of the Bible, that which is merely physical. Even doctrine and teaching are included in this realm, because they are the physical part of the Book, able to be memorized and understood by the wise. But the Bible has still another part. "The words that I have spoken to you are spirit and are life," declared the Lord Jesus (John 6.63). This is the spirit and life side. It is God who speaks in man. Neither the wise nor the understanding know it. It requires an organ other than the eyes, ears, or brain for its apprehension. . . .

What is inspiration? And what is revelation? Inspiration means God has once breathed upon this book the Bible. Without inspiration something cannot be written so as to become a part of the Bible. Consequently, inspiration is the foundation of the Bible. God inspired Paul to write Romans; that is, God breathed on him that he might write the Letter to the Romans.

What, then, is revelation? Revelation means God again breathes on His word when I read Romans two thousand years later in order that I may know it as the word of God. Inspiration is given only once; revelation is given repeatedly. By revelation we mean that today God again breathes on His word, the Holy Spirit imparts light to me; the anointing of the Holy Spirit is upon this word so that once again I see what Paul saw in his day. God does something today to make alive the inspiration of yesterday. This is a tremendous event! It is a most glorious act!!

What again is revelation? Revelation occurs when God reactivates His word by His Spirit that it may be living and full of life as at the time when it was first written. As in the beginning when Paul, full of life, was used by God to write and thus the word became so living, so today the Holy Spirit once more anoints and fills His word that it may have the same power, light and life as it had formerly. This is revelation. It is futile to simply read, for a person can read through the Book without ever hearing God speak once to him. The Bible is the word of God: God has indeed once spoken these words. But to make it living a person must ask God to speak afresh. When God speaks again, things will happen—God's word, light and life come forth. Unless there is this speaking afresh, the Bible will remain a sealed book. . . .

In the ministry of the word there must be God's word beyond man's word; in addition to man opening his mouth, God must open His mouth. Should God keep His mouth shut, nothing spiritual can be done. These are two diametrical worlds. The one is the world of doctrine, truth, teaching, letters, language, phraseology; those who are diligent, clever and wise, and possessing a good memory, may be able to comprehend the one world. But the other is wholly at variance, for God speaks again what He had once spoken before. Do we now see the difference? The Bible records without any error what God once promised, but the word of God today is His speaking to us again what He has said before. In God's word there is the need for Him to again speak to us; in God's light there needs to be another enlightenment from Him; in God's revelation, there awaits a fresh revealing of what has already been revealed. This is the foundation of the ministry of God's word. . . .

Every minister of God's word must learn one lesson. Not because I understand something of the letters of the Bible, not because I see somewhat concerning the truth in the Bible, nor because I am able to quote Scripture verses am I a minister of the word. I need to understand, see, and be able to quote, but besides these there is a still more basic requirement. The possession or lack of possession of this basic requirement determines whether or not I have the ministry of the word. This determining factor is the revelation of the Holy Spirit. The ministry of the word requires the revelation of the Holy Spirit. There must not only be similar words; there must also be corresponding revelation. The absence of corresponding revelation terminates the presence of ministry. This we must know deep in our heart. . . .

The principle is: one inspiration but many revelations; one word but spoken repeatedly by God; one Bible but frequent anointings of the Holy Spirit. Thus is the ministry of God's word established. Whenever anointing, enlightenment and revelation are lacking and hence what is left is but the outward expounding of the Scriptures, the ministry of the word has ceased. We must take note of this before God. Useful indeed are man's diligence, memory, understanding, and cleverness, yet these by themselves are inadequate. To be effective, there must be God's further mercy and renewed speaking. As a matter of fact, unless God is willing to speak, men will never hear the word of God. It is something beyond human ability. If the Lord is silent, the speakings of all the ministers are in vain. It is therefore of the greatest importance that the Lord should speak. Anyone who has learned to speak in the spirit has seen the utter uselessness of human competency alone. The words may be the same, even the tone or feeling seems to correspond, yet what is spoken can be vastly different in effect.

Always remember that God's word needs to be spoken by God. The Bible is the word of God and it requires of Him to speak again. The work of a minister is to allow God to speak through him. He is to serve God in this spiritual realm. Ministering the word of God and ministering theology are separated by an unbridgeable gulf. Whenever listening to a sermon, do not pay attention only to the correctness of the doctrine, teaching, or truth. We do not think lightly of these things, but all who have learned before God and have had their eyes opened search for something more. Perhaps the one who is speaking has very good thoughts, but he just does not have the word of God. Another speaker may not be as gifted in thinking; he nonetheless has the word of God in his delivery. Whether God is speaking or not marks the great divide. . . .

"In the beginning was the Word, and the Word was with God, and the Word was God. He was in the beginning with God" (John 1.1–2). This definitely indicates that the Son of God is this word; Christ is the word. Hence the ministry of the Word is the ministration of God's Son. Serving the church with God's word is ministering the Son of God. If the seven deacons in Acts 6 were those who served tables, the ministers of God's word are those who serve people with God's word. But this word is more than simply a word; it is a Person, even Christ himself.

Some can only serve with the doctrines of the Bible. They have no way to minister the Lord Jesus because they live in the realm of the letter. Their service ends with truths, doctrines and teachings. It is beyond their ability to minister the Christ behind the doctrine. This is a difficulty to many—they cannot impart Christ to others. Yet the written word of God is Christ. The Bible is more than simply a book in whose pages certain doctrines and teachings can be found. If the Bible is divorced from the Person of Christ it becomes a dead book. In one realm it is just a book, but in another realm it is Christ himself. He who lives in the first realm, seeing the Bible merely as a book, is not qualified to be a minister of God's word. He can only serve with doctrines, truths and teachings; he is unable to serve with Christ. . . .

What is the ministry of the word? It touches what is hidden behind the parables or words and what can only be seen when the person is right before God. If the people's hearts have grown dull they naturally cannot hear. A dull heart brings in closed eyes and heavy ears. Today's difficulty does not stem from a scarcity of God's word; rather does it arise from a lack of understanding among God's children. How people incorrectly take parables and external words as the word of God! Brethren, the man who touches the Bible does not necessarily touch the word of God. It is a fact that to touch God's word one needs to touch the Bible. But touching the Bible alone is not enough. You should ask the Lord, "Oh Lord, let me see Your word behind the words; let me see Your light in the light; and let me receive revelation in Your revelation." If you fail to touch what lies behind, then your words have little to offer to people, for you cannot communicate Christ to them.

The Lord is not to be known by merely understanding the truth of the doctrine of the Bible; He is known when you see the light of His countenance. Because you know the Lord, so you know the Bible as the word of God. This is the only way to supply the church with Christ. After you have seen Christ you can easily find a given aspect of Him in the Bible. Hence it is said, and said truly, that there is no page in the Bible which does not speak of Christ. Yes, when you know Him, everything in the Bible becomes living.

So the issue here is whether or not you have the revelation of Christ. If you have the revelation of Christ, Bible knowledge will strengthen your apprehension of Him. Without that revelation, the Bible and the Lord remain two distinct and separate entities. You may supply the church with the Bible, but you are not able to supply Christ to the church. How do you supply the church with Christ? By presenting something of Him that corresponds to each portion of Scripture which you use. You not only use Bible terms and words, you actually supply Christ to the church. Oh, the futility of just the bare studying and expounding of the Scriptures! Always remember that helping others to know the Bible and helping others to know Christ are two opposite matters. . . .

The Christ we know in revelation gradually becomes the word in us. We have found Him in the Bible, perhaps in one, two, or nine or ten different passages. We progressively see the reality of Christ in the word, and so we are able to supply Him along with the word. By the mercy of God, those people who receive such a word will find the Holy Spirit working in them to transform the word into Christ in them. This is called the supply of Christ, that is, Christ is supplied through the word of the Bible; and men receive Him when they receive the word. This forms the basis for all ministry of the word. . . .

A minister of the word is one who has the revelation of Christ, one in whom God has been pleased to reveal His Son (see Gal. 1.16). It is more than that he just says this is so, but he inwardly knows that Jesus is the Christ, the Son of the living God. To say so takes only two or three minutes to recite, but the Lord says:

"Flesh and blood has not revealed this to you, but my Father who is in the heavens." To know Christ is better than to know words; it is a seeing. As one sees this vision of the Son of God everything but Christ recedes, be it sanctification, righteousness, or life. Out of this entire universe nothing can be compared with Christ; no spiritual thing can vie with Him, for Christ is all and in all.

Outside of Christ there is neither life nor light, sanctification nor righteousness. Once a man is brought by God into this revelation of Christ, he begins to realize there is nothing apart from Christ. Christ is everything: He is the Son of God as well as the word of God; He is love, sanctification, righteousness, salvation, redemption, deliverance, grace, light and work. He fills everything. All which we have seen in the past, however much it may be, fades away before Him. Nothing can stand its ground before this grand revelation. Moses and Elijah disappear, so do Peter, James, and John. The Lord Jesus alone remains. He fills all and is all. Christ is the center as well as the circumference. God's center and periphery are found in Christ.

After a person passes through this basic experience of being brought by God to Christ for a true knowledge of His Son, he begins to know the word of God. Thus shall he be able to supply Christ. Without this revelation of Christ, no one is able to minister Him to others. One cannot minister the Christ one does not know, nor can one serve with only a fragmentary knowledge of Christ. Ministry cannot be based on fragmentary knowledge. From the days of Peter and Paul up to this present hour, all who before God possess the ministry of the word have had a basic vision of the Lord Jesus. To minister Christ one needs to be brought into a face-to-face knowledge of God's Son, he must know the Son of God in the depth of his being, know Him as preeminent over all things, as the All and in all. Then and only then can he supply people with Christ. The Bible thereafter becomes a living book to him. . . .

The salient question therefore is this: Are you merely supplying people with the Bible or are you one who has met Christ and so possesses that basic knowledge of Christ? If you are one who has that basic seeing, you will naturally thank God for making many words of the Bible clear to you. Daily you discover the accuracy of the word as you pore over the Bible. You first know the Lord inwardly, next you know Him in the Bible. Once you have had that subjective knowledge of the Lord, you find all the words of God in the Bible to be correct—fitting in, one with the other. What you considered in the past as difficulties now turns to be profitable; what was unimportant before today becomes significant. Every point falls into perfect place; none can be rejected. Henceforward your days are days of knowing the Bible. You do not see everything all at once, but gradually there is an increasing harmony between what you have been shown and the word of the Bible. We know the things of the Bible through inner light and revelation, not through the Bible itself. . . .

Who is a minister of the word? He is one who translates Christ into the Bible; that is, he tells people of the Christ he knows in the words of the Bible so that in those who receive the Bible the Holy Spirit will translate it back into Christ. This may sound strange, yet this is the fact. The Christ he knows is a living person, and the Bible is also full of this living Christ. He sees the Lord Jesus through the mercy of God, yet he sees Him in the Bible too. When he speaks on the Bible he translates Christ into the Bible.

We know that as far as heaven is from earth, so far is the distance between a word with a translation and one without a translation. Some in their speaking move from the Bible to Christ, since they make the Bible the starting point; others, though, start with Christ and transform the living Christ into the word of the Bible. They put Him in the words of the Book and present this to the people. The Holy Spirit is then responsible for opening up these words and imparting Christ to the hearers. If there is no knowledge of Him the presentation will stop short, with just the words of the Bible being uttered; nothing will happen to the audience since only the Bible is being passed on. . . .

A minister of the word is one who is able to impart the Lord through the words he speaks. As the words are given, the Holy Spirit works to enable men to touch and to know Christ. Only in this way can the church be profited. Do not say that the hearers must bear all the responsibility. We ought to know better: that the primary responsibility is ours. It has become almost habitual for people to hear some teachings or expositions of the Bible. Everything starts with the Book and ends with the Book. They are not shown the revelation of Christ behind this Book. And consequently the church becomes poor and desolate.

To translate the Christ we know into the words of the Bible and to retranslate, by the Holy Spirit, these words back into Christ in people constitute the ministry of the word of God. We need to translate the Personal Word into spoken word, and the Holy Spirit will translate the spoken word back into the Personal Word. A minister of the word is able to make the Personal Word and the spoken word one. When he stands up to speak, people see the Christ of God in his words. With his words the word of God is sent forth. The Bible is sent out and so is Christ, for these two are one. . . .

In considering the matter of the word of God we saw two important factors. First, that all latter revelations must follow the preceding ones. Since all the ministries of the New Testament words are based upon those of the Old Testament words, today's ministry of the word must be founded on the revelation of both the Old and the New Testaments. The Bible is therefore the basis of the word. God does not speak extraneously or independently; He speaks once again through His word and releases new light from the light already given. Today God does not give light independently. He imparts fresh revelation according to His past revelations.

Second, that it is imperative for those who would be ministers of God's word to have a fundamental encounter with Christ. They need to have this basic revelation before they can use the Bible as the foundation to their ministry. These two factors are not at all contradictory. On the one hand, today's ministry of the word must be based unquestionably upon the past ministries of the word—even as the New Testament is based on the Old Testament; on the other hand, we must also recognize the fact that all who minister the word must first have met the Lord and received the revelation of Christ before they can speak according to the word in the Bible. This latter point cannot be overlooked. For me to speak by my merely taking hold of the word already given in the Bible would be inadequate; I must first possess this fundamental unveiling of Christ before I can minister according to the word in the Bible.

### *Each Ministry Issues from a Revelation*

When we touch the subject of ministry we should understand that there are two kinds of revelation; the basic, which is given once for all, and the detailed, which is given time and again. When you receive the revelation of Christ you obtain the basic revelation, the same which Paul once received. Later on, you discover from the Bible that what you have already seen before the Lord is this basic revelation. In seeing the Lord your total being has fallen down before God. You know that nothing you once possessed can now stand, not even your zealousness in serving God—much as Paul had once done. Let us realize that Saul of Tarsus was felled to the ground. This prostration of his was not that of sin but was that of work, not of coldness but of zeal. He knew the law, he was familiar with the Old Testament, he was more zealous than his contemporary Pharisees. He was so full of zeal that he laid aside everything to persecute the church. He felt that this was serving God, and he served in an absolute way. Setting aside his error for the moment, it must be admitted that his zeal was very real. Yet he instantly fell down when struck by light. He quickly saw that his past had been spent in persecuting the Lord, not in serving Him at all.

Many may be saved and yet still be blind in this matter of service or work, even as Saul was blind. Saul thought he was in the way of serving God, yet when he was enlightened by the Lord he cried out from the depth of his being, "What shall I do, Lord?" Perhaps this is a question which many have never encountered. They have never been moved by the Holy Spirit to address the Lord as Lord. They may only be calling "Lord, Lord," just as those in Matthew 7, but never have called Jesus as Lord according to 1 Corinthians 12. Here in Saul we see one who confessed for the first time Jesus of Nazareth as Lord and who also asked for the first time, "What shall I do, Lord?" He had fallen down—down from his work, his zeal, his righteousness. Upon his experiencing this fundamental seeing, the Bible became a new book—an opened book—to him.

Many people depend on instructions or references in studying the Bible; they do not know the Scriptures through meeting the Lord. But how marvelous: as soon as anyone meets the Lord and receives enlightenment the Bible becomes a new book to him. One brother, speaking out of his experience, once said, "When the Lord puts me under His light, what I get that day is enough for me to speak for a month." First you must have this basic revelation; and out of that, many more revelations will be given to you. When you have received this fundamental revelation you will discover God speaking here and there throughout the Scriptures. Day after day you will receive many fragmentary revelations which you can use in serving people. This is called ministry.

Ministry, therefore, is based upon our getting a word before God. We have met Christ, and we want to serve the church with the Christ we know; and for this we need to have revelation each time we serve. Ministry requires our seeing something before God and in freshness presenting this thing to the church. Revelations, we have said, are of two kinds: the basic and the detailed, the "once for all" and "the time and again." Without possessing the first it is impossible to have the second. Only after you have secured the basic is your spirit usable; only then is your knowledge of the Lord and that of the Bible usable, and only then too are you usable.

Even so, you still cannot simply go out and minister. It is true that this basic revelation makes you a minister, but when you do minister you need detailed revelations added to the foundational one. Ministry is founded on the basic understanding and revelation, but when God sends you out to speak today you must learn how to receive the particular revelation for that day before God. Not because I have once received revelation am I therefore able to speak. Each time I minister I need to receive special revelation for the occasion. Each revelation brings in service, each revelation gives a special supply, each revelation constitutes a ministry.

The basic revelation once given will not supply enough for a lifetime; it only serves as the basis for a fuller and continuous revelation before God. The first revelation brings in many more revelations. Without the first there can be no additional; but with the first, many more will be given. Not because a person has once received the basic revelation can he thereafter minister with that revelation for years or for a lifetime. If we need to depend momentarily on the Lord for our life, we in like measure need to do so for our work. Each revelation we receive gives birth to each new ministry. It requires many revelations for many times of ministry. Let us keep in mind that each revelation is only sufficient for one occasion of ministry, not for two. Nevertheless, all these detailed revelations are based on the fundamental one. . . .

Let us remember that all spiritual things must be nurtured by revelation. God desires to have all things concerning Christ maintained livingly and nurtured through revelation. Only God's revelation can ever make an old thing new in us. Whatever is in Christ must always be kept in revelation; the absence of revelation will deaden everything. You may assume that since you have seen it before, surely you can speak on it today. But the result will be that you are unable to give people anything. The same thing can be applied to preaching of the gospel. You well recall how the Lord is your Savior and how your sins were forgiven. And in preaching the gospel you sometimes do touch this reality; but at other times the longer you speak the less you sense it, like a paste which has lost its adhesiveness. The one is in revelation while the other is not. Only what is in revelation is fresh, living, and powerful. Remember, death comes to all spiritual matters if separated from revelation.

Consequently, when we go before people to minister the word we cannot depend on our memory, we cannot draw on the experience and word which we once had. It may have been good during that first time, but not for now. For if you speak in such a way as this, you will sense that something is wrong. You have not touched the thing; it is at a distance.

The wonder of revelation lies here: that it is not teaching. Many people make a fundamental mistake. They think they can always teach. But let us realize that mere doctrine or teaching is useless. Never think because you are able to preach, that that is good enough. You may preach the truth and others may tell you how much they enjoy your preaching, but you should be your own judge, because inwardly you will sense that something is amiss. Many people are often vaguely, dimly helped; hence do not be elated if people tell you they have been helped by you. They may say so, yet it may not really be that they have gotten something. You yourself, though, will know whether the word has been near or far, old or new, dead or living. If you have received revelation from the Lord then you shall surely touch the thing when you speak. You will have touched the living reality. You will know it was living, and that solves every problem. So do remember that each time you minister, you need to have a new revelation. . . .

### *The Two Different Realms*

We ought to recognize two different realms: one is that of doctrine (which we can learn in school through textbooks and instructors), and the other is that of revelation. The first can be attained with a little effort, a little cleverness, and a little eloquence; the second, however, is beyond human ability. We must see that in the ministry of God's word men are absolutely helpless if God withholds His revelation. If God does not speak, nothing can be forced out. If God does not give revelation, nothing can be done. With revelation there is ministry; without it there is no ministry. Each time we minister we have God's present revelation as our foundation. In this realm we have to be rightly related to God, we have to be before the Lord; otherwise we cannot stand before men. But in the other realm, that of doctrine, men are able to do something. Memory, cleverness and eloquence will all help. Yet in the realm of revelation you cannot minister if God does not speak. This is known by all those who have learned before the Lord. They can easily discern in what realm one is speaking. The ignorant person mistakes eloquence and cleverness as the criteria. He thinks preaching is strictly a matter of eloquence. However, the Bible shows us that prophecy is a matter of whether or not there is revelation; it is not a matter of eloquence. Preaching without revelation can only edify people's mind and thought; it does not produce revelation. . . .

The starting point of the ministry of the word is revelation. When revelation comes to us, it is God enlightening us; we seem to receive a little light by which we are able to see something. Nevertheless this light appears to be fleeting. If we claim to have seen something it may be that we have not actually seen anything; but should we say we have not seen anything we seem to have distinctly seen something. We see it one moment and then we do not. . . .

We will now see the second point, which is, how to translate light into thought. When revelation comes, it is God who enlightens you. This is the starting point of the ministry of the word. God has shone in your heart; He has enlightened you. But this light has come and gone so swiftly that you cannot remember nor hold it fast. How can one utilize this swift-passing light in the ministry of the word? It is utterly impossible to do so. Hence something needs to be added to light.

This added element is thought. If anyone has been dealt with by God so that his outward man is being broken, that person will actually have very rich thoughts. Only the man with rich thoughts can translate light into thought. Only such individuals can understand the meaning of the light. It is similar to the idea expressed by some brethren who say, "Because I know Greek I am able to grasp the meaning more precisely and translate it more accurately for my understanding." In like manner, the light is the word of God, for it represents God's mind. If our thought life is poor we will not be able to know the meaning nor understand the content when light is given. But if our thought life is rich and strong enough, then we will be able to interpret the light we see and translate it into something which we understand. After we have translated light into something we can understand, we will be able to remember what we have seen, since we can only remember thoughts—we cannot do so with light. To put it another way, the light which is remembered is that which has been translated into thought. Before it is translated into thought we have no way to know it or to call it back to mind. After being translated, however, we are well able to recall the light. . . .

Light first shines into the spirit, but God does not purpose to have the light remain there. He wishes this light to reach the understanding. After light has reached the understanding, it no longer passes away but can be fixed. Revelation is not permanent in nature; it is like lightning which flashes and passes away. But when light shines and man's understanding takes it in and knows its meaning, then the light is *fixed* and we know its content. When the light is only in the spirit it comes and goes freely, but once it enters our thought and understanding it becomes anchored. From then on we are able to use the light. . . .

### *The Breaking of the Outward Man*

Perhaps some will raise the question as to how we should

regard the scriptural teaching that in spiritual things man's wisdom should not be employed. This question points to the need for the outward man to be broken. If our thoughts, like a servant standing at a door, are waiting for enlightenment so as to understand the meaning of what is revealed in the spirit, then they become the best of servants; without them, there can be no ministry of the word. But if our thoughts, instead of trying to understand the light, tend to advocate their own ideas, then they turn into the worst master.

There is a great difference between thoughts as a servant and thoughts as a master. When thoughts assume the role of a master, they try in themselves to conceive God's light, create God's thought, and manufacture God's word. This is what we call man's wisdom. For a man to think independently is human wisdom, but it is condemned by God. Such independent thought needs to be broken. Our thoughts ought to wait at the door as a servant, waiting and ready to be used by God. Do not think to conceive light; it is God who shines in our spirits. Instead, our thoughts should be prepared to fix the light, to understand and to translate it.

We may say that in the ministry of God's word thought is an indispensable servant. What a difference there is between conceiving light and fixing light. Anyone who has truly learned before the Lord knows immediately whether the thoughts of the person speaking are master or servant. Whenever man's thought wedges itself into the things of God and usurps the place of a master it becomes a distraction to God. Therefore, the outward man needs to be broken. When one's thought has been broken, it is no longer confused and independent.

Simply realize that the power of thinking is increased instead of destroyed once the outward man is broken. To have the thought broken means to have that thought which initiates and centers upon itself broken. Afterwards it will be more usable than before. For example, one whose mind is taken over by one thing and is made to think on that one thing day and night will soon become obsessed. In such a mental condition, how can he ever understand the Bible? Yet from God's viewpoint, our thoughts too are more or less like an obsessed person's, because they always revolve around ourselves. There is no strength left to think of the things of God. Brethren, do you see the seriousness of this matter?

One important requirement for the ministry of the word is that a minister have a fine mind and an unfettered understanding for God to use. By the outward man being broken we do not mean to say that our mind is so destroyed that we can no longer think. It only means that we will no longer think in and of ourselves nor will we be occupied with external matters. After the wisdom of the wise is destroyed and the understanding of the prudent is brought to nothing, then our mind becomes a usable instrument for it ceases to be our life and master. . . .

What is the minding of the Spirit? It is to think on the things of the Spirit. If one's thought is scattered and confused the whole day long, naturally he belongs to the flesh. If he is always thinking on matters strange and alien to the Spirit, he of course is of the flesh. If one is brought by the Lord to the place where he can think on the things of the Holy Spirit, he will be a spiritual person, able to understand spiritual things. How can one whose mind is fully occupied with earthly matters live by the law of the Spirit? This is impossible. None can live by the Holy Spirit if his mind is set on the things of the flesh throughout the day and night.

Just remember that our thought ought not be the center of our being. It should be a servant listening carefully to its master's voice. Otherwise, we are not listening attentively to the Holy Spirit, but are thinking of many things according to our own desire. And the natural consequence is that we fall into that which we think. With the breaking of the outward man, though, we no longer make our self the center, nor do we think as we wish. We learn to hear God's voice, waiting before Him as an obedient servant. As soon as God's light flashes in us, our spirit catches the light and our understanding apprehends its meaning.

Never is the ministry of the word to be merely a matter of

knowing doctrines. If such were the case, Christianity would be a carnal religion. But Christianity is not a carnal religion; it is a spiritual revelation. Our spirit knows the things of God, and our mind reads and interprets what is spoken to our spirit. Accordingly, our thought cannot afford to be scattered. A scattered mind is unable to fix the light of God, nor can a low mind hold God's light. . . .

The question therefore narrows down to this: when God's light passes through our spirit and mind, how much is it damaged or how much is it perfected? We truly need the mercy of the Lord. If our mind lacks the dealings of the Lord, it will fail to read and interpret fully God's light. The result will be that the word of God will be presented weakly. Our words cannot be strong if our thought is weak. Our ministry will be weak because our thought is weak. We are God's channels, and channels determine the volume of water passing through. Channels can be leaky and defective. Either we deliver the word of God strongly to the brothers and sisters or we defile God's word and present it in damaged form. How serious is our responsibility.

We shall always stress the necessity of having the wounds of the cross upon us. We insist on having the outward man broken because we are fully persuaded that without brokenness there can be no ministry. This is so very basic that we simply cannot overlook it. If you wish to be used of God as a minister of the word, your outward man must be broken. If you expect to supply others with Christ, with God's word, your outward man needs to be dealt with drastically. Again and again we come up against the problem of man. It is unavoidable. If we are suitable we will be used; if unsuitable, then we shall not. The issue is man. . . .

In addition to having the light of God's revelation and in addition to fixing this light, a minister of God's word must also have burden in his heart. The Hebrew word "massam" has two different usages. One is that of a burden to be lifted or carried, as suggested in the Pentateuch. Examples are Exodus 23.5;

Numbers 4.15,19,24,27,31,32,49; 11.11,17; and Deuteronomy 1.12. The other usage of "Massam" is to convey the idea of an oracle or revelation to the prophet, as found in such prophetic writings as Isaiah 13.1; 14.28; 17.1; 19.1; 21.1,11,13; 22.1; 23.1; 30.6; Jeremiah 23.33,34,36,38; Nahum 1.1; Habakkuk 1.1; Zechariah 9.1; 12.1; and Malachi 1.1. This indicates that the oracle which comes to the prophet is the burden he gets. This matter of burden plays a very important part in the ministry of the word. The prophet carries out the ministry of the word through his "massam," that is, his burden. When there is no burden, there is no ministry of the word. Therefore, a minister of the word must possess burden. . . .

Why is it called a burden? Because inwardly we have touched a thought while yet under enlightenment and so we feel heavy within, uncomfortable and even pained. This is the burden of God's word. Such burden as the prophets have can only be discharged in words. Without appropriate words this burden cannot be lifted.

In learning to be ministers of the word we cannot overlook the relationship between light, thought, and word. First we receive light, then we have thought, and finally we get the word. The usefulness of the word is in the discharging of God's light. From God's side it is light turned to thought in us; from our side it is thought precipitated into word. When we try to share God's light with others we seem to be discharging a burden upon them. The light and thought in us are like a burden upon us. Under this burden we cannot breathe freely, for we feel heavily pressed even to the extent of pain. It is only after we deliver this burden to God's children that our spirit is once more lightened and our thought is once again free. The burden upon our shoulders seems to have been placed elsewhere. . . .

What enlightens my spirit is revelation, for without revelation there can be no enlightenment. Enlightenment is God's work, but fixing the light as thought is the work of one who is instructed of God. Following the translation of light into thought there must be the conversion of such thought into words. To interpret the light with my thought and go no further is to serve my own purpose, but to interpret thought by converting it into inner words is to minister to others. For my own use, thought is enough; that is as far as it must go; yet to help others, thought needs to be turned into words. Light void of thought almost appears to be abstract to me, though spiritually it is quite real. It becomes concrete in me only after it is transformed into thought. In a similar manner, light becomes concrete in others if thought is converted into words. . . .

There are therefore two ways of fixing the light: first, I use my thought to fix God's light; or second, God gives me words to fix His light. My mind holds fast the light shown me in my spirit or God grants me words to hold His light. The revelation I get in word is one with the revelation I get in my spirit. In my spirit I see for a split second. The time for seeing is so short, yet the thing beheld is timeless. What is seen in one second can never be expressed in one second, for in my spirit I have seen a great deal in that split second. If my understanding is strong and my mind is rich, I will be able to fix more of God's light. When God gives words, however, He seemingly gives only a few words. God employs a few words to transfix His light.

These words may be few in number yet inclusive in content, because they contain the whole revelation. In ordinary speech, if there are eight or ten words you are finished after those eight or ten words. Worldly speech is measured by counting words or counting time. Words of revelation, however, are enormously different. Perhaps there are but a few words, yet the words of revelation are as rich as the revelation of God. What is revealed is rich, what is enlightened in a split second is rich; so are the few words given by God rich in content. Just as God can reveal so much in a second, so He is able to show that much in a word. Just as what is seen in a second may take several months to unveil, so what is shown in one word may require several months to deliver too.

Here is the distinction between the words within and the words spoken without. The words within are never long but are rich in content. They do not come in long messages for us to deliver, since we are usually given only a few words. But what spiritual wealth is hidden in those few words! When they come, they come with one distinctive characteristic; which is, that these few words are life-releasing. . . .

However heavy the weight, you must wait before God, for His words shall come to you. Sometimes you may have to pray for days before the words are given. At times you are able to fix the light with thought but you have no way to express it. At other times words flow with the thought: as soon as the burden is felt, appropriate words are given. We cannot decide when we will have the words. God may impart them immediately after you have seen the light, or He may wait until your burden becomes nearly unbearable.

In any event, the words when given are most appropriate. They hold the light which you have seen. The entire revelation seems to be completely uncovered by these few words. The revelation is rich, and so are the words. It is like unscrewing a cork—the entire contents of the bottle can be poured out. You must seek to have these few words granted to you. These we designate as the words within. They are God's, and they contain the whole of the revelation you have received. God hides what He has revealed in these few words, and through these same words His revelation is also unveiled. In the delivery of these words of revelation, God's enlightenment is also delivered.

Let us understand beyond a shadow of a doubt that there can be no ministry without enlightenment, no ministry without translating light into thought by our understanding, and no ministry without having the words of revelation to express the thought. This is what Paul means by "combining spiritual thoughts with spiritual words" (1 Cor. 2.13). The Holy Spirit grants us words. He imparts not only revelation but the words of revelation as well. It may be only a few words, yet these few puncture the vessel and let out life. You may say many words, yet without these few God-given words life simply will not flow.

God's life is released through revelation. Take the crucifixion of the Lord Jesus as an example. The Lord has in truth already died for the whole world. Yet why is it that not all the people of the world have life? It is because not all have received this revelation. One can endlessly recite the sentence that the Lord Jesus has died for all, but if a person has no revelation he will not be in the good of the death of the Lord. Another person who has received the revelation can thank and praise God from the bottom of his heart, for such seeing has given him life. The Holy Spirit quickens us through His word.

Today God desires to supply the church with His words. He intends to give Christ—the life of Christ—to the church. And this life is released through the discharge of the burden in us. It requires appropriate words to puncture a hole so that life may flow. A person could be speaking for two hours and life would still not be released, or a person could merely commence to speak and life at once begins to flow. It all depends upon revelation and words. Each time revelation is given, a few appropriate words must accompany it, otherwise life will not flow. With such words, life is given. Without them, life is not even touched.

If God accords you a burden, He must also grant you words to discharge that burden. These two are both imparted by God. He who gives burden is also the One who gives words to release the burden. It is God who gives you burden, and it is God who helps you to discharge it. He will supply you with words. With these few words life is released. Hence do not go away still ladened with your burden; learn how to release life or else you cannot serve God. Do not merely bring the leather bag to your brethren, but puncture it so as to give them water to drink. The way to let the water out is to obtain some words from God. Frequently we meet a brother who speaks much but says little. He speaks with great effort, yet he is not able to bring out the thing within. He is going around in circles, always missing the spot where the water can be let out. If only he could add a few right words, life would flow; however, he does not possess the words within. He cannot be a minister of the word if he does not know how to secure these necessary words. The longer he talks, the farther he drifts.

How essential for us, therefore, to wait before God for these words. It is best if we have the words the moment we are able to fix the light with thought. But if no word is forthcoming at that moment, we must ask God for it. The day will come when we will realize how incompetent is our own eloquence. Is it not all too true that before we begin to learn to be a minister of God's word, we think very highly of our eloquence? Let us admit that man's natural eloquence is good for anything else except for the things of God. Man's eloquence is futile in the affairs of God; no amount of it will impart life. The words of life are only found in revelation.

We must acknowledge that Paul is naturally eloquent, yet he asks in Ephesians 6.19 "that utterance may be given to me in the opening of my mouth, to make known with boldness the mystery of the gospel." Paul requests the Ephesian believers to pray for him that he might be granted words to proclaim the mystery of the gospel. In things spiritual, natural eloquence is useless. God must give words; and these words come from within. The difficulty with many is that they talk a great deal but cannot express their inward feeling. Do not try to find words while on the platform; have them within you beforehand. Find the words and afterwards speak. A minister of God's word must learn to know the words within. May the Lord make us those who have the appropriate words. We need burden—plus the words to discharge it. . . .

Hence we must wait on God and read the Bible, asking Him to grant us the words. When the words do come, we are instantly assured of what we should speak today. We have learned the secret of utterance. We are able to express the light we have seen and the thought which is within us. Before we secure the words, however hard we try, we simply cannot speak forth the inward revelation. There is no way to release the light of revelation other than by the words of revelation. He who has the revealed light but lacks revealed words should not attempt to release his light. The greater the lack of revealed words the longer should be the waiting before God. Pray, commune, wait, and lay the Bible before God. This is not an ordinary waiting, nor ordinary prayer and communion. This is waiting before God with the Bible, praying to God with the Bible, and communing with God over the Bible. It is a convenient time for the Lord to speak, and so it is relatively easy to obtain the words of revelation. As soon as you receive a few words you are able to win sinners to Christ and to help the believers. These few words are God's words, not the word written much earlier, but God's most recent word. These can be used for life. Whenever you use these words, if your spirit is right the Holy Spirit will honor them. They are God's words; the Holy Spirit is at the back. They are not common words; they are extraordinary and powerful. . . .

God calls us to be ministers of His word. He knows the inadequacy of our words. Accordingly, He speaks "in many portions and in many ways" to us (Heb. 1.1). We must spend time to read the Scriptures. There is much of doctrine, knowledge, and teaching in the Bible which can be added to our speech. We must have Scriptural basis, Scriptural teaching and truth, to make what we say acceptable to God's children. There needs to be a ground for acceptance. Upon receiving inward enlightenment with its corresponding thought and words, we will think of quite a number of similar experiences and similar subjects recorded in the Bible. We remember them and use them to bring out our message. We may ourselves only have a few words, perhaps ten-odd sentences, for what we say must be based on our experience. But if we are familiar with the Bible we can use the words there to help complete the delivery. This is not expounding the Scriptures objectively. It is on the contrary a highly subjective approach to the understanding of the Bible. We are not talking about the

Bible but about the revelation we have received. We use the Bible because we find in it things similar to our experience. Something happened to Peter and to John; something was recorded in Genesis or in Psalms. These fit in perfectly with what we intend to say, and thus we clothe our message with them. We have noticed how Paul, how Peter, how David, how Moses, and how the Lord spoke about certain matters. When we are now given a few words concerning a particular matter, we clothe them with the words of Paul, Peter, David, Moses, and even our Lord. We still base our speech on the light and burden we have received from God, so that in speaking, the light shines out and the burden is discharged. . . .

### *The Formation of the Word*

Just as God's word is a Person in the Lord Jesus, so it must today be personified in us. The Lord Jesus is the Word become flesh; thus God spoke in the flesh. Today God intends to have His words become flesh once more, that is, He still wishes to speak through human flesh. That is why He deals with this flesh of ours, hoping that through it His word may come forth. To arrive at this goal there must be the constituting work of the Holy Spirit in us. By the indwelling Spirit God is able to incorporate something in us so that when we think and speak, the word of God comes through. What is incorporated in us by the Holy Spirit converts God's word into our subjective words. A minister of the word must allow the Holy Spirit to so reconstitute him that he may have this kind of subjective words. His thought must not only *agree* with God's thought but is to *be* God's thought. His words become God's word, not just coincide with God's word. This is the result of the Holy Spirit's incorporating work in us. And this is New Testament ministry. The man is there, and so is God. Man speaks, and God speaks too. What dealing must that man go through if the word of God is destined to come through him! . . .

By this, then, let us understand that God is forming words in you as He puts you through this dual process of clarity and obscurity. In our trials, in the dual process we go through, God is creating words in us. We appear to be getting through but nevertheless are stuck; we appear undone, yet not completely beaten. After some days the Lord finally carries us through. This carrying through constitutes God's word. The farther you get through the clearer you become and the more words you possess. This is how words are formed. The word of the ministry is not something thought out but rather created. How different are thought-out words from created words. You are groping in the dark; you faintly see something; it becomes a little more definite. By adding together these times of clarity, you secure the word. What you have passed through becomes your word. . . .

Missing a discipline means forfeiting the possibility of receiving a revelation. When we accept a dealing by God we may receive a revelation, a new revelation. We should recognize the hand of our Lord. Frequently His hand is upon us, touching us and dealing with us in point after point; and so we yield little by little. Or He may have to touch us many times before we consent somewhat by saying, "Lord, now I am willing to yield and to strive no more." Then and there we receive enlightenment. The Lord continues to deal with us and so we gradually yield to Him. Each yielding brings enlightenment to our spirit. Thus we see light, and in this light we receive the word. Through testing, God gives us word as well as light. The words we use in preaching are not something we ourselves conceive; they are created through God's discipline of us. . . .

We therefore declare that a minister of the word ministers with Spirit-taught words. Not only does the Holy Spirit speak words of wisdom with my lips; He teaches me how to speak. I am instructed by the Holy Spirit; I have learned in the fiery furnace; I have the word. Otherwise, all which is said is merely empty words. How basic this is: that we need to learn in each dealing.

Our words must be burned into being through fire, else they shall be ineffective. *We* cannot comfort those who are sorrowful. What is merely external is futile. In order to be truly useful, we must be those who have been dealt with by God. . . .

The memory we need is of two kinds: the outward memory and the Holy Spirit memory. A minister of the word needs both. The outward memory points to the memory of the outward man, that which is produced in a man's brain. It occupies a very important place in testifying the word of God. The Holy Spirit memory is what the Lord Jesus mentions in John 14.26: "But the Helper, the Holy Spirit, whom the Father will send in My name, He will teach you all things, and bring to your remembrance all that I said to you." This is the Holy Spirit memory, for it is the Holy Spirit who brings things to your remembrance, not you yourself. . . .

Such words need memory to accommodate them. I must remember two things: the words and the light. Let us call the recollection of the words the outward memory, and that of the light the Holy Spirit memory. Wherein does our difficulty today lie? It is that often we remember the words with our outward memory, but lose the Holy Spirit memory—that is, we cannot recall the light. Words we recollect, but sight we forget. There is no such problem in the realm of doctrine or teaching, because we can memorize and deliver every word and so our task is done. Doctrine stops at the outward. The ministry of the word, however, is to touch life. The more doctrinal, the easier to be remembered and to be uttered. The more full of life the inward seeing is, the easier to be forgotten. We may recall every word but lose sight of the reality. This is due to some defect in our Holy Spirit memory. Only in this way will the words be living. Whenever these inward words are separated from the Holy Spirit memory they change from spiritual to material. All spiritual things can turn material if care is not exercised. . . .

When a minister is speaking, his inner man must be released;

but this in turn depends upon his feeling. If the latter is unusable the spirit is stuck. No matter how much electricity may be stored in the power company, if there is no electric bulb there will be no light. And by the same token, no matter how excellent is the condition of our spirit, it will be severely hampered if our feeling is unusable. The spirit flows through the channel of emotion. A minister of the word must therefore have a usable feeling as well as a free spirit. If emotion refuses to listen to the spirit or fails to cooperate with it, the spirit is inevitably arrested. For the sake of letting his inner being come out freely, man must have a usable feeling. Now we shall see how a feeling can be useful. . . .

Now of course the emotion we here mention is not a matter of performance. In any theatrical performance the feeling is something put on. A minister should never use human ingenuity in putting on a show while speaking. As he is speaking he must actually have the feeling of each word. He should have a mournful feeling when he uses sad words. How does a man's spirit give expression to its mourning? Through his mournful feeling. And when happy words are said his feeling should be one of happiness, for the joy of the spirit comes through a joyful emotion.

Let us understand that the coming forth of words alone is not enough; the spirit must also come out, and when it does it will do so together with feeling. If our feeling lags behind, our words are stripped of the spirit. If our feeling is too hard, it renders itself unusable. Feeling is the most delicate part of man. A little hardening will deprive the word of its spirit. To be useful, a certain kind of word must be accompanied by the same kind of spirit. If it does not agree with the word the latter is damaged and becomes useless. . . .

For the one who is under His dealing God orders all sorts of circumstances by which to break him. Each stroke opens in him a wound which gives him pain. His feeling is automatically wounded, becoming more delicate than before. Man's emotion is naturally the most sensitive area of the soul. It is more tender than will and mind. Nonetheless it does not possess enough sensitivity to be useful to God. It does not possess the degree of tenderness which is demanded of God's word. If His word is to come through, we must be filled with the feeling of His word. We must match our feeling with that of God's word. Our feeling must be able to cope with our words. Whatever emotion the word requires must be fully supplied, else the word will not be strong in others.

Let us take note of this principle: that if there is a ministry of the word there must be spirit as well as word when the message is given. As the word is released, the spirit is released as well. Those who listen not only touch the words, they also touch the spirit. If only the words were touched the message would be common and weak. Even in regard to God's recorded word, if a person does not touch its spirit it will seem common to him. When the spirit is touched, life is touched. "The words that I have spoken to you," declared the Lord, "are spirit and are life" (John 6.63). Only by touching the spirit can anyone know the meaning of that word. . . .

Hence a minister of the word needs the Lord to break down his outward man on the one hand and to strengthen his spirit through training on the other hand. Both of these are done by the discipline of the Holy Spirit. Please note that each one comes out of a trial a different person—either he is stronger or he is weaker. You either murmur against God and go under or you emerge in victory. . . .

Consequently, the exercise of the spirit is the outpouring of our life. We expend all our power in reaching out to the spiritually weary and dead. Each time the spirit launches out, it touches man's weakness and man's death. It goes forth at great cost. It goes out as a burden, with pain and privation. The giving forth of the spirit requires one to forsake something. Whether in private conversation or in public speaking, he encounters spiritual weakness in many people. So he allows his spirit to go forth, he pushes it out to meet these weaknesses so as to destroy them. It is as if the one ministering to these needs and lacks is wrestling with them. He senses spiritual death, coldness, hardness and barrenness in many people, and his spirit therefore goes out to suppress and overcome these deaths. He rises above them and swallows up death.

—MGW 9–20, 23–8, 33, 40–1, 57–60, 61, 63, 63–4, 69, 79, 83–4, 86–7, 88–9, 90, 92, 99, 111–2, 113, 115–6, 118, 124, 125, 130–3, 134–5, 137–8, 143, 145, 146, 150–1, 153–4, 155–6, 159, 160, 162–3, 164–5, 165–8, 169, 174–5, 181–2, 183, 184, 187, 196–7, 197–8, 208, 209, 213, 221, 225, 226–7

# 46 Spiritual Ministry

*The Basis of True Ministry*

We come to consider the divine principle of service to God There are specific principles from which no one who tries to serve the Lord can deviate. The principle which God laid down in His word for service to Him is as definite as are the conditions of salvation. We cannot change the conditions of salvation: no one can ever get saved that way. Similarly, we cannot change the conditions of service to God: no one will ever be used by the Lord that way. The conditions for service to God are just as specific as the conditions of salvation. The conditions of salvation, or, rather, the basis of salvation, is upon the Lord's death and resurrection, and on no other ground. The *ground* of His death and resurrection is the ground of our acceptance with God. The *principle* of the death and resurrection of the Lord is the condition, is the basis of our service to God. Our salvation rests on the *fact* of the death and the *fact* of the resurrection of our Lord, but our service is based on the *principle* of death; not the fact exactly, but the principle of death and the principle of the resurrection of our Lord. . . .

What is this soul power or natural energy? It is simply this, what *you* can do, what *you* are yourself, what *you* have from nature. The power of the soul is present with us all. Those who have been taught by the Lord repudiate that principle as a life principle: they refuse to live by it; they will not let it reign; they will not allow it to be the power-spring of the work of God. But those who have not been taught of God rely upon it: they utilize it; they think it is *the* power. . . .

And then you come to a place which we speak of as resurrection ground. Death in principle has to be wrought out in a crisis to our natural lives, and then you will find God releases you into resurrection, you will come out on resurrection ground. What does it mean? You will find that what you have lost is coming back, though not as before; it is your life-principle that is at work, something that empowers and strengthens you, something which is animating you, giving you life. From henceforth what you have lost will be coming back under [resurrection] power. For instance, if we want to be spiritual there is no need for us to amputate our hands or feet; we can have our body. So we can have our soul, the full use of our faculties, but it is not our life-spring; we are not living in it, we are not living by it, we use it. When the body becomes the life of man, we live like beasts. When the soul becomes the life of man we live as rebels from God, we live apart from the life of God. When we have to live our life in the spirit, and by the spirit, we use our soul faculties just as we use our physical faculties.

—WG 90-1, 98, 103-4

### *The Basis of All True Ministry*

No one can be a true servant of God without knowing the principle of death and the principle of resurrection. Even the Lord Jesus himself served on that basis. You will find in Matthew 3 that, before His public ministry ever began, our Lord submitted himself to baptism. He was baptized not because He had any sin, or anything which needed cleansing. No, we know the meaning of baptism: it is a figure of death and resurrection. The ministry of the Lord did not begin until, in figure, He had taken his stand there. After He had been baptized and had voluntarily taken the ground of death and resurrection, the Holy Spirit came upon Him, and then He ministered. . . .

What is waste? Waste means, among other things, giving more than is necessary. If a shilling will do and you give a pound, it is a waste. If two grams will do and you give a kilogram, it is a waste. If three days will suffice to finish a task well enough and you lavish five days or a week on it, it is a waste. Waste means that you give something too much for something too little. If someone is receiving more than he is considered to be worth, then that is waste.

But remember, we are dealing here with something which the Lord said was to go out with the gospel, wherever that gospel should be carried. Why? Because he intends that the preaching of the gospel should issue something along the very lines of the action of Mary here, namely, that people should come to Him and waste themselves on him. This is the result that He is seeking. . . .

### *Ministering to His Pleasure*

"Wheresoever the gospel shall be preached . . . that also which this woman hath done shall be spoken of" (Mark 14.9).

Why did the Lord say this? Because the gospel is meant to produce this. It is what the gospel is for. The gospel is not just to satisfy sinners. Praise the Lord, sinners will be satisfied! but their satisfaction is, we may say, a blessed by-product of the gospel and not its primary aim. The gospel is preached in the first place so that the *Lord* may be satisfied.

I am afraid we lay too much emphasis on the good of sinners and we have not sufficiently appreciated what the Lord has in view as His goal. We have been thinking how the sinner will fare if there is no gospel, but that is not the main consideration. Yes, Praise God! the sinner has his part. God meets his need and showers him with blessings; but that is not the most important thing. The first thing is this, that everything should be to the satisfaction of the Son of God. It is only when He is satisfied that we shall be satisfied and the sinner will be satisfied. I have never met a soul who has set out to satisfy the Lord and has not been satisfied himself. It is impossible. Our satisfaction comes unfailingly when we satisfy Him first.

But we have to remember this, that He will never be satisfied without our "wasting" ourselves upon Him. Have you ever given too much to the Lord? May I tell you something? One lesson some of us have come to learn is this, that in divine service the principle of waste is the principle of power. The principle which determines usefulness is the very principle of scattering. Real usefulness in the hand of God is measured in terms of "waste." The more you think you can *do*, and the more you employ your gifts up to the very limit (and some even go over the limit!) in order to do it, the more you find that you are applying the principle of the world and not of the Lord. God's ways with us are all designed to establish in us this other principle, namely, that our work *for* Him springs out of our ministering *to* Him. I do not mean that we are going to do nothing; but the first thing for us must be the Lord himself, not His work. . . .

The Lord has to open our eyes to His worth. If there is in the world some precious art treasure, and I pay the high price asked for it, be it one thousand, ten thousand, or even fifty thousand pounds, dare anyone say it is a waste? The idea of waste only comes into our Christianity when we underestimate the worth of our Lord. The whole question is: How precious is He to us now? If we do not think much of Him, then of course to give Him anything at all, however small, will seem to us a wicked waste. But when He is really precious to our souls, nothing will be too good, nothing too costly for Him; everything we have, our dearest, our most priceless treasure, we shall pour out upon Him, and we shall not count it a shame to have done so.

—NCL 245, 269, 275–6, 279–80

Where there is no Cross there is no life, and no ministry of life. The object of suffering is that there may be a full and abundant ministry. Theory is no substitute for this. Poverty of ministry results from the choice of an easy road. Those who have an easy time all too often have little to give. They do not understand men's needs. Of course I don't mean we are to invite trouble, or by austerity to ill-treat our bodies. The Spirit himself takes responsibility for our experience, leading us in paths where we encounter, in body, heart, or spirit, that measure of "the dying of Jesus" that will mean enrichment to our ministry. It is our part only to follow.

You ask me how you can be used to minister life to the Body. Not by setting out deliberately to do a lot, nor indeed by running away into retirement and doing nothing, but simply by letting the Cross operate in the normal course of your walk with the Lord. Those who only serve by words and works find they have no ministry if at any time they are reduced to inactivity or silence. But the measure of your ministry is not determined by the measure of your activity. Only let "the slaying of Jesus" work in you, and life *must* manifest itself in others. It cannot be otherwise, for it is an abiding principle of the Body that "death worketh in us, but life in you." So you need make no special effort to bring increase to the Body in this way, for anything God takes you through by way of the Cross will spontaneously bring increase there. . . .

John of course was no less a "fisherman" in the full sense than was Peter, and equally it would seem that, within his sphere, he was no less a "builder" than was Paul. We find him at the beginning of the Acts sharing fully in the preaching and fellowship of the early phases; and like Paul he too can write authoritatively "to the church" (3 John 9). But seen in the context of the New Testament as a whole, the feature of John's writings that stands out most prominently is surely this particular ministry of recalling things to their original or divinely-intended state.

As we all know, John's is the last of the four Gospels. His Epistles too are the last epistles; and his Revelation is placed last in the whole Book of God. All his writings are in some sense "the last." In John's Gospel you find everywhere the reflection of this fact. John touches on very little of the work of the Lord as it is set forth, for example, in Mark. Neither does he concern himself with the commandments of the Lord as they are dealt with by Matthew in the Sermon on the Mount. He is not so troubled about what you should do if someone takes away your coat, or whether, when pressed by your neighbor, you should go with him one mile or two. That is not his first concern now. His burden relates to the life of the eternities and to your right relation thereto. If you go back to that, he implies, everything else will follow. In this he is quite different, too, from Luke. He is not occupied with outward and temporal things—with dates and genealogies, even though they take you right back to Adam. His whole burden is this, that we must get right behind these various things to *the Life*. Everything here now is in disrepair. Go back to the Life that "came down from heaven," and when you get back there, Peter and all that he stands for will be preserved, and so will Paul. In a sense, John has nothing new to offer. He does not take us further, for the furthest point has already been touched by God. The purpose of the revelation entrusted to John is to bring back people again to that original purpose, by bringing them into a fresh touch with the risen Lord of life himself.

—WSM 125-6, 152-3

What is Peter's testimony? In reading Matthew 16 and Acts 2 we can readily recognize that what Peter is particularly concerned with is *the kingdom of God.* His line of ministry is especially focused on that. What about Paul? I trust all who have read the entire writings of Paul have seen that what he puts forth is none other than *the house of God.* In other words, it is the church of God. All the testimonies and works of Paul's entire life are centered on this point. And finally, John's testimony is different from these two. For example, he never talks about church affairs. Although Peter himself does not speak specifically on the church, nor touch on its organization, he at least mentions something about the elders. John, however, is completely silent on such church affairs as appointments and organization. He talks almost exclusively about the fathers, the young men, and the children. What this signifies with respect to John is a testimony concerning the *family of God.*

—SWR 126

May I ask you most frankly: Whom are we serving?—believers or God? What is the focus of our works—the works themselves or the Lord? To minister to the house and minister to the Lord are vastly different actions. Today many people are serving, but they are in the outer court and not before the table. Indeed, many are ministering to the house but they are not ministering to the Lord. Yet the ministry which the Lord is seeking today is that which truly ministers to Him. What He requires of us is not merely doing His works. Works are important; tilling the ground and tending the sheep are all important. Nevertheless, the Lord is not looking for these He looks instead for ministry to God, a waiting upon God.

"Yet they shall be ministers in my sanctuary, having oversight at the gates of the house, and ministering in the *house*: they shall slay the burnt-offering and the sacrifice for the people, and they shall stand before them to minister unto them. . . . But the priests the Levites, the sons of Zadok, that kept the charge of my sanctuary when the children of Israel went astray from me, they shall come near to me to minister unto *me*; and they shall stand before me to offer unto me the fat and the blood, saith the Lord Jehovah: they shall enter into my sanctuary, and they shall come near to my table, to minister unto *me,* and they shall keep my charge" (Eze. 44.11,15–16). Do we see the great difference between verse 11 and verse 15? It is a fundamental difference. Verse 11 speaks of the ministry to the house, whereas verse 15 speaks of ministry to Jehovah. According to God, the Levites were divided into two parties. Though they were all Levites and all belonged to one tribe and to God, yet the vast majority were fit to serve only the house. Only a small minority among the Levites—the sons of Zadok—could minister to Jehovah.

Do we know what is the ministry to the house and what is the ministry to Jehovah? Do we know the difference between these two? Many confess that there is nothing better than ministering to the house. It truly is the best to them. This is their thought: "See how I exert all my strength to expand my work. I strive for the kingdom of God. I work hard in the name of the Lord. I take up responsibility to help the church. I stir up myself to be the servant and even the bond servant of the brethren. I do my best to assist brothers and sisters. I run here and run there to prosper the church and to advance the work." How numerous are those who consider rescuing souls and increasing church membership as works par excellence. But I would say that all these are solely ministering to the house. In God's eye, however, there is another kind of ministry which is a better one. We must not only minister *before* the Lord but also minister *to* the Lord. Here is a ministry not only to the house but also before the table. How totally different is ministry before the Lord and ministry to the Lord himself. . . .

One thing we must be clear about here—which is, that in outward appearance there does not seem to be much difference between ministering to the house and ministering to the Lord. Many people have really tried their best to help the brethren, to rescue souls, to manage church affairs and to exhort saints to read the Bible and pray. They have endured much and suffered much persecution. They have truly done all they can. Yet the question remains: Why do they do all these things? The issue is whether or not the Lord is the greatest consideration in their heart.

When this morning you rise up to serve brothers and sisters, do you say in your heart, "O Lord, for Your sake I will do these things once again"? Or do you merely call to mind that these are your duties which you must fulfill? If it be the latter, then it is all a matter of need and not a matter of the Lord: you are only seeing your brethren, you are not seeing the Lord. In other words, your heart intention has already settled the issue. The entire question, therefore, revolves around the matter of your heart motivation: Why do you do these things?

Let me tell you frankly that work does indeed have its attraction to the flesh. If, for instance, a person is naturally active and talkative, he will be most happy to run from village to village preaching the gospel. Why does he so work? Because he is active and talkative by nature. Speaking candidly, though, he does not work for the sake of the Lord. For frequently he fails to carry out the work he dislikes but which God also calls him to do. He thinks he is serving the Lord, yet actually he is but serving the house. Here can be seen the great difference. In God's work, there is an element of interest or of adventure or of inclination that can allure the flesh. How lovely and admirable to have many people surrounding you and listening to your preaching; how nice to be praised after you have expounded the Scriptures; and how satisfying to have many souls won to the Lord through your efforts. You sense how exciting it is to be doing these things.

If I am a housekeeper, I am busy from morning till night doing mundane tasks. If I am a laborer in a factory, I hear the grinding sound of machines from dawn to dusk. If I am an office worker, all I see the whole day are black ink on white papers. If I am a house servant, what I do all day long is cleaning tables, sweeping floors and cooking meals. How meaningless these things are! How good it would be if I could go out and do the Lord's work! Many women consider being a wife who must take care of children and carry out endless household chores as highly uninteresting work. How exciting if she be given freedom to go here and there to talk about spiritual things, things of the Lord. Yet that is but the attraction of the flesh; it is not spiritual at all; it is wholly catering to self-delight.

Let us realize that many works and services done before God are not recognized by Him as serving Him. How strange that God himself tells us in His word that while a group of Levites were busily ministering in the house of God He was declaring that they were only ministering to the house and not ministering to Him. We know ministry to the house appears to be very much like ministry to the Lord. There seems to be hardly any difference in outward appearance between the two. There in the tabernacle or later in the temple, they slew peace offerings and burnt offerings. How appealing these works looked. For example, an Israelite would come to worship God. He would offer a peace offering and a burnt offering to Him. But the sheep might refuse to move, the bullock might not budge The Levites would therefore come to help him pull and push the animals and assist him in slaying them. What a good work this was! You see, he is leading another person to draw near to the Lord. He is helping one to know the Lord. Would you not agree that turning back a sinner from his ways or assisting a believer to grow in worship or service is a good thing? In the meantime, the Levite, in his busyness, would perspire all over his body, for he was helping people to succeed in offering up sheep and bullocks to the Lord. We know that both the peace offering and burnt offering typify Christ. We also know that the burnt offering denotes a relationship between the believer and the Lord, while the peace offering bespeaks a relationship between the sinner and the Lord. A peace offering causes the sinner to draw near to the Lord; a burnt offering speaks of the consecration of the believer. And hence, we may say that God's servant expends his energy in inducing sinners to trust in the Lord, and it is a very good thing to bring such people to know the Lord. Moreover, it is a very good thing to persuade a believer to consecrate himself. And these works are all real and nothing false about them. God truly knows these works of His servant. His servant is really helping people to offer up peace offerings and burnt offerings; that is to say, he is truly winning souls and edifying the saints. And he works hard at these things, too. Nonetheless, God declares that he is not ministering unto Him. . . .

To paraphrase the apostle Paul, for me to repeat "the same things to you, to me indeed is not irksome" (Phil. 3.1). What I fear most in my heart is that many launch out to preach the gospel, to win sinners to the Lord and to edify believers, but in the doing of these things they have not ministered to the Lord. To many, their so-called ministry has no other justification than their own pleasure and delight having been satisfied. They cannot stand being shut up at home: they love action: they have to run here and there because activity gives them pleasure. Let me tell you most candidly, that though to whom you outwardly minister may be sinners and brethren, to what you inwardly minister is your own flesh! For unless you are so at work, you are unhappy. In truth, you are not at all seeking to please the Lord. I may seem to be hard on you at this point, but is not this that I have just said a fact? Let us be reminded that there are many natural attractions to God's work. Yet how this can hurt us if we should go ahead in the work of God motivated only by these attractions. If so, how pitiful! Let us ask God to give us grace that we may know what is ministry to God and what is only ministry to the house.

I have a dear friend who now is on the other side of the veil. I loved her dearly in the Lord. One day we were praying together on the hill. Afterwards we read this very portion of Ezekiel 44. She was much older than I. So she said to me, "Little brother, twenty years ago I had already read this Scripture passage." "What did you do after you had read this passage of God's word?" I asked. "As I read this passage of the Scriptures," she answered, "I immediately closed the Bible, knelt down and prayed, 'Lord, let me minister to You, and do not let me minister only to the house.'" I shall never forget this incident, not today, nor forever. Although she has long since gone, I have always remembered her word: "O Lord, let me minister to You, and do not let me minister only to the house." Could we also pray, "O Lord, I want to minister to You and not to the house only"? . . .

What is ministering to the Lord? Ezekiel 44.15 says clearly, "But the priests the Levites, the sons of Zadok, that kept the charge of my sanctuary when the children of Israel went astray from me, they shall come near to me to minister unto me; and they shall stand before me to offer unto me the fat and the blood, saith the Lord Jehovah." Hence, the foundation of ministry to the Lord or the basic condition of ministry to the Lord is to come near to Him. They dare to come before the Lord and are able to stand before Him. Let me ask, do you know how to come near to the Lord? Is it not that we frequently must drag ourselves with all our strength to come before Him? Many are fearful of a darkened room, of being alone. They cannot stand to be shut in all by themselves. Sometimes they may be present physically in the prayer closet, but their hearts have already gone outside. They cannot draw near to the Lord and learn to pray before Him alone and in solitude. How many find great pleasure in activities and crowds. They love to preach before people. But how many are able to draw near to God in the Holiest of All? Alas, many find it impossible to come near to God in the Holy Place, in the midst of darkness, quietness and solitude. Yet none can minister to the Lord without coming near to Him. Nor can anyone serve the Lord without drawing nigh to God in prayer. Spiritual power is not seen in the power of preaching but in the power of praying. How much one can pray demonstrates how much is the inner strength. No spiritual matter demands more strength than prayer. You may study God's word without exerting yourself much at all. I do not mean that it is totally effortless; only that it is easily done. You may also preach the gospel without expending much effort and may be able to help the brethren, too, without much spiritual power being required. For you can preach or give counsel about what you are able to remember. But to kneel before God for an hour requires all your strength. Indeed, unless you are violent to yourself, you are not able to continue. This is something we naturally cannot stand. Nonetheless, everyone who ministers to the Lord knows its preciousness. How sweet is the one hour of prayer after being awakened at midnight. How good is the early hour of morning prayer before going back to sleep again. Let me tell you most honestly, except we come near to God, we cannot minister to Him. You cannot on the one side stand afar off and on the other side minister to the Lord. The disciples may have followed the Lord at a distance, but no one who is far apart from Him can serve Him. Yes, it is possible to follow the Lord distantly and secretly, but it is impossible to minister to the Lord in such a way. There is only one place where people can minister to the Lord, and that is, in the Holy Place. In the outer court you can come near to people; but in the sanctuary you come near to God. The fact of the matter is that only those who are near to God could help the Church and do the work. How very poor is our work if all we can do before God is minister to the brothers and sisters.

What should be our manner before the Lord? We should "stand" before Him. We, however, always like to move on. It seems almost impossible for us to stand still. Today so many brothers and sisters look so very busy. They have so many things before them that they have to go straight ahead. If they are told to stand and wait a while, they cannot comply. Yet all spiritual men know how to *stand* before the Lord.

What is meant by standing? It means waiting for orders, waiting for God to make known His will. How many works today have long been planned and decided beforehand. I am not speaking here of secular works such as characterize the factories and business offices. Christians should be absolutely faithful to their earthly masters. They should serve them most faithfully. But spiritual work is quite another matter. Let me speak especially to my fellow-workers. Have your works been planned long ago? Do you carry them out quickly? Or is it true that you must stand a while and wait a little? Is everything already programmed and thus you can simply follow the list on the program and do them according to the instruction of the organization? Is it that you have everything and nothing is lacking? If so, may it be that you are required to wait for three days or to stand by and be temporarily inactive. For that is what standing means. Just as no one who does not come near the Lord can minister to Him, so no one who cannot stand before the Lord can minister to Him. Consider the example of a servant who must first wait for an order from his master before he can proceed to do it.

Let me illustrate this matter further. All sins before God are of two kinds: One is a trespassing against the Lord's command; that is to say, if He gives an order and you do not carry it out, this is sin. But there is another kind of sin: an action which you take *without* the Lord's command. The first kind is the sin of rebellion; the second kind is the sin of presumption. One is not hearkening to what the Lord *has* said, the other is doing what the Lord has *not* said. To "stand" is to deal with the temptation of proceeding to work without having the Lord's command. Let me ask this: How much of our spiritual works is done after we are crystal clear of God's will? How many of us enter into work because we have received the command of the Lord? Or do we work as we are driven along by our own zeal or work because we reckon it a good thing to do? Let me assert here that nothing hurts God's will more than a *good* thing, for a *good* thing can most easily and seriously hinder God. A mere glance at all obviously sinful, unclean and wicked things enables us to know them as *bad* things which Christians ought not to do. And hence they can hardly do damage to God's will. But what obstructs His will the most are the *good* things which are so close to His heart and will. And accordingly, we think there is nothing wrong in doing them. We may even consider that there can be nothing better than these good things; with the result that we go ahead and do them without ever inquiring if they be God's will or not. Good things, therefore, become the greatest enemy to God and His work. Indeed, each time we think we are doing something good for God, we more than likely are rebelling against Him! We who are God's children know we should not do anything unclean or wicked; but alas, how often we do other sinful things—these so-called good things—because our conscience has not condemned us.

The thing you contemplate doing may well be the very best, but have you *stood* before God? We must stand. By so standing it means that you can neither walk nor move at all. Stop and wait for the Lord's order. And if you do, then this is a ministering to the Lord. The work of slaughtering sheep and cattle is something done whenever people come to the outer court. But in the Holy Place, it is all quiet because nobody else enters. There, no brother or sister has power to manage us. There, no council can decide for us, no committee has authority to send us. There is only one authority there that can control you and me, and that is the Lord. If the Lord bid me do or go, I do or go; if the Lord does not bid me do or go, I do not do so. Are we really able to stand?

In order to minister to the Lord in the Holy Place, we need to spend time in prayer before Him. Otherwise, it will not be adequate. Through prayer we are brought to the presence of God. Through prayer we draw near to Him. Consequently, prayer is such standing—that is, a standing before God to seek His mind and will. Thank the Lord that even if not every believer is doing so, at least some of God's children are standing there. They follow the Lord faithfully in His footsteps.

Those who stand before God must do one thing, which is, "to offer unto me the fat and the blood." We know God in His sanctuary is holy and righteous, but God in the Holiest of All is glorious. The glory of God fills the Holiest of All, and His holiness and righteousness fill the Holy Place. The blood is there for God's holiness and righteousness. The fat is there for His glory. The blood has relation to God's holiness and righteousness; the fat is meant for His gain. We know God is holy and righteous, and therefore He cannot accept men who are unclean and sinful. Without the shedding of blood there is no remission of sins. Without receiving the payment for sins, God cannot pass us by. For this reason, there must be the Blood, otherwise no one can draw near to God. Under the Old Covenant, men were always set aside, unable to come before God. Only the high priest could do so—and that but once a year on behalf of all the people. But today we all can come before God because of the Lord Jesus' blood. Furthermore, we can today offer the fat—which is to say, that which is chubby, the best. We may be well aware that blood is symbolic of our sins being dealt with; the fat, however, is symbolic of our satisfying God's heart. Being plump—the best—the fat can indeed satisfy His heart; and hence, it is for the glory of God.

All who wish to come before God and minister to Him must deal with the glory of God as well as the holiness and righteousness of God. We know that what the entire Bible, in both the Old Testament and the New, emphasizes are three things: God's holiness, God's righteousness and God's glory. We also know that God's glory speaks of God himself: of His holiness, His nature, His righteousness, His way. In other words, God's working is righteous, His nature is holy, and He himself is beyond description; and thus it is glory. Each time we come before God, the first thing we marvel at is how people such as we are can possibly stand before Him! How holy, how righteous He is! How, then, can sinners ever see God? Never mind, however, for here is the Blood which can atone and cleanse us of our sins. Consequently, we can approach God without any objection from Him. His Son's blood has cleansed us from all our unrighteousness. Even so, there is not only holiness and righteousness to consider, there is also God himself who is glorious. Hence, the fat must also be offered; that is, we ourselves must offer our best to God to satisfy His heart. To put it another way, the Blood is offered to deal with all that belongs to the old creation, but the fat bespeaks all which is of the new creation. The Blood casts out all the old creation, thus resolving the matter of holiness and righteousness. The fat bespeaks the new creation and signifies the presenting of ourselves to God, thus resolving the matter of His glory.

One who does not know what death and resurrection mean cannot serve God. The death I refer to here is not merely some doctrine or Biblical idea. It means the experience of a co-death with Christ. Through the flowing out of His incorruptible blood, you too have been drained out. Thank God, our Lord today has no blood. What He has is a body of flesh and bones. All which belongs to the natural life has been poured out. The shedding of the Lord's blood at Calvary meant the pouring out of all the natural life: He poured out His soul even unto death. This is the meaning of the blood. Consequently, the shedding of blood denotes the removal of all which belongs to the natural life.

In order to come to God to minister to Him, we must draw

near to Him. We must stand before Him, waiting for His will. But please be aware that two things are absolutely needed: death and resurrection. On the one side we must continuously pour out our blood. In other words, we need to confess persistently that all which we possess by birth and which is subject to death has been poured out. Many often ask me, What does the natural life really mean? To which my response has always been this: all which comes by birth and vanishes with death belongs to the natural life. Praise the Lord, He has drained out all our natural life, all that we possess by birth. When our Lord shed His blood, He let out not only His own life but *our* natural life as well. Therefore, we ought to stand on this fact and resist our own natural life.

Let me repeat that this is not merely a doctrine. This is absolute truth to be worked out in experience. Before God, whatever belongs to the natural life has been set aside. This is not an ideal which we cannot reach, because in Christ all of our soul life has been drained away. For this reason (and for this reason alone), we are able to be selfless persons. Praise God, that we *can* be selfless people because of the fact that in the shedding of the Lord's blood He has flushed out our "self"—the life of self. Without question, we cannot possibly accomplish this by ourselves. No one is able to put himself to death on his own. But thank God, His Son has accomplished this feat. By trusting in Him we may die—that is to say, we may deny ourselves.

Nevertheless, death alone is not sufficient, for death is only the negative side. What we must also pay attention to before God is the other side, the positive side of resurrection. When the Lord Jesus was raised from the dead, we were in Him as well. Consequently, we are now the new creation. He not only died, He also was resurrected. He lives forever unto God. Wherefore, His all is for the satisfaction of God's heart. Nothing is for His own self. And this is what God desires all of us to see and to experience, for such constitutes ministering to the Lord. We therefore need to give Him, as it were, both the blood and the fat.

"They shall enter into my sanctuary, and they shall come near to my table, to minister unto me, and they shall keep my charge" (v.16). Here it tells how ministry to the Lord has its confined location. It is inside the sanctuary, in a quiet place that unlike the outer court is hidden from public view. Let us ask God for grace that we may not consider this to be something painful. Actually, to be but one day *there* is far better than to be elsewhere for a thousand days. Yet how we are afraid of the Holy Place and love the outer court. In the outer court, people can see us and recognize us. How very good the outer court is! There we are well known. There we are welcome without any attack or slander. How excellent this is! Yet, where God really wants us to be is in the sanctuary with Him. But we are fearful of being *there* because we may be criticized as being too lazy or as doing nothing. Few of us realize that what is done in the Holy Place far exceeds the effort of ministering to the people in the outer court. Have those of you who have spent time ministering to the Lord ever heard people say you are too small or too narrow? Have you ever heard men criticizing you as being too strict, saying that you will not do this or that? People complain that you are too lazy because of many things you do not do. Let me say that if our heart is right, then it will not be straitened at all by such things since we have but one aim: to minister to the Lord in the sanctuary: we will ask nothing of men: we are not willing to stand at the door to be seen by many. Far from wishing to minister to the house, we hope instead to do a greater thing. We would have a heart like Paul's: no heart was more ambitious than his, for he constantly aimed at being well-pleasing to his Lord (see 2 Cor. 5.9).

So, what we are seeking after here is a greater work, one that is greater than many so-called great works. Our hearts are bigger than most people, who would nonetheless regard us as being too small, too narrow when it comes to doing God's work. For we are really aiming at the highest, since we will not only seek to minister to the house but even more so seek to minister to the Lord. Let us make no move if it is not God's will. Let people criticize if they wish. Yet if we truly love the Lord, we shall maintain but two positions: one, that having died we forsake all which is of the old creation; and two, that having been resurrected we learn to minister to God by standing before Him, waiting upon Him and listening for His order. We shall care for nothing else. Let me therefore put the following questions before you as a challenge: Does the will of God satisfy your heart? Is it enough for you to do God's will? Is God's will good enough? Or must you seek something else? Is what God has ordained for you good enough? Oh how we need to learn to minister to Him. . . .

### *The Qualifications and Conditions of Those Who Minister to the Lord*

"And it shall be that, when they enter in at the gates of the inner court, they shall be clothed with linen garments; and no wool shall come upon them, while they minister in the gates of the inner court, and within. They shall have linen tires upon their heads, and shall have linen breeches upon their loins; they shall not gird themselves with anything that causeth sweat" (vv.17–18). Here we are told what kind of dress those who minister to God must wear. They are to wear linen garments, linen tires upon their heads and linen breeches upon their loins—thus clothing the entire body with nothing but linen. No wool was to come upon them. No one who ministers to the Lord can wear woolen things. Before God he is forever forbidden to wear anything made of wool. And should some ask why this prohibition against wool, the answer is given thus: "they shall not gird themselves with anything that causeth sweat." What it therefore means here is that no one who serves must ever sweat. All "sweating works" are unacceptable to God and are therefore rejected by Him. What is the spiritual significance that attaches to this word sweat in the Bible? We know that the first instance of sweating which happened in the world came upon Adam after he had been driven from the garden of Eden. Genesis 3 tells us that due to Adam's sin, God had set forth His punishment of him by declaring that "in toil shalt thou eat . . . ; in the sweat of thy face shalt thou eat bread" (vv.17c,19a). Sweat bespeaks curse because the ground was cursed in that it could not and would not bring forth food naturally. Now lacking God's blessing, man must toil, thus producing perspiration. For this reason, "sweating works" refer to the works of the flesh—that work which is done without the blessing of God the Father. All who minister to God should not do these sweating works. Yet how many works are done before God today through running hither and thither! But the works which those who minister to God perform must not be sweating works at all. For every one of God's works is done calmly—which is to say that it is done through sitting and not by running. Though God's minister may be outwardly busy, he nonetheless is inwardly peaceful. Though he may be outwardly zealous, inwardly he is calm. And hence these works of God are done, as it were, while sitting: most certainly are they all accomplished without sweating. As a matter of fact, nothing before God can be done in accidental fashion, nothing is to be done through natural strength. How sad today that many works cannot be accomplished without the sweat of man. How terrible that many works are done by human planning, managing, promoting, running, encouraging and reminding. Without men's own strength or fleshly power, they simply cannot be accomplished. How lamentable that today "no sweat" means "no work."

Please notice that sweating is permitted on the outside where the sheep and cattle are killed; where the sinners are saved and the believers are ministered to. In doing such works as these it is allowed for man to sweat. But all who would minister to the Lord in the Holy Place are absolutely forbidden to sweat since God has no need for such ones to perspire. No doubt, all works are busy, but God's works do not require the energy of the flesh. I do not say here that there is no need for spiritual power. Actually, it is hard to decide just how much spiritual power is needed inasmuch as it is impossible to know how much suffering is involved. Today men make no distinction between spiritual works and those so-called works of God which are obviously carnal works. They generalize that no work of God can be accomplished without running, contacting, discussing, proposing, approving and passing. They cannot wait quietly before God and listen to His word. For this is impossible to the flesh. Indeed, all the works of the flesh demand perspiration; else, they cannot be done.

However, the greatest portion of a truly spiritual work lies in dealing with God. And in this case the first person to be contacted is God, not man. How different, though, is the work of the flesh, for in that context the first contact is man. A work that cannot succeed without man is definitely not God's work. How very precious to be before God, for the one whom we deal with there is none other than God himself. Here it is not a case that we are doing nothing, but that we are doing a work which does not need any sweat. How is this to be explained? If you have already had dealings with God, you will not need to sweat before men. You are able to use the least strength to do the most work. The reason why today men in God's work of winning the lost and helping the needy saints have to resort to many advertisements and promotional techniques is because they have not prayed before God. Let me tell you that all spiritual works are done before God. If they are done before Him, lost men and needy believers will listen to you. You have no need to resort to many methods in order to help the people. For here it is God who works, and therefore there is no need for fleshly energy and sweat.

Accordingly, we must honestly examine ourselves before the Lord, asking Him: "O Lord, is what I do a serving of you or a serving of the work? Am I ministering to the house or ministering to the Lord?" If your work requires you to sweat from dawn to dusk, you can conclude that you are ministering to the house and not to the Lord. If what you are busily occupied with is entirely a matter of meeting outside needs, you can conclude that you are serving the people and not serving the Lord. I do not in the least despise those who serve the people, for they too are doing God's work. There *must* be those who are involved in slaughtering sheep and cattle. There *must* be those who lead and help the needy. The children of Israel certainly needed help, as do the believers of today. Yet what God desired back in those days and desires today is something deeper. Hence we should pray, "O God, save me from falling into only ministering to the people." Many of God's workers are doing only that. Why do you wish to join their ranks? Today God is not able to persuade all to minister to Him for this is something many will not do. It seems impossible that the entire Church can be revived or that everyone will be faithful to God, simply because so many are unwilling. Many are truly saved and have life, but they would rather minister to the people. There is no way to turn them around. They are unable to forsake outward noise and bustle or to lay down outward work. They highly esteem their fields of work. I recognize, of course, that somebody must do these works. But the question to be asked is this: Does God want me to be one of them or does He have something deeper for me? I hope we can say today, "O God, I want to minister to You. I am willing to cast aside all things, lay down all works and forsake all that is outward which is not of You. I want to come and minister to You and do spiritual works. I will put down the outward and enter more deeply into the inward."

In the days of Israel, God was not able to cause all the hearts to come. He could only choose the sons of Zadok. Why? Because when the children of Israel went astray from God, the sons of Zadok were the only ones who kept the charge of the sanctuary. They recognized that the outward—the outer court—was beyond repair, that it was broken down and defiled. So they let it go and concentrated on keeping the holiness of the sanctuary. Are you able to let the outside remain broken down? Or will you try to support it with boards to keep it from falling further into disrepair? Yet God has already proclaimed: "I do not want these anymore. Now I will keep my sanctuary so as to retain a holy place for My children." Today there needs to be a place which is wholly sanctified, where the difference between right and wrong may be discerned. For what God wants to keep is His sanctuary. The outside will fall, and God allows it to fall. Only the sons of Zadok kept the charge, so God chose them. Indeed, God today cannot deal in this way with all of His people, but only with those who—like the sons of Zadok—are willing to stand before Him within the sanctuary. Whom will He seek if you are unwilling to lay down all that is outside? Let me declare to you that those whom God seeks today are those who will wholly minister to Him. In our day too many are ministering on the outside and too few are ministering to God within. Henceforth, the cry of God today is, Who will enter My sanctuary to minister to Me? . . .

I say again that ministering to the Lord does not mean to leave all the outside works or to quit going to the countryside. What I would say is this, that all these outside works must be based on the ministry to the Lord. We are to go forth to do these outer works as a consequence of our ministering to the Lord and not because of our garnering from them our own pleasure. The difference between these two heart attitudes is so vast that it is as great as that between heaven and earth. All who are experienced know that there is nothing more different than this between ministering to the Lord and ministering to the house.

—MHMG 1-4, 5-8, 9-10, 11-21, 21-6, 27-8

# 47 The Work

God has His work. This work is not your work or mine, nor is it the work of this mission or that group. It is God's own work.

Genesis 1 tells us that God worked and then He rested. In the beginning God created light, living creatures, man, and so forth. None but He could do this work of creation. And today He also has His work, which is not any man's work, and which no man is able to do. God's work can be done by none other than God himself. The earlier we acknowledge this the better. For man's works, man's thoughts, man's methods, man's zeal and earnestness and efforts and tireless activities have absolutely no place in what God is doing. Man can no more have a part in God's work today than he could have had way back then in creation.

In Philippians Paul says: "That I may lay hold on that for which also I was laid hold on by Christ Jesus." The Lord Jesus has a special, specific purpose in laying hold on us—and that specific purpose is the thing we want to lay hold of. He has a purpose, and this purpose is that He might get *us* and that we might be co-workers with Him. Nonetheless it is still true that we *cannot do* God's work, since it all is absolutely and wholly His. But on the other hand we *are* His co-workers. So that on the one hand we must recognize and acknowledge that we cannot touch with even one little finger the work of God, yet on the other hand we are called to be co-workers with Him! And this is that for which He has laid hold on us. The Lord has a definite purpose in salvation—and a clear and specific purpose in saving us—which is, that He might have us as His co-workers....

...God's work in this dispensation is to form the body of Christ. And the work of the church is precisely the same—to form the body of Christ: "All the body... maketh the increase of the body unto the building up of itself in love." No mission, no Bible school, no evangelistic band, etc., etc., can ever take the place of the church or do the work of the church....

The eternal purpose of God can never be understood or grasped by the mind. It has to come by revelation. All work for God begins with consecration or is based on surrender. But such consecration or surrender only comes through revelation. As a matter of fact, the work of God (not our work, but God's work through us) begins only when revelation comes. Outwardly is the heavenly vision, inwardly is the revelation.

God does not want us to just do a kind of general, miscellaneous sort of work for Him. He desires us to know His whole plan and to be working with Him toward a clear purpose and plan. For we are not only His servants but also His friends.

All surrender and consecration is valuable, but when it comes right down to it, it is only after revelation that surrender and consecration can be of much value, because only then can it be complete. Our surrender before this revelation is only in view of salvation. He has bought me with His blood, His love toward me is unspeakable. Therefore, I *ought* to give myself to Him. I ought to give myself and all that I have to Him because of His saving grace and love. But after revelation it is a different matter. When we see God's eternal purpose, it calls for a tremendous giving of ourselves to this purpose, with a surrender we have never dreamed of before—something deeper and more utter. Paul said, "I was not disobedient unto the heavenly vision" (Acts 26.19). He could go through anything and bear anything because of the heavenly vision....

### *Spiritual Work Based on Revelation*

All spiritual work for God comes out of revelation. Apart from revelation on God's eternal purpose, there can be no truly spiritual work. There can be scattered, miscellaneous work for God which is blessed by Him, but it cannot be truly called spiritual work or co-working with Him unless it issues out of revelation as to God's eternal purpose. It must be revelation and not just a mental grasp of it—not just an understanding it and seeing it intellectually, for this is useless. It needs to be a "seeing" in your spirit: a seeing what the sphere and limitation of God's working are.

Now only revelation can deal with both work and worker. This light from heaven smashes us to bits. It shatters and slays *us* and *our work.* If it is mere doctrine or teaching it will leave us after a while. It goes, it evaporates as it were. But if it is light or revelation it is our *life,* and we cannot get away from it. . . .

Here, then, do we have the two ways by which the church is to be built up: (a) 1 Corinthians 12, by the gifts of the Spirit; and (b) 2 Corinthians 4, by death working in us that life may work in others.

Which way has built you up the most? Has your inner life been built up the most by the gifts of the Spirit, or by those whom you have known who know the cross applied to their inmost lives—who always bear about in them the dying of Jesus that the life of Jesus may be manifested? This is cross-bearing. Let death never cease to work in you and me that life may never cease to flow out to others. . . .

What really edifies and helps most is not the gifts or utterances of those who have these gifts, but the life of those we come in contact with who *deeply know the cross,* who know the cross within and bear it daily. Take, for example, a company of newly-saved Christians. Now for the first few years the Lord may give them gifts to cause them to wonder at His power and glory and to strengthen their weak faith. But once it is strong enough, He will remove the gifts and bring in the cross. There are grave dangers associated with the gifts, the greatest of which is "spiritual" pride. One can stand up in the Spirit (that is, the outpoured Spirit) and utter a few wonderful sentences that no one else can utter. "I feel I am really something!" he thinks. Yet his inner life may be infantile compared to another believer who has not the gifts but who deeply knows the cross. . . .

### *Not Doing, But Being*

The organized church today emphasizes what a person says and what a person does but pays little attention to what a person *is*. Many young workers earnestly desire to be able to speak with power, long for eloquence, yearn to be able to preach brilliantly in order to move and help people. They fail to realize that this is not the vital point. The vital issue is: Who and what are *you?* The thing of value, the preeminently important matter is, not that you are given a gift and therefore you are able to speak, but that you know the Lord and therefore you speak. . . .

Are the gifts needed? Yes, they are, up to a certain point; but they are not to continue beyond that point where the Lord seeks to discontinue them and to bring in the working of the cross, to bring in the breaking, the weakening, and the knowing of the Lord—wherein we need no supernatural utterances. Because of the fact that out of the fullness of the heart the mouth speaks, and because Christ has been inwrought by the indwelling Holy Spirit, therefore I can speak out of His life within. We may say today exactly the same thing as we said ten or fifteen years ago, but it is entirely different. Yes, I knew and believed it then, but now it has been inwrought into my very being. It is myself, that is, Christ in me. . . .

### *Prophetic Ministry*

If you would be a prophet, three things are necessary:

(1) Your preparation as a vessel—the Holy Spirit breaking you, dealing with you, applying the cross, taking you down into

death, and working into you the life of Christ. In other words, a secret history with God.

(2) A burden within, which God gives—a thought which becomes a burden.

(3) Utterance for that burden, expression for that thought—an interpretation and clear expression of it. . . .

### *The Cross—the Basis of Ministry of Life*

2 Corinthians is beyond everything else a book of suffering. We see there God's servant—His chosen vessel—going through terrific, fiery trials and suffering such as perhaps no other apostle or servant of the Lord has ever had to go through. We see sufferings written all through the book: some are physical, some mental, some spiritual; some are temporary while some others are continuous. But he gives the reason for these sufferings when he says, "Always bearing about in the body the dying of Jesus, that the life also of Jesus may be manifested in our body." This is the basis of all ministry *in life.* There *must* be suffering, there must be pain, there must be the *cross*—if there is ever going to be the life of Christ manifested. "So then death worketh in us, but life in you."

Whenever there is a shrinking from the cross, a dodging of Calvary, a refusal of the pathway of pain and suffering, an unwillingness to pay the price and to suffer pain and loss, then there will be poverty, death, and shallowness, an emptiness that can give out, nothing with which to minister to God's people. "Let death never cease to work in me that life may never cease to flow out to others." . . .

All ministry which has lost its priestly emphasis over all things else has broken down. If a person has not first of all gone into the presence of God, he cannot come forth out of the presence of God with any message or service of value. If we have not stood in the presence of God as priest, all our work, all our witnessing, all our running about, all our wearing ourselves out, will only be a ministry to man and not to the Lord. . . .

It is still true that all God's people are priests. Hallelujah, it is indeed still true. Nevertheless, it is equally true that we cannot execute that office without special qualifications. We cannot exercise our appointed function as priests as we naturally are. Spiritually speaking, only Moses and Aaron and the Levites could execute that office. We see this principle in the case of Korah, Dathan, and Abiram. When the two hundred and fifty princes of the congregation offered false fire in their incense burners, they were consumed.

Afterwards Aaron's rod and the representative rods of the other tribes were laid up in the tabernacle. On the next day only Aaron's rod budded. This of course means resurrection: life out of death. Only those can minister to the Lord who have been through death and have come out into resurrection life. They must have known the death of the cross.

You cannot possibly take anything of the old creation into the tabernacle, into the ministry of the Lord: neither your old mind nor your old creation brilliancy or cleverness, nor your old creation eloquence, nor your old creation strength of any kind. All this has to go right down into death and to come out into resurrection life. Unless your rod has budded, you cannot serve God. In short, you cannot serve God if you only know the blood but do not know the cross.

### *Through Death into Life*

It is true that positionally we are all priests, but only after we have accepted the subjective working of the cross and have had our natural life absolutely and utterly dealt with can we execute that priestly office.

Resurrection has only one meaning, which is, that a person *has been through death* and received new life. The resurrection we see in Philippians 3 is the positive side of resurrection. It is not a matter of something dead going through death and coming out alive. No, resurrection is *life going into death and emerging in new life.* Whatever is good and living in us, whatever comes from the new birth, all the pure, new, born-again life that God has given us—all this *has to go down into death,* has to go *through death,* and to be purified again by death, thrice purified by three days (which typifies fullness and perfection and completeness of death) and to come out in life. That is resurrection life indeed; and life having passed through death and having had everything consumed that it had collected of self or earth can never be touched by death. That is life in which there is no death.

All which we naturally have as gifts and all which God has given us as gifts of the Spirit *must* pass through death. If we have been a gifted conversationalist or a great talker, we may find that all this disappears when we go through death. Because although it has been good and helpful and "spiritual" conversation, it has not been wholly the Spirit of God. It has at best been a mixture; and because of this it will all be purified in going through death. Our natural strength and ability will never emerge from death. Our intellectual power must all of it go through death or else it can never minister to God. And this death is not the death of Romans 6 and Galatians 2.20; it is *something beyond this!* This death and resurrection is the basis and the only basis for priestly ministry.

Thank God, we refuse all service which is only to man. We do not serve man, we serve God; for we are first ministers of Christ, and afterwards to man, to the church. But the basis of it all is *death* and *resurrection* which issues in a priestly ministry Godward, and which then issues in ministry to man. May the Lord give us grace to enter into the Holy of Holies because all of self and all of man and all of mixture and all of earth has been destroyed in death but what is indestructible and what is deathless has emerged in resurrection life. . . .

### *The Iniquity of the Sanctuary*

God said to Aaron: (1) "Thou and thy sons and thy fathers' house with thee shall bear the iniquity of the sanctuary"; (2) "They [the tribe of Levi] shall keep thy charge . . . : only they shall not come nigh unto the vessels of the sanctuary and unto the altar", and later, (3) "A stranger shall not come nigh unto you." God shows us very clearly what He thinks of sin and goes through the whole list, yet those sins are not punished by death. But "the iniquity of the sanctuary"—the iniquity of ministry—is alone punishable by death, with no possible escape nor pardon. This kind of iniquity, unlike lying or killing or pride or breaking the law in any way, is not easy to be atoned for. This sin—the iniquity of ministry—is not to be forgiven. This sort of thing just cannot be permitted, overlooked, or forgiven. Every other sin can be cleansed and forgiven, but not this one.

What are these sins of the sanctuary? We must go back and see again what ministry is. We have seen that all ministry issues from death and resurrection. The dead rod of Aaron had to be laid up before God and to go through death. The rod had absolutely no life in itself. It was a dead thing. We have to acknowledge that we, like the rod, are dead things: useless—utterly useless, without anything whatever to give, without any hope, without the least little fragment to give to a needy world, without one atom of anything of value to God or which He can use. But when God has taken this dead rod through death, it will blossom. It simply has to be laid up before the Lord for Him to put His own life into it. Into the earthen vessel He puts that exceedingly precious treasure: His very own life which itself has been through death and resurrection. It is *His* death and *His* resurrection that He gives us to experience as is mentioned in Philippians 3. For instance, take a brilliant person who tries to serve the Lord with his brilliancy. Such a ministry as his just does not issue forth in life. On the contrary, whatever he touches issues in death because he himself has not been through the death of Philippians 3.

What then is the iniquity of the sanctuary? *It is bringing into the service of the Lord something other than resurrection life.* Many people are just naturally burning for the Lord; they bring their warm enthusiasm into His service. This is an iniquity of the sanctuary. Many servants of God bring their strong wills into the service of the Lord. This is a sin of the sanctuary. Other people have everything in the mental. They have strong clear minds and they grasp things quickly. They greatly love to be in spiritual circles and with spiritual people. They like to hear spiritual messages. But they as it were are watching it all through a window; it has never been made life to them. God has never really touched their spirits and given them revelation. They have never been through death to all that is good and strong and natural. They instead bring their natural minds and talents and whatever into the service of God. It is abhorrent to Him, and is a sin of the sanctuary.

—GW 5-6, 12, 18-9, 20, 26-7, 27, 32, 33, 40, 45-6, 51, 53-5, 59-61

In like manner, God has His foreordained plan as to the work of the building of the church. Regardless of large or small matters, He has His own specific way. As Moses was not responsible for the design of the tabernacle but only responsible to build it according to the pattern of the mount, so the glory of a servant of Christ lies not in his ingenuity in doing God's work but rather in his careful execution of what he understands to be the will of God. To know the Lord's counsel and to execute accordingly is the glory of Christ's servant.

A sister who has served the Lord for many years once said, "Man has absolutely no liberty in God's work." When Moses built the tabernacle, he had no freedom in deciding whether a small nail should be made of silver or of gold. He made every item according to what the Lord had commanded. . . .

The greatest blessing to a servant of Christ is to arrive at the mountain of God's direction, to know what work is appointed to him, and to be acquainted with the foreordained pattern of that work. When you as a servant of Christ come before the Lord and seek for an appointment, do you come to ask Him to show you the time and the way of your labor? Or do you perform the work according to man's counsel, plan and decision? . .

"Keep back thy servant also from presumptuous sins; let them not have dominion over me: then shall I be upright, and I shall be clear from great transgression" (Ps. 19.13). From this verse of David's psalm we are shown that there are two kinds of sin before God: one is the sin of rebellion, the other is that of presumption. Not doing what one is told to do constitutes the sin of rebellion. Now we all know the sinfulness of this kind of sin; and from this sin we wish to be delivered. But please take note that besides the sin of rebellion there is also that of presumption, which is, that we do what we are not ordered to do. Rebellion is failing to do what God has charged, whereas presumption is doing what God has not commanded at all. To be active outside of the Lord's will is to be presumptuous. On the one hand God says, Do not commit adultery, Do not steal. If anyone should commit such an act, he is guilty. This we all know. But on the other hand, do we know that it is equally sinful for us to act without God's order? It is reckoned as sin before the Lord if we work for Him without His command and instead work according to our own idea, even though we may view what we do to be most excellent. The prayer of David is for Jehovah to keep him away from presumptuous sin.

God knows what He wants. He therefore tells us, either through the Bible or through the Holy Spirit, what He wishes us to do. For spiritual work depends not on its quantity but on its fitting in to God's purpose and meeting God's use. What matters most to a servant of Christ is to know what God wants him to do, and at what time and by what means. One who serves the Lord has absolutely no need to design his work. One of the characteristics of the New Covenant is that everyone may know God's will. A servant of Christ may receive in his spirit the revelation of the Holy Spirit, thus discerning clearly what God requires of him. Such knowledge is real; it comes neither from his imagination nor from the encouragement or direction of other people. It is based on the teaching of the letter of the Bible and revealed as God's command in the deepest recess of his being by the Holy Spirit who dwells in his spirit.

Yet how many today really know spiritual revelation? How many can truly say, "I have seen it clearly"? Many there are who substitute for the work of God that which they deem to be good and spiritual, much to be desired, and calculated to be most profitable. In the Lord's work there are probably more volunteers than actually chosen by Him. Many can only say "I come"; but they cannot say "I am sent"! Hence a great deal of so-called divine work is full of death. Numerous are the endeavors which are not desired by God but are designed by men according to their own zeal and supposition. They call all these labors works of God, yet in reality they have almost nothing of God in them.

The prime mover of true spiritual work is the Lord, not us. We are only made responsible to know the divine will. Whatever is spiritually effective must originate from God's heart; we are merely to do what the Holy Spirit has revealed to us. As a matter of fact, all services can be traced to either of two sources: one proceeds from God, the other proceeds from man; one is desired by God while the other is what man thinks God may desire. Oh do let us inquire as to what kind of work we have done.

It is most regrettable that many servants of God overlook or little understand this sin of presumption. They have not been brought by the Holy Spirit to the place where they will judge themselves rigorously and acknowledge that in divine work they are not given liberty to voice their opinion because God himself is the sole Lord. How we need the Holy Spirit to convict us of what the sin of presumption is and how terrible is such sin. We should realize that doing what God has *not* charged is as sinful as not doing what He *has* charged us. We must not habitually say, "Since the Lord has not prohibited, why can I not do it?" Rather, we ought frequently to maintain this attitude of heart: "How can I do what God has not charged?" Those who know the Lord only superficially assume that they can do anything which is not prohibited in the Bible; but those who know Him more deeply understand that they would be committing a presumptuous sin if they attempted to do what the Scriptures have not forbidden and yet God has not commanded them to do.

Do recognize this fact, that when you are brought one day to a deeper place with God, you will see that you should not do what He has not ordered just as you must not rebel against what He has ordered. You will be perfect and usable if you do not follow your own thought in things unadvised by God. A perfect man will not commit presumptuous sin. If God has not given an order, such a one will wait in quietness. Such a person is usable and can be used to do the Lord's work. . . .

What is the cause for presumption? Nothing can account for it but the expression of the self-life. Though many people are willing to obey when commanded, their hearts take no delight in God's will because they still like their own idea. Consequently, they tend to act presumptuously whenever the Lord is silent. Let me say that unless we judge our flesh and take up the cross which deals with our self-life, we on the one hand may perhaps struggle to obey God when ordered but on the other hand will certainly act with our own thought if unadvised.

To be presumptuous in the Lord's work does not necessarily mean to have a wrong intention. Before we were converted, our self-life did not like to serve God; but once saved, we do like to serve Him. This, then, becomes a most dangerous time. For whereas formerly we absolutely refused to serve the Lord, we now desire to do so, yet only to serve Him in our own way. God, however, demands that we not only serve Him but also serve according to the way He prefers. How frequently His people are mistaken, thinking that God only requires service and leaves the way of service to man's discretion. May we be enlightened to see that the Lord is not pleased with any service which is not done in accordance with His will. Moreover, we should also be assured that both the time and the way to proceed in the work have likewise been ordained of the Lord.

We ought to recognize that however correct man's motive is, it cannot be a substitute for God's will; no matter how successful a man's endeavor may appear to be, it can fall short of the divine pleasure. How many have been the works which were done not in obedience to the Lord's command but rather in meeting circumstantial needs, in helping believers' spiritual life, or in saving sinners' souls. Such labors may not be fruitless, yet neither the workers nor the works satisfy the Lord's heart. What we must consider first is God's need at the moment, not the outward demands of saints or sinners. The primary objective of our labor is to fulfill *God's* needs, not those of saints and sinners.

Oh do let us see that we are *God's* servants. Though He has entrusted His work to us, He nevertheless reserves for himself the authority to direct His servants. For do recall that at Antioch the Holy Spirit called the Lord's servants to the work, yet Paul and Silas could not go to Asia by their own choice. The authority over the movement of the Lord's servants is forever in the hands of the Holy Spirit (see Acts 16.6ff.). The question lies not in whether there is need in Asia but whether God has a need in Asia *at that particular time.* How marvelously the book of Acts shows that the Holy Spirit who gives us power to work is also the One who sets the direction and timing of our work. Our responsibility in the work is simply to supply God's current need. . . .

Who knows how much of our zeal is strange fire! Ofttimes people conjecture over how to prosper the Lord's work and to please God: such conjecturing is all according to their fleshly thoughts without themselves having been dealt with by the cross or having had their cleverness denied. Zeal yes, but not of God. It indeed is fire, but it is foreign fire instead of altar fire. Whatever does not come from the cross, that is to say, from the self-denying altar, is merely strange fire. Such fire is nothing but "self-fire"—that which proceeds from the soul life. It is the fire and power of the natural life. And hence it is the self-life intervening in God's affairs. The affair may unquestionably belong to God, nonetheless self-life decides how it is to be done. If we depend on our wisdom, use our method, or insist on our opinion in the Lord's affairs, we are offering strange fire—fire which is not only unacceptable to God but even causes our death in His presence.

—TG 58–9, 59–60, 61–4, 64–6, 68

As we learn to serve God in the church, it is important that we be faithful in all our works; but we should also pay special attention to the increase of spiritual value. The purpose for doing all things well is to impart spiritual reality. If we merely have the business side without having sufficient measure on the spiritual side, we have departed from the original aim of serving God. For He has laid upon us a spiritual responsibility, and it will be a great loss if we only attend to the business side and neglect the life side. If we have lack on the life side, our services will only be activities—we will not be able to meet the needs of God's children, for what can truly meet the needs of His children is life. Therefore, we should strive for real progress in spiritual life before we are in a position to supply life through work and service to the brothers and sisters. . . .

Let us never imagine that spiritual worth lies in the realm of excitement and enthusiasm. No, spiritual value lies in the manifestation of holiness while serving because there is the presence of God. Many brothers and sisters can testify that when they serve in the church they are like the priests of old entering the holy place. By the blood of the Lamb sins are cleansed; by the renewal of the Holy Spirit uncleanness is washed away; and by the "Holiness" of the holy place the self life is eliminated. Each time we serve God we should have such a consciousness and such an expression. But if there be no inward awareness of sin, uncleanness and self about us, I am afraid there is little of the presence of the Lord. . . .

### *Service in Time and Eternity*

In spiritual matters we should recognize the fact that "time" is for "eternity"; that the service we render in time is preparation for the service in eternity. God places us in the here and now for the purpose of training us to be useful in eternity. Time is like a school in which we receive spiritual training and education. Whatever spiritual training and education we receive in time makes us truly fit for God's use in eternity. Consequently, the service performed today prepares us for the service in the hereafter. . . .

From the day we are saved the Lord puts His life in us and trains us gradually but continually through practical matters that we may learn to cooperate with Him more and more. He is with us to develop His nature in us so that we may become useful in His hand. In the measure of God's life in us is the measure of our usefulness to Him. As the measure of God increases, so our usefulness increases too. The measure of God's life does not increase only at the time of prayer and Bible reading; God uses also the things in our hand by which to incorporate himself in us. Let us therefore see that in time God has no other purpose than to increase His measure of life in us day by day. Due to the thick impenetrableness of our own self, He is unable to make any perforation through its walls. But after some time of dealing with us, He is able to get through us a little; and after a little more time, He can perforate the shell of resistance somewhat more. Finally, after many years of working further, He will penetrate through us almost completely.

Hence it takes considerable time for God's life to be organized in us. But this activity in turn establishes our usefulness. Every spiritual usefulness comes from the incorporation of God's life in us. Our usefulness before the Lord is none else than His nature developed in us. God imparts His life to us, and when this life in us is released, there is to be found our usefulness.

—WSS 50, 53-4, 55-6, 56-7

God has one objective, and that is, to increase His Son. He purposes to have people come under the name of His Son and to share the life of His Son so that they become His own children. He designs to use these people for the increase of His Son in order that the personal Christ may also be the corporate Christ.

For all the purposes of God are in His Son and all His works are intended to extend His Son!

The tragedy surrounding the events in the Garden of Eden lies in the fact that instead of receiving the life of God's Son man sinned, thereby turning himself against God and becoming a slave to Satan. And hence, thereafter the work of God first lay, negatively, in solving the question of man's sin by delivering him from the bondage of the devil, and, positively, in causing man to accept His Son's life. God would then be able to give increase to His Son so that His Son might fill all in all. Before the fall, God only required man to accept His life. But since his fall, man needs to have the double problem of sin and the power of Satan solved before he can receive the life of God. The redemptive work of God is therefore to deliver man from sin and Satan and to cause man to partake of His Son's life. . . .

. . . In the Bible there is not only in view the personal Christ but also the corporate Christ. The first has the total victory, but the second has yet to experience this victory. The personal Christ is the Head of the corporate Christ. Christ is the Head, the Church is the Body. Christ plus the Church is the corporate Christ. Christ himself has fully overcome, but the Church is yet to experience His victory. The triumph of the Head must be experienced by the Body.

Moreover, the Church has not fully known Christ, nor is she absolutely clear on the faith. Though the believers are people with divine life, they are babes nonetheless and have yet to be fully grown up unto the measure of the stature of the fulness of Christ. The Church must arrive at a certain measure before she can satisfy God's heart. God does everything for the sake of Christ, because Christ is His objective. God wishes all the redeemed to receive life only from Christ, to know Him fully, and to be like Him completely. It is the will of God that all the grace and life in the Head would flow into the Body. All the facts in Christ must become experiences in the Church.

Hence before Christ will bind Satan and bless the whole world by himself, He must first establish His Church, thereby causing His people to partake of His victory, as well as arrive at the full measure ordained for them. Consequently, God has His own Work to do *today*. He is building the Body of Christ until all who compose it arrive at the unity of the faith and of the full knowledge of the Son of God, until they attain unto the measure of the stature of the fullness of Christ (see Eph. 4.12–13). Such an undertaking of building the Body of Christ is God's *current* Work. It occupies a large place in all the works of God. His today's Work is centered upon this one thing: He is especially concerned with the upbuilding of the Body of Christ. . . .

. . In the Bible there are at least three passages which resemble the one in Ephesians 4; namely 1 Corinthians 12.8–10, 1 Corinthians 12.28, and Romans 12.6–8. In these three passages, various ministries, various persons, and various gifts are mentioned. Only in Ephesians, however, is the term "the Ministry" used. In order to know the distinction between Ephesians 4 and the other passages, we must compare them.

"For to one is given through the Spirit the word of wisdom; and to another the word of knowledge, according to the same Spirit: to another faith, in the same Spirit; and to another gifts of healings, in the one Spirit; and to another workings of miracles; and to another prophecy; and to another discernings of spirits: to another divers kinds of tongues; and to another the interpretation of tongues" (1 Cor. 12.8–10).

"And God hath set some in the church, first apostles, secondly prophets, thirdly teachers, then miracles, then gifts of healings, helps, governments, divers kinds of tongues" (1 Cor. 12.28).

"And having gifts differing according to the grace that was given to us, whether prophecy, let us prophesy according to the proportion of our faith; or ministry, let us give ourselves to our ministry; or he that teacheth, to his teaching; or he that exhorteth, to his exhorting: he that giveth, let him do it with liberality; he that ruleth, with diligence; he that showeth mercy, with cheerfulness" (Rom. 12.6–8).

1 Corinthians 12.8–10 enumerates the gifts given to *individual* believers. Ephesians 4.11–12 speaks of the persons whom the Lord gives as gifts to the *Church.* The gifts in 1 Corinthians 12 are *supernatural,* whilst the gifts in Romans 12 are *ordinary* as a result of the Lord's grace and our faith. The nine gifts mentioned in 1 Corinthians are those received when men are under the power of the Holy Spirit. Hence in verse 1 it says this: "Now concerning spirituals" (original Greek). The gifts in Romans 12 are based upon the grace of God. God gives men grace so that they may manifest His grace by fulfilling their various functions as members of the Body. Consequently, the gifts enumerated are neither miraculous nor Spirit-moved but are rather of life. Even "giveth" and "showeth mercy" are viewed as gifts, for all of them are gifts according to grace. In Ephesians 4, however, those persons mentioned are the Lord's gifts given to the Church. The persons *themselves* are gifts, and the gifts they receive are such gifts as those enumerated in 1 Corinthians 12 and Romans 12. The emphasis of 1 Corinthians is power, whilst the emphasis in Romans is life. Ephesians speaks of the persons who possess these two different kinds of gifts, for the persons themselves are God's gifts to the Church.

"*The* Ministry" in Ephesians is unique and special. 1 Corinthians 12 also speaks of ministry, but there it is the ministries (see verse 5, original Greek) which are of the common ordinary kind, of which the children of God receive severally, before the Lord. The four gifts to the Church as cited in Ephesians 4 are for "the work of the Ministry"; the nine gifts to individuals listed in 1 Corinthians 12.8–10 are for the ministries as each person possesses a different gift for a different service.

1 Corinthians 12.28 enumerates eight (or nine) classes of persons God has set in the Church. It is different from the gifts enumerated earlier in verses 8–10. For the earlier passage in 1 Corinthians refers to the *gifts* of the Holy Spirit, whilst verse 28 refers to the *workings* (or operations) of God. The first alludes to the gifts which the Holy Spirit gives to the church *local,* whereas

the latter passage alludes to the workings of God in the Church *universal.* Verses 8–10 have reference to the gifts individuals receive from the Holy Spirit, but in verse 28 we see that God sets in the Church those men who have received gifts for His operation. So that there are eight (or nine) classes of persons cited in 1 Corinthians 12.28 whom God has set in the Church, whereas in Ephesians there are only four classes of persons whom God gives to the Church for "the Ministry." In the Church of God there are many who function, yet the four classes of persons mentioned in Ephesians 4 alone take part in the special work of building up the Body of Christ. All the others have their usefulness and services, but only the four classes of persons enumerated in Ephesians are especially used for "the Ministry." . . .

Who are the apostles, then? Apostles are those gifted persons whom God has chosen to be His fitted vessels by sending them out to preach the Word and to build up the Church. They are those gifted ones who have received a special office, they being appointed by God to travel around for the work of the Ministry. Although apostleship is an office, the apostles without doubt have their personal gifts. . . .

The greatest test for a false apostle is money. Whoever is not clear of money and harbors the ulterior motive of gain in his heart is doubtless a false apostle. A false apostle will be one who either seeks for fame or for wealth. In sending relief to the saints in Jerusalem, Paul especially appointed two other brothers to accompany him and his apostolic party: "avoiding this, that any man should blame us in the matter of this bounty which is ministered by us: for we take thought for things honorable, not only in the sight of the Lord, but also in the sight of men" (2 Cor. 8.20–21). All who are greedy of money are false apostles. Whenever money has its hold on us, our work shall cease to be wholly for the Lord. And thus there is the possibility of our turning from being real apostles to becoming false ones! We need to learn how to test those who call themselves apostles and are not, just as the Ephesian believers did. . . .

## *The Holy Spirit's Call*

In the first two verses of Acts 13 we read: "Now there were in the church that was at Antioch certain prophets and teachers; as Barnabas and Simeon that was called Niger, and Lucius of Cyrene, and Manaen, which had been brought up with Herod the tetrarch, and Saul. As they ministered to the Lord, and fasted, the Holy Ghost said, Separate me Barnabas and Saul for the work whereunto I have called them." Let us note a few facts here. There was a local church in Antioch, there were certain prophets and teachers who were ministers in that church, and it was from amongst those that the Holy Spirit separated two for another sphere of service. Barnabas and Saul were two ministers of the Lord already engaged in the Ministry when the call of the Spirit came. The Holy Spirit only sends to other parts such as are already equipped for the Work and are bearing responsibility where they are, not those who are burying their talents and neglecting local needs whilst they dream of some future day when the call will come to special service. Barnabas and Saul were bearing the burden of the local situation when the Spirit put the burden of other parts upon them; their hands were full of local work when He thrust them out to work further afield. Let us note first that the Holy Spirit chooses apostles from amongst the prophets and teachers.

"And as they ministered to the Lord, and fasted, the Holy Ghost said, Separate me Barnabas and Saul for the work whereunto I have called them." These prophets and teachers ministered so wholeheartedly to the Lord, that when occasion demanded they even ignored the legitimate claims of their physical being and fasted. What filled the thoughts of those prophets and teachers at Antioch was ministry to the Lord, not work for Him. Their devotion was to the Lord himself, not to His service. No one can truly work for the Lord who has not first learned to minister to Him. It was while Barnabas and Saul ministered to the Lord that the voice of the Spirit was heard calling them to special service.

It was to the divine call they responded, not to the call of human need. They had heard no reports of man-eaters or head-hunting savages; their compassions had not been stirred by doleful tales of child-marriage, or foot-binding, or opium-smoking. They had heard no voice but the voice of the Spirit; they had seen no claims but the claims of Christ. No appeal had been made to their natural heroism or love of adventure; they knew only one appeal—the appeal of their Lord. It was the lordship of Christ that claimed their service, and it was on His authority alone that they went forth. Their call was a spiritual call, no natural factor entered into it. It was the Holy Spirit who said, "Separate me Barnabas and Saul for the work whereunto I have called them." All spiritual work must begin with the Spirit's call; all divine work must be divinely initiated. The plan conceived for the work may be splendid, the reason adequate, the need urgent, and the man chosen to carry it out may be eminently suitable; but if the Holy Spirit has not said, "Separate me that man for the work to which I have called him," he can never be an apostle. He may be a prophet or a teacher, but he is no apostle. Of old all true apostles were separated by the Holy Ghost for the work to which He called them, and to-day all true apostles must just as surely be set apart for the work by Him. God desires the service of His children, but He makes conscripts, He wants no volunteers. The Work is His, and He is its only legitimate Originator. Human intention, however good, can never take the place of divine initiation. Earnest desires for the salvation of sinners, or the edification of saints, will never qualify a man for God's Work. One qualification, and only one, is necessary—God must send him.

It was the Holy Spirit who said, "Separate me Barnabas and Saul for the work whereunto *I have called them*." Only the divine call can qualify for the apostolic office. In earthly governments there can be no service without commission, and the same holds true in the government of God. The tragedy in Christian work today is that so many of the workers have simply *gone* out, they have not been sent. It is divine commission that constitutes the call to divine work. Personal desire, friendly persuasions, the advice of one's elders and the urge of opportunity—all these are factors on the natural plane, and they can never take the place of a spiritual call. That is something which must be registered in the human spirit by the Spirit of God....

The calling of an apostle is the Holy Spirit speaking directly to the one called; the separating of an apostle is the Holy Spirit speaking indirectly through the fellow-workers of the called one. It is the Holy Spirit who takes the initiative both in the calling and separation of workers; therefore, if the representative brethren of any assembly set men apart for the service of the Lord, they must ask themselves, Are we doing this on our own initiative, or as representing the Spirit of God? If they move without absolute assurance that they are acting on behalf of the Holy Ghost, then the separation of the worker has no spiritual value. They must be able to say of every worker they send forth, He was sent out by the Holy Ghost, not by man. No separation of workers should be done hastily or lightly. It was for this reason that fasting and prayer preceded the sending forth of Barnabas and Saul.

When Barnabas and Saul were separated for the Work there was prayer and fasting and the laying on of hands. The prayer and fasting was not merely in view of the immediate need of clear discernment regarding the will of God, but in view also of the coming need when the apostles would actually go forth. And the laying on of hands was not by way of ordination, for Barnabas and Saul were already ordained by the Holy Ghost; here, as in the Old Testament, it was an expression of the perfect oneness of the two parties represented. It was as though the three sending forth the two said to them: When you two members of the Body of Christ go forth, all the other members go with you. Your going is our going, and your work is our work. The laying on of hands was a testimony to the oneness of the Body of Christ. It meant that those who remained behind were one with those who went forth, and in full sympathy with them; and that, as they went, those at the base pledged themselves to follow them continually with prayerful interest and loving sympathy....

Nowhere did the apostles settle down and assume responsibility for the local church, but in every church they founded they chose from amongst the *local* believers faithful ones upon whom such responsibility could be placed. When they had chosen elders in each church, with prayer and fasting they committed them to the Lord, just as, with prayer and fasting, they themselves had been committed to the Lord by the prophets and teachers when they were sent out on their apostolic ministry. If this committal of elders to the Lord is to be of spiritual value, and no mere official ceremony, a vital knowledge of the Lord will be required on the part of the apostles. It is easy to become so occupied with the problems and needs of the situation, that one instinctively takes the burden upon oneself, even whilst admitting the truth that the Lord is responsible for His own Church. We need to know Christ as Head of His Church in no mere intellectual way if we are to let all its management pass out of *our* hands at the very outset. Only an utter distrust of themselves, and a living trust in God, could enable the early apostles to commit the affairs of every local church into the hands of local men who had but recently come to know the Lord. All who are engaged in apostolic work, and are seeking to follow the example of the first apostles in leaving the churches to the management of the local elders, must be spiritually equipped for the task; for if things pass out of human hands and are not committed in faith to Divine hands, the result will be disaster. Oh, how we need a living faith and a living knowledge of the living God! . . .

In the appointment of elders the apostles did not follow their personal preferences; they only appointed those whom God had already chosen. That is why Paul could say to the elders in Ephesus, "The Holy Ghost hath made you bishops" (Acts 20.28). The apostles did not take the initiative in the matter. They merely established as elders those whom the Holy Spirit *had already* made overseers in the church. In a man-made organization the appointment of an individual to office entitles him to occupy that office; but not so in the Church of God. Everything there is on a spiritual basis, and it is only divine appointment that qualifies a man for office. If the Holy Ghost does not make men bishops, then no apostolic appointment will ever avail to do so. In the Church of God everything is under the sovereignty of the Spirit; man is ruled out. Elders are not men who think themselves capable to control church affairs, or men whom the apostles consider suitable, but men whom the *Holy Ghost* has set to be overseers in the Church. Those whom the Spirit chooses to be shepherds of the flock, to them He also gives grace and gifts to qualify them for spiritual leadership. It is their spiritual call and their spiritual equipment, not their official appointment, that constitutes them elders. In a spiritual sense they are already elders before they hold the position officially, and it is because they actually *are* elders that they are publicly appointed to be elders. In the early Church it was the Holy Spirit who first signified His choice of elders, then the apostles confirmed the choice by appointing them to office. . . .

As we have already observed, the Holy Spirit said, "Separate me Barnabas and Saul for *the Work* whereunto I have called them." The service that followed the apostles' separation, which we generally refer to as their missionary campaigns, the Holy Spirit referred to as "the Work." "The Work" was the object of the Spirit's call, and all that was accomplished by Paul and his associates in after days, all that for which they were responsible, was included in this one term, "the Work." (The term, "the Work," is used in a specific sense in this book, and relates to all that is included in the missionary efforts of the apostles.) . . .

The Work belongs to the apostles, whilst the churches belong to the local believers. The apostles are responsible for the Work in any place, and the church is responsible for all the children of God there. In the matter of church-fellowship the apostles regard themselves as the *brethren* of all the believers in the city, but in the matter of Work, they regard themselves as its personnel, and maintain a distinction between themselves and the church. As members of the Body, they meet for mutual edification with all their fellow-members in the locality; but as ministering members of the Body, their specific ministry constitutes them a group of workers apart from the church. It is wrong for the apostles to interfere with the affairs of the church, but it is equally wrong for the church to interfere with the affairs of the Work. The apostles manage the Work; the elders manage the church. It follows then that we must be clear about our call. Has God called us to be elders, or to be apostles? If elders, then our responsibility is confined to local affairs: if apostles, then our responsibility is extra-local: if elders, then our sphere is the church: if apostles, then our sphere lies beyond the church, in the Work. . . .

### *Responsibility—Spiritual and Official*

Just as the apostles have *spiritual* but no *official* responsibility regarding the church, so the elders, and the whole church, have *spiritual* but no *official* responsibility regarding the Work. It is commendable if a local church seeks to help in the Work; but it is under no official obligation to do so. If the members of the church are spiritual, they cannot but regard the Work of God as their work, in which case they will count it a joy to help in any way. They will recognize that, whilst the official responsibility for the Work rests on the apostles, the spiritual responsibility is shared by all the children of God, and consequently by them. *There is a vast difference between spiritual and official responsibility.* In the matter of official responsibility there are certain prescribed duties, and one is in the wrong if one fails to perform them; but in the matter of spiritual responsibility there are no legal obligations, therefore any neglect of responsibility does not register as an official shortcoming, but it does register a low spiritual state. From an official point of view, the responsibility of the Work rests upon the apostles. If they lack the needed help they cannot demand it, but if the church is spiritual, its members will see the meaning of the Body and will gladly assist in the Work and give towards it. If the church fails in spiritual responsibility the apostles may have difficulties which they should not have, and the church will suffer spiritually. On the other hand, the responsibility of the church rests officially upon the elders, therefore the apostles should not take upon themselves to do anything directly there. They may and should assist the church by their counsel and exhortations, and if the local believers are spiritual they will willingly receive such help; but should they be unspiritual, and in consequence reject the proffered help of the apostles, their failure is spiritual and not official, and the apostles have no option but to leave them to their own resources. The church does not come within the sphere of the Work and is consequently outside the sphere of their authority. Again let us repeat, the churches are local, intensely local: the Work is extra-local, and always extra-local. . . .

The churches in Scripture are intensely local. We never find any federation of churches there; they are all independent units. The position is quite otherwise as regards the workers. Amongst them we find a certain amount of association; we see here a little group, and there another, linked together for the Work. Paul and those with him—as for instance Luke, Silas, Timothy, Titus and Apollos—formed one group; Peter, James and John, and those with them, formed another. One group came out from Antioch, another from Jerusalem. Paul refers to "those who were with me" (Acts 20.34), which indicates that whilst there was no organization of the workers into different missions, still they had their own special associates in the Work. Even in the beginning, when our Lord chose the Twelve, He sent them out two by two. *All* were fellow-workers, but *each* had his special fellow-worker. Such grouping of workers was ordained and ordered by the Lord.

*These apostolic companies were not formed along partisan or doctrinal lines;* they were formed under the sovereignty of the Spirit, who so ordered the circumstances of the different workers as to link them together in the Work. It was not that they were really divided from other workers, but merely that in the Spirit's ordering of their ways, they had not been led into special association with them. It was the Holy Spirit, not men, who said, "Separate me Barnabas *and* Saul." Everything hinged on the sovereignty of the Spirit. The apostolic companies were subject to the will and ordering of the Lord. As we have seen, the Twelve were divided into pairs, but it was not left to their personal discretion to choose their associates, it was the Lord who coupled them together and sent them forth. Each had a special fellow-worker, but that fellow-worker was of the Lord's appointing, not of their choosing. It was not because of natural affinity that they associated specially with some, nor was it because of difference in doctrine or practice that they did not associate specially with others. The deciding factor was *always* the ordering of the Lord.

We recognize that the Lord is the Head of the Church, and that the apostles were the first order "set" by the Lord in the Church (1 Cor. 12.18). Although they were formed into associations, having their special fellow-workers appointed by the Lord, still they had no special name, system, or organization. They did not make a company smaller than the Body to be the basis of their Work; all was on the ground of the Body; therefore, although on account of difference of locality and the providential ordering of their ways, they formed different groups, still they had no organization outside the Body; their Work was always an expression of the ministry of the Body. They were constituted into separate companies, but each company stood on the ground of the Body, expressing the ministry of the Body.

The Lord is the Head of the Body and *not the Head of any organization;* therefore whether we work for a society, a mission, or an institution, and not for the Body alone, we lose the Headship of the Lord. We must see clearly that the Work is the Work of the Body of Christ and that, whilst the Lord did divide His workers into different companies (not different organizations), their Work was always on the ground of the Body. And we must recognize that every individual worker and every company represents the ministry of the Body of Christ, each office held being held in the Body, and for the furtherance of the Work of

God. Then, and only then, can we have one ministry—the upbuilding of the Body of Christ. If we recognized clearly the oneness of the Body, what blessed results we should see! Wherever the principle of the oneness of the Body operates, all possibility of rivalry is ruled out. It does not matter if I decrease and you increase; there will neither be jealousy on my part, nor pride on yours. Once we see that all the Work and all its fruits are for the increase of the Body of Christ, then no man will be counted yours and no man mine; it will not matter then whether you are used or I. All carnal strife amongst the workers of God will be at an end once the Body is clearly seen as the principle of the Work. But life and work in the Body necessitates drastic dealings with the flesh, and that in turn necessitates a deep knowledge of the Cross of Christ. . . .

But in divinely constituted companies of workers there is no organization. Authority *is* exercised amongst them but such authority is spiritual, not official. It is an authority based upon spirituality, an authority which is the outcome of a deep knowledge of the Lord, and intimate fellowship with Him. Spiritual life is the source of such authority. The reason why Paul could direct others was not because of his superior position, but because of his greater spirituality. If he had lost his spirituality, he would have lost his authority. In an organization those who are spiritual do not necessarily hold any office, and those who hold office are not necessarily spiritual; but in Scripture it is otherwise. There it is those who know the Lord who superintend affairs. It is those who are spiritual that direct others, and if those others are spiritual, they will recognize spiritual authority and will submit to it. In an organization its workers are obliged to obey, but in a spiritual association they are not, and from an official point of view no fault can be found with them if they do not obey. In a spiritual association there is no compulsion; direction and submission alike are on the ground of spirituality. . . .

To-day we must learn on the one hand to maintain a right

relationship with our fellow-workers, and on the other hand to be guided by the Holy Spirit. We must maintain both relationships, and also maintain the balance between the two. In the first and second epistles to Timothy there are many passages which illustrate how fellow-workers should co-operate, and how a younger worker should submit to an older. A young Timothy ought to obey the commands of the Holy Spirit, but he ought also to receive the instructions of an elderly Paul. Timothy was sent out by Paul, Timothy was left by Paul at Ephesus, and Timothy obeyed Paul in the Lord. Here is an example for young servants of God. It is most important in His Work to learn how to be led by the Spirit and how, at the same time, to co-operate with our fellow-workers. The responsibility must not be wholly upon Timothy, neither must it rest wholly upon Paul. In the Work Timothy must learn to fit in with Paul, and Paul must also learn to fit in with Timothy. Not only must the younger learn to submit to the instructions of the elder, but the elder must learn how to instruct the younger. The one who is in a position to "leave," or "send," or "persuade" others, must learn not to follow the dictates of his own nature, acting according to personal inclination or desire, for in that case he will make it difficult for those under his authority. Paul must direct Timothy in such a way that he will not find it hard to obey both the Holy Spirit and the Apostle.

However, that does not mean that every company could just go on independently, knowing no relatedness or fellowship with other companies. The principle of the oneness of the Body holds good here as in all other relationships between the children of God. In Scripture we not only see the principle of "the laying on of hands," but also that of giving "the right hands" (Gal. 2.9). The former speaks of *identification:* the latter of *fellowship.* In Antioch hands were laid on Paul and Barnabas; in Jerusalem there was no laying on of hands, but the right hands of fellowship given them by James, Cephas and John. In Antioch the sphere in view was *one* apostolic company, and the point *emphasized* was identification; consequently hands were laid on them. But in Jerusalem the sphere in view was the relationship between *different* apostolic companies, and the point *emphasized* was fellowship, consequently, the right hands were extended to them.

Many are called to work for the Lord, but their sphere of service is not the same, so it follows that their associates cannot be the same. But the various companies must all be identified with the Body, coming under the Headship of the Lord, and having fellowship amongst themselves. There is no laying on of hands between Antioch and Jerusalem, but there is the giving of the right hands of fellowship. So the word of God does not warrant the forming of one central company, neither does it warrant the forming of various scattered, unrelated and isolated companies. There is no one central place for the laying on of hands, nor is there *merely* the laying on of hands and nothing else in any one of the various groups; but amongst them there is also the giving of the right hands of fellowship one to the other. Each company should recognize what God is doing with the other companies and should extend fellowship to them, acknowledging that they are also ministers in the Body. Under the ordering of God they may work in different companies, but all must work as one Body. The extending of the right hands of fellowship implies a recognition that other people are in the Body and we are in fellowship with them, working together in a related way, as becomes functioning members of the same Body. "When they saw that I had been intrusted with the gospel of the uncircumcision . . . and when they perceived the grace that was given unto me, James and Cephas and John, they who were reputed to be pillars, gave to me and Barnabas the right hands of fellowship, that we should go unto the Gentiles, and they unto the circumcision" (Gal. 2.7–9). The unrelated, scattered, disrupted and conflicting organizations in Christendom, which do not recognize the principle of the Body, and do not come under the soverignty and Headship of Christ, are never according to the mind of the Lord. . . .

Here is the most important principle in the Work of God—a worker must not seek to establish a branch of the church from which he goes out, but to establish a church in the locality to which he comes. He does not make the church in the place to which he goes to be an extension of the church in the place from which he comes, but he founds a church in that locality. Wherever he goes, he establishes a church in *that* place. He does not extend the church of his place of origin, but establishes the church in the place of his adoption. Since in Scripture all churches are local, Jerusalem and Antioch can have no branch-churches. We cannot extend one local church to another locality, we can only form a *new* church in that locality. The church which the apostles established in Ephesus is the church in Ephesus: the church which they established in Philippi is the church in Philippi: the churches which they established in other places are the churches of those different places. There is no precedent in Scripture for establishing any other than local churches. It is all right to extend *the* Church of God, but it is all wrong to extend *a* local church of God. What is the place in which I intend to work? It is the church in *that* place I must seek to establish. . . .

This question of finance has most important issues, so let us devote a little time to it. In grace God is the greatest power, but in the world mammon is the greatest. If God's servants do not clearly settle the question of finance, then they leave a vast number of other questions unsettled too. Once the financial problem is solved, it is amazing how many other problems are automatically solved with it. The attitude of Christian workers to financial matters will be a fairly good indication as to whether or not they have been commissioned of God. If the work is of God it will be spiritual, and if the work is spiritual the way of supply will be spiritual. If supplies are not on a spiritual plane then the work itself will speedily drift on to the plane of secular business. If spirituality does not characterize the financial side of the work, then the spirituality of its other departments is merely theoretical. There is no feature of the work that touches practical issues as truly as its finance. You can be theoretical in any other department, but not in that one.

## *The Importance of the Life of Faith*

Every worker, no matter what his ministry, must exercise faith for the meeting of all his personal needs and all the needs of his work. In God's word we read of no worker asking for, or receiving, a salary for his services. Paul made no contract with the church in Ephesus, or with any other church, that he should receive a certain remuneration for a certain period of service. That God's servants should look to human sources for the supply of their needs has no precedent in Scripture. We do read there of a Balaam who sought to make merchandise of his gift of prophecy, but he is denounced in no uncertain terms; and we read also of a Gehazi who sought to make gain of the grace of God, but he was stricken with leprosy for his sin. No servant of God should look to any human agency, whether an individual or a society, for the meeting of his temporal needs. If they can be met by the labour of his own hands, or from a private income, *well and good;* otherwise he should be directly dependent on God alone for their supply, as were the early apostles. The Twelve Apostles sent out by the Lord had no fixed salary, nor had any of the apostles sent out by the Spirit; they simply looked to the Lord to meet all their requirements. The apostles of to-day, like those of the early days, should regard no man as their employer, but should trust Him who has sent them forth to bear the responsibility of all that the doing of His will involves, in temporal as well as spiritual matters. . . .

Faith is a most important factor in God's service, for without it there can be no truly spiritual work; but our faith requires training and strengthening, and material needs are a means used in God's hand toward that end. We may profess to have faith in God for a vast variety of intangible things, and we may deceive ourselves into believing we really trust Him when we have no trust at all, simply because there is nothing concrete to demonstrate our distrust; but when it comes to financial needs, the matter is so practical that the reality of our faith is put to the test at once. If we cannot trust God to supply our temporal needs, then we cannot trust Him to supply our spiritual needs; but if we truly prove His trustworthiness in the very practical realm of material wants, we shall be able also to trust Him when spiritual difficulties arise either in connection with the Work or with our personal lives. What a contradiction it is if we proclaim to others that God is the living God, yet we ourselves dare not trust Him for the meeting of our material needs. . . .

The first question anyone should face who believes himself truly called of God is the financial question. If he cannot look to the Lord alone for the meeting of his daily wants, then he is not qualified to be engaged in His Work, for if he is not financially independent of men, the work cannot be independent of men either. If he cannot trust God for the supply of needed funds, can he trust Him in all the problems and difficulties of the Work? If we are utterly dependent on God for our supplies, then we are responsible to Him alone for our work, and in that case it need not come under human direction. May I advise all who are not prepared for the walk of faith, to continue with their secular duties and not engage in spiritual service? Every worker for God must be able to trust Him.

If we have real faith in God, then we have to bear all the responsibility of our own needs and the needs of the Work. We must not secretly hope for help from some human source. We must have faith in God alone, not in God plus man. If the brethren show their love, let us thank God, but if they do not, let us thank Him still. It is a shameful thing for a servant of God to have one eye on Him and one eye on man or circumstance. It is unworthy of any Christian worker to profess to trust in God and yet hope for help from other sources. This is sheer disbelief. I have constantly said, and say it again, that as soon as our eyes turn to the brethren, we bring disgrace on our fellow-workers and on the Name of the Lord. Our living by faith must be absolutely real, and not deteriorate into a "living by charity." We dare to be utterly independent of men in financial matters, because we dare to believe utterly in God; we dare to cast away all hope in them, because we have full confidence in Him. . . .

From the study of God's word we note two things concerning the attitude of His children to financial matters. On the one hand, workers should be careful to disclose their needs to none but God; on the other hand, the churches should be faithful in remembering the needs both of the workers and their work, and they should not only send gifts to those who are working in their vicinity, or to those who have been called out from their midst, but, like the Philippians and the Macedonians, they should frequently minister to a far-off Paul. The horizon of the churches should be much wider than it is. The present method of a church supporting its own "minister" or its own missionary, was a thing unknown in apostolic days. If, with the present-day facilities for transmitting money to distant parts, the children of God only minister to the material needs of those in their own locality, they certainly lack spiritual insight and largeness of heart. On the part of the workers there must be no expectation from man, and on the part of the churches there should be a faithful remembrance of the Work and the workers both at home and abroad. It is essential to the spiritual life of the churches that they take a practical interest in the Work. *God has no use for an unbelieving worker, nor has He any use for a loveless church.*

—CW, II: 11, 13–4, 18–21, 28, 46, 50–2, 54–5, 72–3, 76, 137, 138–9, 140–1, 159–61, 165, 167–8, 170–2, 175, 181–3, 183–4, 184–5, 195–6

*The Work Is Regional*

Among several things which have been shown to us, the first is *the important principle of region* or area. Whereas the churches are local, the Work, we have come to see, is regional. To us this is something which has become crystal clear from the Scriptures. To put the matter differently, a church is in one locality, whereas for purposes of the Work, many such localities together form one region. . .

### *The Region Has a Center*

We come now to a *second principle.* Each region, we find, has a center; whereas the churches, of course, have no such center. The church in Jerusalem cannot—as a "central church"—rule the church in Samaria. No local church can control another local church, nor can one church control several churches. The widest scope of a church's authority is its locality; no more. There is no such thing as a regional church or an association of churches. The Church has neither regional council nor headquarters. But with the Work it is otherwise. The Work has a region and the region has a center, and that is why in the book of Acts we see Jerusalem as a center and Antioch as another center. . . .

*Hence we have discovered three things:* that the Work is regional, that it operates from divinely chosen centers, and that the movement out is two-fold, by workers who go and return, and by the migration of scattered saints. . . .

In this matter of coordination of the Work, the first principle is authority, as we have seen. The second principle is fellowship.

### *Co-Workers: People to Whom You Can Open Your Heart*

There is a basic need among co-workers for people who work together to be able to open their hearts to one another in real fellowship. Coordination opposes individualism. Coordination is for the sake of body ministry. I serve indeed, yet I serve according to the principle of the body. There must therefore be the kind of fellowship where heart is opened to heart and where there is mutual help given. If one member is honored, the whole body rejoices. If one member suffers, the whole body suffers with it. If one member is sorrowful, the whole body is sorrowful. This is coordination. . . .

### *Whatever We Do Is to Serve God*

If we want to serve, then everything we do must be done for His service. We must give our all. We need to realize that not only *not* making tents is for the sake of being an apostle, even *making* tents can be for that purpose. I therefore hope all who are working as apostles will not upset the priority, and that all who serve God locally will not miss the point. Serving God is our vocation, our basic occupation. Whatever we do is for the purpose of serving Him. Earning money is for the purpose of serving God, and likewise *not* earning money. Devoting all our time is for that purpose, and devoting part of our time can be also. Whichever way we take, we serve God. Even our very life is all given to him. This is how the problem of occupation is to be solved. . . .

—CW, III: 2, 3, 7, 142, 173

# 48 Miscellaneous

*[The Spirit of the Gospel]*

The coming of the Lord Jesus to earth is the casting of the fire of the gospel. He begins with the callings of the twelve and of the seventy to preach the gospel. After He has accomplished the work of redemption by His death, He then commissions His disciples to preach the gospel throughout the world.

With the coming of the Holy Spirit, the church was born and was commissioned to preach the gospel. It is instructive that the four canonical Gospels are placed in the New Testament before the Acts of the Apostles, for the words of the apostles are based on the Gospels. These men not only preach the truth of the gospel but also propagate the spirit of the gospel. Ever since sin entered the world, it has caused great pain to God as well as insurmountable difficulty to men. Even before men were conscious of their being lost, God had sensed the loss of children. With the burden pressed upon His heart, He designed to deliver men out of hell. Because of this love, God sacrificed His only begotten Son in order to gain many sons in us (cf. Heb. 2.10). This fire of love was in Christ. It compelled Him to travel a far distance to this earth to save sinners. This fire of love burned in Him, driving Him to the cross to die for sinners. "Many waters cannot quench love, neither can floods drown it" (S.S. 8.7a). Such love shakes heaven and earth. All who are consumed by this love cannot but cry out, "Woe is unto me if I preach not the gospel" (1 Cor. 9.16b). This fire burned in the apostles enabling them to die by the sword and by being boiled in caldrons of hot oil.

The mark of being filled with the Holy Spirit is defined in one place in Scripture as the act of getting drunk (see Eph. 5.18). Having been saved by the Lord, we cannot but lose our usual cool. The recovery of the church is the recovery of the entire range of God's word. Hence the ministry of the gospel must be recovered. The fire of the gospel must be burning in the church and the gospel must be preached to the ends of the earth before our Lord will return (see Matt. 24.14). That the fire fails to spread abroad is a basic problem. It is because the outward man is not broken. The outward man must be broken; otherwise the gospel will not be able to spread. For the nature of the outward man is opposite to that of the fire. Paul wept for the sake of the gospel. And so did the psalmist of an earlier day: "They that sow in tears shall reap in joy. He that goeth forth and weepeth, bearing seed for sowing, shall doubtless come again with joy, bringing his sheaves with him" (Ps. 126.5-6).

*A need to be gentle, a need to be zealous.* The fire should not be suppressed. There is not much fire in the first place. It will die out if it is suppressed. In preaching the gospel, the spirit of the cross and the spirit of the throne must be present in the meeting.

*Not simply a preaching, but a kindling.* The fire needs to be cast forth from us. We must not think of ourselves. We cannot be lazy. We must weep and cry for the sinners. Our Lord wept over Jerusalem: and such is the spirit of the gospel. The Holy Spirit is the Spirit of Christ, and the Spirit of Christ is the Spirit of the cross. In preaching the gospel of the cross, our whole being is to be the channel by which the fire comes forth. . . .

He who preaches the gospel must be filled with the love of Christ. His eyes will be full of tears. He will shout, for he sees the sufferings of sinners. He will pray to God because of the penalty he knows sinners will one day receive.

The gospel must live and develop in the spirit. If our spirit is usable, a right atmosphere will be created when the gospel is preached.

The love of God is something the world has never known. That Christ died to save is also beyond the reasoning of the world. The gospel is totally new to the world. There is no common ground between the gospel and the world.

Today the spirit of the gospel must burn like fire; otherwise, the gospel will be quenched by sinners. As the mouth is responsible for proclaiming the gospel, so the person is responsible for sending out the spirit of the gospel. The gospel must be like manna which is fresh every day. But for the spirit to launch forth, the outward man needs to be broken.

To send forth the truth of the gospel with the highest thought is but half the work. The other half is to touch sinners with the spirit of the gospel. He who loves himself has used up all his feelings on himself. We should learn to reserve our feeling for the gospel.

Fire need not be big, so long as it burns. The first one to be kindled is yourself. For the sake of the gospel, you need to be beside yourself before God like David of old was. You lay aside shame, glory and pride. All who are zealous in soul-winning are beside themselves for the gospel's sake

—SG 2-4, 12-3

### *Three Enemies*

The Bible tells us we have three different enemies: (1) *the flesh*—in us, (2) *the world*—outside of us, and (3) *Satan*— above and below us. According to the ascended position of the church, Satan is under us.

The Old Testament uses three different tribes to typify these enemies. The Amalekites typify the flesh, which is to be overcome through constant prayer. The Egyptians signify the world, which needs to be buried in the Red Sea. And the Caananites represent the powers of Satan, which must be conquered and destroyed one by one.

The flesh is set against the Holy Spirit: "the flesh lusteth against the Spirit, and the Spirit against the flesh; for these are contrary the one to the other" (Gal. 5.17). The world opposes the Father: "If any man love the world, the love of the Father is not in him" (1 John 2.15). And Satan contends with Christ: "To this end was the Son of God manifested, that he might destroy the works of the devil" (1 John 3.8). We thus see that the flesh is overcome by walking after the Holy Spirit; the world is overcome by loving the Father; and Satan is overcome by believing in Christ.

—GP 49–50

### *[Pressure and Power]*

. . . Let us see what the Bible teaches on the relationship between pressure and power. First of all, I would say that these two are directly proportional to each other. Wherever there is pressure there is also power. If a Christian does not know what pressure is, he has no knowledge of what power is. Only those who have experienced being weighed down under pressure know what power is. The greater the pressure the more power. . . .

Let me ask, how great is your pressure? You can only measure your power by your pressure. The power of steam is measured by the pressure of the boiler. In like manner, the power of a believer can never be greater than the pressure he undergoes. If anyone wants to know how great his power is before God, he ought to understand that it cannot exceed the pressure he receives from God. This is a basic spiritual law.

You as a believer may sometimes pray, "O God, give me power." Do you know what you are actually praying for? If God answers your prayer, He will most certainly put you under pressure. For He knows that the power of life is generated from the pressure of life. A life under pressure is a life with power, whereas a life without pressure is a life without power. Great pressure in life produces great power of life, but little pressure in life results in little power of life. Yet the power under discussion here is the power of life, not the power from other sources.

—FF 68, 70

*[Tears]*

. . . I wonder if you know the significance of tears? It is a good sign if a person is able to shed tears. An individual who had had much experience in spiritual matters once made this statement: Giving your love to a person who cannot shed tears is like handing over your money bag to a thief to keep. This is quite true. A person often feels uneasy about giving his love to one who cannot shed tears. For tears are the one thing that is indispensable in this world. It can rightly be said that a person who is unable to shed tears has lost something of the very essence of man: he can no longer be considered as being human.

I strongly repudiate any man who is so haughty as to condemn tears in men. He may think himself brave for not shedding tears. He may deem himself as nobler and superior to others. But facts just do not bear this out! Let me tell you, a dry eye reveals a dry and hard heart. Such a heart has become rebellious, void of feeling, insensitive as wood and stone. Oftentimes tears betray the true heart condition of a person. It may be said that nothing discloses the inward state of a human heart more than do tears. Let me say from conviction that tears are the outlet of the heart. . . .

Although tears sometimes flow forth out of sheer joy, usually they are caused by extreme sorrow or pressure beyond measure. Tears are shed because the sorrow, sadness, or pressure within us has become unbearable. Nevertheless, a most surprising thing happens at this juncture. As your tears flow, the many burdens within you are suddenly lightened. What was of tremendous importance before is now loosened up. It would appear as though something has gone out of you because of your tears. Otherwise, how could the many burdens inside you have been lessened? How could the pressure built up in you have decreased? Here may we see the meaning of tears. Tears discharge what is in the heart. Tears are the outlet of the heart. . . .

David was brought by God into such depth and had so much

experience because he shed many tears. The profusion of his tears showed the multitude of his sufferings and adversities. Many lessons were learned in distress, just as Romans indicates: "tribulation works endurance" (5.3 Darby). Let us understand that David became what he was partly because of his tears. Had there been no tears to develop him, he would not have been any deeper than the ordinary person. . . .

I would say that in this world tears excel the smile. This world full of sin and perversity is fortunate indeed to have a few drops of tears with which to wash itself; otherwise, this world would probably be far worse. It is fortunate, in this blind and wicked generation, to have a few warm tears to betoken one final trace of human feeling. Were there not even a few tears evident, this world would truly be darker than hell. Due to God's providential care, many beautiful flowers today are watered by tears in the form of rain-drops falling from heaven; or else they would all be withered. . . .

I personally treasure very much this word in 2 Kings 20.5: "I have seen thy tears." Each time we meet a difficult situation which is heartbreaking, distressing, pressed beyond measure and with no way out, we can lift up our heads and drop a few tears before God, for He surely sees. Yet be clear of this, that tears are futile if they are not shed before God. Naturally, there are many people in this world who are prone to weeping. Man's cry simply expresses his own sorrow and distress; it in itself will not produce any positive result. Tears with prayer, however, *is* effective. Every time you cry in distress, why not add to it prayer? You may tell God your sorrow and distress through prayer. The Bible shows us not only the tearful prayer of Hezekiah but also the prayers and supplications of our Lord which came with strong crying and tears (see Heb. 5.7).

Oftentimes it is useless to cry to each other; but if one cries to God it is effective, since God sees one's tears and will hear one's prayer. Indeed, every drop of tears shed before God will be counted by Him—"Thou numberest my wanderings: put thou my tears into thy bottle; are they not in thy book?" (Ps. 56.8) Please note that such is the advantage of having tears before God. O sorrowful heart, if life makes you suffer, and you are pressed beyond measure, passing your days in misery, and weary in battling many problems, why not cry before God? Let me tell you, this will never never fail. God will record the tears you shed each time. He will put them in His bottle, which means He will remember all your sufferings. Thank God, our tears do not fall to the ground and mix with the dust; rather, they are stored in God's bottle of remembrance; for are they not in His record-books? God will not forget; He will always remember our tears. . . .

For this reason, each one who works for the Lord must have experience in tears. Whenever you see a brother fall or defeated you are not worthy to do the Lord's work nor worthy to either reprimand or persuade if you shed no tears. Before you chide a brother or a sister, before you tell him his error, you first must be afflicted and hurt by the sharpness of the words to be spoken. Only in this way are you qualified. How easy it is to speak of people's weakness, but how hard to speak it with tears. Yet only the person who has tears is ever really qualified to speak.

Thank God, the blood of His Son once fallen to the ground has never turned back, so that people may still be saved through its efficacy. Thank God, too, that the *tears* of His Son have not turned back either, so that we today may know His heart of concern and learn to shed tears before God and men. Let us follow the footsteps of our Lord and shed some more tears in our prayer and work. . . .

### *[Temper]*

The Lord exhorts us to deny ourselves. He wants us to learn to be self-denying people. It is obvious that a man who is willing to deny himself and to lay down his personal rights will not lose his temper. The reason for losing temper is self-seeking. If a person does not strive for himself, he will hardly lose his temper. We who are children of God ought to deny rather than preserve ourselves.

Sometimes people are really unreasonable towards us and many things done to us are truly irritating, but the Bible informs us that love "is not provoked" (1 Cor. 13.5). And the Lord shows us at the same time that we ought to bear with one another. If the Lord allows anything to come our way, He will certainly enable us to bear with it. The Lord's command is that our Christian life be a life of patience and endurance. If we endure, there is no possibility of losing our temper. . . .

This matter of losing one's temper is a considerably big problem to us, yet in the Bible we are not even able to find the word "temper." What we view as a most common fault seems to be ignored completely in the Bible. Why? Because *the losing of temper is a symptom, not a disease.* Disease and symptom are two different things. A person may have appendicitis—and this is a disease. His fever runs high—but this is a symptom. The symptom is caused by the disease. It is futile to treat only the symptom without treating the disease as well. The fever may subside temporarily, but it will return if the disease is still present. Losing control of temper is not a disease, it is a symptom. Hence we must search out the source of the disease. If the root is found and eliminated, the symptom will quite naturally disappear. Should we mistake the loss of temper as a disease, we miss the way; and no wonder, then, that we cannot solve the problem. . . .

What, then, is the root of the disease which causes the symptom of losing the temper? There is a simple answer: losing the temper has to do with one's "self." A person's search for a solution ends at the wrong place if he does not deal with his own self but instead thinks of dealing with his temper. He loses his temper because of his own self. *That self of his is his disease,* his temper is not at all his disease. Due to the fact of this self, there is the outburst of such temper. If his self is being dealt with before God, his temper will naturally fade away. For this reason, the Bible pays attention to the self rather than to the temper. Were the problem of self solved, the problem of temper would automatically be solved also. If the basic problem of self is not solved, the secondary problem of temper will not be solved either.

As to this "self," let us look into several of its characteristics. *First,* some people are highly subjective. A subjective person must be full of self. He has his opinion on every matter, and he has his conviction on every subject. He considers his own opinion and conviction as infallible. And he insists on seeing his own idea adopted. He cannot tolerate any obstruction or frustration or rejection. His view must be accepted and his opinion must be carried through. If on any day his opinion is not respected and his view not adopted, his subjectiveness is unable to bear with it. And what will be the outcome? He will lose his temper and be thrown into a fit. . . .

*Second,* some people lose their temper because they deem themselves to be extraordinary and look upon themselves as superior. In short, they are proud. The proud not only think highly of their own selves but also desire others to admire them and look up to them. They are never satisfied with their speaking good of themselves; they want other people to praise them too. In other words, the "self" of the proud will not stop at themselves but will try to extend such self-exaltation through others. They wish to be admired and exalted by all the brothers and sisters. If any brother should come to them and fail to discover how valuable and important they are, or what spiritual position or high spirituality they have, they will feel hurt and their temper will break lose. What causes the temper? Pride of self. People show bad temper because they are proud. *If you get rid of your pride you will get rid of your temper.* How impossible it is to try getting rid of your temper without getting rid of your pride. *The root of temper is pride.*

*Third,* in the very concept of self-exaltation is the thought that no one else could be as high as one's own self. A person will expect himself to rise higher while expecting others not to rise at all. He anticipates gain for himself but not for other people. He rejoices at others' failure and grieves at peoples' success. This concept is called jealousy. Such jealousy is evident in spiritual affairs as well as in worldly affairs. The proud is pleased with his brother's fall but is unhappy with his brother's progress. Such an attitude is the meanest of all attitudes; there is no mentality lower than this one. If a person delights in another's fall, he shares the attitude of Satan, for Satan loves to see people fall. How shameful it is for God's children to harbor Satan's feeling! To be happy rather than burdened over the stumbling of a brother is the most despicable and vilest of all feelings. . . .

*Fourth,* some people show their self in another area—that is, self-love, the loving of one's own self. Among so many people, the one he loves most will be his own self. The center of attention and affection is himself. He considers himself to be the most important person in eating and lodging and in all the affairs of life. He hopes his profit will increase, and that he will be more comfortable. All his thoughts are woven around his own self. He is aware of only himself and treasures himself dearly. If he encounters anything that would cause discomfort to him, he will respond with an outbreak of temper. Many lose their temper because their self-love is wounded. . . .

*Fifth,* some brothers and sisters love themselves to such a degree that they look only to their own things and have no concern or interest for the things of others. They have no desire to help other people. All their deeds and thoughts are centered upon their own selves. They themselves are the most important persons in the world, and their affairs are the most urgent. For a person whose thoughts and deeds are all for himself and who is always busily occupied with his own self, how will he have the leisure for other people? If someone should come and seek him out too much, he will feel annoyed, and his temper will break out. This is because all his activities are centered on himself, so that he has no sympathy for anybody else. He loves his own self so much that he has no time to sympathize with other people. He is so busy with himself that he has no strength to bear the sufferings of others. Many lose their temper simply because of the intrusion by others upon their self-centered love. They are irritated, agitated, and therefore blow up. . . .

*Sixth,* some people not only love their own selves, they also have another kind of love, which is, that they love things, they love money. This kind of people has never been delivered from things or wealth. To them goods and money are precious. Their "self" is a self which loves material things. Their self is expressed in loving these things. If any one thing belonging to such a person should be overturned, broken, or lost by other people, he cannot keep back his temper. His self is being wounded, his love of things is being hurt; therefore, he is bound to blow up. . . .

To sum up, then, temper comes from within one's self. Whoever loses his temper only proves that one specific area or several areas of his self has or have not been dealt with. Whether or not the problem of the temper is solved depends on how much one's self is being dealt with before God. The deeper his self is taken care of, the greater is his deliverance from temper. If his self is not dealt with, his temper will remain with him. Do not be so foolish as to treat the temper only. Let us always remember that the problem of self is much deeper than that of the temper. With self left undealt with, the matter of the temper will never be solved. In the process of learning, we receive enlightenment which causes us to see, on the one hand, the actual conditions of our "self," and, on the other hand, God's mercy in making all sorts of arrangements in our circumstances. When things begin to come to us, one after another, and if we have learned anything before God, we will bow our heads and say to the Lord: "Lord, what You have arranged is the best. Your way in dealing with my self is the best. I submit and I accept." Thus shall we find the impossibility of losing the temper. . . .

*[Tongue]*

"He that guardeth his mouth keepeth his life; but he that openeth wide his lips shall have destruction" (Prov. 13.3). We dare not rule dogmatically either way that when Solomon wrote this proverb he was referring to physical life or to spiritual life. But we may take its principle and apply it to the spiritual realm. This word shows us one thing, which is, that a person who seeks the Lord and who desires to supply the church with the life he receives must be careful in word. If he is not careful in word his life will leak away. Why is it that some people are not of much use in God's hand? It is because there has been a leakage of life. You can only touch death and not life in them because life has been drained away through their words. Because of this, we need to guard our mouth—and guard it vigilantly—before the Lord. Many stories can be told how an idle word drains away life more than does anything else. This does not imply that sin is better than an idle word. But we can say that aside from sin what dissipates life most is our idle word.

"Every idle word that men shall speak, they shall give account thereof in the day of judgment" (Matt. 12.36). Does the Lord here speak of an unclean word? No. Does He here speak of a slanderous word? Not at all. Of an evil word? Again, the answer is no. What is spoken of here is an *idle* word. Idle words are superfluous words, irrelevant words, unnecessary words, or words of rumor which cause dispute. "They shall give account thereof in the day of judgment. For by thy words thou shalt be justified, and by thy words thou shalt be condemned" (v.36b,37). This is what the Lord Jesus has said. May we see the seriousness of *idle* words as well as slanderous words. Not only the speaking of unclean words is grave, the speaking of idle words is also of solemn significance. In the case of certain things and particular sins we are able to make some kind of restitution; but there are other things and other sins which cannot be recompensed at all. How can you make amends for idle words spoken against people? You may go to the person and confess your sin, you may say to that person that you take back your words; but their sound has already entered people's ears and no way is available to eliminate it. You may reimburse someone for things stolen, but by what means can you repay the damage done through idle words? Such a sin will be presented before God. Hence the Lord says: "Every idle word that men shall speak, they shall give account thereof in the day of judgment. For by thy words thou shalt be justified, and by thy words thou shalt be condemned."

"A gentle tongue is a tree of life; but perverseness therein is a breaking of the spirit" (Prov. 15.4). "Gentle" is a not being overheated; it is being moderate and proper in tone. With much speaking, the tongue becomes heated; and when the tongue gets overheated, there is no more tree of life. Only a *gentle* tongue is a tree of life. A gentle tongue is one that is neither hasty nor foolish nor babbling. Such a tongue is like a tree of life. You cannot smell the fragrance of Christ in a Christian who loves to chatter with idle words. He who delights in speaking idly is unable to supply others with life. For an idle word is but the creation of a big opening through which your life is leaked away.

Knowing that an idle word is a dissipation of life, what should we do about it? In order to guard our mouth we need first to deal with our heart. "For out of the abundance of the heart the mouth speaketh," says the Lord. The mouth utters whatever is in the heart. If you have something in your heart, your mouth sooner or later will express it. If you do not say it here, you will say it there: if not in this house, then it will be in another house. What the heart is filled with, that the mouth will spill out. Consequently, learning not to say idle words before God must begin with the dealing of the heart. If your heart is not dealt with, neither will your mouth ever be dealt with. For out of all the various things that fill the heart the mouth speaks them forth. Never excuse yourself by saying that you are a person who speaks without your heart being in it. Judging by the word of the Lord Jesus, there simply is no such possibility. With the mouth comes the heart. The mouth merely expresses what is in the heart. Hence the heart must be dealt with before the mouth can truly be dealt with.

—PI 1–2, 8–9, 11, 13, 20–2, 28–9, 38, 40–1, 41–2, 43–4, 45, 46, 47, 48, 49–50, 54–7

### *The Offence of the Lord*

On one occasion, involving John the Baptist, the Lord said. "blessed is he, whosoever shall find no occasion of stumbling in me" (Matt. 11.6). In Darby's version it reads: "blessed is whosoever shall not be offended in me." What does this mean? It means that we do not like what the Lord does. And from our perspective we have good reason for not liking it. In our own eyes we ought to be offended. *That* is the offence of the Lord. What the Lord did or did not do caused John the Baptist to be offended. John was not offended by the Pharisees or the publicans, but by the Lord. And from his standpoint he had reason to be offended.

Why was he offended? He had hoped that Israel would be restored as a nation—that the kingdom would be re-established in justice and righteousness. He had hoped the Lord would bring in a revival. The first Elijah had gone up to Mount Carmel and had wrought mightily. Israel was revived and Elijah's ministry vindicated. But the second Elijah, John the Baptist (see Matt. 17.9–13), was put into prison and was soon to be killed, and yet no national restoration was in sight. So John sent a message to the Lord, because he was greatly offended. He thought, if *I* am not to accomplish anything, then surely *You,* Lord, are to do so! *You* ought to do something! Couched in a sting of rebuke, John's message to Jesus was: "Art thou he that cometh, or look we for another?" (Matt. 11.3) He wanted something done by the Lord by which to demonstrate who he, John, was. From John's viewpoint, nothing had been done thus far by Jesus to show who he indeed was, and thus nothing done by which to vindicate his ministry which had now by his imprisonment come to an end.

To "not be offended in me" is not to be offended by what the Lord does or does not do. We feel the Lord does not do what we want, what we feel He ought to do—that He does not vindicate us. Are we pleased with the *way* of the Lord with us? This is not just a matter of knowing and doing God's will, but a matter of whether or not we *like His ways.* Often we *can* do God's will, even though we may do it weeping; even so, we are offended by the way He does things. We are offended with His way, His road, His method, and so forth. And thus it would seem as if we have a legitimate reason to be displeased.

This has nothing to do with our Lord's dealings with our flesh, our sacrifice, and so on. For such dealings are on a far lower plane. But I am here speaking of those who have been brought to a place where the *whole* heart is for God, such as was the case with John the Baptist. We have sought to know His will; we have sought nothing for ourselves; we only want glory for God alone; and yet, in many of God's ways with us, we are disappointed. For example, we have come to a great difficulty, and yet no way through is opened up; we are ill and expect Him to heal us, and yet we are not healed; we are weak, and yet no strength is given; we are short of money, and yet no money comes. It seems as if God does not measure up to our expectations of Him. When such happens again and again, this is what we call "the offence of the Lord." Many people lack the qualifications to be offended by the Lord. On the contrary, their fall is because of the flesh and the world. When the Lord seems to disappoint them it is *they* who have been wrong, and they know and ultimately acknowledge it.

Not to be offended in the Lord is the highest and deepest form of discipline. Often we feel the Lord *must* come in because of His testimony, because His honor and His faithfulness are at stake; yet He does *not* come in. God led the children of Israel out of Egypt, and then they were pursued. They got to a place where they were shut in by the enemy from behind, mountains were to the right and left, and the Red Sea was in front. But then God opened a way through the sea. So whenever we too get to the place where we are shut in, we always expect God to open a way through for us; yet often He does not do so: the prison gates do not open, the money does not come, the situation is not dealt with. Nevertheless, just here lies the test. Those who love the ways of the Lord can look up and say, "You were not pleased for us to die in Egypt, but You are pleased for us to die near the Red Sea. Whether the Red Sea opens or not we are content, we are glad."

Madame Guyon once said, "I believe God more than His word." Even though God does not seem to keep His promise, we believe Him in spite of that. Now *this* is to not be offended in the Lord.

When there has been an utter consecration, more than when we are saved, more than when we give ourselves to His service—when there is a mighty consecration, an awesome devotion to Him—it is when we get to *that* place, that *then* we expect God to do something for us. If we have such an utterness towards the Lord, then we have a great expectancy. (If, of course, we have not got to that stage, we can explain away much of everything which happens to us on the ground of our *own* weakness—that it is because *we* were wrong or mistaken, etc., etc.) But if we get to that place of utterness with the Lord just now described wherein we expect to see God's deliverance and yet He does not come in, wherein we feel we have a *right* for God to do such and such and He does not do it—*that* is the offence of the Lord of which we have been speaking. Yet it is those who are not offended who are blessed. We need, therefore, to get to a point where we have a liking *for His ways,* where we can say: "If You, Lord, (I state it reverently here) act according to Your promise, good; but if not, it is also good."

There will indeed come a day when all things shall be explained and we shall *see* that God was right. At the present moment, however, His ways are much higher than our ways, and so we at times cannot see and understand. But when we stand before the judgment seat, not only will it be the occasion at which we shall be judged, it will also be the occasion at which God (again, I reverently state it) will have to explain things to us. There will be many cases in which I thought I was right but I was wrong, yet there will also be other cases about which God will say, "I was right, but you were right also." . . .

*[The Limitations of God]*

How does it come about that the omnipotence of God becomes limited by man? And will limitation be continued for eternity? We find in the word of God that in eternity past and eternity to come God is omnipotent and is not subject to limitation. But in the eternal purpose of God, He wants a people to share the life of His own Son and to manifest His Son. In order to bring this about, He created man, a free-willed being; and then the limitation of God began. There are now three wills at work, the Divine, the satanic and the human. God will not destroy the human will. He wants the will of the creature to be put on His side instead of on the side of Satan, and so He has accepted a position of limitation. If man is not on the side of God, God cannot do anything with him. God will not compel him to do anything.

But God is working toward a goal. There is One whose will is absolutely identified with the Father's. There is One who will not limit God; and by His death and resurrection His life is imparted to us. A Body is being formed by the power of the Spirit, and God is looking to the members of the Body to function in such a way that they will not limit Him—they will be responsive to Him; and in this new creation, identified with His will, His limitations will be for ever put out of the way. God will be able to go back to His omnipotence without limitation. We must first come to the place where God has a free way in us, before He can bring the whole creation back to that. The Church is a first fruit in God's creation [see James 1.18], so what is going to be true universally in the kingdom-age should be true at least of the overcoming company of the people of God today.

What is the kingdom? "Thy will be done in earth, as it is in heaven" [see Matt. 6.10]. That means that there will be no human will coming out to limit Him. When the question of the will is settled, then the question of power is also settled. What is the secret of really serving the Lord? It is not doing a hundred and one things for the Lord. Service is really submission to the Lord—knowing the true meaning of that word, "to obey is better than sacrifice" [1 Sam. 15.22b]. Abraham was one who obeyed God's voice; and the Lord is after such utter responsiveness to himself, so that He can have a free way unhindered.

—WG 55-9, 86-7

### *God's Skilled Craftsmen*

The calling of God is a distinctive calling. In some degree at least, this statement is true of all whom He calls. Their commissioning is always personal; it never stops at being general—to all men. "It was the good pleasure of God," says Paul, "to reveal His Son in *me*."

Moreover its object is always precise; never merely haphazard or undefined. By this I mean that, when God commits to you or me a ministry, He does so not merely to occupy us in His service, but always to accomplish through each of us something definite towards the attaining of His goal. It is of course true that there is a general commission to His Church to "make disciples of all the nations"; but to any one of us, God's charge represents, and must always represent, a personal trust. He calls us to serve Him in the sphere of His choice, whether to confront His people with some special aspect of the fullness of Christ, or in some other particular relation to the divine plan. To some degree at least, every ministry should be in that sense a specific ministry.

It follows from this that, since God does not call each of His servants to precisely identical tasks, neither does He use precisely identical means for their preparation. As the Lord of all operations, God retains the right to use particular forms of discipline or training, and often, too, the added test of suffering, as means to His end. For His goal is a ministry that is not merely common or general, but rather, one specially designed for the service of His people in a given hour. To the servant himself, such a ministry must become peculiarly his own—something to be specially expressed because specially experienced. It is personal because it is firsthand; and it cannot be escaped because, in so far as it directly relates to the purpose of God, that purpose itself demands that it be fulfilled.

Every Spirit-taught reader of the New Testament will have noticed something of this. In its pages we can, I think, recognize at least three such distinctive emphases in ministry, represented by the particular historic contributions of three leading apostles. These three men, while certainly having very much in common, nevertheless display, at certain points in the record, differences of emphasis sufficiently striking to suggest that something quite original was being committed by God to each of them. I allude, of course, to the special contributions of Peter, Paul and John. In the New Testament it is, I suggest, possible to trace three lines of thought, expressed no doubt in varying measure by all the apostles, but specially defined and illustrated by the unique contributions of these three in particular.

It will be seen that the distinctiveness of their three ministries is in part chronological, each apostle bringing, in the course of the history, his own fresh and timely emphasis to the fore. Moreover, it is certainly never such as to set the three men apart from or in conflict with one another, for what each one has is not something opposed, but rather, complementary to what the others have got. And perhaps, too, the difference between them lies less in their ministry as a whole than in what is recorded of it for our instruction. Yet I think it can be shown that the Petrine, the Pauline and the Johannine strands or themes running through the Scriptures indicate three main historic emphases given by God to His people for all time. All the many and diverse ministries of the New Testament—those for example of Philip and Barnabas, Silas and Apollos, Timothy and James—together with the countless more that should follow in history, contain in differing proportions the distinctive elements of these three. It will be well, therefore, if we seek to understand what God is saying to us through the experiences of these three typical men and this will be the aim of our present study.

### "CASTING A NET INTO THE SEA"

We begin with Peter. It is generally held that Mark, in writing his Gospel, was placing on record what were in fact Peter's recollections of the Lord. Added to these we have Peter's own Epistles, and of course the incidents of his life recorded by the other Evangelists in the four Gospels and the book of the Acts. These together form the special contribution of Peter. What, then, was his ministry? Well, his Epistles certainly indicate to us how widely representative it was of all that made up the work of an apostle; but in the narrative passages one thing perhaps stands out above others. It is the thing to which I think the Lord drew special attention when, in calling him to follow, He used the term "fishers of men." That was to be Peter's distinctive task, and the one that fell first to him. He was to bring men, urgently and in great numbers, into the kingdom. Further on in the story Jesus reaffirmed this, when, at Caesarea Philippi, Peter had confessed Him to be the Christ of God. The Lord would build His Church, and Peter might later be called to a pastoral ministry of "feeding His sheep" therein; but, in relation to that Church, Jesus' first words to him were: "I will give unto thee the keys of the kingdom of heaven."

A key implies, among other things, an entry, a beginning. You come in by a door, and you use a key for opening it, or for letting others in. In the outcome, Peter's ministry often issued in such a beginning of things, and his was in fact the first to do so. The Church in Jerusalem began when three thousand souls received his word, and the church in Caesarea began when, in his presence, the Holy Spirit fell on Cornelius and his household. Thus we may say that, when Peter stood up with the eleven, he opened the door to the Jews, and when later he preached

Christ in that Roman home, he opened it again to the Gentiles. So although on neither occasion Peter was alone, for the commission extends always to others beside him, and although later on we find that Paul too was a man chosen of God to have a still wider ministry of the gospel among the Gentiles, yet in a true sense Peter was the pioneer. Historically he held the key and he opened the door. His task was to initiate something. He was ordained by God to make the beginnings.

The burden of Peter's message was salvation—a salvation not for its own sake, but always with a view to the kingdom in fullness, and in relation to Jesus, its exalted King. Yet when first he preached the kingdom it was inevitably to lay stress, not upon its other aspects, but upon the beginning. It was to emphasize the keys, and their function of introducing the kingdom to men. It may be more than a coincidence that this was, as we have said, in keeping with the details of his own call. For Peter was called under circumstances quite different from Paul, and even, as we shall see, from John. Since those circumstances are recorded for us in Scripture, we should not discount them as fortuitous. They are worthy of notice.

Peter, we are told, was called while engaged in the main skill of his trade, namely, "casting a net into the sea." That occupation seems (speaking figuratively) to have given character to his ministry throughout his life. He was to be first and foremost an evangelist: one who starts something by "taking men alive." By casting a net you draw in fish—all sorts of fish. That is Peter; and without for one moment forgetting the wider range of what he did and wrote, it is nevertheless true to say that the main emphasis of what is recorded of his active ministry is placed there.

### "THEY WERE TENTMAKERS"

We come next to Paul. He is a servant of the Lord, but he is a different one. No one would suggest that Paul did not preach the gospel. Of course he did. To have done otherwise would have been to repudiate the pioneer work of Peter and throw away the ground gained by him. Do not let us make the mistake of thinking there was some basic conflict between the ministries of these two men, or that the ministries of God's servants should ever be in conflict. Paul makes it clear, in writing to the Galatians, that such differences as there were related to geography and race, and that in essence their tasks were complementary, not only by mutual consent, but in their value to and attestation by God (Gal. 2.7–12).

But the point is that there came a day when Paul was required to go further. Whereas Peter initiated things, Paul's task was to construct. God entrusted to him in a special way the work of building His Church, or in other words, the task of presenting Christ in His fullness to men, and of bringing those men *as one* into all that God had in His mind for them in Christ. Paul had glimpsed that heavenly reality in all its greatness, and his commission was to build together the gathered people of God, according to that reality.

Let me illustrate. You recall the vision that was granted to Peter before he set out to go to the Gentiles in Caesarea. He saw a sheet coming down out of heaven, held by the four corners and containing every kind of beast, clean and unclean. That vision signified the inclusive and universal intention of the gospel. It is directed *to every creature*. And that, again, is Peter first and foremost. His ministry is a ministry with a sheet—or a net, if you like—putting something of everything into it. It is God-ordained, for it comes to him "out of heaven." His commission from God, renewed and interpreted here at Joppa, was to bring as many as possible of every kind to the Savior.

But our brother Paul is different in this, that he is not a man holding a sheet; he is a tentmaker. The sheet of Peter's vision—again I speak figurativly—becomes in Paul's hand a tent. What do I mean? I mean this, that a sheet is something as yet without form; is not yet "made up" into anything. But now Paul comes onto the scene as a tentmaker, and under the direction of the Spirit of God—under the constraint of a vision that, equally with Peter's, came to him out of heaven (2 Cor. 12.2–4; Eph. 3.2–10)—

he gives that formless "sheet" a form and a meaning. He becomes, by God's sovereign grace, a builder of the House of God. . . .

## "MENDING THEIR NETS"

The ministry of John is quite different from that of Peter. John was not personally or uniquely commissioned, as was Peter, to originate something. So far as our record tells us, the Lord only used him at the beginning *alongside* Peter. Nor is he shown to have been entrusted in any distinctive way with the task of making known the mystery of the Church. No doubt he was as concerned as were the other apostles in its foundation (Eph. 2.20), but in this too his calling was in no sense unique. Doctrinally he has nothing to add to the revelation given through Paul. In Paul's ministry the things of God reach a climax, an absolute, and you cannot improve on that. Paul's concern is with the full realization of divine counsels that had been formed in the Godhead before the foundation of the world. Those counsels in His Son—that plan for man's redemption and glory—God had caused to be unfolded age by age, glimpse by glimpse, until at last, in this special age of grace, it was made fully manifest in the birth and death, resurrection and exaltation, of His Christ. The presentation of that plan in its wholeness, and the bringing of it to full realization in the people of God, was Paul's special burden. His task was to express, for the benefit of us all, something coming out of the very heart of God—something from the eternities, now brought to light in time. To improve, therefore, on what God entrusted to Paul, you would have to improve on God, and that is inconceivable. The divine plan is absolute.

Then why to Paul add John? What need is there for this further ministry? The answer is that, at the end of the New Testament period, the enemy of souls found entry into the house of God, and caused God's own people, the very heirs of redemption themselves, to turn aside from His ways. Even those entrusted with the "Ephesian" vision failed and fell away, and indeed the church in Ephesus was foremost in that failure. If you compare the first epistle to the Ephesians with the second epistle to the Ephesians—that of Paul with that of Jesus through John (Rev.2.1–7)—the two letters show you where these people are. Something terrible has happened; and now John is brought in and commissioned—for what? Not to lead further, but to restore. You will find that, throughout the New Testament, the ministry of John is always restorative. He does not say anything startlingly new and original. He does not introduce anything further (though it is true that in the Apocalypse he carries what has already been given to its consummation). What distinguishes John, whether in Gospel, Epistles or Revelation, is his concern to bring the people of God back to a position they have lost.

Once more, this is in keeping with the circumstances of John's call to be a disciple. Peter was called to follow when he was casting a net into the sea; Paul was (presumably) already by trade a tent-maker when God named him a "chosen vessel unto me"; and John was called quite differently again. Like Peter, John was a fisherman, but unlike him he was not in the boat but on the shore of the lake at the moment of his call, and we are told that he and his brother were "mending their nets." When you set yourself to mend something, you seek to bring it back to its original condition. Something has been damaged or lost, and your task is to repair and recover it; and that is the special ministry of John. He is always bringing us back to God's original. . . .

So we have before us these three representative men. We have Peter, concerned first, with the ingathering of souls; we have Paul, the wise masterbuilder, building according to the heavenly vision given to him; and then, when failure threatens, we have John introduced to reaffirm that there is an original purpose still in view, and one that, in the mind of God, has never been abandoned. There is still something which He intends to fulfill and from that intention He will never be deflected.

The practical point of what we have been saying is this, that it takes these three complementary and interrelated ministries to make the Church perfect. It takes the ministry of Peter to initiate things in any given situation; it takes the ministry of Paul to build upon that beginning; and it takes the ministry of John to bring things back, where that has become necessary, into line with God's original intention. Few will deny that the need of each of these three ministries is with us today or that the third, that of recovery, is perhaps the greatest need of all in this closing period of the age. . . .

## "CALCULATING THAT GOD HAD CALLED US"

We must now consider this matter of divine committal to the Church along three lines—those of guidance, discipline, and prayer. God has made a threefold provision for our guidance in the Christian pathway: we have the Holy Spirit, we have the word of God, and we have the Body of Christ. The word of God shows me the will of God for me; the Holy Spirit reveals the will of God in me; the Body, by putting that will into the larger perspective of the divine purpose, shows me how it is to affect my relationships as a member. . . . Unhappily, because of our reaction against the tyranny of Rome which has made so much of the political world-Church, we are inclined to discard altogether the third of these divine gifts. But every error arises out of a distortion of truth. The truth here is that the Body *is* one, and that fellowship in the Body remains an essential factor in my spiritual illumination. I must know the mind of God, not only by the word of God to me, nor yet alone by the Spirit of God in me, but together with both of these, by taking also my place among God's people in His house.

We would all agree that there is such a thing as individual prayer and there is also such a thing as Church prayer. But equally there is such a thing as light given to the individual and there is also such a thing as light given to the Church. Is it not true that, without the nature of our problem being known to anyone, we often receive light in a church meeting that we cannot discover at home with the Word? Why is this? Surely because the Church is the House of God, the place of manifestation of divine light. Outside we may have the light of nature, but in the sanctuary there is no light, natural or artificial, save the Shekinah of God himself.

This principle of fellowship in guidance was one of the foundations of Paul's life and ministry. We see it in Acts 13, where, as with several others he is found waiting on the Lord, the Holy Spirit says to them "Separate me Barnabas and Saul for the work whereunto I have called them." We said earlier that the anointing of the Spirit is given for the personal guidance of every individual believer, and in keeping with this, we know that on at least two occasions Saul had earlier received a personal call of God to go to the Gentiles (Acts 26.16–18; 22.21). But now the time and way of that leading forth is revealed to several together. Luke says "they sent them away," but he also describes them as "sent forth by the Holy Ghost" (13.3–4). Here we have the Church and the Spirit acting in conjunction, the initiative of the one Spirit being expressed in the one Body.

Again, at the end of chapter 15 we find Paul and Silas being "commended by the brethren to the grace of the Lord" as they set out for Syria and Cilicia. Though it is never safe to argue from silence, it may be significant that the going forth of Barnabas to Cyprus, which is not covered by a similar statement of commissioning by the Church but seems to have been a more personal move, takes him also at that point out of the Scripture record (verses 36–41).

A little later, in Troas, a vision appeared to Paul: "Come over into Macedonia and help us," and after describing it Luke goes on: "We sought to go forth . . . concluding that God had called us to preach the gospel unto them" (16.9–10). The Lord often gives a vision to an individual, but the movement is not based on that individual alone. It is based on a corporate seeking of God. And in this passage too it is the Holy Spirit who takes the initiative (verses 6–7). It is because we move with the Holy Spirit that we are found moving with the Body. The real test of the vision will always be that the Spirit of truth witnesses to it.

—WSM 9–13, 16–8, 18, 134–6

## *Our Dual Problem: Sins and Sin*

The first eight chapters of Romans form a self-contained unit. The four-and-a-half chapters from 1.1 to 5.11 form the first half of this unit and the three-and-a-half chapters from 5.12 to 8.39 the second half. A careful reading will show us that the subject matter of the two halves is not the same. For example, in the argument of the first section we find the plural word "sins" given prominence. In the second section, however, this is changed, for while the word "sins" hardly occurs once, the singular word "sin" is used again and again and is the subject mainly dealt with. Why is this?

It is because in the first section it is a question of the sins I have committed before God, which are many and can be enumerated, whereas in the second it is a question of sin as a principle working in me. No matter how many sins I commit, it is always the one sin principle that leads to them. I need forgiveness for my sins, but I need also deliverance from the power of sin. The former touches my conscience, the latter my life. I may receive forgiveness for all my sins, but because of my sin I have, even then, no abiding peace of mind.

When God's light first shines into my heart my one cry is for forgiveness, for I realize I have committed sins before Him; but when once I have received forgiveness of sins I make a new discovery, namely, the discovery of sin, and I realize not only that I have committed sins before God but that there is something wrong within. I discover that I have the nature of a sinner. There is an inward inclination to sin, a power within that draws to sin. When that power breaks out I commit sins. I may seek and receive forgiveness, but then I sin once more. So life goes on in a vicious circle of sinning and being forgiven and then sinning again. I appreciate the blessed fact of God's forgiveness, but I want something more than that: I want deliverance. I need forgiveness for what I have done, but I need also deliverance from what I am.

### *God's Dual Remedy: the Blood and the Cross*

Thus in the first eight chapters of Romans two aspects of salvation are presented to us: firstly, the forgiveness of our sins, and secondly, our deliverance from sin. But now, in keeping with this fact, we must notice a further difference.

In the first part of Romans 1 to 8, we twice have reference to the blood of the Lord Jesus, in chapter 3.25 and in chapter 5.9. In the second, a new idea is introduced in chapter 6.6, where we are said to have been "crucified" with Christ. The argument of the first part gathers around that aspect of the work of the Lord Jesus which is represented by "the Blood" shed for our justification through "the remission of sins." This terminology is, however, not carried on into the second section, where the argument centers now in the aspect of His work represented by "the Cross," that is to say, by our union with Christ in His death, burial and resurrection. This distinction is a valuable one. We shall see that Blood deals with what we have done, whereas the Cross deals with what we are. The Blood disposes of our sins, while the Cross strikes at the root of our capacity for sin. . . .

### *Romans 5:12–6:23: "In Adam" and "In Christ"*
### *Romans 7:1–8:39: "In the Flesh" and "In the Spirit"*

We need to understand the relationship of these four things. The former two are "objective" and set forth our *position*, firstly as we were by nature and secondly, as we now are by faith in the redemptive work of Christ. The latter two are "subjective" and relate to our *walk* as a matter of practical experience. Scripture makes it clear that the first two give us only a part of the picture and that the second two are required to complete it. We think it enough to be "in Christ," but we learn now that we must also walk "in the spirit" (Rom. 8.9). The frequent occurrence of "the Spirit" in the early part of Romans 8 serves to emphasize this further important lesson of the Christian life. . . .

It is in chapter 8 that Paul presents to us in detail the positive side of life in the Spirit. "There is therefore now no condemnation," he begins, and this statement may at first seem out of place here. Surely condemnation was met by the Blood, through which we found peace with God and salvation from wrath (Rom. 5.1,9). But there are two kinds of condemnation, namely, that before God and that before myself (just as earlier we saw there are two kinds of peace) and the second may at times seem to us even more awful than the first. When I see that the blood of Christ has satisfied God, then I know my sins are forgiven, and there is for me no more condemnation before God. Yet I may still be knowing defeat, and the sense of inward condemnation on this account may be very real, as Romans 7 shows. But if I have learned to live by Christ as my life, then I have discovered the secret of victory, and, praise God, in the inward sense also, "there is therefore now no condemnation." "The mind of the spirit is life and peace" (Rom. 8.6), and this becomes my experience as I learn to walk in the Spirit. With peace in my heart I have no time to feel condemned, but only to praise Him who leads me on from one fresh victory to another.

—NCL 13–5, 174–5, 184

## EPHESIANS

*A. Doctrinal (Chapters 1 to 3)*
*1. Our Position in Christ (1.1–3.21)*
*B. Practical (Chapters 4 to 6)*
*2. Our Life in the World (4.1–6.9)*
*3. Our Attitude to the Enemy (6.10–24)*

Of all Paul's epistles, it is in Ephesians that we find the highest spiritual truths concerning the Christian life. The letter abounds with spiritual riches, and yet at the same time it is intensely practical. The first half of the letter reveals our life in Christ to be one of union with Him in the highest heavens. The second half shows us in very practical terms how such a heavenly life is to be lived by us down here on the earth. We do not here propose to study the letter in detail. We shall, however, touch on a few principles lying at its heart. For this purpose we shall select one key word in each of the above three sections to express what we believe to be its central or governing idea.

In the first section of the letter we note the word *sit* (2.6) which is the key to that section and the secret of a true Christian experience. God has made us to sit with Christ in the heavenly places, and every Christian must begin his spiritual life from that place of rest. In the second part we select the word *walk* (4.1) as expressive of our life in the world, which is its subject. We are challenged there to display in our Christian walk conduct that is in keeping with our high calling. And finally, in the third part we find the key to our attitude towards the enemy contained in the one word *stand* (6.11), expressive of our place of triumph at the end. Thus we have:

KEY WORDS IN EPHESIANS

1. *Our Position in Christ*—"SIT" *(2.6)*
2. *Our Life in the World*—"WALK" *(4.1)*
3. *Our Attitude to the Enemy*—"STAND" *(6.11)*

The life of the believer always presents these three aspects—to God, to man, and to the Satanic powers. To be useful in God's hand a man must be properly adjusted in respect of all three: his position, his life, and his warfare. He falls short of God's requirements if he underestimates the importance of any one of them, for each is a sphere in which God would express "the glory of his grace, which he freely bestowed on us in the Beloved" (1.6).

We will take, then, these three words—"Sit," "Walk," "Stand"—as guides to the teaching of the Epistle, and as the text for its present message to our hearts. We shall find it most instructive to note both the order and the connection in which they come.*

*Excerpts with respect to "sit" and "walk" follow here; but for the excerpts with regard to "stand," the reader is directed to consult the end of Ch. 42 above (Spiritual Warfare).

> The God of our Lord Jesus Christ, . . . raised him from the dead, and made him to sit at his right hand in the heavenly places, far above all rule, and authority, and power, and dominion, and every name that is named, not only in this world, but also in that which is to come (1.17–21).
>
> And raised us up with him, and made us to sit with him in the heavenly places, in Christ Jesus: . . . for by grace have ye been saved through faith; and that not of yourselves: it is the gift of God: not of works, that no man should glory (2.6–9).

"God . . . made him to sit . . . and made us to sit with him." Let us first consider the implications of this word "sit." As we have said, it reveals the secret of a heavenly life. Christianity does not begin with walking; it begins with sitting. The Christian era began with Christ, of whom we are told that, when he had made purification of sins, he "sat down on the right hand of the Majesty on high" (Heb. 1.3). With equal truth we can say that the individual Christian life begins with a man "in Christ"—that is to say, when by faith we see ourselves seated together with him in the heavens.

Most Christians make the mistake of trying to walk in order to be able to sit, but that is a reversal of the true order. Our natural reason says, If we do not walk, how can we ever reach the goal? What can we attain without effort? How can we ever get anywhere if we do not move? But Christianity is a queer business! If at the outset we try to do anything, we get nothing; if we seek to attain something, we miss everything. For Christianity begins not with a big DO, but with a big DONE. Thus Ephesians opens with the statement that God *has* "blessed us with every spiritual blessing in the heavenly places in Christ" (1.3) and we are invited at the very outset to sit down and enjoy what God has done for us; not to set out to try and attain it for ourselves.

Walking implies effort, whereas God says that we are saved, not by works, but "by grace . . . through faith" (2.8). We constantly speak of being "saved through faith," but what do we mean by it? We mean this, that we are saved by reposing in the Lord Jesus.

We did nothing whatever to save ourselves; we simply laid upon Him the burden of our sin-sick souls. We began our Christian life by depending not upon our own doing but upon what He had done. Until a man does this he is no Christian; for to say "I can do nothing to save myself; but by his grace God *has done* everything for me in Christ" is to take the first step in the life of faith. The Christian life from start to finish is based upon this principle of utter dependence upon the Lord Jesus. There is no limit to the grace God is willing to bestow upon us. He will give us everything, but we can receive none of it except as we rest in Him. "Sitting" is an attitude of rest. Something has been finished, work stops, and we sit. It is paradoxical, but true, that we only advance in the Christian life as we learn first of all to sit down. . . .

. . . Christian experience proceeds as it began, not on the basis of our own work but always on that of the finished work of Another. Every new spiritual experience begins with an acceptance by faith of what God has done—with a new "sitting down," if you like. This is a principle of life, and one which God himself has appointed; and from beginning to end, each successive stage of the Christian life follows on the same divinely determined principle. . . .

. . . Though the Christian life begins with sitting, sitting is always followed by walking. When once we have been well and truly seated and have found our strength in sitting down, then we do in fact begin to walk. Sitting describes our position with Christ in the heavenlies. Walking is the practical outworking of that heavenly position here on earth. As a heavenly people we are required to bear the stamp of that heavenliness upon us in our earthly conduct, and this raises new problems. What then, we must now ask, has Ephesians to say to us about walking? We shall find that the Epistle urges upon us [what is found in the following representative passages].

> I therefore, the prisoner in the Lord, beseech you to walk worthily of the calling wherewith ye were called, with all lowliness and meekness . . . (4.1–2).
>
> This I say . . . that ye no longer walk as the Gentiles also walk, in the vanity of their mind . . . But . . . that ye be renewed in the spirit of your mind (4.17,23).
>
> Walk in love, even as Christ also loved you, and gave himself up for you (5.2, mg.).
>
> Walk as children of light, . . . proving what is well-pleasing unto the Lord" (5.8,10).

Eight times in Ephesians the word "walk" is used. It means literally "to walk around," and is used here figuratively by Paul to mean "to deport oneself," "to order one's behavior." It brings immediately before us the subject of Christian conduct, and the second section of the letter is largely taken up with this. . . .

—SWS 11–5, 17–8, 27–8